Using 1-2-3®

Geoffrey T. LeBlond
Douglas Ford Cobb

Revised for Release 2
by Thomas W. Carlton

Que™ Corporation
Indianapolis, Indiana

Dedication

To Laura
—G.L.

To my wife, Gena
—D.F.C.

Editorial Director
David F. Noble, Ph.D.

Managing Editor
Gregory Croy

Editors
Charles O. Stewart III, M.A.
Bill Nolan
Gail S. Burlakoff
Ann Holcombe, M.S.Ed.

Technical Editor
Timothy S. Stanley

Screen reproductions in this book were created by means of the PRINT SCREEN program from DOMUS Software, Limited, Ottawa, Ontario, Canada.

Composed by Que Corporation in
Garamond

Cover designed by
Cargill Associates
Atlanta, Georgia

About the Authors

Douglas Ford Cobb

Douglas Ford Cobb received his B.A. degree, magna cum laude, from Williams College and his M.S. in accounting from New York University's Graduate School of Business Administration. He has worked for Arthur Andersen & Co. and was president of Cobb Associates, Inc., a Boston-based microcomputer consulting firm. He coauthored *Spreadsheet Software: From VisiCalc to 1-2-3; Using 1-2-3; 1-2-3 Tips, Tricks, and Traps;* and *1-2-3 for Business,* all published by Que Corporation. He is president of The Cobb Group, Inc., a microcomputer information firm in Louisville, Kentucky.

Geoffrey T. LeBlond

Geoffrey T. LeBlond, president of LeBlond Software, received his B.A. degree from Brown University and M.B.A. in finance from Indiana University's Graduate School of Business. Mr. LeBlond coauthored *Using 1-2-3* and *Using Symphony* and is a contributing author to *1-2-3 for Business,* all published by Que Corporation. Prior to his current position, Mr. LeBlond was also a technical editor at Que Corporation for the *IBM PC UPDATE* magazine and Editor-in-Chief of *Absolute Reference: The Journal for 1-2-3 and Symphony Users.*

Acknowledgments

The authors would like to make the following acknowledgments:

Dr. John Boquist, for his helpful insights in comparing 1-2-3 to VisiCalc and VisiTrend/Plot

Dr. Hugh McLaughlin, for his help in getting started with 1-2-3

Steve Miller, Chris Morgan, and Ezra Gottheil of Lotus Development Corporation

Rex Hancock of ComputerLand of Castleton, Indiana

Thomas D. Perkins, Editor-in-Chief, *Absolute Reference: The Journal for 1-2-3 and Symphony Users*, and Technical Editor, *IBM PC UPDATE: New Techniques for Professionals*; Tom Henderson; and Ann de Calonne, for their assistance with this project

Table of Contents

7 File Operations 231

8 Printing Reports 249

12   Macros and Command Language 377

13 A Comprehensive Model 471

Trademark Acknowledgments

Conventions Used
In This Book

A number of conventions are used in *Using 1-2-3* to help you learn the program. One example is provided of each convention to help you distinguish among the different elements in 1-2-3.

References to keys are as they appear on the keyboard of the IBM Personal Computer. Direct quotations of words that appear on the screen are spelled as they appear on the screen and are printed in a `special typeface`. Information you are asked to type is printed in *italic*.

The "NEW WITH R2" symbol in the margin indicates that a paragraph or section discusses commands, operations, or program applications that have changed or are new with Release 2 of Lotus 1-2-3.

The first letter of each command from 1-2-3's menu system appears in boldface: **/R**ange **F**ormat **C**urrency. Abbreviated commands appear as in the following example: /rfc. **/R**ange **F**ormat **C**urrency indicates that you type /rfc to select this command if you were entering it manually. The first letter of menu choices also appears in boldface: **C**opy.

Words printed in uppercase include range names (SALES), functions (@PMT), modes (READY), and cell references (A1..G5).

Conventions that pertain to macros deserve special mention here:

1. Macro names (Alt-character combinations) appear with the backslash (\ ) and single character name in lowercase: \a. In this macro command example, the \ indicates that you press the Alt key and hold it down while you press also the A key.

2. All /x macro commands, such as /xm or /xn, appear in lowercase, but macro commands from Release 2's command language within braces should be uppercase: {WAIT}.

3. 1-2-3 menu keystrokes in a macro line should be lowercase: /rnc.

4. Range names within macros should be uppercase: /rncTEST.

5. In macros, representations of cursor keys, such as {DOWN}; function keys, such as {CALC}; and editing keys, such as {DEL}, appear in uppercase letters and are surrounded by braces.

6. Enter is represented by the tilde ($\sim$). (Note that throughout the text, Enter is used instead of Return.)

The function keys, F1 through F10, are used for special situations in 1-2-3. In the text, the function key number is usually followed by the name in parentheses: F10 (Graph).

Ctrl-Break indicates that you press the Ctrl key and hold it down while you press also the Break key. Other hyphenated key combinations, such as Alt-F10, are performed in the same manner.

Key sequences, such as End+Home, are performed by pressing and releasing each key in turn.

Introduction

1-2-3® is the most exciting program for microcomputers on the market today. This "all-in-one" program combines the best of the popular electronic spreadsheets, business graphics software, and personal data managers into one integrated software package. Thanks to its power and sophistication, 1-2-3 is the hottest product in the microcomputer industry.

Although 1-2-3 is in many ways similar to VisiCalc, Multiplan, and the other electronic spreadsheet programs, 1-2-3 is a dramatic improvement on the basic concept of a spreadsheet. If 1-2-3 were only a spreadsheet, it would still be an excellent product; but 1-2-3 combines exceptional graphics and useful data management functions with its state-of-the-art spreadsheet. 1-2-3 does not provide all the functions of such "integrated" packages as Symphony and Framework, but you can have all the capabilities of these programs by combining 1-2-3 with your favorite word processor and communications package.

Using 1-2-3

With the sophistication of 1-2-3 comes complexity. Although the basics of 1-2-3 are easy to learn, especially for the experienced PC user, the fine points of the program can take months to master. As a result, many users are not taking full advantage of the power of 1-2-3.

Using 1-2-3 helps solve this problem. This book explains 1-2-3's commands and functions in a clear, easy-to-understand style. It includes examples of 1-2-3's commands and functions that will help you apply 1-2-3 to your business problems. The unique elements of 1-2-3— graphics, data management, and keyboard macros—are covered in detail.

Using 1-2-3 is not a substitute for 1-2-3's good manual, but rather a user's guide that goes beyond the basics of the manual to give examples and practical hints on using the program. This book should be used with the Lotus manual to gain a complete understanding of the power of 1-2-3.

Who Should Use This Book?

If you own 1-2-3, you should own this book. *Using 1-2-3* picks up where the 1-2-3 manual leaves off to explain both the basics and the fine points of the program. Every chapter includes clear explanations and examples, and special care has been taken to cover in detail those topics that are not thoroughly explained in the 1-2-3 manual. For example, Chapter 6 demonstrates 1-2-3's built-in functions, and Chapter 12 covers 1-2-3's macros and command language. The explanations and examples in this book help put the full power of 1-2-3 at your fingertips.

If you do not own 1-2-3 but are considering purchasing the program, this book is also for you. Chapter 1, "An Overview of 1-2-3," will help you understand the unique features of this powerful program. If you are an experienced spreadsheeter who is considering trading up to 1-2-3, you will appreciate the special attention this book pays to those elements of the program that may be unfamiliar to the users of other spreadsheet programs. And if you are a 1-2-3 user who has upgraded from Release 1A to Release 2, you will appreciate the notations throughout this book indicating features that are new with Release 2.

About This Book

Chapter 1, "An Overview of 1-2-3," discusses 1-2-3 in the context of the spreadsheet programs that preceded it. This chapter explains the basic concepts of 1-2-3 as well as the new features in Release 2 that make 1-2-3 the most powerful spreadsheet program available today. You will also learn the story behind the development of 1-2-3.

Chapter 2, "Getting Started," covers the process of readying 1-2-3 for your computer and describes the Lotus Access System, the six disks that come with the program, and the program's exceptional help screen facility.

Chapter 3, "The 1-2-3 Spreadsheet," introduces the basic element of 1-2-3—the spreadsheet. This chapter covers the size and memory capacity of the spreadsheet and teaches you the fundamentals of entering data into it.

Chapter 4, "Commands," discusses the basic 1-2-3 spreadsheet commands, including **Range**, **Worksheet**, **Move**, and **Copy**.

The process of formatting the spreadsheet is covered in Chapter 5. This chapter includes descriptions and examples of all of 1-2-3's range and global formats.

The next chapter, "Functions," explains 1-2-3's built-in spreadsheet functions, including @HLOOKUP, @VLOOKUP, and @IRR. This chapter also deals with 1-2-3's exciting date arithmetic capabilities, string functions, and special functions that return information about the locations or contents of cells and ranges.

Chapter 7, "File Management," covers the commands used to store and retrieve worksheets. This chapter also shows the commands that are used to merge and consolidate worksheets.

Chapter 8, "Printing Reports," provides explanations and examples of 1-2-3's report printing commands. This chapter goes beyond the 1-2-3 manual to give examples of 1-2-3's powerful report formatting features.

Chapters 9 and 10, "Creating and Displaying Graphs" and "Printing Graphs," cover 1-2-3's built-in graphics capabilities. Chapter 9 provides an example of each of 1-2-3's graph types—bar, stacked bar, line, XY, and pie—and explains all of the 1-2-3 graph display options. Chapter 10 covers the process of printing a graph, using the Print-Graph program. The examples and illustrations will help you make productive use of 1-2-3's graphics.

1-2-3's built-in database commands are discussed in Chapter 11, "Data Management." This chapter includes all of 1-2-3's /Data commands, including the **Sort**, **Query**, and **Data Table** commands, as well as 1-2-3's built-in database statistical functions.

Macros and 1-2-3's command language are covered in Chapter 12. This chapter explains each macro command and function and presents a number of interesting and useful macro examples. If you are a 1-2-3 user, you know that the program's manual leaves much to be desired in its explanations of this exciting capability. *Using 1-2-3* gives you all the instructions you will need to begin using 1-2-3's macros and command language.

The final chapter, "A Comprehensive Model," draws together all of the concepts developed in the earlier chapters into one comprehensive 1-2-3 application. This model includes a spreadsheet, a database, a set of graphs, and a menu macro system. The comprehensive model will show you how the knowledge you have gained from *Using 1-2-3* can be applied to your needs.

Inserted in the back of this book is a command menu map picturing all of 1-2-3's commands. This map will help beginners and experienced users to quickly locate commands included in the sublevels of 1-2-3's main menu. For users who have upgraded from Release 1A to Release 2, the map highlights all the commands that are new to Release 2.

A comprehensive index is also included.

More 1-2-3 Knowledge
1-2-3 for Business

Que's book *1-2-3 for Business*, by Hugh McLaughlin, Leith Anderson, and Douglas Ford Cobb, makes an excellent companion to *Using 1-2-3*. Where *Using 1-2-3* concentrates on explaining the fundamentals of 1-2-3, *1-2-3 for Business* offers 14 interesting and useful business applications for 1-2-3. You may be able to use many of these applications in your business. All of them will help you learn more about 1-2-3. Once you have read *Using 1-2-3,* you may want to polish further your 1-2-3 skills with *1-2-3 for Business*.

For users who want to learn more about 1-2-3's macros, two other Que books are available. *1-2-3 Macro Library,* by David P. Ewing, is an easy-to-use reference that contains more than 100 examples of 1-2-3 macros. *1-2-3 Financial Macros*, by Thomas W. Carlton, expands on the applications introduced in *1-2-3 Macro Library* and shows how to develop complex spreadsheet and database models controlled by macros.

Absolute Reference

If you would like to receive a continual flow of information about 1-2-3, you should consider subscribing to Que's publication, *Absolute Reference: The Journal for 1-2-3 and Symphony Users*. For more on this exciting opportunity, see the announcement inside the back cover of this book.

1
An Overview of 1-2-3

Introduced in 1983, 1-2-3 was hailed immediately as the most significant new software product since VisiCalc, which appeared in 1978. 1-2-3 required only three months to displace VisiCalc on the software best-seller lists, and remains firmly entrenched as the best-selling software program for the IBM PC and compatible computers.

The excitement over 1-2-3 comes primarily from the program's tremendous power. 1-2-3 is one of the first integrated office management software programs. 1-2-3 means 3 in 1. It combines three of the most popular business applications programs—electronic spreadsheet, business graphics, and data management—into one sophisticated program. Unlike other programs that attempt to accomplish this feat, the various elements of 1-2-3 are not compromised to achieve this interactivity. Each element is competitive with stand-alone programs designed to accomplish the same task.

1-2-3 was one of the first members of a new generation of microcomputer software programs designed specifically for powerful 16-bit computers like the IBM Personal Computer. Designed to take full advantage of the computer's speed and memory capacity, 1-2-3 quickly became the standard for judging all other software programs with similar capabilities.

Lotus Development Corporation, 1-2-3's publisher, works hard to keep the program state-of-the-art. The most recent upgrade, Release 2, adds a host of exciting new features and capabilities that significantly increase 1-2-3's power. Release 2 includes such new features as a larger worksheet, new and more powerful spreadsheet functions, and a greatly expanded macro command language. Furthermore, Release 2 offers the capability of using optional hardware to expand memory to four megabytes and to speed up spreadsheet calculation and graph printing.

Table 1.1
1-2-3 Release 2 at a Glance

Published by:
Lotus Development Corporation
55 Wheeler Street
Cambridge, Massachusetts 02138

System requirements:
IBM Personal Computer or compatible
Display: color or monochrome
Disk capacity: two 360K double-sided disk drives
Memory size: 256K
Maximum usable memory size: 640K
Operating system: PC DOS V2.0 or above
Other hardware: color/graphics adapter, printer,
     plotter, expanded memory (to 4 megabytes),
     8087 coprocessor

Price: $495.00

Also available for:
IBM Personal Computer AT
IBM 3270 PC
COMPAQ Portable Computer
COMPAQ PLUS
COMPAQ DESKPRO
COMPAQ 286
AT&T PC 6300
1-2-3 certified compatibles

Basically, 1-2-3 is an electronic spreadsheet. The framework of this spreadsheet contains the graphics and data management elements of the program. Graphics are produced through the use of spreadsheet commands. Data management occurs in the standard row-column spreadsheet layout. Because 1-2-3 is primarily a spreadsheet, it owes a great deal to the spreadsheet programs that came before 1-2-3— especially VisiCalc. This relationship has led to the description of 1-2-3 as an evolutionary development of the basic features pioneered by VisiCalc. 1-2-3 is regarded as the logical next step in the development of the electronic spreadsheet.

Because 1-2-3 owes so much to the programs that came before, an understanding of the developments that led up to the creation of 1-2-3 in 1983 is important.

The History of 1-2-3

The history of 1-2-3 begins with the history of computing. Our discussion, therefore, begins with the origins of computers.

The first computers were developed during World War II. They were used exclusively for military applications, such as breaking coded messages and computing shell trajectories.

During the 1950s these large computers began to find their way into the nation's largest businesses. By the 1970s, virtually every large corporation had at least one large computer, and many small and medium-sized firms had the smaller minicomputers. These machines were used primarily for accounting and payroll applications and for specialized functions, such as processing banking records—jobs that required rapid processing of large volumes of data.

Because these computers required a carefully controlled, secure environment, they were sequestered in special computer rooms. Since the computers were expensive to purchase and operate, they were run 24 hours a day on tight schedules to achieve the highest possible return on investment. Work on these machines usually was scheduled to make the most efficient use of the computer, but not to meet the needs of the user. These two factors combined to make the computer inaccessible to the average manager. Special requests for programming time were frequently put off to a later date. "You want it when?" became a popular poster in data-processing departments everywhere.

The First Microcomputers

In 1974 Intel Corporation developed the first microprocessor, the 8008. It condensed thousands of electronic circuits on a single, tiny silicon chip. The processing power of the room-sized computers of a few years earlier could now fit on a piece of silicon less than one inch square. Intel soon followed the 8008 with the 8080 microprocessor, which was selected by early computer hobbyists as *the* chip for many microcomputer kits.

About the same time, another integrated circuit manufacturer, MOS Technologies (later purchased by Commodore Business Machines), developed a more advanced processor, the 6502. This processor was selected for several early microcomputers, including the Commodore PET and the Apple II.

Soon, these microprocessors were integrated with other components to make the first commercial microcomputers. These early machines were sold as kits. The most famous computer kit was the Altair MITS. Kit computers did not look much like the popular computers we know today. Instead of the familiar video displays and keyboards, the front panels consisted of lights and programming switches. All programming was done in machine language. Printers and disk drives were not available for these early machines. Needless to say, the first micros were as inaccessible and impractical for the average businessperson as the mainframe computers. Not surprisingly, when microcomputers were first developed, they were used by only a few hardy individuals with advanced technical abilities.

Appliance Computers

In 1977 Steve Wozniak and Steve Jobs introduced a microcomputer kit called the Apple I. About 500 units of this machine were eventually sold. Wozniak and Jobs soon offered the Apple II. Unlike all of the computers that had gone before it, the Apple II was sold preassembled. It also had a disk drive and a powerful Disk Operating System (both developed by Wozniak).

Near that time, Tandy/Radio Shack also developed a microcomputer, the TRS-80 Model I, around an advanced derivative of the 8080 chip, the Z80 (manufactured by Zilog).

These appliance microcomputers opened the doors of microcomputing to nontechnical users. Because the machines did not have to be assembled, no advanced technical knowledge was required. Both machines were shipped fully assembled and factory tested and were sold through a new kind of store, the computer store. Computer stores offered some help in acquiring the computer as well as factory-authorized service. Both computers had several *expansion slots* that could be used to attach devices like printers, disk drives, and telephone modems to the computer.

Chips inside the appliance microcomputers contained the BASIC programming language. (Occasionally, the language was provided on a floppy disk packaged with the computer.) Because BASIC is easier to learn and use than machine or assembly language, users of these computers found it practical to write their own programs in BASIC.

Although BASIC uses English-like words to develop relationships, programs designed to accomplish simple tasks, such as multiplying two numbers, could require 8 to 10 lines of code. Imagine the complexity of using BASIC to solve sophisticated problems. A program written in BASIC to produce a financial report for a large company would be quite large, containing hundreds, or even thousands, of code lines.

In the early days of microcomputers, canned software (prewritten for a specific purpose and sold by a software publisher) was available. This left users with three choices: become experts in programming, pay a programmer, or accomplish little with the expensive microcomputers. Because most businesspersons were too busy (or too intimidated) to learn BASIC, many of those who bought micros during this period found themselves "all dressed up with no place to go." Countless others simply avoided microcomputers altogether.

The First Generation of Spreadsheet Programs

This situation changed with the introduction of VisiCalc, the first spreadsheet program for microcomputers, in 1978. From the time of its introduction until 1983, VisiCalc was the most popular computer program of all time. VisiCalc sold well over 400,000 copies. Some observers argue that VisiCalc launched the entire microcomputer industry. There is no question that VisiCalc "wrote the rules" for all the spreadsheet programs that have followed it, including 1-2-3.

VisiCalc was created in 1978 by Robert Frankston and Dan Bricklin in Cambridge, Massachusetts. Bricklin, a student at Harvard Business School, was frustrated with the tedium of analyzing three business cases a night, five days a week. Many of these cases required the preparation of intricate financial analyses. He decided there had to be a better way to do that sort of work. Teaming up with his programmer friend Frankston, Bricklin established Software Arts and began to develop VisiCalc. Another student, Dan Fylstra, acquired the rights to market the program and founded Personal Software (renamed VisiCorp, after its most famous product) to do so. One year later, VisiCalc was offered to the public.

VisiCalc arrived on the scene shortly after Steve Wozniak and Steve Jobs began selling the Apple II. The combination of VisiCalc and Apple had a tremendous impact on the infant microcomputer industry. For the first time, there was a legitimate business and professional application for desktop computers. VisiCalc met a clear need in the business world for a personal analysis tool. The Apple II was an attractive, reliable, readily available vehicle for the program. For about two years, this combination ruled the market for business microcomputers.

Advantages of VisiCalc

Although financial analysis software had been available for years on mainframe computers, VisiCalc offered several major improvements. First, VisiCalc ran on personal computers. This meant that, for the first time, a financial, sales, or production manager had a personal tool for numerical analysis. Computer time didn't have to be shared with every other manager in the firm. Analyses could be readjusted until correct, and there were no worries about mainframe computer-user budgets or EDP procedures. The manager did not have to wait to see the results of the analyses. The procedure was simply to boot the computer, load the model, and go to work.

VisiCalc brought about another important change. Unlike mainframe analysis programs, which require that input be in list form, VisiCalc is a *visible calculator*. Data and assumptions are entered in the model at the intersection of rows and columns on the sheet in much the same way that the information would appear on an accountant's pad. The model flows in a logical, understandable way.

Because the appearance of the model on the computer's screen is essentially the same as on a piece of paper, the user can quickly grasp the relationships in the model. The model is, therefore, much easier to use and modify. Editing requires only a few moments with a visible processor, instead of the hours that might be needed with mainframe planning tools.

VisiCalc had one more attractive feature. Its price, less than $200 when first introduced, knocked the mainframe competition out of the ring.

Limitations of VisiCalc

The earliest version of VisiCalc lacked some of the powerful features common to today's spreadsheets, including later editions of VisiCalc itself. Although it had the capability to sum; count; average; and look up and calculate maximums, minimums, trigonometric functions, and net present values, VisiCalc did not have Boolean functions (if, or, and, not). The earliest VisiCalcs also lacked the power to communicate with other software programs. Finally, the formatting capabilities of the first version were fairly limited. Despite these limitations, VisiCalc was clearly one of the most powerful and functional programs ever introduced.

As more people became experienced with VisiCalc, they attempted to expand its applications to include such things as tax computations, financial statement production, and more sophisticated budget analysis. Users wanted if-then-else logic, the ability to represent models graphically, and a tool that could transfer VisiCalc data to word processing and other software. Users also wanted more flexibility in the setup and formatting of models.

Changes in VisiCalc

These desires led to improvements in VisiCalc itself and the introduction of companion programs that expanded the power of the product. One major improvement was the introduction of the Data Interchange Format (DIF), developed by Software Arts as an answer to the problem of transferring data among different programs. DIF allows the user to move the results of a VisiCalc planning session into a word processor, a graphics generator, or a database manager.

The first programs to take advantage of this capability were the other members of the "Visi" family: VisiTrend/Plot and VisiFile. These programs are all completely interactive with VisiCalc through the DIF format. This family was, in effect, one of the first attempts at an all-in-one software system. Interestingly enough, the developer of VisiPlot, the graphics element of the family, was Mitch Kapor, the founder of Lotus Development Corporation.

Enter SuperCalc

VisiCalc was first introduced on the Apple II and TRS-80 Model I microcomputers. However, VisiCalc soon became available for a large number of desktop computers, including the Atari 800, the Commodore PET, the TRS-80 models II and III, the Hewlett-Packard 80 series and 125, and the Apple III. Personal Software (now VisiCorp) chose not to make its product available to the growing CP/M market. Because many businesses were selecting CP/M micros for accounting and word processing, a large segment of potential spreadsheet users was left without a satisfactory program.

This situation left the door open for Sorcim Corporation's SuperCalc, the first major CP/M spreadsheet and the most important spreadsheet program after VisiCalc. Sorcim Corporation (Sorcim is micros spelled backward) introduced SuperCalc in 1980. SuperCalc met with immediate success and is the second largest selling electronic spreadsheet in the world. SuperCalc is available for more than 125 different computers—by far the most versatile availability of any spreadsheet program.

SuperCalc was clearly designed with the intention of surpassing VisiCalc. SuperCalc contains many features and functions not found in VisiCalc. However, the experienced VisiCalc user immediately recognizes many of SuperCalc's features. Like VisiCalc, SuperCalc is a visible processor spreadsheet program with cells for entry of information or equations at the intersection of 63 columns and 254 rows. SuperCalc includes all of the basic spreadsheet functions found in VisiCalc, such as SUM, MAX, LOOKUP, and NPV. Like VisiCalc (and 1-2-3) SuperCalc uses the / symbol to activate commands. In fact, most VisiCalc functions and commands are also found in SuperCalc.

Summary of First-Generation Programs

The first-generation programs were significant when they were first introduced. VisiCalc, SuperCalc, and the other spreadsheets in this group were a vast improvement on the traditional analysis tools—the accountant's pad, pencil, and calculator. These programs were an important force in the early success of the microcomputer industry. In fact, VisiCalc helped to legitimize the industry. VisiCalc's practicality and flexibility made it the most popular program in the history of microcomputing. These programs dominated the sales of business software for five years, and SuperCalc continues to be among the biggest sellers.

The Second Generation of Spreadsheet Programs

Several software packages emerged in 1983 that expanded the capabilities of the first-generation spreadsheets. This group of programs included new releases of the first-generation packages as well as several important new software packages such as 1-2-3 and Context Management Systems' Context MBA.

Of the many factors that influenced the development of these second-generation spreadsheet programs, two were critical. First, widespread use of VisiCalc and its imitators resulted in a "wish list" of new features that served as the basis for developing the new programs. This wish list included the desire for more memory; the ability to link individual spreadsheets into an integrated system of sheets; the need for more powerful arithmetic and formatting functions; and the desire for fully integrated graphics, database management, and word processing.

The second important factor was the introduction of IBM's Personal Computer, the first of a new generation of 16-bit computers. These computers combined greatly expanded memory and processing power with upward compatibility for the VisiCalc program from the 8-bit CP/M computers that dominated the business market in the early 1980s.

The IBM Personal Computer quickly became a new hardware standard for business applications. To take advantage of the PC's powerful features, software developers created new, exciting software programs. The memory capacity and processing power of the new 16-bit computers allowed the second generation of spreadsheet packages to offer tremendous power and sophistication.

These packages have been created also in response to the growing Fortune 1000 market for microcomputers and microcomputer software. As microcomputers become more pervasive in business, the market for new software becomes increasingly more attractive.

The second-generation programs that appeared in 1983 included new versions of several familiar programs as well as some new names. At least three of the second-generation programs were descendants of first-generation sheets: SuperCalc, VisiCalc Advanced Version, and ProCalc. Others, like Multiplan, Context MBA, and 1-2-3, were exciting new efforts. All of the second-generation programs incorporated the features of the first generation and added major new features.

For example, Sorcim Corporation, responsive to the desires of SuperCalc users for a more advanced spreadsheet, introduced SuperCalc^2. This program offered dramatic improvements over the basic SuperCalc capabilities. SuperCalc^2 had a variety of new built-in functions, including date arithmetic, the ability to manipulate text entries, and a command that allows you to consolidate different sheets into summary sheets.

Multiplan introduced the capability of linking several different worksheets, like pages in a book, into one large model. This capability makes Multiplan a natural choice for applications where data from several subsidiary worksheets must be combined into a summary sheet. For example, multiple departmental income statements can be built and consolidated easily into a company-wide statement.

In response to the "wish list" that developed from the first-generation spreadsheets, second-generation spreadsheets were designed to run on the hundreds of thousands of existing Apple II and 8-bit CP/M computers. However, these programs did not utilize fully the power and memory capabilities of such 16-bit computers like the IBM PC. It was left to two other packages, Context MBA and 1-2-3, to usher in the era of integrated business software on the IBM PC.

The Integrated Approach

Context MBA and 1-2-3 stand out from the other second-generation programs by integrating graphics and data management with advanced spreadsheets. (Context MBA also includes simple text processing and data communications.) These programs incorporate all of these applications in a single, extremely powerful package.

Context MBA, the first integrated program to be introduced, was the first program to incorporate all five applications into one package. The MBA program was the result of a long study done by the Arthur D. Little Company on the needs and desires of businesspersons for desktop management software.

Context MBA suffered from some unfavorable criticisms about its speed and jack-of-all-trades orientation. These criticisms, and the introduction of 1-2-3, affected Context MBA's acceptance by the market.

Enter 1-2-3

If VisiCalc is the grandfather of electronic spreadsheets, then 1-2-3 is the wonder child. 1-2-3 is an extremely advanced spreadsheet that combines the features of an easy-to-use spreadsheet program with graphics and data management functions.

1-2-3 is the brainchild of Mitch Kapor, president of Lotus Development Corporation, and Jonathan Sachs, vice president of Research and Development at Lotus. Like so many of the early leaders of the microcomputer industry, Kapor taught himself the art of programming. He learned well. Prior to founding Lotus, Kapor scored one of the largest successes in the young microcomputer software industry with VisiTrend/Plot, a graphics and statistical package that he sold to VisiCorp. After working for VisiCorp for a brief time following the sale, he left and founded Lotus with the intention of producing the ultimate spreadsheet software program. Sachs had been involved in three spreadsheet development projects prior to joining Lotus.

Kapor's first step was to assemble an experienced team of financiers and business managers to help launch his new product. Ben Rosen, one of the most respected businessmen in the industry (Rosen was one of the original VisiCorp investors and is the chairman of COMPAQ Computer Corporation), was one of the first investors in Lotus, and is a member of the board of directors of Lotus. Kapor also recruited Chris Morgan, previously editor-in-chief of *Byte Magazine* and *Popular Computing Magazine*, to be vice president of Communications. Because every member of the Lotus team had prior experience in the microcomputer industry, Kapor calls Lotus a "second-generation" software company.

1-2-3 was designed by Kapor and Sachs to beat VisiCalc at its own game. 1-2-3's overall design, command syntax, and built-in functions are based on the conventions used by VisiCalc. In fact, according to one rumor, Kapor's experience working at VisiCorp after the VisiPlot sale was the spark that ignited his desire to create 1-2-3.

While Sachs and company worked to create the program, Kapor was working to build excitement about 1-2-3 in the marketplace. Articles praising the product appeared in *The Wall Street Journal*, *The New York Times*, *Business Week*, and other national publications. Nearly every magazine in the microcomputer industry carried a feature story about the program.

Since its introduction in 1983, 1-2-3 has become one of the most successful software programs ever produced. By the end of April, 1983, 1-2-3 was outselling VisiCalc. By the end of the year, 1-2-3 had become the leading software program for spreadsheet applications. 1-2-3 still dominates sales of spreadsheet software for IBM PC-compatible computers. With Lotus 1-2-3 as the software industry's standard, a host of compatible spreadsheet packages has developed in much the same way that the IBM PC-compatible hardware industry developed.

Beyond the Spreadsheet

Since the introduction of 1-2-3, business software has evolved in the direction paved by Context MBA. In 1984, Lotus and several other software developers introduced new software packages that integrated spreadsheet, data management, and graphics capabilities similar to those in 1-2-3, with word processing and communications.

Six months after 1-2-3's initial release, Lotus upgraded 1-2-3 to Release 1A. Release 1A, prompted in part by the proliferation of new personal computer models and the need to support hardware other than the standard IBM PC, also included new features. Notable among these features were upgraded 1-2-3 keyboard macros.

In mid-1984, Lotus introduced Symphony, an integrated software package that includes spreadsheet, data management, and graphics as well as word-processing and communications functions. All Symphony functions, like those in 1-2-3, are based on the spreadsheet. Symphony also incorporated several improvements to 1-2-3's spreadsheet, graphics, and keyboard macros.

Ashton-Tate (the publisher of dBASE) introduced its integrated package, Framework, at the same time that Lotus introduced Symphony. Framework and Symphony contain the same five functions, but Framework organizes the functions around an outline processor instead of a spreadsheet. Subsequently, several other software developers have introduced integrated packages that offer similar capabilities.

However, the introduction of these integrated software packages has not reduced 1-2-3's popularity. 1-2-3 continues to outsell all other integrated packages combined. Instead of buying an integrated package, people seem to prefer buying 1-2-3 and a separate word-processing package as well as a separate communications package (if needed). Therefore, in mid-1985, Lotus announced Release 2 of 1-2-3. Release 2 upgrades 1-2-3's spreadsheet and keyboard macros to include all the features offered in the latest release of Symphony. Once again, 1-2-3 is the state-of-the-art in spreadsheet software.

In late 1985, 1-2-3 seems sure to remain firmly entrenched as the most popular business software, a position that will be reinforced by such windowing packages as IBM's Top View or Microsoft Windows. These packages allow the user to run two or more compatible application packages at once, passing data back and forth. By using 1-2-3 with your favorite word processor and a compatible windowing package, you can achieve nearly the same level of integration that the integrated software packages offer.

One sign of 1-2-3's continuing dominance is the recent appearance of many less expensive imitations that claim 1-2-3 spreadsheet compatibility, and the introduction of more expensive integrated packages that claim to be able to read and write 1-2-3 worksheets.

How Is 1-2-3 Like Other Spreadsheets?

As we have observed, 1-2-3 is primarily an electronic spreadsheet. Like all spreadsheet programs, 1-2-3 is an electronic replacement for the traditional financial modeling tools: the accountant's columnar pad, pencil, and calculator. In some ways, spreadsheet programs are to those tools what word processors are to typewriters. Spreadsheets offer dramatic improvements in ease of creating, editing, and using financial models.

The typical electronic spreadsheet configures the memory of a computer to resemble an accountant's columnar pad. Because this "pad" exists in the dynamic world of the computer's memory, the pad is different from paper pads in some important ways. For one thing, electronic spreadsheets are much larger than their paper counterparts. Most electronic spreadsheets have 254 rows and 64 columns. 1-2-3 has 8,192 rows and 256 columns!

Each row in 1-2-3 is assigned a number, and each column a letter. The intersections of the rows and columns are called *cells*. Cells are identified by their row-column coordinates. For example, the cell located at the intersection of column A and row 15 is called A15. The cell at the intersection of column X and row 55 is called X55. These cells can be filled with three kinds of information: numbers; mathematical formulas, including special spreadsheet functions; and text (or labels).

A *cursor* allows you to write information into the cells much as a pencil lets you write on a piece of paper. In 1-2-3, as in most spreadsheets, the cursor looks like a bright rectangle on the computer's screen. The cursor typically is one row high and one column wide.

Because the 1-2-3 grid is so large, the entire spreadsheet cannot be viewed on the screen at one time. The screen thus serves as a window onto the worksheet. To view other parts of the sheet, you *scroll* the cursor across the worksheet with that cursor-movement keys. When the cursor reaches the edge of the current window, the window begins to shift to follow the cursor across the sheet.

To illustrate the window concept, imagine cutting a hole one inch square in a piece of cardboard. If you placed the cardboard over this page, you would be able to see only a one-inch square piece of text. Naturally, the rest of the text is still on the page; it is simply hidden from view. When you move the cardboard around the page (in much the same way that the window moves when the cursor keys are used), different parts of the page become visible.

Formulas

Electronic spreadsheets allow mathematical relationships to be created between cells. For example, if a cell named C1 contains the formula

C1 = A1+B1

then C1 will display the sum of the contents of cells A1 and B1. The cell references serve as variables in the equation. No matter what numbers are entered in A1 and B1, cell C1 will always return their sum. For example, if cell A1 contained the number 5 and cell B1 contained the number 10, the formula in cell C1 would return the value 15. If the number in cell A1 were changed to 4, C1 would also change to 14. Of course, spreadsheet formulas can be much more complex than this simple example. A cell can be added to, subtracted from, multiplied by, or divided by any other cell. In addition, spreadsheet functions may be applied to the cells.

Functions

Spreadsheet functions are shortcuts that help the user perform common mathematical computations with a minimum of typing. Functions are like abbreviations for otherwise long and cumbersome formulas. 1-2-3 contains all of the basic functions found in the first-generation programs like VisiCalc: SUM, COUNT, AVERAGE, MAX, and MIN; the basic Boolean functions, such as IF, AND, and OR; and trigonometric functions, including SIN, COS, TAN, and PI. Newer spreadsheets like 1-2-3 include many advanced functions.

Likewise, most worksheets use an @ symbol to signal a function. For instance, the SUM function in 1-2-3 is written as @SUM(A1..C1).

Commands

Like other spreadsheet programs, 1-2-3 includes several important commands that manipulate the worksheet in various ways. For example, all electronic spreadsheets include a command (or commands) that can be used to format the appearance of the contents of cells in the sheet. These commands can alter the display to make numbers appear in a variety of forms. In most spreadsheets, commands are activated by pressing the slash (/) key. After the slash is typed, a *menu* of commands appears on the screen. The user must then select the command to be implemented.

Most electronic spreadsheets use this basic command structure pioneered by VisiCalc. Many competitive programs even use the same letters to stand for these commands. There are, however, noticeable differences between the precise effects of the commands on different spreadsheets. Some spreadsheet programs use different letters to stand for a command with an exact parallel in VisiCalc. SuperCalc, for example, uses the /c command to stand for COPY. To CLEAR a SuperCalc sheet, a /z is used, representing the word zap. In 1-2-3, the worksheet is cleared by typing /we (for /Worksheet Erase).

Spreadsheet commands can be used at every phase of building and using a model. Because a spreadsheet holds in the computer's memory a model while you build it, you are not bound by the physical limitations of the printed page. Are some of your formulas repeated in different sections of your model? Use the spreadsheet's copy feature to project quickly your assumptions from one cell to another. Did you forget a row or a column? Simply insert the row or column at the appropriate point. Is one of your assumptions or formulas incorrect, or is there a typographical error in one of your headings? Correct the error instantly with the edit command.

Playing "What If"

The act of building a model on a spreadsheet defines all of the mathematical relationships in the model. Until you decide to change the relationships, every sum, product, division, subtraction, average, and net present value will remain the same. Each time you enter data into the model, computations will be calculated at your command with no effort on your part. All of these computations will be calculated correctly; spreadsheets don't make math errors. And next month, when you decide to use the same model again, the formulas will still be set, ready to calculate at your command.

Even more important, spreadsheet software allows you to play "what if" with your model. After a set of mathematical relationships has been built into the worksheet, the worksheet can be recalculated with amazing speed, using different sets of assumptions. If you use only paper, a pencil, and a calculator to build your models, every change to the model will require recalculating every relationship in the model. If the model has 100 formulas and you change the first one, you must make 100 calculations by hand so that the change flows through the entire model. If, on the other hand, you use a spreadsheet, the same change requires the press of only a few keys—the program does the rest. This capability permits extensive "what if" analysis.

For example, suppose you build a financial projection for your business for the years 1986 through 1991. In building this forecast, you assume that your sales will grow at an annual rate of 10 percent. But what happens to your projections if the rate of growth is only 3 percent? What if the rate is 15 percent? If you were using a pencil and a calculator to do this analysis, it might take hours to compute the effects of these changes. With 1-2-3 or other electronic spreadsheets, all that is required is to change the growth rate you entered in the sheet and strike one key to recompute. The entire process takes just seconds.

As your models become more complex, this capability becomes more and more valuable.

What Makes 1-2-3 Different?

1-2-3 took the microcomputer world by storm. Within six months after its introduction, 1-2-3 zoomed to the number one position on *Softalk*'s IBM Personal Computer best-seller list. Except for VisiCalc, no other program has demonstrated such complete dominance of the software market. 1-2-3 has achieved this dominance by combining outstanding performance with expertly coordinated publicity and advertising.

But what makes 1-2-3 exciting? 1-2-3 integrates graphics and information management with a first-rate spreadsheet, but that description obviously only scratches the surface. The following discussion will help you understand more about the features and capabilities of 1-2-3.

NEW WITH
R2

The 1-2-3 Disks

It is obvious that 1-2-3 is a formidable product from the moment you open the package. The program is so large that it is distributed on six disks: System disk, Backup System disk, Install Library disk, Utility disk, PrintGraph disk, and A View of 1-2-3 disk. Glancing through the manual will show you just how much there is to this program.

The program also comes with a shirt-pocket summary of 1-2-3's commands, functions, and options. 1-2-3's on-line help function is so good, however, that most users will probably not use this card.

1-2-3 on the IBM PC

The IBM PC, with its expandable memory and excellent video display, is the best spreadsheeting machine available today. Many corporations and individuals have found the IBM-plus-spreadsheet combination to be a terrific investment, saving time and effort while improving analysis.

For the first six months of its life, 1-2-3 was available only for the IBM Personal Computer. 1-2-3 was one of the first programs specifically designed for the IBM PC. 1-2-3 uses virtually every key on the PC's keyboard, including all of the function keys, the scroll key, the delete key, and the alternate key. The function keys serve several purposes. The F1 key activates 1-2-3's on-line help facility. F2 activates the program's editor. The F10 key replots graphics. The PgUp key jumps the cursor one screen, and the PgDn key moves the cursor down one key. The Home key returns the cursor to cell A1.

The plastic function-key template included in every 1-2-3 package contains one-word explanations of the action performed by each key. It is designed to be placed over the function keys on the PC's keyboard. The Lotus template both looks and feels substantial. Lotus could have saved money by using a less expensive template. But, in typical form, Lotus chose the best. This emphasis on quality down to the smallest detail is one of the things that has made 1-2-3 so popular.

1-2-3 on Other Computers

Lotus makes 1-2-3 available for a variety of computers that are not fully compatible with the IBM. Included in this list are the Zenith Data Systems Z-100, the DEC Rainbow, the Texas Instruments Professional Computer, the AT&T 6300, the Wang Professional, and the NEC Advanced Personal Computer.

Because the first release of 1-2-3 ran only on the IBM PC, program installation was not necessary, The program was ready to run fresh out of the box. With the program's availability for non-IBM computers, however, installation requirements have changed. The newest version of 1-2-3 comes with an installation program and a library that contains drivers for customizing the program to a particular computer.

These drivers also allow you to take full advantage of any optional hardware, such as plotters and graphics printers, that you purchased to accompany the computer. (More information on installing 1-2-3 can be found in Chapter 2.)

Hardware Requirements and Extras

1-2-3 requires a considerable investment in hardware to make full use of its capabilities. Two double-sided, double-density floppy disk drives are suggested. 1-2-3 will run on a system with only one double-sided disk drive, but the disk swapping that is required on a one-drive system can be confusing even for advanced users. A minimum of 256K of random-access memory (RAM) is required to use the program. This amount has increased from 192K for Release 1A and 128K for Release 1. In contrast, VisiCalc required a system with only one disk drive, 64K of RAM, and only one color or monochrome display.

A color monitor is required if you want to view 1-2-3's spectacular color graphics. If you have only a monochrome monitor, you will be able to see the spreadsheet and database parts of 1-2-3 and produce hard-copy graphs. If you use a Hercules Graphics card or another 1-2-3-compatible monochrome graphics adapter, you will be able to view your graphs in black and white on your monochrome monitor.

For maximum use of 1-2-3's capabilities, you may also want to invest in up to 640K of RAM memory, up to four megabytes of expanded memory, and an 8087 or 80287 coprocessor chip. These hardware extras greatly expand the practical size of 1-2-3's spreadsheet, and speed up calculations. You will need a printer with graphics capabilities (like an EPSON FX or LQ series printer) or a plotter to produce hard copies of your graphs.

The Access System and On-Line Help

When you first load 1-2-3 (either by typing *LOTUS* from the system level or by doing a warm boot), you come into the Lotus Access System. The access system is a five-part menu that gives you the choice of entering the 1-2-3 spreadsheet or the PrintGraph program, or performing various file handling and disk maintenance operations. This handy menu system helps tie together the various elements of 1-2-3 into one neat package. (For more information on the Access System, see Chapter 2.)

On-line help is becoming a must for virtually all spreadsheet programs. No spreadsheet publisher takes on-line help as seriously as Lotus. 1-2-3 offers an extensive on-line help facility. The help screens are keyed to the user's location in the program and are accessed by pressing the F1 key. The level of detail depends on how deeply the user is embedded in the commands. (See Chapter 2 for more information.)

The 1-2-3 Spreadsheet

NEW WITH
R2

As we have seen, the design of the 1-2-3 spreadsheet is much like that of VisiCalc. This should be reassuring to those with electronic spreadsheet experience. Remember, though, that the 1-2-3 sheet is much larger than VisiCalc's sheet. 1-2-3 offers 256 columns by 8,192 rows, or more than 2,000,000 cells. VisiCalc and SuperCalc offer just over 16,000 cells. To take advantage of all of that space, however, you'll need a great deal of memory in your machine. 1-2-3 can accommodate up to 640K of RAM memory plus up to 4 megabytes of extended memory. (See Chapter 3 for more information on the 1-2-3 worksheet and the memory requirements of the program.)

Operating Speed of 1-2-3

Given the staggering size of the 1-2-3 spreadsheet, it is reasonable to expect the program to be a bit slow. This is not the case. 1-2-3's spreadsheet is one of the fastest, if not *the* fastest, spreadsheet program available today. In some tests, 1-2-3 was 300 percent faster than VisiCalc. 1-2-3 outperformed Context MBA, the other all-in-one program introduced in 1983, by a wide margin in every test.

1-2-3 is written in assembly language, the closest language to the hexadecimal numbers the computer uses. The program is well designed, and 1-2-3 retains its advantage in speed over competing spreadsheets and integrated packages.

Built-In Functions

All of the second-generation software packages responded to the need for more powerful built-in spreadsheet functions. 1-2-3 offers all of the spreadsheet functions that you would expect to find in a powerful spreadsheet program, and more. The functions available in 1-2-3 have become a standard that is eventually matched by every competing spreadsheet and integrated package. With Release 2, 1-2-3 has added more functions to that standard.

1-2-3 offers a complete set of mathematical functions, not only for use in business, but also for engineering and scientific use. 1-2-3 includes such common mathematical functions as @LOG, @EXP, @SQRT, @INT, and @ABS; a complete set of common trigonometric functions; a random-number-generator function; and functions for rounding and determining remainders.

1-2-3 has a wealth of financial functions. In addition to the basic financial functions for net present value and internal rate of return calculations, there is a complete set of functions for annuity and compound growth rate calculations. In Release 2, 1-2-3 has even added functions for calculating depreciation by several common methods—straight line, sum of the years digits, and double declining balance.

1-2-3 offers basic statistical functions to calculate the sum, average, minimum, maximum, count, variance, and standard deviation of a range of values. These functions provide the worksheet's basic statistical capabilities. Corresponding database statistical functions perform the same calculations on those rows of a 1-2-3 database that meet specified selection criteria.

NEW WITH
R2

For those who need greater statistical capabilities, Release 2 of 1-2-3 also includes a multiple regression command (not a function) that can perform a regression with up to 16 independent variables.

NEW WITH
R2

String Functions

1-2-3's new string functions give you the power to manipulate strings in much the same way that you manipulate numbers in the spreadsheet. The @FIND function, for example, allows you to locate the starting position of one string within another string. With the @MID, @LEFT, and @RIGHT functions, you can extract one string from another. 1-2-3 includes several other string functions that provide a complete capability for manipulating alphanumeric data. These functions significantly enhance the integration of 1-2-3's spreadsheet and database capabilities.

The 1-2-3 date and time functions give you tremendous flexibility for manipulating dates and times in your worksheets. With the basic @NOW function, you can capture the current date and time from your system clock. The @DATE and @DATEVALUE functions allow you to enter dates in numeric or string formats, whereas @TIME and @TIMEVALUE give you the same capability for times.

Once dates and times are stored as date serial numbers in the worksheet, you can use ordinary mathematical commands to perform date and time arithmetic. A complete set of functions lets you extract the second, minute, hour, day, month, and year from a date serial number. 1-2-3 also has a variety of formats for displaying date serial numbers as dates and times in the worksheet.

Special Functions

NEW WITH
R2

Special 1-2-3 functions include those to change numeric entries to strings (and vice versa), and others that help you manage the use of both numbers and strings in your worksheets. Also included are such special functions as @@, the indirect addressing function, and @CELL.

@CELL provides information about the contents of spreadsheet cells. If, for example, you enter @CELL("width",b12..b12), 1-2-3 will return the width of column B as viewed in the current window. In addition to indicating width, the @CELL function can indicate a cell's address, type of value, label prefix, format, or row and column number location.

1-2-3 Spreadsheet Commands

1-2-3 has many commands that allow the user to perform a number of tasks in the spreadsheet. Commands are available to format the worksheet, name ranges, edit and copy data, perform calculations, store files, etc.

Formatting the Worksheet

1-2-3 offers a wide variety of formats for numeric entries. These new formats include the ability to display or print numbers with embedded commas, dollar signs, parentheses, or percent signs, and to specify the exact number of digits that will be displayed to the right of the decimal. For example, 1-2-3 can format the number 12345 to look like $12,345.00, 12,345, 1.2345, or 12345; the number –12345 to look like ($12,345.00) or –12,345; and the number .45 to look like 45% or $.45. (The details of all of 1-2-3's cell formats are covered in Chapter 5.)

These new formatting features allow users to create finished reports and financial statements directly from analyses. Numbers can appear as you would expect them to in a formal document, and eye-pleasing spacing can be achieved by varying column widths.

In 1-2-3, formats are always assigned to a range of cells. In fact, the format command is an option of a higher level command called /Range. A range in 1-2-3 can be as small as a single cell or as large as the entire worksheet. When you assign a format, the program prompts you to provide the appropriate range for that format by pointing to its limits with the cursor.

Naming Ranges

1-2-3 also allows a name to be assigned to a range. This feature lets you label an area for use in formulas or as the range for a command. For example, if a part of your worksheet has been named SUMMARY, you can tell 1-2-3 to print the section of the sheet called SUMMARY. Only the cells contained in that region will be printed. Similarly, if you have created a temporary area called SCRATCH, you can use that name with 1-2-3's /re (for /Range Erase) command to blank that part of the screen. (This exciting feature is discussed in Chapter 4.)

Copying Cell Entries

1-2-3 uses a /Copy command to make replicas of values, labels, or formulas in other cells. This replication allows the user to develop quickly a model by building a few key relationships, then replicating them over the entire workspace.

1-2-3 allows cell references to be defined as relative or absolute at the time the cell is defined. Relative cell references are entered in the normal way. Absolute references are entered with a dollar sign ($) preceding the reference. For example, in the formula

A1+$A2+A$3+$A$4

the reference to cell A1 is relative. The references to cells A2 and A3 are mixed: relative in one direction and absolute in the other. The reference to A4 is absolute in both directions.

This method of determining absolute and relative references has some interesting advantages. For example, you can /Copy a single cell into a block of cells without making complicated formula adjustments. (See Chapter 4 for complete details of this important feature.)

Recalculating the Worksheet

Earlier spreadsheets like VisiCalc and SuperCalc use a simple linear form of recalculation. The model recalculates by starting at the upper left corner of the spreadsheet (cell A1) and proceeding either row by row or column by column through the worksheet. The user must be careful to build dependencies in the worksheet to avoid *forward references* (a cell whose value depends on other cells below it in the recalculation order) and *circular references* (two or more cells defined by each other). These references can create calculation nightmares.

1-2-3 addresses these limitations by offering a *natural* mode of recalculation. Natural recalculation begins by discerning the most fundamental cell in the worksheet (that is, the cell on which most other cells are based). This cell is evaluated first. Next, the program searches for the second most basic formula in the worksheet and evaluates that cell. This process continues until the entire worksheet is recomputed.

Accompanying natural recalculation is the capability to perform iterative calculations. In 1-2-3, the user can specify the number of passes the program should make through the same worksheet each time the worksheet is recalculated. Iterative calculation helps to relieve the problem of circular references.

The addition of these two features simplifies the design and use of complex spreadsheets. With 1-2-3, the user does not have to be as careful about planning the locations of the various model sections. Instead, the computer can manage the order of recalculation. (More details on recalculation are provided in Chapter 4.)

Printing the Worksheet

1-2-3 has more printing flexibility than any other spreadsheet. The user has the choice of printing the entire worksheet or any part of the worksheet. In addition, the user can alter the left, right, top, and bottom margins on the page; change the page length and width; insert page headers and footers, which can even contain the date and page number; and send setup codes to the printer to alter the size and style of type used to print. (For more information on printing, see Chapter 8.)

Storing Files

1-2-3 offers the basic loading and saving commands found in other electronic spreadsheets. Three types of files can be created: normal spreadsheet files (.WK1), text files (.PRN), and graph files (.PIC). In addition, the program has the ability to load a text file created by another program, including a WordStar word-processing file. This feature allows you to load information from other sources into 1-2-3.

1-2-3 also has the capability to import files created by dBASE II, dBASE III, Jazz, and VisiCalc. Release 2 of 1-2-3 has a utility that translates a dBASE file into a .WK1 file. The file will appear in standard 1-2-3 database format, with each row representing a record and each column representing a field.

1-2-3 has a utility that translates a VisiCalc file into a .WK1 file. This utility converts all of the formulas and functions in the file into 1-2-3 syntax. Although there are usually some adjustments to be made after the file is loaded, this utility makes it easy for a VisiCalc user to convert existing worksheets into 1-2-3 templates. (Chapter 7 covers in detail the use of 1-2-3's storage commands.)

Finally, 1-2-3 Release 2 has the capability to read directly both Release 1A and Symphony worksheets. Release 2 also has utilities to write worksheets that those two programs can read.

1-2-3 Graphics

Mitch Kapor's background in graphics software design is evident in the graphics portion of 1-2-3. The program has definitely benefited from his experience.

The capability to convert spreadsheet data into graphs is not unique to the second-generation spreadsheets. Kapor's own program, VisiPlot, made graphics available to VisiCalc users. However, 1-2-3 ties the graphics capability directly into the spreadsheet so that there is no need to use a DIF (VisiCalc), SDI (SuperCalc), SYLK (Multiplan), or other communications file. 1-2-3's graphics capability is also remarkably versatile, easy to use, and even allows you to do "what if" analysis on the graphs.

1-2-3 has five basic graph types: bar, stacked bar, line, scatter, and pie. Up to six ranges of data can be represented on a single graph (except for pie graphs and scatter diagrams). This means, for example, that a line graph with six different lines can be created.

Graphs are created with 1-2-3's **/Graph** command. Although the program has a number of options, the user need specify only a graph type and a single data range. After providing the required information, the user simply types *v*, for **View**. This will plot the graph to the screen. If the computer has both a color and a monochrome display, the graph will appear on the color screen while the spreadsheet remains on the monochrome monitor. If there is only a color monitor, the graph will replace the spreadsheet on the display until a key is pressed.

1-2-3 gives the user an exceptional amount of flexibility in formatting graphs. Up to three different colors can be used to represent graphs on a color monitor. On a black-and-white monitor, the user can choose different shading patterns. The *color legend*, which defines the color or pattern for each data range, can also be displayed on the screen.

Labels can be inserted in graphs by referencing a list in the worksheet. Although 1-2-3 automatically scales the x- and y-axes to fit the data being plotted, users are free to adjust the scaling to suit their tastes. A grid can be placed over the worksheet. The user can specify a title and a subtitle for each graph, as well as labels for both the vertical and horizontal axes. In line and scatter graphs, the user has the option of selecting the type of symbol that will represent the data on the graph and connecting the data points with a line.

Because 1-2-3 lets the user name graphs after they are created, these graphs can be replotted by typing /gnu (for **/Graph Name Use**) and supplying the graphs' names. With this feature, you can create a slide show of graphs that are recalled, one after another, and plotted.

"What If" with Graphics

The most exciting thing about 1-2-3's graphics is not the variety of graphs, but the degree to which the graphics and spreadsheet elements are interrelated. With 1-2-3, graphs can be quickly designed and altered as worksheet data changes. This means that graphs may be changed almost as fast as the data is recalculated.

True graphics "what if" analysis can be performed with 1-2-3. In fact, the F10 function key on the IBM PC allows the user to replot a graph after making changes to the worksheet, without having to redefine the graph with the /g command. This replotting immediately shows the effects of changes on the current graph.

Printing Graphics

Because the basic 1-2-3 program is not capable of producing hard-copy graphics, the program is accompanied by a second program, called PrintGraph, which is used to create printed or plotted copies of graphs.

After a graph is created by 1-2-3, the graph can be saved in a file on a disk. These files, called .PIC files, are created with the /gs (for /Graph Save) command. The graph files can then be read into the PrintGraph program for additional formatting and printing.

The PrintGraph program offers a number of options for further formatting before the graphs are printed. The Color option allows parts of the graph to be assigned different colors. The Font option allows the labels and titles in the graph to be printed in one or several of eight different fonts, including a script face and a block face. The Size option allows the user to specify the size of the printed graph. A graph can be printed full size to occupy an entire printed page, or half size to fill half a page; or a manual option can be chosen. After the options have been selected, the PrintGraph program will print the graph to the specified graphics device.

The professional results that can be obtained from the PrintGraph program are another indication of the overall high quality of the 1-2-3 program. The user friendliness of 1-2-3's graphics capability is also important.

With previous graphics software, the time and trouble involved in creating and changing graphs often outweighed the benefits. 1-2-3 graphs, however, can be quickly and easily created and changed. With 1-2-3, managers will use graphs more frequently both to increase their own understanding and to communicate their analyses to others.

1-2-3 Information Management

The column-row structure used to store data in a spreadsheet program is similar to the structure of a relational database. The similarity between a database and a spreadsheet is demonstrated by the expanded Lookup capabilities of the second-generation spreadsheets. 1-2-3 has expanded Lookup capability like ProCalc and Multiplan, but goes one step further and provides a true database management function as well. One important advantage of 1-2-3's database manager over independent DBM systems is that its commands are similar to the other commands used in the 1-2-3 program. The user can, therefore, learn how to use the 1-2-3 database manager along with the rest of the 1-2-3 program.

Database Functions and Commands

Once a database has been built in 1-2-3 (which is no different from building any other spreadsheet table), a variety of functions can be performed on the database. Some of the tasks you will want to perform on a 1-2-3 database can be accomplished with standard 1-2-3 commands. For example, records can be added to a database with the /wir (/Worksheet Insert Row) command. Fields can be added with the /wic (/Worksheet Insert Column) command. Editing the contents of a database cell is as easy as editing any other cell; you simply move the cursor to that location, press F2 to call up the editor, and start typing.

Data can also be sorted. Sorts can be done with both a primary and a secondary key, in ascending or descending order, using alphabetic or numeric keys. In addition, various kinds of mathematical analyses can be performed on a field of data over a specified range of records. For example, you can count the number of items in a database that match a set of criteria; compute a mean, variance, or standard deviation; and find the maximum or minimum value in the range. The capability to perform statistical analysis on a database is an advanced feature for database management systems on any microcomputer.

Other database operations require database commands, such as /dqu (/Data Query Unique) and /dqf (/Data Query Find). A 1-2-3 database can be queried in several ways. After specifying the criteria on which you are basing your search, you can ask the program to point to each selected record in turn, or to extract the selected records to a separate area of the spreadsheet. You can also ask the program to delete records that fit your specified criteria.

Several commands help the user make inquiries and clean the data of duplications. All of these commands are subcommands of the /dq (/Data Query) command. These commands require that the user specify one or more criteria for searching the database. The criteria refer to a field in the database and set the conditions that data must meet in order to be selected.

1-2-3 allows a great deal of latitude in defining criteria. As many as 32 cells across, each containing multiple criteria, can be included in the criteria range. Criteria can include complex formulas as well as simple numbers and text entries. Two or more criteria in the same row are considered to be joined with an *and*. Criteria in different rows are assumed to be combined with an *or*. Criteria can also include "wild card" characters that stand for other characters.

1-2-3 also has a special set of statistical functions that operate only on information stored in the database. Like the query commands, the statistical functions use criteria to determine which records they will operate on.

The following database functions are supported: @DCOUNT, @DSUM, @DAVG, @DSTD, @DMAX, and @DMIN. These functions perform essentially the same tasks as their spreadsheet counterparts. For example, @DMIN finds the minimum number in a given range. @DCOUNT counts all of the nonzero entries in a range. @DSTD computes the standard deviation of the items in the range.

The combination of these functions and 1-2-3's database commands makes this program a capable data manager. 1-2-3's data management capabilities, however, do not put it in competition with more sophisticated database languages, such as dBASE III or R:base. Both of these programs use a database language to translate the user's requests to the computer. By comparison, 1-2-3's data management is fairly simple.

When compared to less powerful data managers, however, such as VisiDex and PFS:FILE, 1-2-3 looks good. 1-2-3 is fast and has adequate capacity (at 8,192 records) for most data management tasks. Because 1-2-3's data management uses the same basic command structure as the rest of 1-2-3, the program is easy to learn. In summary, the database function of 1-2-3 is valuable and sets 1-2-3 apart from the generic spreadsheet. (1-2-3's data management capabilities are covered in detail in Chapter 11.)

Using the /Data Table Command

/Data Table is 1-2-3's most misunderstood command. A data table is simply a way to look at all of the outcomes of a set of conditions without having to enter manually each set into the equation. The command simply allows you to build a table that defines the formula you wish to evaluate and contains all of the values you wish to test. A data table is very similar to the X-Y decision grids you probably built as a math student in high school.

The /Data Table command can be used to structure a variety of "what if" problems. It can also be combined with 1-2-3's database and statistical functions to solve far more complex problems. (Chapter 11 explains in detail the data table command and gives examples that will help you master this tricky tool.)

International Formats

International formats and an international character set are available as a new Release 2 feature. First, through the /Worksheet Global Default command, you have the options of changing Currency, Date, and Time formats to International formats. The Currency option, for example, enables you to change the default dollar sign ($) to a foreign currency sign like that for the British pound (£) if you plan to use that format regularly throughout your worksheet. Second, the international character set, referred to as the Lotus International Character Set (LICS), provides characters from many languages. In the 1-2-3 manual, you will find a complete list of the international and special characters available in LICS.

Security System

1-2-3 allows you to protect cells in a worksheet so that changes cannot be made, for example, in cells that contain important formulas. With Release 2, you can also hide ranges of cells and use passwords to protect your worksheets when you save them on disk.

Whenever you protect an area of your worksheet, you use two commands: the /Worksheet Global Protection command and the /Range Protect command. These commands prevent someone from erasing, moving, or changing the cells even though the cell contents are displayed on the screen. If you also want to prevent the display of cell contents, you can use the /Range Format Hidden command.

1-2-3 also lets you password protect your worksheet files when you save them. A password-protected file is encrypted and cannot be examined or retrieved without the password. Your confidential or sensitive data is protected from use by anyone who does not have the correct password.

Multiple Regression and Simultaneous Equations

1-2-3's powerful multiple regression command significantly expands the program's capabilities for statistical analysis. If you use regression analysis, the regression command could save you the cost of a stand-

NEW WITH
R2

alone statistical package. For business applications, the new /**Data Regression** command probably will meet all your regression analysis needs.

A /**Data Matrix** command can be used to solve systems of simultaneous equations. This capability, although likely to be of more interest to scientific and engineering users, is available to all.

Keyboard Macros and the Macro Command Language

One of 1-2-3's most exciting features is its macro capability, which allows you to automate and customize 1-2-3 for your special applications. 1-2-3's macro capability allows you to create, inside the 1-2-3 spreadsheet, user-defined programs that can be used for a variety of purposes. At the simplest level, these programs are "typing alternatives"—programs that reduce, from many to two, the number of keystrokes for a 1-2-3 operation. At a more complex level, 1-2-3's macro capability with Release 2 gives the user a full-featured programming language—1-2-3's command language. The macro capability with Releases 1 and 1A can be used as a programming language, but in a much more limited fashion.

Whether you use 1-2-3's macro capability as a typing alternative or as a programming language, you'll find that it can simplify and automate many of your 1-2-3 applications. When you create typing-alternative macros, you group together and name a series of normal 1-2-3 commands, text, or numbers. Once you have named a macro, you can activate its series of commands and input data by pressing two keys—the Alt key and a letter key.

The implications for such typing-alternative macros are limited only by 1-2-3's capabilities. For example, typing the names of months as column headings is a task frequently performed in budget building. This task can be easily turned into a 1-2-3 macro, thereby reducing multiple keystrokes to a two-keystroke combination—the Alt key and a letter key. An Alt sequence in 1-2-3 can be structured to make decisions when the sequence is executed. These decisions can be based either on values found in the spreadsheet or on input from the user at the time the sequence is executed. By combining the typing-alternative features of 1-2-3's macro capability with the capability's programming language, you can cause the macro to pause and wait for user input.

When you begin to use 1-2-3's sophisticated command language, you'll discover the power available for your special applications of 1-2-3. For the application developer, the macro command language is much like a programming language (such as BASIC), but the programming process is significantly simplified by all the powerful features of 1-2-3's spreadsheet, database, and graphics commands. Whether you want to use 1-2-3's command language to create typing alternatives or to program, Chapter 12 gives you the information you need to get started.

NEW WITH
R2

Conclusion

1-2-3 has become an extraordinarily popular program for many reasons. First, it combines several sought-after functions into one program. Second, and more important, the program is "done right." 1-2-3 is one of the first microcomputer programs ever released that is not filled with compromises. Third, the program is fun to use, especially for those who have used VisiCalc.

Although 1-2-3 should not be mistaken for a full-featured office automation system, the program does represent a bridge between traditional spreadsheets and the integrated programs such as Symphony and Framework. Each element of the program is a full-fledged application program in its own right. Together, these elements offer unprecedented power and flexibility.

2
Getting Started

The First Step

The first step in getting started with 1-2-3 is to tailor the program to your particular computer system. There are three different considerations here. First, 1-2-3 has to know what kind of display hardware you have. For example, different graphics control characters are used to display color graphs on a color monitor instead of displaying regular black-and-white graphs on a monochrome display equipped with a Hercules Graphics Card.

The second consideration is the printer configuration. Depending on the particular printer model and the size and shape of the report you want to print, certain special settings must be selected. In many cases, the system defaults can be used. But if you have a 132-character printer, for example, you will want to change some of the settings. If your printer is capable of printing graphs, you will want also to install the printer for 1-2-3 graphics.

The third and final consideration is the preparation of data disks for use with 1-2-3.

Installing 1-2-3 System Disks

Installing the 1-2-3 system disks is a fairly easy procedure and a necessary part of configuring the program to your system. Without this step, the 1-2-3 program will run, but you will not be able to use your printer with 1-2-3 or display graphs on the screen.

Six disks come in the 1-2-3 package, and all of them must be installed. They are as follows:

System disk
Backup System disk
PrintGraph disk
Utility disk
A View of 1-2-3 disk
Install Library disk

The most important of these disks, the System disk, contains all of 1-2-3's operations excluding one: the commands for printing graphs. Printing graphs requires the use of the separate PrintGraph disk (see Chapter 10).

Note that the 1-2-3 System disk contains a hidden copy protection scheme. Individual files on the System disk can be copied, but you cannot use a "copy" of the System disk to start up the program. When 1-2-3 starts up, the program checks the System disk for the copy protection scheme. If 1-2-3 cannot find the scheme, the program will not run. Lotus provides a Backup System disk in case the System disk should be lost or damaged.

The Utility disk contains programs for installation and data transfer. The Install program on the Utility disk enables you to tailor 1-2-3 for your computer system. The Utility disk also contains a Translate program that you use to transfer data between 1-2-3 and VisiCalc, dBASE II, dBASE III, Symphony, Jazz, and earlier releases of 1-2-3. Choices from the Translate program screen are made in columns rather than rows.

The A View of 1-2-3 disk contains a brief, on-line demonstration of some of 1-2-3's features. If you are a new user, you should spend a few minutes with this demonstration to become familiar with the program. If you are an experienced user who is upgrading to Release 2 from an earlier release, you can use this demonstration to get the feel of the new release.

The remaining disk, the Install Library disk, contains the library of drivers that you use with the Install program to set up 1-2-3 for your system. Drivers, briefly, are programs that 1-2-3 uses to control your hardware. Different drivers are used to control, for example, a color monitor and a black-and-white monitor.

You must take several steps to prepare your disks before you can run the Install program to set up 1-2-3 for your system. The steps required before you can run the Install program depend on whether you are going to use 1-2-3 on a computer with two floppy disk drives or on a computer with a hard disk drive.

Two-Disk System

The general procedure for preparing and then using the six disks that come with 1-2-3 on a system with two floppy disk drives is as follows:

1. Make backup copies of the PrintGraph disk, the Utility disk, the Install Library disk, and the A View of 1-2-3 disk.

2. Add the DOS file COMMAND.COM to the System disk, the Backup System disk, and the copies of the PrintGraph disk, the Utility disk, and the A View of 1-2-3 disk.

Making Backup Copies

Lotus provides you with a backup copy of the System disk, but you must make backup copies of the other disks. You cannot copy the System disk or the Backup System disk, either one of which must be used to start the program. It is a good idea to work with backup copies of your other master disks and store the masters in a safe place. Should you damage one of the backup disks in any way, you can use the master disk to make a replacement copy.

Before making backup copies, you should become familiar with your computer's disk operating system. Refer to the books mentioned in the Introduction or to your system's manual for specific explanations of formatting disks and copying files. Keep in mind that you can use Release 2 of 1-2-3 with DOS V2.0 or later, but not with DOS V1.0 or V1.1. Follow these steps for creating backup copies and adding the COMMAND.COM file from your DOS disk to the 1-2-3 disks.

To copy disks with a system that has two floppy disk drives, do the following:

1. Format four blank disks, using the DOS FORMAT.COM program.

2. Label these four disks as follows:

    Backup Copy: PrintGraph disk
    Backup Copy: Utility disk
    Backup Copy: A View of 1-2-3 disk
    Backup Copy: Install Library disk

3. Copy each 1-2-3 master disk, with the exception of the System disk, onto the appropriate formatted blank disk as follows:

a. With DOS operating, place the master 1-2-3 disk in drive A and the formatted blank disk in drive B.

b. At the A> prompt, type *copy a:*.* b:/v* and press Enter. The /v will verify the copy. (Lotus suggests using the COPY command instead of the DISKCOPY command.)

c. Once all files have been copied from the master disk onto the formatted disk, remove the master disk from drive A and the backup copy from drive B.

d. Repeat steps 3a through 3c for the PrintGraph Disk, the Utility disk, the A View of 1-2-3 disk, and the Install Library disk.

Adding COMMAND.COM to the 1-2-3 Disks

Lotus suggests that you copy the file COMMAND.COM from your DOS disk to the System disk, the Backup System disk, and your copies of the PrintGraph disk, the Utility Disk, and the A View of 1-2-3 disk. If the COMMAND.COM file is not present on any of these 1-2-3 disks, the error message Insert disk with \COMMAND.COM in drive A and strike any key when ready appears on the screen when you attempt to exit 1-2-3.

You can't boot your computer with the System disk in drive A because there isn't enough room on the System disk for the necessary DOS files.

With the DOS A> prompt on the screen and your DOS disk in drive A, proceed through the steps that follow.

1. Place the 1-2-3 System disk in drive B. Make sure there is no write-protect tab on the disk.

2. Type the command *copy a:command.com b:/v* and press the Enter key.

3. Remove the disk from drive B.

4. Repeat steps 1 through 3 for the Backup System disk and your backup copies of the PrintGraph disk, the Utility disk, and the A View of 1-2-3 disk.

Finally, put the 1-2-3 master disks (except the System disk) in a safe location.

Hard Disk System

The following steps are required to copy the 1-2-3 disks onto your hard disk drive so that all the 1-2-3 programs can be started from your hard disk. (Because of the copy protection, however, you'll still need the System disk in drive A each time you start the 1-2-3 program from the hard disk.)

1. Start your computer with DOS.

2. Type *c:* and press Enter if the hard disk is not the default start-up drive.

3. Create a subdirectory to hold the 1-2-3 files (for example, MD \123 to create a subdirectory of the current directory named 123). Make that directory the current directory (for example, CD C:\123 to make the subdirectory C:\123 the current directory.)

4. Copy the contents of each 1-2-3 master disk, starting with the System disk, onto the hard disk.

   a. Place the master 1-2-3 disk in drive A.

   b. Type *copy a:*.*/v* and press Enter. (DOS recognizes that you want the files copied to the current directory.)

   c. When copying is completed, remove the master 1-2-3 disk from drive A.

   d. Repeat steps 4a through 4c for the System disk, the PrintGraph disk, the Utility disk, the A View of 1-2-3 disk, and the Install Library disk.

Finally, put all the master 1-2-3 disks (except the System disk) in a safe location.

Normally, you must place the System disk in drive A as a key disk when starting the 1-2-3 program. The System disk is used only to verify that you have a legitimate copy of 1-2-3, with the rest of the 1-2-3 program read off the hard disk. After 1-2-3 has started up, you can remove the System disk from drive A.

As an alternative, Lotus provides a program to write the copy protection information onto your hard disk. If you use this special program, then you don't need to place the System disk in drive A to start 1-2-3. In fact, the copy protection on the System disk is altered so that you can't use the System disk while the copy protection is installed on the hard disk. You must use the uninstall option of the hard disk copy-protect program to restore the System disk to operation.

Think carefully before writing the copy protection onto the hard disk. If something happens to the hard disk, you may lose the copy protection information. Warning: You should not install the copy protection on your hard disk if you use a tape backup for your hard disk. If you do a file-by-file backup and restore, you erase all the copy protection information on the hard disk. If the copy protection information is lost for any reason, you have to use your Backup System disk to run 1-2-3 and seek a replacement for your nonfunctional System disk.

NEW WITH
R2

Installing Drivers

Installing driver programs is the next step in tailoring 1-2-3 disks to your particular system. The drivers are small programs that reside in the driver library on the Install Library disk. This step was not necessary with the original version of 1-2-3, Version 1.0. Lotus later decided, however, and wisely so, that rather than carry the overhead for all the different system configurations, the company would give you a way to match the 1-2-3 program to your particular system.

NEW WITH
R2

Using the Install Program

The driver files store information about your computer system, such as information about the display(s), printer(s), and plotter. You can create one or many driver files, depending on your needs. If, for example, you want to run 1-2-3 on an IBM PC that is capable of displaying graphics in color, and also run the program on a COMPAQ displaying graphics and text in one color, then two separate driver files will enable you to run 1-2-3 on both computers whenever you like.

When you make your driver selection, review carefully the options. Whether your system can display graphs and text at the same time and in color depends on a number of factors: the type of monitor(s) you will be using; the type of color cards, if any; the adapter (whether it will produce only text or also graphics and color); and the number of colors that are displayed.

Some equipment selections enable you to view text and graphics only at different times on the screen (One Monitor mode). An IBM color monitor with a color card, for example, will display graphs and text in color, but not at the same time. Some dual monitor combinations, on the other hand, enable you to view color graphs on one screen and text on the other at the same time (Two Monitor mode).

NEW WITH
R2

Before you run the Install program, prepare a list of your equipment. First, you need to indicate to 1-2-3 what display hardware you have. For example, a color monitor uses graphics control characters that are different from those for a monochrome monitor equipped with a Hercules Graphics Card, which displays regular black-and-white graphs.

Second, you need to indicate to the program what kind of printer(s) you have. You can specify more than one printer at installation, then select the proper one from within 1-2-3.

Third, 1-2-3 will ask you to indicate the graphics printer(s) or plotter(s) you will be using. Again, if you specify several graphics printers during installation, you can later select the proper one from within 1-2-3. Keep in mind that multiple printer drivers take up space on your 1-2-3 disk. If disk space is a problem, keep the list of printers down to a minimum.

Another installation option you can choose is the sort order, an option that is not affected by the kind of equipment you are using. (Note: to set the sort order, you must select the Advanced Options at the main Installation menu.)

Two data sort options are available:

1. English-like language with numbers first

2. English-like language with numbers last

The data sort selection regulates whether 1-2-3 sorts database entries beginning with numbers before (selection 1) or after (selection 2) it sorts entries beginning with letters. For example, consider a database containing inventory codes, some beginning with numbers and some beginning with letters. 1-2-3 will sort those beginning with numbers first and then those with letters, if you have selected numbers first for your driver set.

When installing drivers, you provide information for required equipment and any optional equipment you plan to use. The monitor you specify is considered required equipment. You can skip the steps in the Install program that are addressed to optional equipment if you do not plan to use any optional equipment. If, for example, you are not

NEW WITH R2

going to use a graphics printer or a plotter, the 1-2-3 Install program allows you to skip the steps for adding these pieces of equipment to the driver set.

The procedure for setting drivers to run 1-2-3 with your equipment is as follows:

1. Place the Utility disk in drive A if your system has two floppy disk drives, or change the current directory to the subdirectory containing the 1-2-3 programs if your system has a hard disk drive. Then, at the DOS A> prompt (C> is the prompt for hard disk drives), type *install*.

2. Begin the install process. If you have a system with two floppy disk drives, you replace the Utility disk with the Install Library disk when 1-2-3 prompts you to do so. When the main install menu appears, select First Time Installation for step-by-step guidance through the installation process. (You can also edit an existing driver set with Change Selected Equipment and change certain installation settings like the sort order with Advanced Options.)

3. Follow the step-by-step directions that appear on the screen for creating and naming the driver. If you are creating only one driver, you may use the default driver name 123.SET. If you are creating two or more drivers, you must name each driver.

4. Follow the directions for saving the driver(s). If your system has two floppy disks, you save the driver(s) on the System disk, the PrintGraph disk, and the A View of 1-2-3 disk. If your system has a hard disk drive, you save the driver(s) in the subdirectory that contains the 1-2-3 programs.

After you have completed installing your 1-2-3 disks, they should be ready to run with your equipment.

Replacing Your 1-2-3 System Disk

As mentioned previously, Lotus provides the Backup System disk in case your master System disk is lost or destroyed. For information on replacing your 1-2-3 System disk, refer to the Customer Assurance Plan that comes with the 1-2-3 disks.

Configuring the Printer and the Data Disk

After the drivers are installed, the configuration must be set for the printer and the default drive for disk storage. 1-2-3 helps in this process by saving certain default settings from session to session. Lotus provides a default configuration for all settings, but you will want to change some of the settings.

The actual settings for the printer are accessed by entering the /Worksheet Global Default Printer command (see Chapter 8). The settings for the default drive for disk storage are accessed with the /Worksheet Global Default Disk command (see Chapter 7). The default drive for transferring data to and from disk storage is drive B. This drive assignment may have to be changed if you have a hard disk system.

Preparing Data Disks

The final procedure in getting started with 1-2-3 is preparing data disks. For those who are unfamiliar with preparing disks, all disks must be properly formatted using the DOS FORMAT command before they can be used. By using the 1-2-3 /System command, you can initialize a blank disk without exiting from the program (see Chapter 4).

Using the Lotus Access System

Lotus devised the Lotus Access System as a way to tie all the different functions of 1-2-3 together in one unit (fig. 2.1). This system is a series of menus that gives you the ability to move back and forth between 1-2-3 and other Lotus programs for printing graphs; to transfer files between 1-2-3 and other outside programs, such as dBASE, Symphony, and VisiCalc; and to access the Install and the A View of 1-2-3 programs within 1-2-3.

To enter the Lotus Access System, you must first load the System disk into drive A and enter *lotus* at the A> system prompt. The Lotus Access System command menu will appear after a few seconds. There are six different functions available in the command menu:

    1-2-3   PrintGraph   Translate   Install   View   Exit

These options should not intimidate you. Taken individually, they are very easy to understand and use. If you have any questions when you are in the Access System, you can always get help by pressing F1, just

NEW WITH

R2

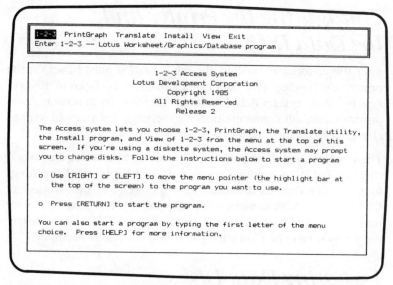

```
┌──────────────────────────────────────────────────────────────┐
│ │1-2-3│ PrintGraph  Translate  Install  View  Exit            │
│ Enter 1-2-3 -- Lotus Worksheet/Graphics/Database program       │
│ ┌────────────────────────────────────────────────────────────┐│
│ │                   1-2-3 Access System                      ││
│ │               Lotus Development Corporation                ││
│ │                     Copyright 1985                         ││
│ │                    All Rights Reserved                     ││
│ │                        Release 2                           ││
│ │                                                            ││
│ │ The Access system lets you choose 1-2-3, PrintGraph, the Translate utility, ││
│ │ the Install program, and View of 1-2-3 from the menu at the top of this ││
│ │ screen.  If you're using a diskette system, the Access system may prompt ││
│ │ you to change disks.  Follow the instructions below to start a program ││
│ │                                                            ││
│ │ o  Use [RIGHT] or [LEFT] to move the menu pointer (the highlight bar at ││
│ │      the top of the screen) to the program you want to use. ││
│ │                                                            ││
│ │ o  Press [RETURN] to start the program.                    ││
│ │                                                            ││
│ │ You can also start a program by typing the first letter of the menu ││
│ │ choice.  Press [HELP] for more information.                ││
│ └────────────────────────────────────────────────────────────┘│
└──────────────────────────────────────────────────────────────┘
```

Fig. 2.1. The Lotus Access System.

as in 1-2-3. The help screen lists the different Access System options and their use. If you have questions about a particular option, you can press F1 to get information.

Entering and Exiting from 1-2-3

The first option in the Lotus Access System menu is to enter 1-2-3. To do this, either point to 1-2-3 by using the right- or left-arrow keys and press Enter, or type *1* and press Enter. It will take several seconds for the 1-2-3 logo to appear on the screen. The 1-2-3 logo will appear on the screen for a few seconds; then the worksheet will appear.

You can also enter 1-2-3 without going through the Lotus Access System by typing *123* at the DOS prompt and pressing Enter. This method saves time and memory space. You can also save more time later by not having to exit from the Access System at the end of the session.

Whatever way you choose to enter 1-2-3, you should make sure that the date and time have been entered correctly with the DOS DATE command. (When a worksheet is saved, the date and time are saved with all other data. This can be helpful if you want to see the last time a file was accessed.) 1-2-3's @NOW function takes the date and time from the entries you make in DOS. If this function is not entered correctly, DOS and 1-2-3 assume the default time; the @NOW function will return that default date. (Remember that computer time increments and the default date and time will not remain the same unless the computer is shut off.)

If your system has an internal clock or you don't intend to use the @NOW function, you won't have to worry about entering the time and date.

To exit the 1-2-3 program, enter /Quit from the 1-2-3 main command menu (fig. 2.2). This command is used by all the programs in the Lotus Access system. If you look at the 1-2-3 command menu, you will see the Quit option at the end of the list of menu items. If you enter 1-2-3 directly from DOS, without going through the Lotus Access system, the DOS command prompt A> will appear right after you select Quit.

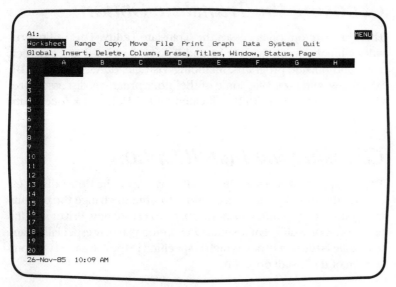

Fig. 2.2. The 1-2-3 main command menu.

If you entered 1-2-3 from the Lotus Access System, Quit will return you to it. To exit from the Access System, select Exit from the command menu.

Exit is the final option in the Lotus Access System menu. You must choose Exit (Release 1A and 2) or PC DOS (Release 1) to end the Lotus Access System program. When you do so, the DOS prompt A> will appear.

If you exit from the Lotus Access System prematurely, you can easily reenter it by typing *lotus* at the DOS prompt A>.

Choosing the PrintGraph Option

The **PrintGraph** option in the Access System menu initiates the PrintGraph program for printing graph files. After this option is chosen, the PrintGraph disk must be placed in the disk drive to run the program (see Chapter 10).

You can also go directly to the PrintGraph program without going through the Lotus Access System. To do this, with the PrintGraph disk in the drive, you enter the word *graph* at the DOS prompt.

NEW WITH
R2

Choosing the Translate Option

The **Translate** option accesses the Translate Utility. This utility provides a link between Release 1A and Release 2 of 1-2-3 and between 1-2-3 and outside programs, including VisiCalc, dBASE II, dBASE III, Symphony, and Jazz. Like some of the other programs discussed previously, the Translate Utility is located on the Utility disk (see Chapter 7).

NEW WITH
R2

Choosing the Install Option

The **Install** option accesses the Install program on the Utility disk. You can use the Install program from time to time to change the options that you set during initial installation, or to create new driver sets for using 1-2-3 on a different system. One option you may especially want to change is the sort order, which is specified in the Advanced Options section of the Install program.

Choosing the View Option

The **View** option simply accesses the A View of 1-2-3 disk (see the following section).

1-2-3 User Friendliness

One of the biggest selling points of 1-2-3 is its user friendliness. Lotus obviously went to a great deal of trouble to ensure that the spreadsheet is easy to learn and use.

The most outstanding user-friendly feature of 1-2-3 is the tremendous support Lotus provides for the new user who is learning 1-2-3. Lotus provides A View of 1-2-3, an on-line introduction to the features and business applications of 1-2-3; and the Tutorial, a self-paced instructional manual that leads you through the creation of a series of actual 1-2-3 worksheets that use important features of 1-2-3.

The A View of 1-2-3 Disk

NEW WITH
R2

A View of 1-2-3, shown in figure 2.3, has three sections: an introductory section that presents an overview of 1-2-3 for the new user, a sample business analysis session that shows how 1-2-3 can be used to evaluate alternative business strategies, and for the experienced Release 1 or 1A user a section that describes the differences between Release 2 and Release 1A.

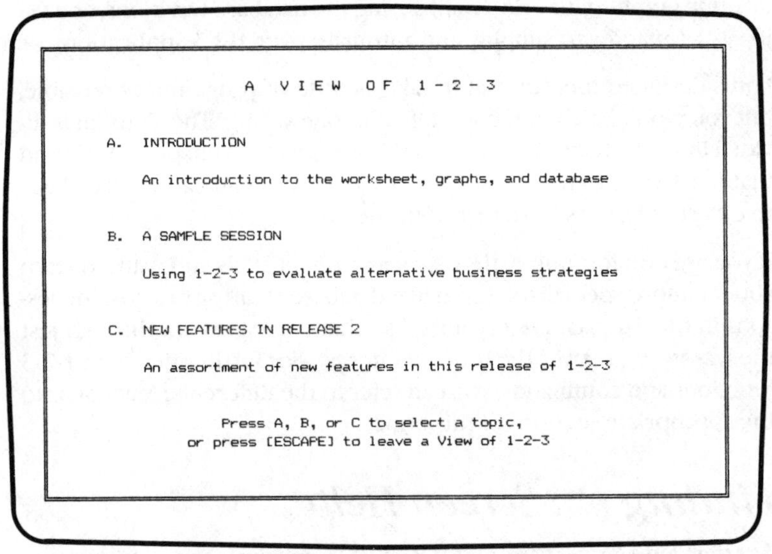

```
                    A   V I E W   O F   1 - 2 - 3


      A.   INTRODUCTION

           An introduction to the worksheet, graphs, and database


      B.   A SAMPLE SESSION

           Using 1-2-3 to evaluate alternative business strategies


      C.   NEW FEATURES IN RELEASE 2

           An assortment of new features in this release of 1-2-3


                   Press A, B, or C to select a topic,
                 or press [ESCAPE] to leave a View of 1-2-3
```

Fig. 2.3. Sample screen display from the A View of 1-2-3 disk.

If you are a new 1-2-3 user, we recommend that you work through the introductory section and the sample business analysis section of A View of 1-2-3. Each section takes from a half hour to a couple of hours to complete, and you gain a good overview of how 1-2-3 operates and what its capabilities are.

NEW WITH
R2

Taking the 1-2-3 Tutorial

The second part of the learning materials is the Tutorial manual, a self-paced guide to learning 1-2-3. The Tutorial goes through a series of lessons on 1-2-3 in a step-by-step fashion. The lessons are arranged in order of increasing difficulty and build on each other. The Tutorial does not cover all of 1-2-3's functions and commands but covers enough to give you a basic understanding of the program.

The Tutorial assumes that you have successfully installed your 1-2-3 disks and have worked through A View of 1-2-3. The Tutorial begins by providing complete instructions for starting up your computer with 1-2-3, moving the cursor around the worksheet, and accessing the 1-2-3 command menu.

The Tutorial progresses through lessons on basic worksheet skills, more advanced worksheet skills, printing reports from the worksheet, printing graphs with PrintGraph, using the database functions, and using 1-2-3 macros to simplify and automate your 1-2-3 applications.

Lotus designed the Tutorial to take as little of your time as possible, but you won't be able to complete it in one sitting. The Tutorial is divided into six chapters with several lessons in each chapter. We found that it is better to do a lesson or two at a time. You can go back later to different lessons to refresh your memory.

If you are comfortable with basic spreadsheet skills and want to learn about a more specialized topic like database skills or macros, the lessons in the Tutorial are organized so that you can work through just the lessons that cover the topic of interest. For further detail on 1-2-3 functions and commands, you can refer to the Reference Manual or to the appropriate sections of this book.

Finding On-Screen Help

Another friendly feature of 1-2-3 is its extensive series of interconnected help screens. By pressing the Help (F1) key, you can gain access to the Help Index screen, shown in figure 2.4. This screen has headings that can connect you to more than 200 Help screens (fig. 2.5).

Each screen contains information about a single topic as well as reverse video headings positioned at the foot of the screen. These headings allow you to move to other topics or back to the Help Index screen.

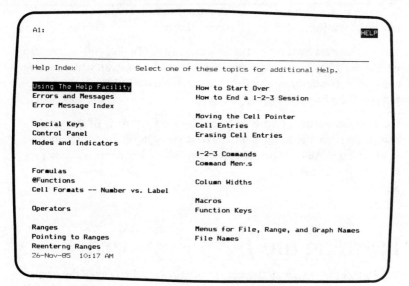

Fig. 2.4. Help Index screen.

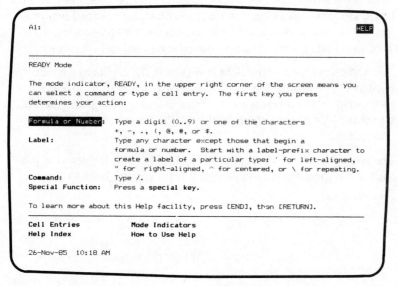

Fig. 2.5. Help screen.

To move to another topic, use the cursor-movement keys to move the cursor to another heading, then press Enter.

One of the best features of the on-screen help facility is that you can press the F1 key at any time during a 1-2-3 session, even while issuing a command or defining a cell. Once you have the information, you return to 1-2-3 by pressing the Esc key.

Other good features of this help facility are that many of the screens refer to pages in the 1-2-3 manual so that you can get more explanation if you need it. Also, by pressing the Backspace key, you can view previous help screens again.

Learning the 1-2-3 Keyboard

1-2-3 makes more use of the keys of the IBM PC than any of the earlier spreadsheet programs. The keyboard, shown in figure 2.6, is divided into three sections: the alphanumeric keyboard in the center, the numeric keypad on the right, and the special-function key section on the left. This arrangement makes it easier to take a general look at how groups of keys are used in 1-2-3.

Most of the keys in the alphanumeric section at the center of the keyboard are found on a typewriter and maintain their normal functions in 1-2-3. Several keys, however, take on new and unique functions: Esc, Tab, Shift, and Alt (which is not found on typewriter keyboards).

The numeric keypad on the right-hand side of the keyboard is normally used for entering numbers in most programs on the IBM PC. The main purpose in 1-2-3, however, is cursor movement. Although this method works well for moving the cursor, it limits the use of these keys for entering numbers.

The special-function keys on the left-hand side of the keyboard are designed for special situations ranging from getting help to drawing graphs.

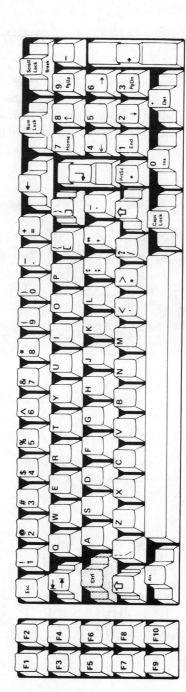

Fig. 2.6. Keyboard diagram.

The Alphanumeric Keyboard

Although most of the alphanumeric keys shown in figure 2.7 have the same functions as on a typewriter, several keys have special functions in 1-2-3, which are listed in table 2.1. If some of the functions do not make much sense the first time through, don't worry. Their meaning will become clearer as you read more of this chapter and subsequent ones.

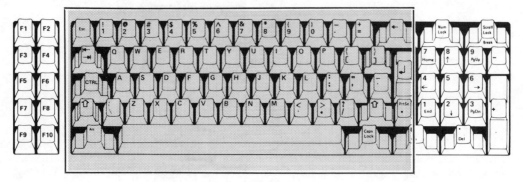

Fig. 2.7. The alphanumeric keyboard.

The Numeric Keypad

The keys in the numeric keypad on the right-hand side of the keyboard are mainly used for cursor movement (fig. 2.8). The keys and their functions are listed in table 2.2.

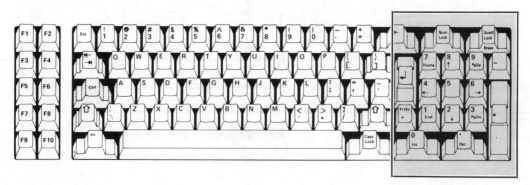

Fig. 2.8. The numeric keypad.

Table 2.1
Alphanumeric Key Operation

Key	Function
Esc	Erases current entry when specifying a command line or range, erases a command menu, or returns from a help screen
→ (Tab)	Moves cursor one screen to the right when used alone, and one screen to the left when used with the Shift key
Alt	Used simultaneously with other individual alpha keys to invoke keyboard macros. (See Chapter 12, "Keyboard Macros and CommandLanguage.")
↑ (Shift)	Changes the central section of the keyboard to uppercase letters and characters. It also allows you to key in numbers, using the numeric keypad on the right (equivalent of a temporary Num Lock).
← (Backspace)	When defining the contents of a cell, erases the previous character in the definition
/ (Slash)	Used to start a command. Also used in its normal function as a division sign.
. (Period)	Used to separate cell addresses when ranges of cells are defined and, in a different manner, to anchor cell addresses when pointing. (For more on ranges, see Chapter 4.) It is also used as a decimal point.

Table 2.2
Numeric Key Operation

Keys	Function
Home	Returns to cell A1 from any location in the worksheet. Also used after the End key to position the cursor at the active end of the worksheet. Also used in EDIT mode to jump to the beginning of the edit line.
End	When entered prior to any of the arrow keys, positions the cursor in the direction of the arrow key to the cell on the boundary of an empty and filled space. Also used in EDIT mode to jump to the end of the edit line.
← →	Left- and right-arrow keys. Used to position the cursor one column left or right.
↑ ↓	Up- and down-arrow keys. Used to position the cursor one row up or down.
Num Lock	Activates the numeric character of the keys in the numeric keypad
Del	Used in editing command lines (covered under F2 in the next section) to delete the character above the cursor.
Scroll Lock/ Break	In Scroll Lock position, used to scroll the entire screen one row or column in any direction each time the cell pointer is moved. In the Break position, used with Ctrl to return 1-2-3 to READY mode.
PgUp	Used to move up an entire screen
PgDn	Used to move down an entire screen

1-2-3 uses the End key in a unique way. When you press an arrow key after you have pressed and released the End key, the cursor will move in the direction of the arrow key to the next boundary between a blank cell and a cell that contains data. Although this process may sound complex, in practice it's useful. We'll look at several interesting applications for the End key in the following chapters. Figure 2.9 demonstrates the movement of the cursor with the End key. Figure 2.10 shows all the cursor movement types mentioned previously.

When you want to use the numeric keypad to enter numbers rather than to position the cursor, you can do one of two things. First, you can use the Num Lock key before entering the numbers, and press the key again when you are done. (This is the method used in most IBM PC software.) The second way is to hold down the Shift key while simultaneously pressing the number keys. Neither way is ideal, but this is one of the trade-offs that Lotus made when it decided to use the numeric keypad for cursor movement.

In Chapter 12, you will learn how to create a macro that will enter numbers down a column of cells without having to press the Num Lock key or hold down the Shift key. You can easily apply the macro to entering numbers in any direction.

The Special-Function Keys

The special-function keys, F1 through F10, are used for special situations in 1-2-3. Lotus provides a plastic function-key template that fits over the function keys of the IBM PC. A special version of this template is also available for COMPAQ owners who send the purchase registration card to Lotus. Unfortunately, the template does not give you enough information when you are first starting out. To help you in the first sessions until you have memorized the functions, we have provided table 2.3, which lists the function keys, an explanation of what each key does, and a reference to subsequent discussion.

The special-function key table refers you to different sections in this book for further explanations of the various function keys. Because all of the keys except F5 are explained sufficiently elsewhere, only F5 is discussed here.

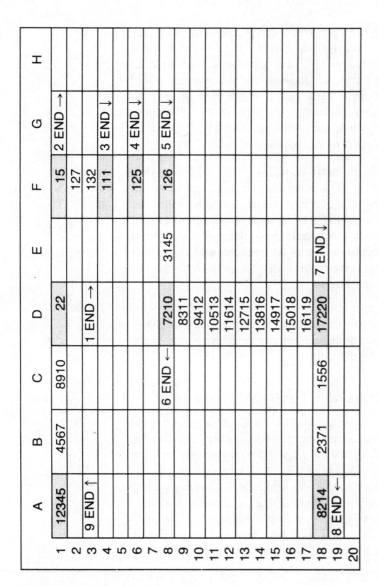

	A	B	C	D	E	F	G	H
1	12345	4567	8910	22		15	2 END →	
2						127		
3	9 END ←			1 END →		132		
4						111	3 END →	
5								
6						125	4 END →	
7								
8			6 END ←	7210	3145	126	5 END →	
9				8311				
10				9412				
11				10513				
12				11614				
13				12715				
14				13816				
15				14917				
16				15018				
17				16119				
18	8214	2371	1556	17220	7 END →			
19	8 END ←							
20								

Fig. 2.9. Using the End key.

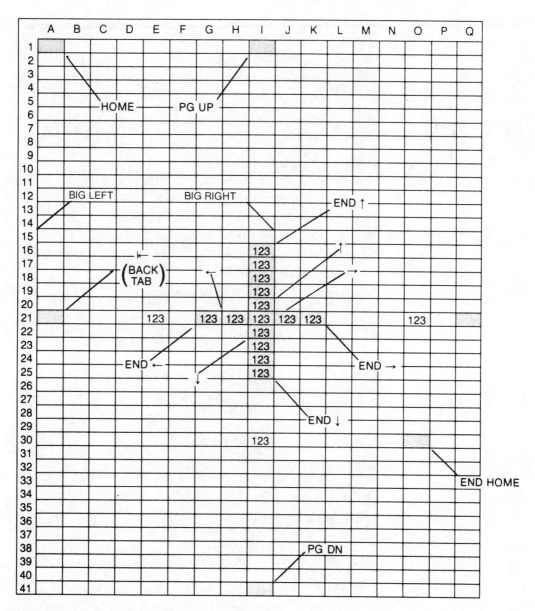

Fig. 2.10. Cursor-movement chart.

NEW WITH
R2

Table 2.3
Function Key Operation

Key	Function	Discussion
Alt–F1 (Compose)	Used with other keys to make International Characters	Chapter 3, "Special Characters in Labels"
Alt–F2 (Step)	Shifts 1-2-3 into single-step mode for debugging macros	Chapter 12, "Debugging a Macro"
F1 (Help)	Accesses 1-2-3's on-line help facility	Chapter 2, "On-Screen Help"
F2 (Edit)	Shifts 1-2-3 into EDIT mode. Allows contents of cells to be altered without retyping the entire cell.	Chapter 3, "Editing"
F3 (Name)	In POINT mode, displays a list of the range names in the current worksheet. Pressing F3 a second time switches to a full screen display of range names.	Chapter 4, "Examples Using Range Names"
F4 (Abs)	Used during cell definition to change a relative cell address into an absolute or mixed address	Chapter 4, "Setting Absolute and Relative References"
F5 (GoTo)	Moves the cursor to the cell coordinates (or range name) provided	Chapter 2, "The Special-Function Keys"
F6 (Window)	Moves the cursor to the other side of a split screen	Chapter 4, "Splitting the Screen"

F7 (Query)	Repeats the most recent Data Query operation	Chapter 11, "Output Range"
F8 (Table)	Repeats the most recent Data Table operation	Chapter 11, "Table-Building"
F9 (Calc)	Recalculates the worksheet	Chapter 4, "Iteration"
F10 (Graph)	Redraws the graph defined by the current graph settings	Chapter 9, "Redrawing the Graph"

Jumping to a Cell

The F5 (Goto) key saves you from having to position the cursor manually to a cell location. When 1-2-3 is in READY mode, F5 allows you to move directly to a cell. F5 cannot be used when you are in the middle of entering a 1-2-3 command or making a cell entry (that is, when you are not in READY mode). For VisiCalc users, 1-2-3's F5 is the equivalent of VisiCalc's >.

Another nice feature of the F5 key is that you can combine the key with range names. When 1-2-3 asks you for the address "to go to," you can enter *Ratios* instead of *A94*, for example. (This is covered in the "Naming Ranges" section of Chapter 4.)

Learning the 1-2-3 Screen Display

The main 1-2-3 display is divided into two parts: the control panel at the top of the screen, and the worksheet area itself. A reverse video border separates the two areas. This border contains the letters and numbers that mark columns and rows.

Other important areas of the screen are the mode indicators (upper right corner), the "lock" key indicator (lower right corner), and the error messages area in the lower left corner.

The Control Panel

The control panel is the area above the reverse video border. This area has three lines, each with a special purpose. As figure 2.11 indicates, the first line contains all the information about the *current cell*. A current cell is the cell where the pointer is currently located. The first item in the line is the address of the cell. The second item is the display format, which is always displayed in parentheses. (Display formats are covered in detail in Chapter 5.) The last item in the first line is the actual contents of the current cell.

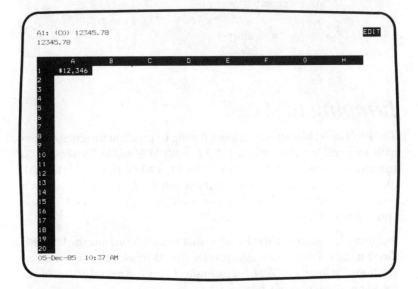

Fig. 2.11. The 1-2-3 display.

The second line in the control panel contains the characters that are being entered or edited. The third line contains explanations of the current command menu item. If you move the pointer from one item to the next in a command menu, the explanation on the third line of the control panel will change each time. If a command menu is not in effect, this line will be blank.

The Mode Indicators

There are several modes in 1-2-3, one of which is always in effect depending on what you are doing. The mode indicator is located in the upper right corner of the screen and always shows the current mode

Table 2.4
Mode Indicators and Descriptions

Mode Indicator	Description
READY	1-2-3 is waiting for you to enter a command or make a cell entry.
VALUE	A number or formula is being entered.
LABEL	A label is being entered.
EDIT	A cell entry is being edited.
POINT	A range is being pointed to.
FILES	1-2-3 is waiting for you to select from a file name.
MENU	A menu item is being selected.
HELP	1-2-3 is displaying a help screen.
ERROR	An error has occurred, and 1-2-3 is waiting for you to press Esc or Enter to acknowledge the error.
WAIT	1-2-3 is in the middle of a command and cannot respond to other commands. Flashes on and off.
FIND	1-2-3 is in the middle of a **/Data Query** operation and cannot respond to commands.

that 1-2-3 is in. The mode indicators and descriptions of the functions are listed in table 2.4.

The Lock Key Indicators

There are three "lock" keys on the IBM PC: Num Lock, Caps Lock, and Scroll Lock (see fig. 2.12). In the other spreadsheet programs, it is hard to tell whether these keys are on or off. But in 1-2-3, you always know their status, because a special area of the screen has been set aside to show that information. Each key has its own reverse video indicator that appears in the lower right corner of the screen when the key has been activated.

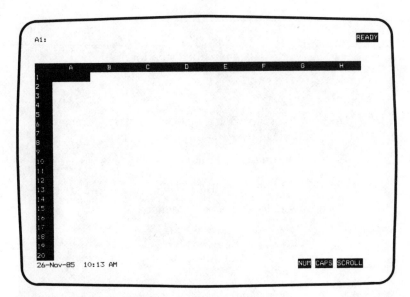

Fig. 2.12. The lock key indicators.

Other Indicators

Other indicators in 1-2-3 also appear in the lower right corner of the screen. They display the status of certain keys and special situations and are listed in table 2.5.

The Error Messages Area

When an error occurs in 1-2-3, a message will appear in the lower left corner of the screen. The error may occur for many reasons: the disk you are trying to save a file to is full, a cell formula is too long, there are no files on disk of the type you are looking for, etc.

To clear the error and get back to the READY mode, you must press Esc or Enter. If you do not press one of these keys, the message will not clear.

Conclusion

The initial steps to getting started with 1-2-3 have included tailoring the program to your particular computer system as well as learning how to use several basic features of the program. In this chapter, you have learned how to use the Lotus Access System, the A View of 1-2-3 disk, the Tutorial, the keyboard, and various parts of the screen. There is only one barrier left to your actually using 1-2-3, and that is how to use the 1-2-3 spreadsheet itself.

Table 2.5
Special Key Indicators and Descriptions

Indicator	Description
CMD	Appears during the execution of a keyboard macro (see Chapter 12).
SST	Appears when in single-step execution of a keyboard macro
STEP	Alt–F2 has been pressed, and you are currently stepping through a macro one cell at a time (see Chapter 12).
END	The End key has been pressed and is now active.
CALC	Global Recalculation has been set to Manual (see "Recalculation" section of Chapter 4).
CIRC	A circular reference has been found in the worksheet (see "Iteration" section of Chapter 4).

3

The 1-2-3 Spreadsheet

The spreadsheet is the foundation of the 1-2-3 program. In fact, if 1-2-3 were simply a spreadsheet program without graphics and database functions, it would still be an amazing software product.

The importance of the spreadsheet as the basis for the whole product cannot be overemphasized. All the commands for the related features are initiated from the same main command menu as the spreadsheet commands, and all the commands are in the same style. For a complete listing of all of 1-2-3's commands, see the Command Menu Map included at the back of the book.

Also, all the special features of 1-2-3 originate from the spreadsheet. For instance, in data management, the database is composed of records that are actually cell entries in a spreadsheet. Similarly, macros are statements that are placed in adjacent cells in out-of-the-way sections of a spreadsheet. Finally, all the commands for displaying graphs refer to entries in the spreadsheet and use these entries to draw graphs on the screen.

As we have seen, the 1-2-3 worksheet contains 8,192 rows and 256 columns, or more that 2,000,000 cells. Each column is assigned a letter value ranging from A for the first column to IV for the last. A good way to visualize the worksheet is as one giant sheet of grid paper that is about 21 feet wide and 171 feet high!

NEW WITH
R2

Like many other spreadsheets, the 1-2-3 worksheet is too large to be viewed at one time on a computer video display. If the default column width of 9 characters is used, only 20 rows and 7 columns can be seen at a time on the screen. As demonstrated in figure 3.1, the screen is like a window over a portion of the 1-2-3 worksheet.

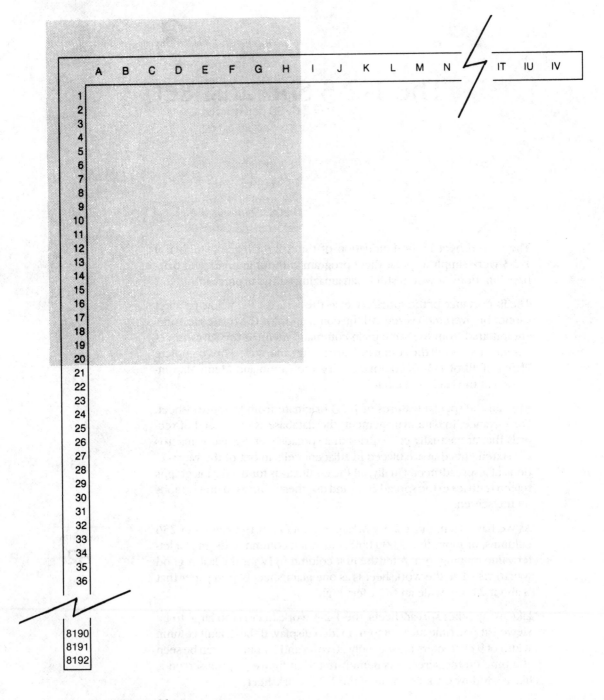

Fig. 3.1. The 1-2-3 spreadsheet.

1-2-3 Spreadsheet Size

The 1-2-3 spreadsheet is more than 131 times larger than the original VisiCalc spreadsheet of 63 columns by 254 rows. Practically speaking, however, there are some limitations to using the entire sheet. If you imagine storing just one character in each of the 2,097,152 cells that are available, you end up with a worksheet that is far larger than the 640K maximum random-access memory (RAM) of an IBM PC.

For Release 2, the program alone requires 215K of RAM. Its large size stems primarily from the programming required for all the extra features that 1-2-3 provides beyond the standard spreadsheet function. Another important reason for the program's size is 1-2-3's extensive memory. 1-2-3 remembers cell formats, worksheet and command ranges, print options, and graph settings. Some information is saved automatically by 1-2-3, but some information must be saved by the user.

NEW WITH
R2

In addition to the size of the 1-2-3 program, the size of the worksheet in RAM must be considered. There is no simple way to equate the number of active cells in a worksheet to its RAM requirements because the contents of cells can vary greatly. Perhaps the best way to get a realistic notion of the potential size of a worksheet is to conduct two simple tests. In the first, we'll relate the size of the worksheet to the number of standard 8 1/2-by-11-inch pages that can fit into it. For the second, we'll experiment with filling cells in the worksheet, using the /Copy command, to learn when we run out of main memory. From these two tests, we can draw conclusions about realistic worksheet size.

To begin the first test, we will use the maximum configuration possible for 1-2-3 without an extended memory card, 640K of RAM. After subtracting the 215K for the 1-2-3 program, 425K of usable memory remains. If we divide the remaining RAM by the number of characters on a standard 8 1/2-by-11-inch page using pica type (66 lines by 80 characters = 5,280 total characters), we get approximately 86 pages. Although this is a rough measure, it points out the tremendous capacity of the 1-2-3 worksheet.

For the second test, we again use a system with 640K of main memory. This time we make various types of entries in cell A1 and copy the entries to other cells until the worksheet is full. Table 3.1 shows the result.

Table 3.1
Spreadsheet Capacity To Hold
Various Types of Entries

Type of Entry	Maximum Number of Cells
Integer (the number 1)	109,580
Real Number (the number 1.1)	36,526
10-Character Label (ABCDEFGHIJ)	27,394
Small Formula (+B1+B2)	10,690
50-Character Label (ABCDEFGHIJKLMNOPQRSTUVWXYZabcdefghijklmnopqrstuvwx)	7,827

As the table shows, the maximum number of nonblank cells in the 1-2-3 spreadsheet depends on the kinds of entries made in those cells. Integer numbers require the least memory per entry; therefore, a spreadsheet containing integer numbers can have substantially more entries than a spreadsheet containing formulas or long labels. In practice, a worksheet for a business application will contain entries of different types, and the maximum number of nonblank cells will be somewhere between the value for all integers and the value for formulas or long labels.

There are few situations in which the size of your worksheet will exceed main memory, unless your system is configured at substantially less than 640K. If you do have an application that exceeds the capacity of your system's main memory, 1-2-3 has the capability to use such special expanded memory boards as the Intel Above Board or the AST Rampage board, to add up to four megabytes of spreadsheet memory to the 640K maximum main memory.

1-2-3 uses the expanded memory to store real numbers, formulas, and labels in the worksheet. Integer numbers are still stored in the main memory, and a pointer is stored in the main memory for each item stored in expanded memory. This expanded memory increases the spreadsheet capacity for any type of entry to the number of integers that can be stored in your system's main memory—approximately 109,000 entries for a system with 640K.

One application that may require large amounts of memory is database management. A computer with 640K of main memory can store about 1,000 four-hundred byte records, or 8,000 fifty-byte records. To handle even larger databases, you will need to invest in an expanded memory card. A database of 8,000 five-hundred byte records requires the maximum four megabytes of expanded memory.

All other things being equal, too much memory is better than too little memory. Because RAM is relatively inexpensive (and is getting even more so) and is important to increasing your productivity with 1-2-3, it makes sense to buy as much RAM as you can.

Remember, though, that an application that requires four megabytes of expanded memory will also require about the same amount of storage on disk. Large spreadsheets or databases that require expanded memory are practical only if you have a hard disk installed in your computer.

If you decide to purchase an expanded memory card, you should not try to install it yourself unless you have had experience "working under the hood" of your computer. Installing the memory card is straightforward for an experienced person, but the average business user would be better off letting his dealer or technical support person install the board.

1-2-3 Release 2 has an advanced memory management scheme that allots main or expanded memory space only to cells with entries. Blank, unformatted cells use no memory space. Earlier spreadsheet programs, including earlier releases of 1-2-3, use memory space for every cell in the active worksheet area (defined as the smallest rectangle that contains all cells with entries). For example, in 1-2-3 Release 2 an entry in cell IV8192, the cell in the lower right corner of the worksheet, takes up no more space than an entry in cell A1. In 1-2-3 Release 1A, however, an attempt to enter a value in cell IV2048 (the lower right corner of 1A's worksheet) results in the error message Memory Full.

When you delete part of a worksheet, 1-2-3 reclaims some of the main memory; you can reuse that memory immediately. This capability is in contrast to earlier spreadsheet programs. After you deleted part of the worksheet in earlier versions of 1-2-3, you had to save and retrieve the worksheet to reclaim memory.

1-2-3 Spreadsheet Speed

NEW WITH
R2

1-2-3's speed of recalculation is another of its outstanding features. 1-2-3 sets a standard for recalculation speed that other programs still have trouble matching. The fact that 1-2-3 is written in 8088 Assembler has a great deal to do with the program's speed. For certain applications involving large spreadsheets with many calculations, you may want to invest in an 8087 or 80287 coprocessor chip. 1-2-3 uses the coprocessor to increase its recalculation speed. The coprocessor is particularly effective in increasing speed when the worksheet contains many calculations involving mathematical functions, such as @SQRT, @EXP, @LN, or the trigonometric functions. However, the coprocessor chip offers little speed improvement for worksheets with simple mathematics: additions and subtractions.

An 8087 coprocessor can improve noticeably 1-2-3's performance in business applications when (1) you use the /Data Table command heavily in your worksheets and (2) in worksheets with simultaneous equations (circular references) that require multiple iterations to solve the worksheet. Interest and debt calculations in a corporate plan, for example, are usually handled by simultaneous equations and iteration.

Again, you should not attempt to install the coprocessor unless you are experienced in adding hardware options. Let your dealer or technical support person install the coprocessor for you.

Two other points to mention with respect to 1-2-3's speed are cursor movement and system loading time. 1-2-3's cursor movement is incredibly fast when compared to other spreadsheet programs. When you press a cursor-movement key, the cursor reacts instantly with almost no visible delay. Unlike several other spreadsheet programs where the screen flickers each time the cursor is moved, 1-2-3 shows almost no flickering. The screen reacts quickly; you can move rapidly to the cell you want without overshooting your mark and ending up several cells beyond.

The system loading time, however, is another story. System loading is probably the slowest thing about 1-2-3 because of the size of the system program itself. On a per-byte basis system loading is relatively fast, but this fact doesn't do you much good when you are waiting to get started. Our tests indicate that loading time takes roughly 23 seconds from the A drive.

Entering Data in the Worksheet

As you recall from earlier spreadsheet experience or from Chapter 1, there are three different types of cell entries: numbers, formulas, and labels. You enter data into a cell simply by positioning the cursor in the cell and typing the entry. 1-2-3 determines the type of cell entry you are making from the first character that you enter. If you start with one of the following characters,

0 1 2 3 4 5 6 7 8 9 + - . (@ # $

1-2-3 will treat your entry as a number or a formula. If you begin by entering a character other than one of the above, 1-2-3 will treat your entry as a label.

Entering Numbers

The rules for entering numbers are simple.

1. A number cannot begin with any character except 0 through 9, a decimal point, or a dollar sign ($).

2. You can end a number with a percent sign (%), which tells 1-2-3 to divide the number that precedes the sign by 100.

3. A number cannot have more than one decimal point.

4. You can enter a number in scientific notation—what 1-2-3 calls the Scientific format (for example, 1.234E+06).

If you do not follow these rules, 1-2-3 will beep when you press Enter while trying to enter the number into the spreadsheet. 1-2-3 also will automatically shift to EDIT mode just as though you had pressed F2. (The "Editing" section later in this chapter explains how to respond.)

Entering Formulas

In addition to simple numbers, formulas can also be entered into cells. Formulas are a complicated topic in 1-2-3 because they incorporate so many different concepts.

Suppose that you want to create a formula that adds a row of numbers. In figure 3.2, you would want to add the amounts in cells B1, C1, D1, and E1, and place the result in cell F1.

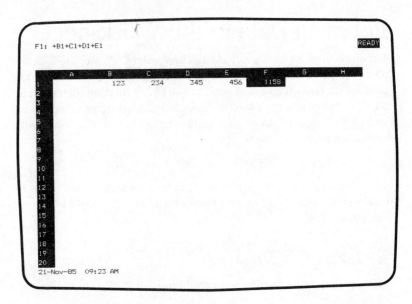

Fig. 3.2. *Simple addition formula.*

One formula that will perform the addition is +B1+C1+D1+E1. Notice the + sign at the beginning of the formula. For 1-2-3 to recognize
the formula as a formula and not a label, the formula must begin with
one of the following characters:

0 1 2 3 4 5 6 7 8 9 . + – (@ # $

Because we started with +, 1-2-3 recognizes our entry as a formula and
switches to VALUE mode, the appropriate mode for entering numbers
and formulas.

Two methods can be used to enter a formula as a cell address: typing
and pointing. Both methods accomplish the same thing, and you can
mix and match the two techniques within the same formula. Typing
cell addresses is self-explanatory, but pointing to cell addresses requires some explanation. The method for pointing to cell addresses is
the same as the method for pointing to cell ranges (see Chapter 4),
but in this case the range is only a single cell.

In figure 3.2, for example, to enter the formula by pointing, you would
move the cell pointer to B1 after entering the first plus sign. Notice
that the address for the cell appears after the plus in the second line
of the control panel—that is, +B1. The mode indicator in the upper
right corner of the screen shifts from VALUE to POINT mode as you
move the cell pointer to cell B1.

To continue to the next address in the formula, you type another plus sign. The cursor will move immediately from cell B1 back to the cell where it was located when you began entering the formula—in this case cell F1. Also, the mode indicator will shift back to VALUE. You continue this sequence of pointing and entering plus signs until you have the formula you want. Remember that you may use a combination of pointing and typing. Use whatever works best for you. Usually, the easiest method is to point at cells that are close to the cell you are defining, and type references to distant cells.

Using Operators in Formulas

Operators indicate arithmetic operations in formulas. Operators can be broken down into two types: mathematical and logical. The mathematical operators are the following:

Operator	Meaning
^	Exponentiation
+, –	Positive, Negative
*, /	Multiplication, Division
+, –	Addition, Subtraction

An important part of understanding operators is knowing their order of precedence. The preceding list is arranged in order of precedence. Operators with the highest order of precedence are at the top. Operators with equal precedence are on the same line. In these cases, the operators are evaluated from left to right. You can always use parentheses to override the order of precedence.

Consider the order of precedence in the following formulas, where B3 = 2, C3 = 3, and D3 = 4, and see if you get the same answers. In the first two formulas notice particularly how parentheses affect the order of precedence and ultimately the answer.

Formula	Answer
C3–D3/B3	1
(C3–D3)/B3	(.5)
D3*C3–B3^C3	4
D3*C3*B3/B3^C3–25/5	(2)

Using Functions

Like most electronic spreadsheets, 1-2-3 includes built-in functions. These functions are simply abbreviations for long or complex mathematical formulas and are considered formulas by 1-2-3. All 1-2-3 functions consist of three parts: the @ sign, a function name, and an argument or range. The @ sign simply signals to 1-2-3 that a function is coming. The name indicates which function is being used. The argument or range is the data required by 1-2-3 to perform the function.

Before we cover functions in detail (in Chapter 6), we will need to cover several other topics, such as the concept of ranges. However, the following example will help you begin to understand 1-2-3 functions.

In figure 3.2, we needed to refer to four cells individually to create the desired formula. We could, however, use the @SUM function to "sum" the numbers in the example. The concept of ranges is important to the @SUM function. (Ranges are also covered in detail later in this chapter and in Chapter 4.) For now, think of a range as simply a continuous group of cells.

The equivalent to the +B1+C1+D1+E1 formula, using the @SUM function, is @SUM(B1..E1). The only difference between the two formulas is one of convenience. If we had several more entries extending down the row, the @SUM function would change only slightly to use the address of the last cell to be summed. For example, @SUM(B1..Z1) would sum the contents of the first row all the way from B to Z.

The following formulas perform the same function in our example; yet each formula is slightly different.

@SUM(B1..E1)	@SUM($B$1..$E$1)
@SUM($B1..$E1)	@SUM($B$1..$E1)
@SUM(B$1..E$1)	@SUM($B1..E1)

Notice the dollar signs in the formulas. These signs are placed strategically to distinguish between relative, absolute, and mixed addressing. (These concepts are covered extensively in the "Copying" section of Chapter 4.)

Entering Labels

The third type of data that can be entered in a cell are labels. Labels are commonly used for row and column headers. Labels can have up to 240 characters, and contain any string of characters and numbers. If a label is too long for the width of a cell, the label will continue across the cells to the right for display purposes as long as there are no other entries in the neighboring cells (fig. 3.3).

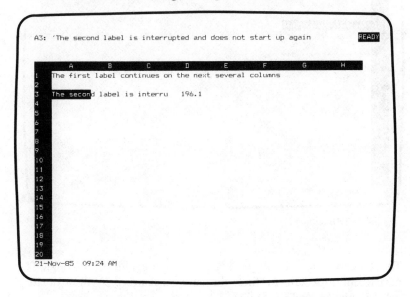

Fig. 3.3. How a label continues across cells.

When you enter a value into a cell and the first character is not an indicator for entering numbers and formulas, 1-2-3 assumes that you are entering a label. As you type the first character, 1-2-3 shifts to the LABEL mode.

One of the advantages of 1-2-3 is that you can left-justify, center, or right-justify labels when you display them (fig. 3.4). To determine the label's position, you must begin the label with one of the following label-prefix characters.

Character	*Action*
'	Left-justifies
^	Centers
"	Right-justifies
\	Repeats

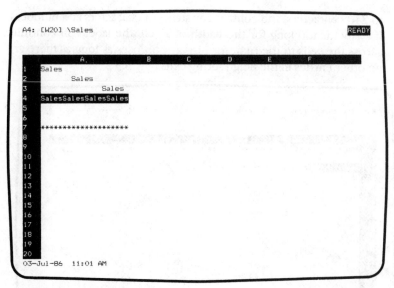

Fig. 3.4. Label alignment.

The standard default for displaying labels is left-justification. You don't have to enter the label prefix in this case because 1-2-3 will automatically supply the prefix for you.

What You Enter	*What 1-2-3 Stores*
Net Income	`'Net Income`

The one exception for all types of alignment occurs when the first character of the label is on the list for entering numbers and formulas mentioned above. For example, suppose that you wanted to enter the number 1983 as a label. If you type *1983*, 1-2-3 will assume that you are entering a value. You will need some way to signal that you intend this numeric entry to be treated as text. You can indicate this by using one of the label-prefix characters. In this case, you could enter 1983 as a centered label by typing ^*1983*.

The most unusual label prefix is the backslash (\ ), which is used for repetition. One of the most frequent uses of this prefix is to create a separator line.

The first step in creating the separator line is to enter * into the first cell (in fig. 3.4, cell A4). This entry causes asterisks to appear across the entire cell. Once you have set up the first cell, you can use the /Copy command to replicate the cell across the page. (For more information about the /Copy command and replication in general, see Chapter 4.)

There are several ways to control label prefixes. For example, suppose that you have entered a series of labels, using the standard default of left-justification, but you decide that you would rather have the labels centered. You could go in and manually change all the label prefixes, or you could change the prefixes all at once, using the /Range Label command.

When you select the /Range Label command, you are given the following choices:

Left   Right   Center

Each choice gives you the appropriate label prefix.

If you select Center, 1-2-3 will ask you to designate a range of cells to change. When you specify a range and press Enter, the cells will be displayed as centered.

Another option for changing label prefixes is to change the default setting for text justification. The command to do this is /Worksheet Global Label-Prefix. This command gives you the same options as the /Range Label command. Previously entered cells, however, are not affected by the /Worksheet Global Label-Prefix command. Only subsequent entries will show the change. In addition, cells that have been previously set, using /Range Label will maintain the alignment set by that command.

Editing Data in the Worksheet

One of the first things you will want to do when you start using 1-2-3 is modify the contents of cells without retyping the complete entry. This modification is quite easy to do in 1-2-3. You begin by moving the cursor to the appropriate cell and pressing the F2 (Edit) key. An alternative is to press F2 when you are entering cell contents. You might press F2 if you discover that you made a mistake earlier.

When you press F2, 1-2-3 enters EDIT mode. Normally, 1-2-3 is in READY mode. The main difference between the two modes is that some keys take on different meanings. (See page 80.)

Key	Action
←	Moves the cursor one position to the left
→	Moves the cursor one position to the right
→| (Tab)	Moves the cursor five characters to the right
|← (Backtab)	Moves the cursor five characters to the left. You must hold down the Shift key when you press |←.
Home	Moves the cursor to the first character in the entry
End	Moves the cursor to the last character in the entry
Backspace	Deletes the character just to the left of the cursor
Ins	Toggles between INSERT and OVERTYPE modes
Del	Deletes the character above the cursor
Esc	Clears the edit line but does not take you out of EDIT mode

After you press F2, the mode indicator in the upper right corner of the screen will change to EDIT. The contents of the cell will then be duplicated in the second line of the control panel (what we call the "edit line") and be ready for editing.

To show how the various keys are used, let's consider two examples. First, suppose you want to edit in cell E4 an entry that reads Sales Comparisson. After you position the cursor to cell E4, the actions are

Keys	Edit Line	Explanation
F2	'Sales Comparisson	The cursor always appears at the end of the edit line when you press F2.
←	'Sales Comparisson	
←	'Sales Comparisson	The cursor now appears
←	'Sales Comparisson	below the errant s.

| Del | ' Sales Comparison | The Del key deletes the character above the cursor. |
| Enter | | You must press Enter to update the entry in the spreadsheet and return to READY mode. |

One thing to remember about using EDIT mode is that you can also use it when you are entering a cell for the first time. If you make a mistake when you are in EDIT mode, you do not have to retype the entire entry.

Now suppose that you want to modify a formula in cell G6 from +D4/H3*(Y5+4000) to +C4/H3*(Y5+4000). After you move the cursor to G6, the actions are

Keys	Edit Line	Explanation
F2	+D4/H3*(Y5+4000)	Again, the cursor always appears at the end of the edit line when you first press F2.
Home	+D4/H3*(Y5+4000)	The Home key takes you to the first position in the edit line.
→	+D4/H3*(Y5+4000)	The → key moves the cursor one position to the right.
C	+CD4/H3*(Y5+4000)	When you enter a character in EDIT mode, the character normally is inserted to the left of the cursor. Entering a character will never cause you to write over another, unless you have pressed Ins to toggle into OVERTYPE mode. Unwanted characters can be eliminated with the Del and Backspace keys.

| Del | +CD4/H3*(Y5+4000)
+C4/H3*(Y5+4000) | Use the Del key to delete the character above the cursor. |
| Enter | | Again, you must press Enter to update the entry in the spreadsheet and return to READY mode. |

The Edit and Calc (F9) functions can be used together to convert a formula stored in a cell to a simple number. As figure 2.11 in Chapter 2 indicates, F9 is normally used for recalculating when /Worksheet Global Recalculation is set to Manual. (This is covered in detail in Chapter 4.) When you are in EDIT mode, however, pressing F9 will cause a formula to be converted to a number, its current value.

For example, suppose that you want to use F9 to convert the formula in the previous example to its current value (which we'll assume is 64,000), and store the result.

Keys	Edit Line	Explanation
F2	+C4/H3*(Y5+4000)	F2 puts 1-2-3 in EDIT mode.
F9	64000	F9 converts the formula to its current value. We picked 64000 at random.
Enter		Stores the entry in the current cell and shifts back to READY mode.

Using Ranges in the Worksheet

1-2-3's commands and functions often require that you deal with a group of cells in aggregate. 1-2-3 calls this type of group a range. Before we go on to learn more about 1-2-3's commands, we need to learn a bit about ranges.

1-2-3's definition of a range is one or more cells in a rectangular group. With this definition, one cell is the smallest possible range, and the largest range is the size of the worksheet itself.

The use of ranges offers you many advantages. Ranges make you work easier and faster. Ranges allow you to process blocks of cells in commands and formulas at the same time. This capability represents a significant change in philosophy from earlier spreadsheet programs, which allowed you to process only individual cells, rows, or columns. These earlier programs hardly ever allowed you to group the cells, rows, or columns together in any significant fashion.

When you actually will use ranges in 1-2-3 depends to some degree on your personal preference. In many cases it is your choice whether to provide ranges. In other cases, however, 1-2-3 will prompt you for ranges.

Ranges are rectangles, as illustrated in figure 3.5. The expanding cursor feature allows you to see the shape of ranges in 1-2-3. When a range is designated, the cells of the range show up in reverse video. Reverse video makes pointing an easy way to designate ranges, because as the cursor moves, the reverse video rectangle expands, as shown in figure 3.6.

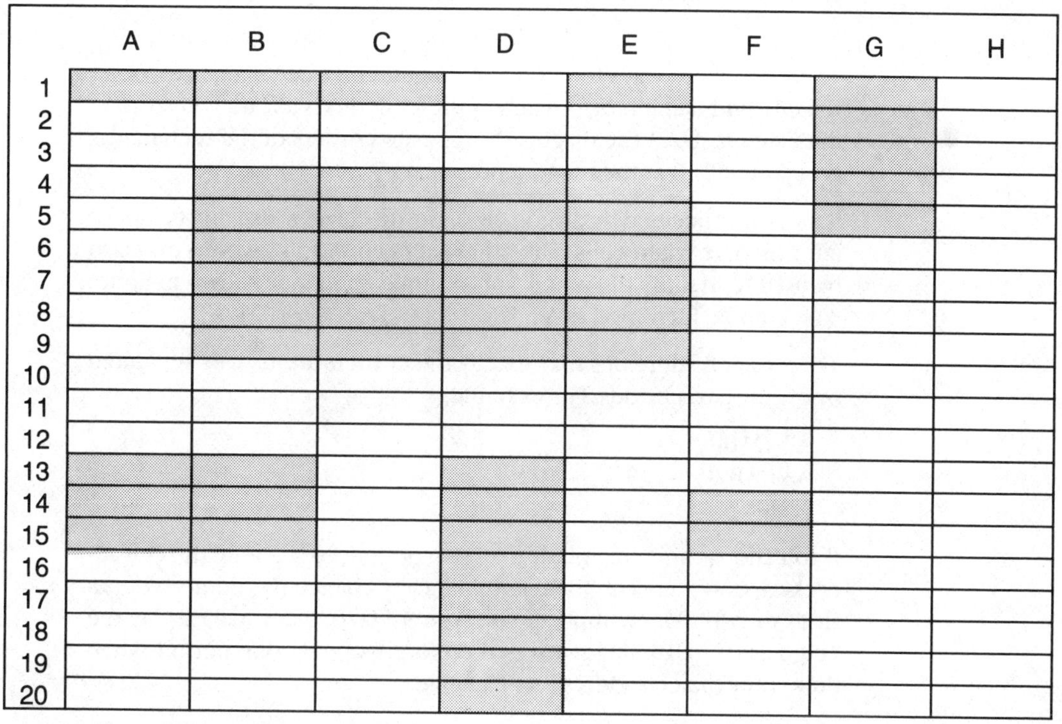

Fig. 3.5. A sample of 1-2-3 ranges.

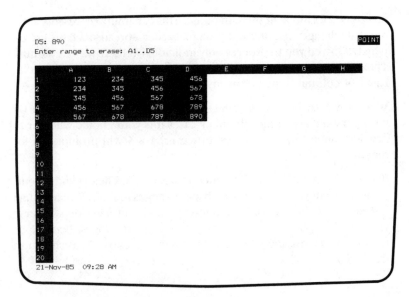

```
D5: 890                                                            POINT
Enter range to erase: A1..D5

         A          B         C         D        E       F       G       H
1        123        234       345       456
2        234        345       456       567
3        345        456       567       678
4        456        567       678       789
5        567        678       789       890
6
7
8
9
10
11
12
13
14
15
16
17
18
19
20
21-Nov-85   09:28 AM
```

Fig. 3.6. Range highlighted by the expanding cursor.

There are three ways to designate ranges: enter cell addresses, point to cells, and name ranges. Each of these methods allows you to communicate to 1-2-3 the diagonally opposite corners of the rectangular group of cells that the range represents.

Ranges are specified by diagonally opposite corners, usually the upper left and lower right cells. The other set of corners, however, may also be used to identify the range. For example, the range shown in figure 3.6 could be identified as A1..D5, A5..D1, D5..A1, or D1..A5.

The two cell addresses that specify the corners are usually separated by one or two periods. For example,

A7..D10
AA1.AB20
J2..K4

If you choose anything other than two periods to separate the cell addresses, however, 1-2-3 will automatically change the number of periods to two. For example, if you type *A7.D10,* 1-2-3 will display the range as A7. . D10. Many users therefore use only one period when they enter the cell addresses of a range.

In the next few chapters, the concept of ranges will be used over and over again. Most of 1-2-3's functions and several of the program's commands require the use of ranges. In addition, 1-2-3 has a whole set of commands that operate on ranges. These commands, and several others, are covered in the next chapter.

4

1-2-3 Commands

Like all electronic spreadsheets, 1-2-3 offers a number of exciting spreadsheet commands. Commands are the instructions you give 1-2-3 to perform a variety of different tasks, such as formatting a worksheet, saving a worksheet, creating a graph, accessing a database, copying data, inserting and deleting rows and columns, moving data, and so forth. For a complete listing of all 1-2-3 commands, please see the 1-2-3 command-menu map included at the back of this book.

Command Menus

Command menus are the devices used by 1-2-3 to present command alternatives to the user. The command menus are especially helpful in 1-2-3 for several reasons. First, 1-2-3 lists the full command words (see fig. 4.1).

To display this menu, you would press the slash (/) key. Remember to press the slash key whenever you want to activate a command.

A second feature of the command menus is illustrated on the third line of the display in figure 4.1. This line contains an explanation of the Worksheet menu item on which the command cursor is sitting. In fact, as you point to the different items in the command menu by moving the cursor across the list, a new explanation will appear in the third line for each command-menu item. This happens in every command menu.

A third friendly aspect of the command menus relates to how a command is initiated. You can either point to the option you want, or you can enter the first letter of the command name. To point to the

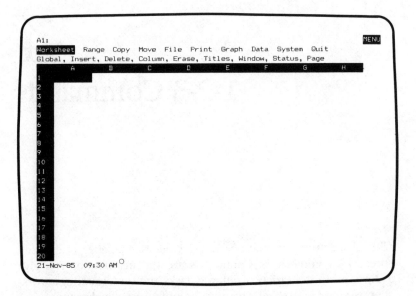

Fig. 4.1. The 1-2-3 Main Menu.

command-menu item, use the left- and right-arrow keys on the right-hand side of the keyboard. When the cursor is positioned at the proper item, press Enter. If you move the cursor to the last item in the list, then press the → again, the menu cursor will "round the horn" and reappear on the first item in the list. Similarly, if the menu cursor is on the first item in the menu, press the ← to move the cursor to the last option. Note that you can move the cursor to the end of the command line also by pressing the End key, and to the beginning of the line by pressing the Home key.

Entering the first letter of the command-menu item is the other way to select a command. For example, to select the /Worksheet Status command, which informs you of the status of several of 1-2-3's global parameters, you would type / to select the main command menu, followed by *w* to select /Worksheet. At this point, another menu appears:

Global   Insert   Delete   Column   Erase   Titles
    Window   Status   Page

From this line, select Status by pressing the S key. A menu similar to figure 4.43 should appear.

If you find that you have made the wrong command selection, you can press Esc at any time to return to the previous command menu. For instance, if you realize that you should not have entered Insert but Delete, press Esc to return to the Worksheet menu. You can enter a series of escapes (for example, press Esc Esc Esc) to return as far back as you want in the series of command menus, even out of MENU mode altogether. One alternative to pressing Esc repeatedly is to press the Ctrl (control) and Break keys simultaneously. This will cancel the entire command and return you to READY mode.

Setting up two alternatives for command selection is just one of the ways that 1-2-3 has successfully oriented itself to both the novice and the experienced user. The novice can point to the different commands and get a full explanation of each one, and the experienced user can enter at high speed a long series of commands, using the first-letter convention without reading the explanations.

If you look back at 1-2-3's main command menu, you will see the wide range of commands offered by 1-2-3. Instead of addressing each command in the order in which it appears in the menu, we have grouped them into several logical divisions. For example, this chapter covers Copy, Move, 1-2-3's Worksheet and Range commands (except Worksheet Format and Range Format, which are discussed in Chapter 5), and the System commands. The Graph commands are covered in Chapter 9. Data commands are explained in Chapter 11, Print in Chapter 8, and File management in Chapter 7.

Range Commands

1-2-3 has a set of commands that operate on ranges. These commands give you the ability to name, erase, format, or protect a range. The command root for the Range commands is /Range. When you type /r from READY mode, the following menu appears:

> Format   Label   Erase   Name   Justify   Protect   Unprotect
> Input   Value   Transpose

The Label command is covered in Chapter 3. The other range commands are discussed here.

Erasing Ranges

The /Range Erase command allows you to erase sections of the worksheet. This command can operate on a range as small as a single cell or as large as the entire worksheet.

For an example of this command, suppose that you created the simple worksheet shown in figure 4.2. Now, suppose that you want to erase

the range from A1 to C3. To remove this range, issue the command
/**Range** Erase. 1-2-3 prompts you to supply a range to delete. Either by
pointing or by entering the coordinates from the keyboard, you instruct 1-2-3 to erase the range A1..C3. After you press Enter, 1-2-3 immediately erases the range.

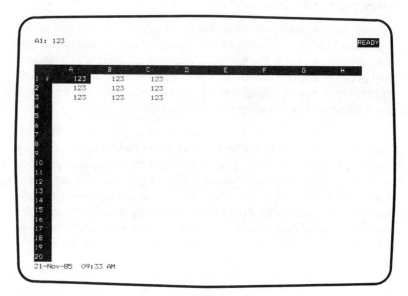

Fig. 4.2. A simple worksheet with values in cells A1..C3.

Be Careful! Once you have erased a range, it cannot be recovered. You
would have to reenter all of the data to restore the range.

Naming Ranges

In 1-2-3, a name can be assigned to a range of cells. Range names can
be up to 15 characters long and should be descriptive. The advantage
to naming ranges is that range names are easier to understand than cell
addresses and allow you to work more intuitively. For example, describing gross margin by the phrase Sales – COGS is more understandable than +A17–B10.

Range names are created with the /**Range Name Create** and /**Range**
Name Labels commands. Once names are established, they can be
easily applied in both commands and formulas.

Specifying Range Names

The /**R**ange **N**ame **C**reate command allows you to specify a name for any range, even one cell. You can specify a range name by any one of two methods: entering the cell addresses or pointing. /**R**ange **N**ame **C**reate can be used also to respecify a range if its location has changed. If minor changes occur to the range, however, such as a column or row of numbers being deleted from the range, 1-2-3 will handle these changes internally without any respecification.

Range names are used also in naming macros. Although macros are covered in detail in Chapter 12, we should note here that macros are named with the same command that names a range.

Using Label Entries for Range Names

The /**R**ange **N**ame **L**abels command is similar to /**R**ange **N**ame **C**reate except that the names for ranges are taken directly from adjacent label entries. Figure 4.3 illustrates one example.

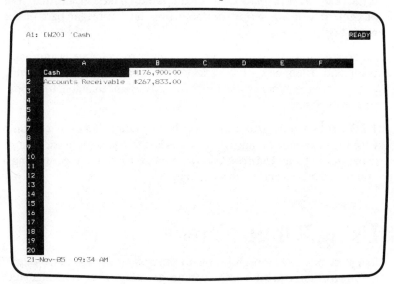

Fig. 4.3. Labels to be used in a /Range Name Labels command.

If you use the /**R**ange **N**ame **L**abels command and specify that the appropriate name for cell B1 is to the left in cell A1, you can assign the name CASH to the range B1. If you also do this for ACCOUNTS RE-CEIVABLE, remember that a range name can be only 15 characters long. The resulting range name will be ACCOUNTS RECEIV. Another alternative would be to use the /Range Name Create command to give cell B2 an appropriate label.

Deleting Range Names

Range names can be deleted individually or all at once. The /Range Name Delete command allows you to delete a single range name, and the /Range Name Reset command causes all range names to be deleted. Because of its power, the latter command should be used with caution.

Creating a Table of Range Names

If you are using range names in a worksheet and have created several range names, you may want to document the names in a table in the worksheet. 1-2-3 provides the /Range Name Table command to perform this task. Creating a range name table is simple, but you must exercise care in your placement of the table. Make certain that your placement will not write the table over an important part of the worksheet.

To create the range name table, you select the /Range Name Table command. Then, when 1-2-3 asks for the location for the table, indicate the range in your worksheet where you want the table to appear, and press Enter.

1-2-3 writes a table that consists of all your range names in a column with the referenced ranges in the cells just to the right of each range name in the table. Figure 4.4 shows a range name table containing a number of names and referenced ranges.

Using Range Names

Range names can be useful tools in processing commands and generating formulas. In both cases, whenever a range must be designated, a name can be entered instead. This eliminates the repetitive task of entering cell addresses or pointing to cell locations each time a range specification is called for. For example, suppose that you had designated the range name SALES for the range A5..J5 in one of your worksheets. The simplest way to compute the sum of this range would be in the formula @SUM(SALES). Similarly, to determine the maximum value in the range, you could use the formula @MAX(SALES). In func-

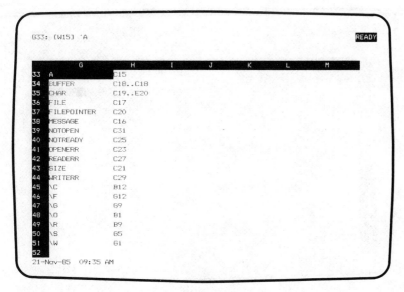

G33: [W15] 'A   READY

```
          G              H         I       J       K       L       M
33  A                C15
34  BUFFER           C18..C18
35  CHAR             C19..E20
36  FILE             C17
37  FILEPOINTER      C20
38  MESSAGE          C16
39  NOTOPEN          C31
40  NOTREADY         C25
41  OPENERR          C23
42  READERR          C27
43  SIZE             C21
44  WRITERR          C29
45  \C               B12
46  \F               G12
47  \G               G9
48  \O               B1
49  \R               B9
50  \S               G5
51  \W               G1
52
21-Nov-85   09:35 AM
```

Fig. 4.4. Range name table created with the /rnt command.

tions and formulas, range names can always be used in place of cell addresses.

Notice that 1-2-3 allows you to use multiple names for the same range. For example, a cell can be given the range names 1978_SALES and SALES_PREV_YR in the same worksheet. We'll see an application for this trick in Chapter 12, which discusses keyboard macros.

Still another advantage is that once a range name has been established, 1-2-3 will automatically use that name throughout the worksheet in place of cell addresses. If a range name is deleted, 1-2-3 will no longer use that name and will revert to cell addresses. The following shows the effect of assigning the name REVENUES to the range A5..J5.

Before Creating Range Name	*After Creating Range Name*
@SUM(A5..J5)	@SUM(REVENUES)

Figure 4.5 is an example of a simple case of adding two rows of numbers together.

If the range name SALES is assigned to the range D3..G3 and the name CGS to range D4..G4, cell H3 can be defined with the formula

@SUM(SALES)

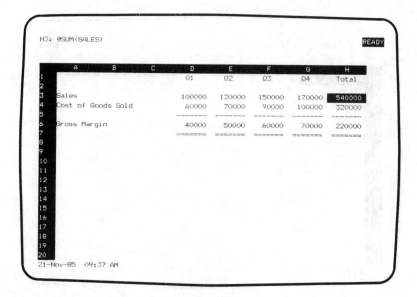

H3: @SUM(SALES)   READY

	A	B	C	D	E	F	G	H
1				Q1	Q2	Q3	Q4	Total
2								
3	Sales			100000	120000	150000	170000	540000
4	Cost of Goods Sold			60000	70000	90000	100000	320000
5								
6	Gross Margin			40000	50000	60000	70000	220000

21-Nov-85   09:37 AM

Fig. 4.5. Range names in @SUM functions.

Similarly, cell H4 can be assigned the formula

@SUM(CGS)

Finally, cell H6 can contain the formula

@SUM(SALES)-@SUM(CGS)

The formulas in cells D6, E6, F6, and G6 cannot be defined in terms of the two ranges SALES and CGS, however, because these ranges refer to the values for all four quarters, not the values for each quarter.

Another example uses names to designate the ranges of cells to be printed or saved. Suppose that you set up special names corresponding to different areas and want to print, or save to another worksheet, the corresponding portions of the current worksheet.

When 1-2-3 prompts you for a range, a predefined name can be entered rather than actual cell addresses. For example, in response to the print range prompt, you could enter the range name PAGE_1 or the name PAGE_5.

A third example using range names involves the F5 (Goto) key. You will recall that the F5 key allows you to move the cell pointer directly to a cell when you specify the cell's address. Another alternative is to provide a range name instead of a cell address. For example, you could enter *Instruct* in response to Enter address to go to. If INSTRUCT was the range name for a set of cells that included a set of instructions, you might get the results shown in figure 4.6.

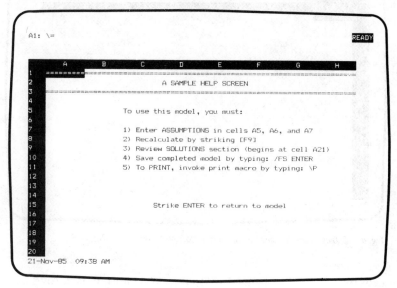

A1: \=   READY

```
      A       B       C       D       E       F       G       H
1  =========================================================================
2                        A SAMPLE HELP SCREEN
3  =========================================================================
4
5                 To use this model, you must:
6
7                 1) Enter ASSUMPTIONS in cells A5, A6, and A7
8                 2) Recalculate by striking [F9]
9                 3) Review SOLUTIONS section (begins at cell A21)
10                4) Save completed model by typing: /FS ENTER
11                5) To PRINT, invoke print macro by typing: \P
12
13
14
15                     Strike ENTER to return to model
16
17
18
19
20
21-Nov-85  09:38 AM
```

Fig. 4.6. A screen display of instructions.

Using the example in figure 4.5 again, suppose that you had assigned the name CGS to the range D4..G4. You could erase this portion of the worksheet by typing /**R**ange **E**rase and entering the range name CGS instead of the cell coordinates D4..G4.

Using figure 4.5 again, suppose that after you typed the /**R**ange **E**rase command, you could not remember the name of the range you wanted to erase. You could press the Names key (F3) to produce a list of the range names in the current worksheet. Figure 4.7 shows the screen at that point. After the list appears, you can use the cursor to point to the first alternative, CGS, and select CGS by pressing Enter. If there are more names than can be displayed at once on the command line, press F3 again to get a full screen display of the range names. The Names key can be used any time the worksheet is in POINT mode.

Protecting Ranges

1-2-3 has special features that protect areas of a worksheet from possible destruction. With a series of commands, you can set up ranges of

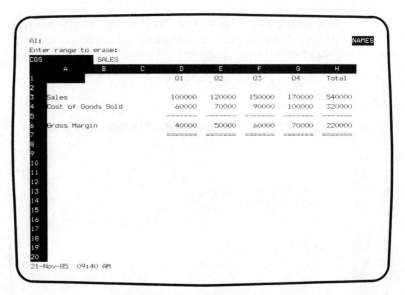

Fig. 4.7. Effect of the Names key during a /Range Erase command.

cells that cannot be changed without special effort. In fact, rows and columns containing protected cells cannot be deleted from the worksheet. These commands are particularly beneficial when you are setting up worksheets in which data will be entered by people who are not familiar with 1-2-3.

When a worksheet is first created, every cell is protected. However, the global protection command is disabled. This means that each cell has the potential of being protected, but is not at the moment. This protection system may be thought of as a series of electric fences that are set up around all the cells in the worksheet. The "juice" to these fences is turned off when the sheet is first loaded. This means that all the cells in the worksheet can be modified, which is appropriate because you will want to have access to everything in the worksheet at this time. Once you have finished making all your entries in the worksheet, however, there may be areas that you do not want modified, or you may want to set up special form-entry areas and not allow cursor movement anywhere else.

To accomplish either of these tasks, you must first enable protection. This is accomplished with the /Worksheet Global Protection Enable command. Once this command is issued, all of the cells in the worksheet are protected. To continue the analogy, this command is like the switch that activates all of the electric fences in the worksheet. Now you can selectively unprotect certain ranges with the /Range Unprotect command. To use the analogy once again, you tear down the fences that surround these cells. You can, of course, reprotect these cells at any time by issuing the /Range Protect command.

Suppose that you created a worksheet which included a number of long and important formulas. You might want to protect these formulas against accidental deletion by using 1-2-3's protection capability. But what if you need to make a change in several of these formulas? You could move around the worksheet, unprotecting cells, changing the formulas, then protecting the cells again. You could also use the /Worksheet Global Protection Disable command to "lower the fences" around all of the cells. After you made the necessary changes, the /Worksheet Global Protection Enable command would restore the protection to all the cells.

For even more protection, you can limit the movement of the cursor by using the /Range Input command. This command will allow movement to only /Range Unprotected cells and must be used when you set up the special form-entry areas mentioned previously.

For example, suppose that you created the simple worksheet in figure 4.8. Every cell in the worksheet is protected except E4, E5, E6, E7, E8, and E9. Note that unprotected cells are indicated in the control panel by the U prefix.

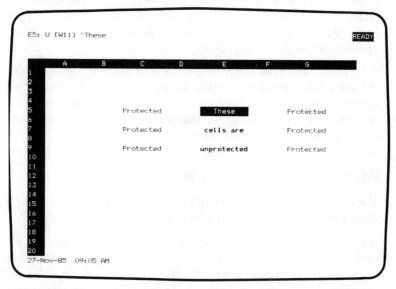

Fig. 4.8. Example of protected and unprotected cells.

Now suppose that you issue the /**Range Input** command. 1-2-3 will prompt you to supply a data input range. In our example, this could be the range A1..F20 or the range E1..E9. The exact size of the range doesn't matter, as long as the range includes all of the unprotected cells. After the range is specified, the cursor will immediately jump to cell E5 and wait for you to enter a number or label. Don't use Enter to terminate the input; use one of the arrow keys. In the example, you might use the down arrow. Notice that the cursor jumps to cell E7. Once again, you will want to make a cell entry and use an arrow key to move on.

The /ri command will remain in effect until you press either the Enter key or the Esc key. When you do, the cursor will return to the upper left corner of the input range.

The /**Range Input** command can be used to automate the process of entering data in the worksheet. This command can be included in a keyboard macro that will automatically execute when a model is loaded into the worksheet. Such a macro would allow a 1-2-3 novice to enter information into the worksheet with no risk of erasing or overwriting important information.

Moving Ranges

In the days of manual spreadsheets, the process of moving data around on the page was called *cutting and pasting* because scissors and glue were used to move sections of the spreadsheet. 1-2-3 contains several commands that move data automatically.

1-2-3 gives you almost complete control over the appearance of worksheets by allowing you to rearrange items in almost any manner. There are three cut-and-paste commands: one that enters blank rows and columns in the worksheet, one that deletes rows and columns, and one that moves the contents of cells.

Moving Cell Contents

The command used to move cell contents is /**Move**. It allows you to move ranges of cells from one part of the worksheet to another.

For example, suppose that you created the sample worksheet shown in figure 4.9. Suppose further that you want to move the contents of range C1..D3 to the range E1..F3. After you enter /**Move**, 1-2-3 will respond with the message Enter range to move FROM. You will notice that a range is already specified after this message. If the cursor was at cell D7 when you started, the range specified is D7..D7. 1-2-3 always tries to stay one step ahead in helping you designate ranges. To enter the appropriate range, start typing. The D7..D7 will immediately disappear. As you type, the characters will appear where the D7..D7 was. To designate the proper FROM range for our example, enter C1..D3. Then press Enter.

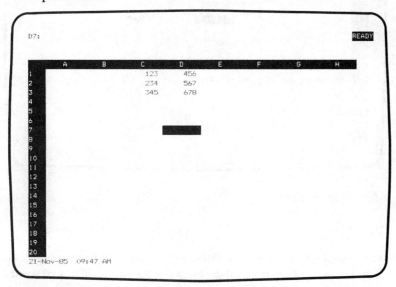

Fig. 4.9. Worksheet before /Move command.

1-2-3 then will ask you to Enter the range to move TO. Again, a range is already specified for you; and just as before, it corresponds to the address of the cell where the pointer was located when you initiated the command. To enter your own range, start typing again. For the TO range, you can specify just the single cell E1. 1-2-3 is smart enough to know that E1..F3 is implied and will use that range. As soon as you finish designating the TO range and pressing Enter, the pointer will return immediately to where it was when you initiated the command. Figure 4.10 shows the results of the /Move operation.

One of the points of this example is that you do not have to have the cursor at the beginning of the TO or FROM ranges when you initiate a command. You can designate a range while the cursor is positioned anywhere on the worksheet.

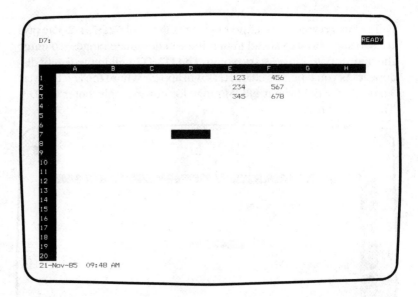

Fig. 4.10. Result of /Move operation.

Reminders for 1-2-3 Spreadsheet Users

All the formulas involved in a /Move operation are updated automatically. For example, suppose that you defined a simple three-cell worksheet that contained the following data:

    A1 = +D1*100
    C1 = 15
    D1 = +C1

Now, suppose that you /Move the contents of cell D1 to cell E1. The formulas would be altered to the following:

    A1 = +E1*100
    C1 = 15
    E1 = +C1

You must be careful about the finality of the /Move command. When you move a range of cells, the TO range is completely overwritten by the FROM range, and the previous contents of those cells are lost forever. If there are other cells whose formulas depend on the cell addresses of the lost cells, the other cells will be given the value ERR instead of the cell address. For example, if you add one more cell to the example above,

    E2 = +E1

and repeat the move operation (/Move D1 E1), the value of cell E2 will change from 0 to ERR, and the contents of that cell will become +ERR. The cell E2 once referred to, E1, has been removed and replaced as a result of the /Move operation.

Reminders for Other Spreadsheet Users

Two features of 1-2-3's method of moving the contents of cells differ from the methods used in earlier spreadsheet programs like VisiCalc. First, in VisiCalc you can move only one column or row of cells at a time. VisiCalc cannot operate on rectangular ranges wider than one column or deeper than one row. 1-2-3's capability to move rectangular blocks is a major improvement over VisiCalc.

On the other hand, when you do move rows or columns in VisiCalc, the contents of the target are automatically shifted to make room for the incoming lines or columns. 1-2-3 overwrites the target area. To duplicate VisiCalc's /M command in 1-2-3, you would have to insert blank rows or columns in the target range before moving a range of cells. If you are an experienced VisiCalc user, be sure to remember this difference between the programs.

Pointing to Cells with the Expanding Cursor

As previously mentioned, the unique pointing capabilities of 1-2-3 can be used to specify a range. This method is somewhat similar to menu pointing, but you will find that pointing to specify a range has a character all its own.

Suppose that you want to shift the contents of the range C1..D3 to E1..F3, but you don't want to enter the cell addresses from the keyboard. We will assume that the cursor was positioned in cell D7 before you initiated the command. When 1-2-3 asks for the FROM range, press Esc.

Esc is used because cell D7 has been automatically "anchored" for you by 1-2-3. This means that 1-2-3 has automatically designated D7 as one corner of the FROM range. If you do not press Esc but move the cursor, you will see the reverse video field begin to expand starting at cell D7. Because you do not want to have cell D7 as one corner of the range, press Esc. (You can also anchor cells yourself by entering a period [.] when you are entering a range.)

Because you want C1 to be one corner of the FROM range, move the cursor up to this cell. As you move the cursor upward from cell to cell, you will see the address designation in the command field change. When you arrive at cell C1, press the period (.) to anchor the cell.

From this point on, cell C1 is referred to as the anchor cell, and the cell diagonally opposite the anchored cell is the free cell. A blinking underscore character is in the middle of the free cell. At this point, cell C1 is both the anchor cell and the free cell. As you move the cursor down to cell E3 to point to the other corner of the range, however, you will see the reverse video field expand as you shift the free cell. You will also see the second part of the range designation change as you move from cell to cell. For example, C1..D1 will appear when the cursor is moved to cell D1.

When you reach cell E1 from cell C1, start moving over to cell E3. Now you will see the reverse video field expand in a columnar fashion. When you reach cell E3, lock in the range by pressing Enter. The designation of the FROM range will appear, as though you entered the range from the keyboard.

The process is similar for designating the TO range. Once you have specified the FROM range, the cursor will automatically return to cell D7. You then move the cursor over to E1 and press Enter. You can designate the TO range by pointing to the entire range, but remember that 1-2-3 knows what you are implying when you enter just E1.

The Esc key can be used also when you are in a command, but no cell has been anchored. Pressing Esc will return you to the previous command step. If you are in the middle of a formula, pressing the Esc key will erase the cell address from the end of the formula and return the cursor to the current cell. In other words, with numbers already in cells A1..A3, if, at cell A4, we type @*SUM(* and then point with the cell pointer to cell A1, our formula so far is @SUM(A1. If we press Esc, our formula again becomes @SUM(and our cell pointer goes to cell A4.

The Backspace key can also be used in pointing to ranges. Pressing Backspace will cancel the range specification, whether or not a cell has been anchored, and return the cell pointer to where you began the command or formula. The Backspace key is slightly more powerful than the Esc key in returning you to where you started when you began entering a command or formula.

Pointing to Cells with the End Key

1-2-3's implementation of the End key makes the job of pointing to large ranges much simpler than in older spreadsheet programs. For example, suppose that you want to move the contents of the range A1..C5 to the range that begins at cell A7. By now, the /Move command should be familiar enough. But the use of the End key to point to the range is not. When the range prompt A1..A1 appears, press the End key followed by ↓. The cursor will jump to cell A5, and the prompt will read A1..A5. Now, move the cursor by pressing End →. The prompt will now read A1..C5.

The End key can really speed up the process of pointing to ranges. Using the End key, we were able to define the range in our example with only four keystrokes. If we had used the two arrow keys instead of the End key, the process would have taken seven keystrokes. The difference is a dramatic one when you work with larger ranges.

The End key can be used even in situations where it appears to be of little value. For example, figure 4.11 shows a worksheet consisting of two rows of information. One row is continuous; the other row is broken. Suppose that you want to erase the contents of the broken row. To do this, issue the /Range Erase command. 1-2-3 then prompts you for a range to delete. You can enter the range either by typing the coordinates or by pointing with the cursor. If you point, you may want to try using the End key; but because the range is not continuous, the End key will not easily move you from one end of the range to the other. Try this trick. When you specify the range, first move the cursor *up* one row to cell A2; use End → to move the cursor to the end of the range; then move the cursor down one row. Presto! The correct range has been specified. Figures 4.12 A, B, and C show this process. This technique is more convenient than simply using the → to point. You should use this technique as often as possible when you define ranges.

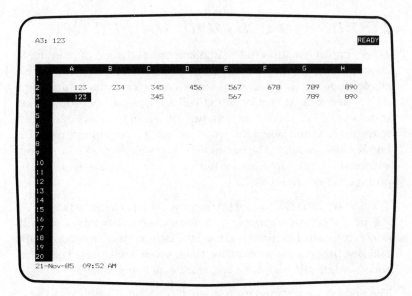

Fig. 4.11. A broken row next to a complete row.

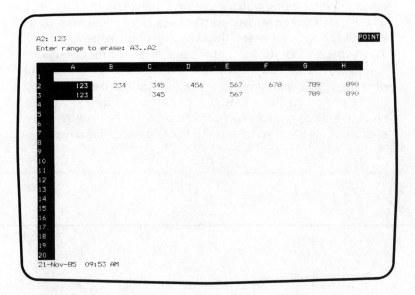

Fig. 4.12A. First step in using the End key on a broken row.

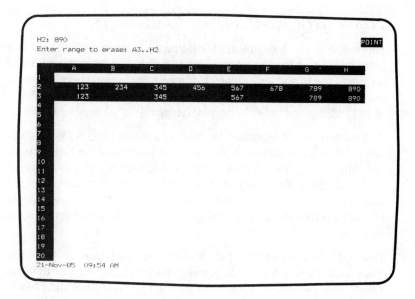

Fig. 4.12B. Second step in using the End key on a broken row.

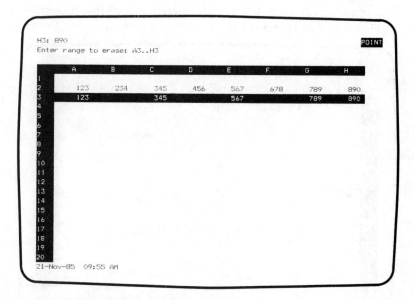

Fig. 4.12C. Final step in using the End key on a broken row.

Inserting Rows and Columns

Suppose that you have finished building a model in a worksheet but want to dress up its general appearance before you show the model to anyone. One of the techniques for improving a worksheet's appearance is to insert blank rows and columns in strategic places to highlight headings and other important items.

The command for inserting rows and columns in 1-2-3 is /Worksheet Insert. You can insert multiple rows and columns each time you invoke this command. After you select /Worksheet Insert, you are asked for the method of insertion, Column or Row. After you have selected one or the other, you are asked for an insert range. Depending on how you set up this range, you will get one or more columns or rows inserted.

Inserted columns appear to the left of the specified range, and inserted rows appear above the specified range. For example, suppose that you created the worksheet shown in figure 4.13. If you issue the /Worksheet Insert Column command and specify an insert range of A10..A10, you will get a single blank column inserted to the left of the values in column A, as shown in figure 4.14. 1-2-3 automatically shifts everything over one column and modifies all the cell formulas for the change. If you then repeat the command, but specify the Row option and a range of A10..A10, 1-2-3 will insert one blank row above row 10. Figure 4.15 illustrates the results of that operation.

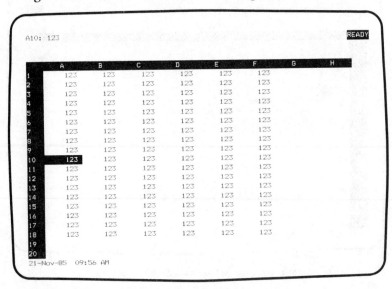

Fig. 4.13. Worksheet before insert commands.

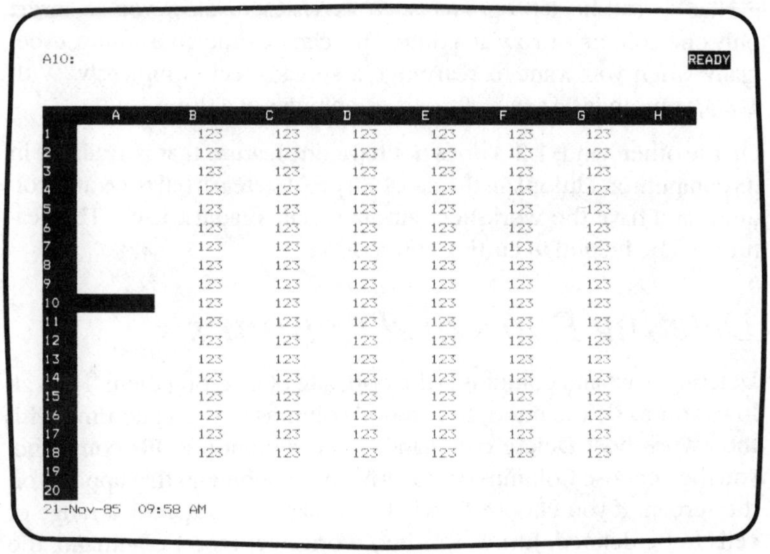

Fig. 4.14. Worksheet after inserting a column.

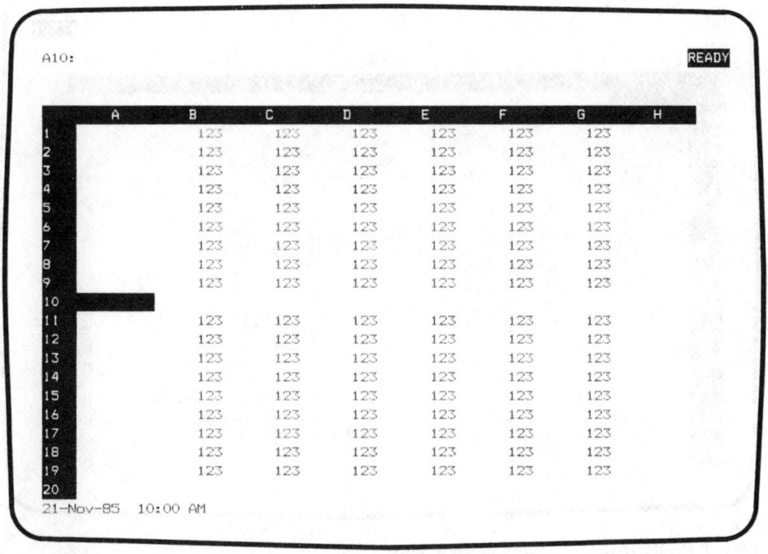

Fig. 4.15. Worksheet after inserting a row.

Earlier spreadsheet programs, such as VisiCalc, allow you to insert only one column or row at a time. This can be time-consuming, especially when you want to rearrange a spreadsheet completely. With 1-2-3, you can insert several rows or columns at a time.

On the other hand, 1-2-3 does not have one feature that is available in its competitor, Multiplan: the capability to delete partial rows and columns and have the worksheet automatically readjust itself. This feature can be helpful in cutting and pasting.

Deleting Rows and Columns

Deleting rows and columns is the opposite of inserting them. 1-2-3 allows you to delete multiple rows or columns at the same time with the /Worksheet Delete command. After you choose this command, you then choose Columns or Rows from the submenu that appears on the screen. If you choose Rows, 1-2-3 asks you to specify a range of cells to be deleted. Just as for the /Worksheet Insert command, the range you specify includes one cell from a given row.

For example, to delete rows 2 and 3 in the worksheet in figure 4.16, you should specify A2..A3. Other acceptable range designations are B2..B3, C2..C3, C2..G3, etc. The results of the deletion are shown in figure 4.17.

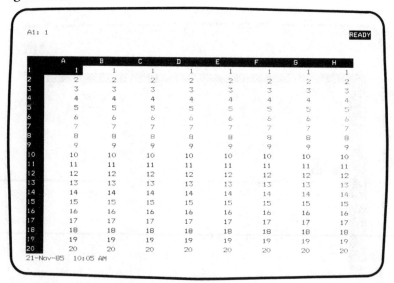

Fig. 4.16. Worksheet before deleting rows.

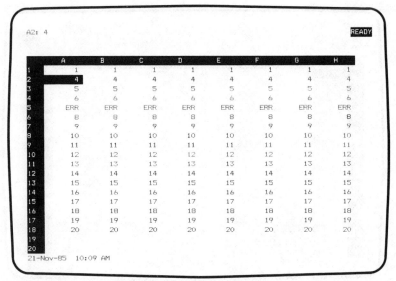

Fig. 4.17. Worksheet after deleting rows.

The easiest way to designate the range to be deleted is by pointing to the appropriate cells. You can also enter the cell addresses from the keyboard. Pointing to cells, however, helps you avoid inadvertently choosing the wrong range. Remember that when you use the /Worksheet Delete command, the rows or columns you delete are gone for good. This includes all the cells in the rows or columns, not just the range of cells you specify. You may be able to get the values back if you have previously saved a copy of the model on disk. If this is not the case, however, the rows and columns are lost.

Notice that the worksheet in figure 4.17 is automatically readjusted so that all the contents below row 3 are shifted up. In addition, all the formulas, command ranges, and named ranges are adjusted for the deletion. Formulas that contain references to the deleted cells are given the value ERR.

The process to delete one or more columns is similar to that for rows. After you select the Columns option from the /wd submenu, specify a range that corresponds to one or more cells in each column to be deleted. For example, suppose that you wanted to delete column B in figure 4.18. A suitable range to designate for the /wd command is B1..B1. Again, pointing is the best way to designate the range so that you avoid selecting the wrong column. Figure 4.19 shows the worksheet after column B is deleted.

A1: 111   READY

	A	B	C	D	E	F	G	H
1	111	222	333	444	555	666	777	888
2	111	222	333	444	555	666	777	888
3	111	222	333	444	555	666	777	888
4	111	222	333	444	555	666	777	888
5	111	222	333	444	555	666	777	888
6	111	222	333	444	555	666	777	888
7	111	222	333	444	555	666	777	888
8	111	222	333	444	555	666	777	888
9	111	222	333	444	555	666	777	888
10	111	222	333	444	555	666	777	888
11	111	222	333	444	555	666	777	888
12	111	222	333	444	555	666	777	888
13	111	222	333	444	555	666	777	888
14	111	222	333	444	555	666	777	888
15	111	222	333	444	555	666	777	888
16	111	222	333	444	555	666	777	888
17	111	222	333	444	555	666	777	888
18	111	222	333	444	555	666	777	888
19	111	222	333	444	555	666	777	888
20	111	222	333	444	555	666	777	888

21-Nov-85 10:11 AM

Fig. 4.18. Worksheet before deleting a column.

B1: 333   READY

	A	B	C	D	E	F	G	H
1	111	333	ERR	555	666	777	888	
2	111	333	ERR	555	666	777	888	
3	111	333	ERR	555	666	777	888	
4	111	333	ERR	555	666	777	888	
5	111	333	ERR	555	666	777	888	
6	111	333	ERR	555	666	777	888	
7	111	333	ERR	555	666	777	888	
8	111	333	ERR	555	666	777	888	
9	111	333	ERR	555	666	777	888	
10	111	333	ERR	555	666	777	888	
11	111	333	ERR	555	666	777	888	
12	111	333	ERR	555	666	777	888	
13	111	333	ERR	555	666	777	888	
14	111	333	ERR	555	666	777	888	
15	111	333	ERR	555	666	777	888	
16	111	333	ERR	555	666	777	888	
17	111	333	ERR	555	666	777	888	
18	111	333	ERR	555	666	777	888	
19	111	333	ERR	555	666	777	888	
20	111	333	ERR	555	666	777	888	

21-Nov-85 10:13 AM

Fig. 4.19. Worksheet after deleting a column.

The /Worksheet Delete command is different from the /Range Erase command. This difference is best explained by using the analogy of a paper spreadsheet. The manual equivalent of the /Worksheet Delete command is to use scissors to cut the columnar sheet apart and remove the unwanted columns and/or rows. Then the sheet is pasted back together again. The /Range Erase command, on the other hand, is like using an eraser to erase ranges of cells in the sheet. Do not forget the difference between these powerful commands.

In native 1-2-3 terms, there are two differences between deleting cells using /Worksheet Delete and erasing cells using /Range Erase. First, /Worksheet Delete deletes entire columns and rows within a worksheet, whereas /Range Erase erases particular ranges of cells, which may be as small or as large as you wish. Second, the worksheet is automatically readjusted to fill in the gaps created by the deleted columns or rows when you use the /wd command. This is not the case, however, for the /Range Erase command. The cells in the range that has been erased are merely blanked.

Copying Ranges

There will be many times when you will want to copy the contents of cells to other locations in a worksheet. These times can be broken down into four different categories.

First, you may want to copy from one cell to another. For example, in the worksheet shown in figure 4.20, you might want to copy the contents of cell A1 to cell A2. To do this, you would issue the command /Copy. 1-2-3 would then prompt you to supply a FROM range with the message Enter range to copy FROM:. Because you want to copy from cell A1, enter A1 in response to this message. (If the cursor were on cell A1, you could also press Enter). Next, 1-2-3 will prompt for a TO range with the message Enter range to copy TO:. Because you want to copy the contents of cell A1 to cell A2, enter A2 as the TO range. Figure 4.21 shows the results of this operation.

The steps required for all copy operations are basically like this simple example: first, issue the /Copy command; second, specify the FROM range; third, specify the TO range. The only things that change are the size, shape, and locations of the FROM and TO ranges.

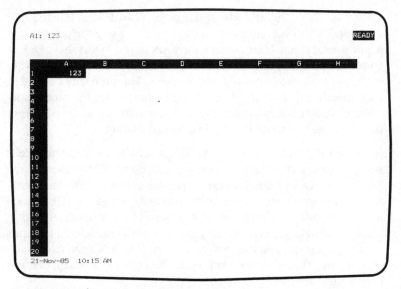

Fig. 4.20. Worksheet before the /Copy command.

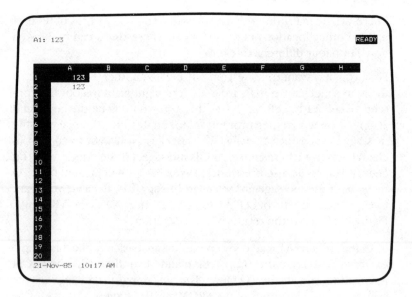

Fig. 4.21. Worksheet after the /Copy command.

A second type of copy operation would be to copy from one cell to a range of cells. Using the same worksheet shown in figure 4.19, suppose that you want to copy the contents of cell A1 into the range A1..H1. To do this, issue the /Copy command, specify A1 as the FROM range, then specify A1..H1 as the TO range. Remember that you can either type the coordinates of the TO range from the keyboard or point to the range, using POINT mode. The results of this copy are shown in figure 4.22.

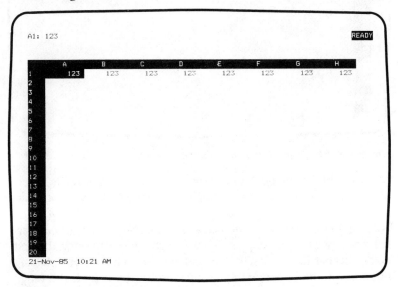

Fig. 4.22. Result of copying from a cell to a range.

The third type of copy operation is a little more complicated. You may want to copy a range of cells to another place in the worksheet. Using the results of our copy in figure 4.22 as an example, suppose that you wanted to copy the range A1..H1 to the range A2..H2. As always, you would begin by issuing the /Copy command. Next, you would specify the FROM range—in this case, A1..H1. Remember that you can either type the coordinates or use the cursor keys to point to the range. Next, specify the TO range. This is where things get a bit tricky. Even though we are copying into the range A2..H2, the TO range in this example would be the single cell A2. The results of this command are shown in figure 4.23.

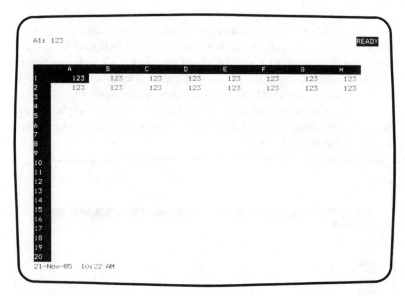

A1: 123   READY

	A	B	C	D	E	F	G	H
1	123	123	123	123	123	123	123	123
2	123	123	123	123	123	123	123	123
3								
4								
5								
6								
7								
8								
9								
10								
11								
12								
13								
14								
15								
16								
17								
18								
19								
20								

21-Nov-85   10:22 AM

Fig. 4.23. Result of copying the partial row A1..H1 to A2.

Although this TO range does not seem to make sense, it really is perfectly logical. Think about selecting the TO range this way. You want to /Copy the eight-cell partial row A1..H1. Because the FROM range is an eight-cell partial row, the TO range must also be an eight-cell partial row. Since the TO range must be an eight-cell partial row, the first cell in that partial row is sufficient to define the range. Given a starting point of A2, the only possible destination for the copy is the range A2..H2. Similarly, specifying the single cell H3 as the TO range would imply a destination of H3..O3. In other words, 1-2-3 is smart enough to deduce the rest of the destination from the single cell provided as the TO range.

The same principle applies to copies of partial columns. For example, looking back at figure 4.21, which shows the results of our first copy example, suppose that you wanted to copy the range A1..A2 to the range B1..B2. The first two steps should be familiar by now: issue the /Copy command and specify the FROM range A1..A2. What would the TO range be? Because we want to copy the two-cell partial column A1..A2 into the two-cell partial column B1..B2, we need supply only the starting point (B1) of the TO range to create figure 4.24.

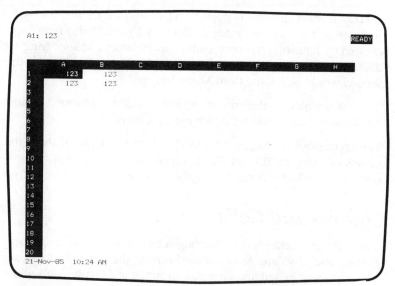

Fig. 4.24. Result of copying the partial column A1..A2 to B1.

Finally, you may want to copy a range of cells to an even larger range of cells somewhere else in the worksheet. Using figure 4.22 once again as an example, suppose that you wanted to copy the range A1..H1 into the rectangular block A2..H20. As before, you would issue the command /Copy and define the FROM range as A1..H1. The TO range would be A2..A20. Figure 4.25 shows the results of this copy.

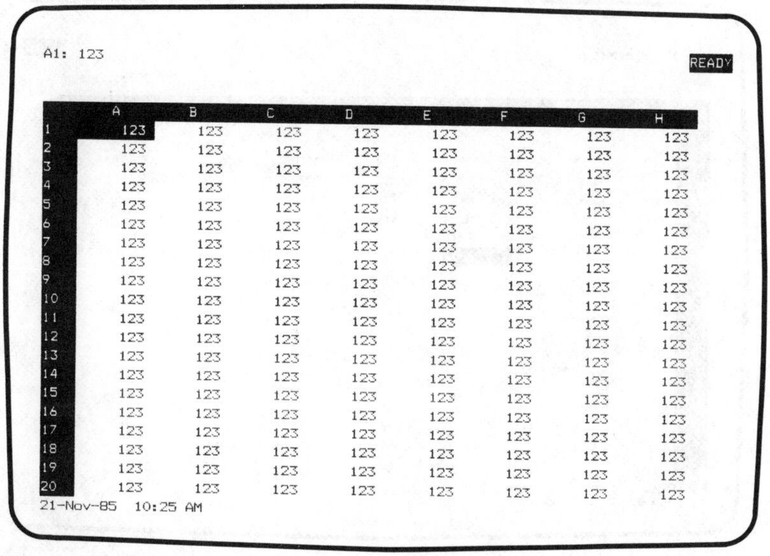

Fig. 4.25. Result of copying the range A1..H1 to the range A2..A20.

You can think of this type of copy as an extension of the previous type. In essence, the copy we made in figure 4.25 could also have been created by repeating the copy command 19 times and specifying 19 different single-row TO ranges. The first TO range would be A2, the second would be A3, the third A4, and so on.

The result would be the same using either method, but you can save much time by using the A2..A20 range as shown.

The concept of TO ranges is tricky. The best way to learn about the effects of different TO and FROM ranges is to experiment on your own. After a while, the rules of copying will be second nature.

Addressing Cells

Two different methods of addressing cells can be used in replication: *relative* and *absolute*. As mentioned earlier, these two methods are also important in building formulas. In fact, it is difficult to talk about the two methods of addressing without treating both topics at once.

Relative Addressing

As an example of relative addressing, suppose that you want to sum the contents of several columns of cells, but you don't want to enter the @SUM function over and over again. Figure 4.26 shows a sample

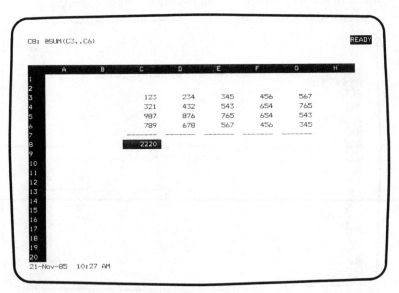

Fig. 4.26. Sample worksheet with one column summed.

worksheet with five columns of numbers. Only column C has been summed, using the formula @SUM(C3..C6) in cell C8.

We want to add the contents of the cells in columns D, E, F, and G in the same manner that the contents of the cells in column C were added. To do this, we use the /Copy command, which is the command for replicating cells in 1-2-3.

To initiate the command, /Copy is chosen from the main command menu. 1-2-3 then asks for a range of cells to copy FROM. We enter C8, and press Enter. Next, 1-2-3 asks for a range of cells to copy TO. Here we enter D8..G8 by either pointing or entering the cell addresses. When we press Enter, 1-2-3 will replicate the @SUM formula in cell C8 to the other cells, as shown in figure 4.27.

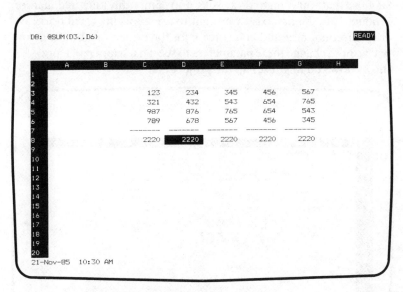

Fig. 4.27. Copied @SUM formulas with relative addressing.

If you look at the formula in the first line of the control panel, you will see that the formula contains the proper cell addresses for adding the cells in column D and not column C, just as the formula should. 1-2-3 was smart enough to know that we actually meant the relative addresses of the cells in column B and not their absolute addresses.

Mixed and Absolute Addressing

In some cases, a formula has an important address that cannot be changed as the formula is copied. In 1-2-3, you can create an address that will not change at all as the address is copied. This is called an absolute address. You can also create an address that will sometimes change, depending on the direction of the copy. This is called a *mixed* address. The following examples will help to make the concepts of absolute and mixed addresses clear.

Mixed Addressing

Mixed cell-addressing refers to a combination of relative and absolute addressing. Because a cell address has two components—a column and a row—it is possible to fix (make absolute) either portion while leaving the other unfixed (relative). The best way to explain this capability is to use an example.

Suppose that you want to do a projection of monthly sales in dollars of Product 1. In the first pass, you want to use a specific retail price, average discount rate, and unit volume for the projection, but later you will want to change these parameters to see what happens. Figure 4.28 shows how you might set up the projection.

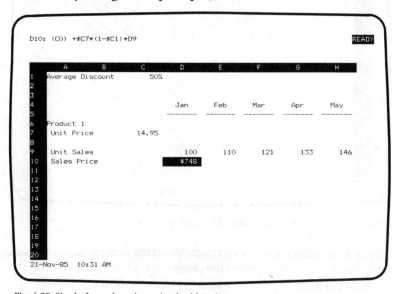

Fig. 4.28. Single formula using mixed addressing.

Notice the dollar signs in the formula for cell D10 in the first line of the control panel. The dollar signs signal 1-2-3 to use absolute addressing on the column portion of the addresses. Because there are no dollar signs in front of the row portion of the addresses, 1-2-3 will use relative addressing there.

To see the importance of this type of referencing, let's /Copy the contents of cell D10 into the range E10..H10. As before, we first issue the /Copy command and designate the FROM range (D10) and the TO range (E10..H10). Figure 4.29 shows the results of the command.

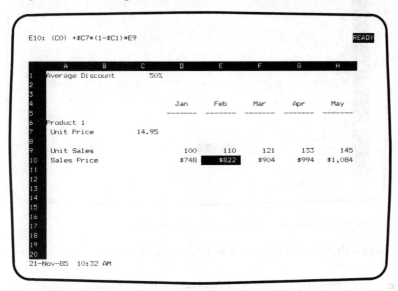

Fig. 4.29. Result of copying the mixed address formula.

Compare the formula in cell E10 with the original formula in cell D10:

E10 = +$C7*(1-$C1)*E9
D10 = +$C7*(1-$C1)*D9

Notice that the formulas are identical except for the last term. 1-2-3 has held the addresses for C7 and C1 constant. Only the reference to cell D9 has been altered. In essence, this formula says, Using a constant price (C7) and a constant discount (C1), compute the dollar sales for Product 1 at each month's sales volume (D9..H9).

Now suppose that you wanted to create a projection for a second product. You would duplicate the labels in column A and change the product name to Product 2. Finally, you would copy the contents of the range C7..H10 to the range C14..H17. Figure 4.30 shows the results of the copy operation.

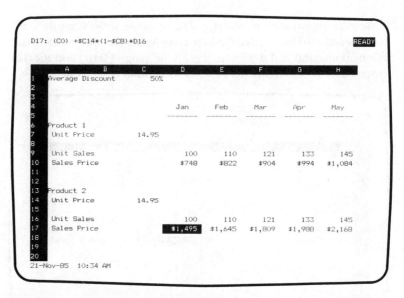

```
D17:  (CO)  +$C14*(1-$C8)*D16                                        READY

         A       B        C        D        E        F        G        H
1   Average Discount       50%
2
3
4                                 Jan      Feb      Mar      Apr      May
5                                ------   ------   ------   ------   ------
6   Product 1
7     Unit Price           14.95
8
9     Unit Sales                  100      110      121      133      145
10    Sales Price                $748     $822     $904     $994   $1,084
11
12
13  Product 2
14    Unit Price           14.95
15
16    Unit Sales                  100      110      121      133      145
17    Sales Price              $1,495   $1,645   $1,809   $1,988   $2,168
18
19
20
21-Nov-85  10:34 AM
```

Fig. 4.30. Worksheet after copying from A7..H10 to A14.

Notice that the numbers in row 17 are not correct. Despite assigning the same price and unit sales volumes to Product 2, that product is showing monthly dollar sales double those for Product 1. To figure out why, look at the formula in cell D17:

   +$C14*(1-$C8)*D16

The references to cell C14 and cell D16 are correct. These cells contain the unit price and unit sales for Product 2. But notice that the reference to cell C1 has changed so that the cell refers to cell C8. This occurred because the row designation in that address—8—was relative and not absolute. When you copied the formulas containing the address $C1 down the worksheet, 1-2-3 assumed you wanted to adjust the row component of the address.

Absolute Addressing

We can correct the problem by changing the reference to cell C1 from a mixed reference to an absolute reference. Going back to the model in figure 4.28, edit cell D10 and change the formula to

   +$C7*(1-$C$1)*D9

The only difference between this formula and its predecessor is the addition of a $ in front of the 1 in the address $C$1. The added $ changes this address from mixed to absolute.

Now you must copy the new formula in cell D10 to the range E10..H10 so that all of the formulas in the row are the same. You can then recopy the areas D9..H10 into the range D16..H17. Figure 4.31 illustrates the adjusted worksheet.

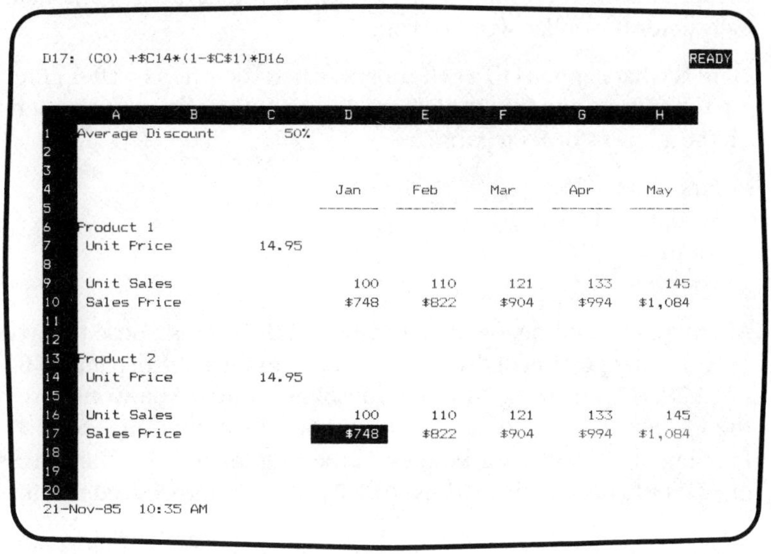

```
D17:  (C0)  +$C14*(1-$C$1)*D16                                    READY

            A        B        C         D      E       F       G       H
  1  Average Discount        50%
  2
  3
  4                                     Jan    Feb     Mar     Apr     May
  5                                   ------- ------- ------- ------- -------
  6  Product 1
  7    Unit Price           14.95
  8
  9    Unit Sales                      100    110     121     133     145
 10    Sales Price                    $748   $822    $904    $994  $1,084
 11
 12
 13  Product 2
 14    Unit Price           14.95
 15
 16    Unit Sales                      100    110     121     133     145
 17    Sales Price                    $748   $822    $904    $994  $1,084
 18
 19
 20
 21-Nov-85  10:35 AM
```

Fig. 4.31. Copied formula using an absolute address.

Notice that the numbers in cells D17..H17 are now correct. If you look at the formula in cell D17:

    +$C14*(1-$C$1)*D16

you will see that the reference to cell C1 has remained fixed during the copy.

To copy cells in 1-2-3 using absolute addressing, you must prepare the cell to be copied before initiating the command. That is, you must enter dollar signs in strategic places when the cell is defined. This is one of the ways that 1-2-3's method of replication differs from earlier spreadsheet programs, such as VisiCalc. In VisiCalc, you normally designate the method of addressing, relative or absolute, at the time of the **R**eplicate (/r) command.

Earlier spreadsheet programs, such as VisiCalc, do not have mixed cell-addressing. To accomplish the replication in figure 4.29 in VisiCalc, you would have to use a hodgepodge of relative and absolute addressing indicators on the end of the replication command and issue the command several times.

Setting Absolute and Relative References

There are two ways that dollar signs can be entered in the formula for cell D10 in the example. You can type in the dollar signs as you enter the formula, or you can use the F4 (Abs) key to have 1-2-3 automatically enter the dollar signs for you.

Here is what happens to a cell address when you press F4 after entering the address or while in EDIT mode. (Note that the cursor must be on the address for F4 to work.)

First time	$C$7
Second	C$7
Third	$C7
Fourth	C7

After typing, pointing, or a combination of the two, suppose that you have the first portion of the formula shown in the control panel of figure 4.28, C7. To change this to an absolute address, you would press the F4 key. The formula in the control panel would change to $C$7. Pressing the F4 key again would shift the address to C$7. A third press of F4 would change the address to $C7, which is the desired result.

A second example of mixed cell-addressing appears in figure 4.32. Here we have created a table to explore the effect of different interest rates and years-to-maturity on the present value of an annuity that pays $1,000 a year. The general format of the built-in @PV function is

@PV(payment,interest,term)

The object of this example is to use a single formula for the entire model, and copy the formula using mixed cell-addressing, as shown in figure 4.32.

Once again, if you look at the command line, you will see the special places where the dollar signs appear. The idea in this example is to use absolute addressing on the column portion of the interest rate address and relative addressing on the row portion ($A4). Conversely, we want to use relative addressing on the column portion of the years-to-maturity address and absolute addressing on the row portion (B$2).

Compare the formula for cell B4 in the control panel in figure 4.32 with the one for cell D8 in figure 4.33. Notice that column A for the interest rate and row 2 for the years-to-maturity have not changed, but the other portions of the addresses have.

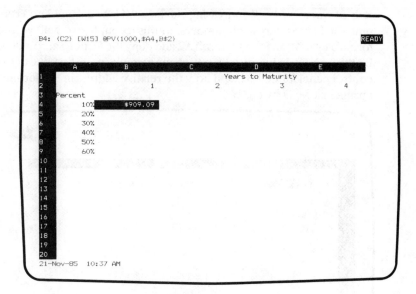

Fig. 4.32. @PV formula with mixed addresses.

```
D8:  (C2)  [W15]  @PV(1000,$A8,D$2)                                    READY

        A           B            C             D             E
1                                          Years to Maturity
2                    1            2             3             4
3   Percent
4        10%     $909.09     $1,735.54     $2,486.85     $3,169.87
5        20%     $833.33     $1,527.78     $2,106.48     $2,588.73
6        30%     $769.23     $1,360.95     $1,816.11     $2,166.24
7        40%     $714.29     $1,224.49     $1,588.92     $1,849.23
8        50%     $666.67     $1,111.11     $1,407.41     $1,604.94
9        60%     $625.00     $1,015.63     $1,259.77     $1,412.35
10
11
12
13
14
15
16
17
18
19
20
21-Nov-85  10:39 AM
```

Fig. 4.33. Result of copying the @PV formula.

A third way mixed cell-addressing can be used is to accumulate a running total across a row of numbers. In this example, we will use the formula @SUM($A$1..B1) in cell A2 and copy the formula across cells B2 through F2. In figure 4.34, notice the formula in the first line of the control panel for cell B2, and how the relative address in the formula changes as we copy the cell.

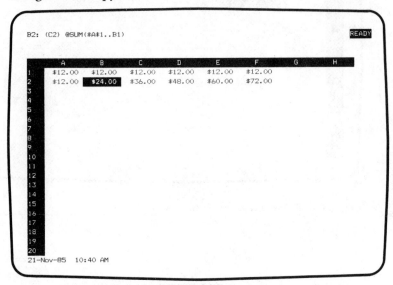

Fig. 4.34. Using absolute addressing to create a running total.

The best way to become comfortable with mixed cell-addressing is to experiment with it. Try several different examples and see what you come up with.

NEW WITH
R2

Using 1-2-3's Specialized Copy Commands

1-2-3 has two specialized copy commands which perform functions that are difficult to perform with 1-2-3's normal copy commands. If you ever have the need for these functions, they are invaluable additions to 1-2-3's command repertoire. They are the /**R**ange **T**ranspose command and the /**R**ange **V**alues command.

Transposing Rows and Columns

The /**Range Transpose** command performs a specialized form of copying where each row of the FROM range is copied into the corresponding column of the TO range. The result is a transposed copy of the FROM range. Figure 4.35 shows the result of using the /**Range Transpose** command to transpose the range at A1..D2 to the range A5..B8.

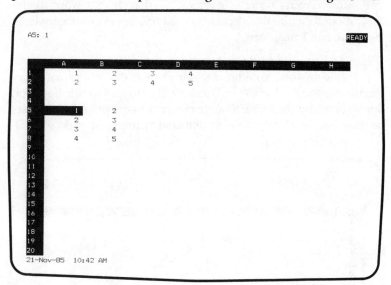

Fig. 4.35. Result of transposing the range A1..D2 to A5..B8.

The /**Range Transpose** command behaves just like the /**Copy** command when copying formulas. When the range is transposed, cell references in the transpose range are adjusted, just as references are adjusted in a normal /**Copy** command. This adjustment of cell references can lead to serious trouble when you use the /**Range Transpose** command to transpose a range containing formulas. The formulas will be incorrect, once transposed; however, values will remain in the same order. Because the cell references are not transposed, the relative and mixed cell references in the transposed range will end up referring to unintended locations after the transposition.

You can avoid the problem of incorrect cell references in transposed ranges by converting the formulas in the FROM range to values before transposing. The /**Range Values** command is a convenient way to convert a range of formulas to values.

NEW WITH
R2

Converting Formulas to Values

The /**R**ange Values command allows you to copy the values of the cells in one range to another range. This command is useful whenever you want to preserve the current values of a range of cells instead of having only the changed values after the worksheet is updated. What is particularly important about the /**R**ange Values command is that the command converts formulas to values. You don't have to worry, therefore, about formulas that depend on cell references (for example, in using /**R**ange **T**ranspose).

Figure 4.36 shows a worksheet with a monthly income statement and a year-to-date total column. As you change the worksheet every month, the year-to-date (Y-T-D) totals will change as well. If, however, you want to save the Y-T-D totals to compare them with previous years or quarters, the /**R**ange Values command enables you to do so, as illustrated in Figure 4.37.

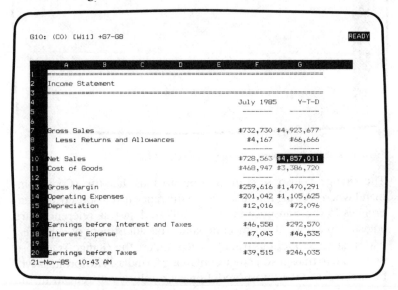

Fig. 4.36. Worksheet with a monthly and a year-to-date income column.

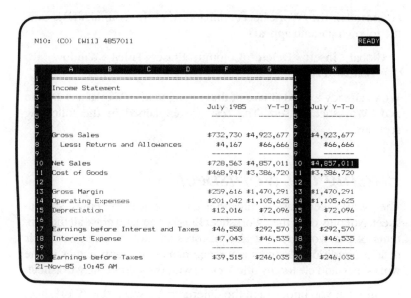

Fig. 4.37. *Saving the year-to-date values with /Range Values.*

Miscellaneous Comments on Copying

When you copy a cell, 1-2-3 automatically copies the format of the cell with it. (See Chapter 5 for more information on formats.) This automatic format copying feature saves you from having to preset the format for an entire range of cells before copying to them.

Sometimes the TO and FROM ranges will overlap when you copy. The general rule is that if you do not overlap the end points for the FROM and TO ranges, there will be no problems in the copy. If you do overlap them, however, you may get mixed results. You can overlap ranges legitimately when the FROM and TO ranges have the same upper left boundary.

You should also note particularly the finality of the /Copy command. If you copy over the contents of a cell, there is no way to retrieve them. Make sure that you have your ranges designated properly before you press Enter.

Worksheet Commands

1-2-3 offers a group of commands that are similar to the range commands but affect the entire worksheet. The command root for all these commands is the /Worksheet command. After this command is issued, the following menu appears:

Global Insert Delete Column Erase Titles Window
    Status Page

We've already looked at two of these commands: /Worksheet Delete and /Worksheet Insert. The rest are explained in the following sections.

Erasing the Worksheet

The /Worksheet Erase command is used to clear the entire spreadsheet. Not only does the /Worksheet Erase command erase all the contents of the worksheet, it also restores all global settings to their default condition, destroys any range names or graph names in the worksheet, and clears any title lock or window split in the worksheet.

Be sure that you understand the difference between the /Worksheet Erase command and the /Range Erase A1..IV8192 command. The /Range Erase command will remove the contents of every cell in the worksheet, except those that are protected. It will not, however, alter any of the global settings, including column widths or print settings. /Worksheet Erase, however, literally restores the 1-2-3 worksheet to its default configuration. After the /we command is issued, the worksheet is exactly as it was when loaded.

Obviously, the /Worksheet Erase command is a powerful and potentially destructive command. For this reason, 1-2-3 will always force you either to type a *y*, for "Yes, I want to erase the entire worksheet," or to point to Yes and press Enter, before this command will be executed. *Be careful!* Once a worksheet has been erased in this way, it cannot be recovered. Always save your worksheets before you erase them.

The /Worksheet Global Commands

The largest subgroup of commands under the /Worksheet command is the Global command. The /Worksheet Global command menu looks like this:

Format Label-Prefix Column-Width Recalculation
    Protection Default Zero

We have already covered the **Protection** command in this chapter, and the **Format** command will be considered in the next chapter. The **Label-Prefix** command was covered in Chapter 3. The **Default** command controls the default settings used by 1-2-3 for printing, file management, and for international display formats. Use of the **Default** command for printing and file management is discussed in Chapters 7 and 8. Setting the defaults for the international display formats is discussed in Chapter 5. The other **Global** commands are **Column-width**, **Recalculation**, and **Zero**.

Recalculating the Worksheet

One of the primary functions of a spreadsheet program is to recalculate all the cells in a worksheet when a value or a formula in one of the cells changes. How this recalculation is actually done says a great deal about where a program fits in the evolution of spreadsheet software. 1-2-3 is among the most advanced spreadsheet programs to date in its method of recalculation, as you can see from the following discussion of the earlier spreadsheet program VisiCalc.

VisiCalc's Recalculation Method

VisiCalc, like most first-generation spreadsheets, gives the option of column-wise or row-wise recalculation. In column-wise recalculation, VisiCalc starts recalculating at the entry in cell A1 and proceeds down column A, then continues at cell B1 and moves down column B, and so on. In contrast, row-wise recalculation starts at cell A1 and proceeds across row 1, then moves down to cell A2 and across row 2, and so on. In VisiCalc, you can specify one method or the other.

These methods of recalculation often can lead to the wrong answer unless you are careful about how you set up the worksheet. Among the recalculative errors that can occur with VisiCalc are forward and circular references.

A forward reference occurs when a cell refers to another cell that is lower in the worksheet. For example, imagine that you created a worksheet with four cells: A1, C1, C2, and C3. Suppose that those cells had the following contents:

    A1 = +C3
    C1 = 100
    C2 = 200
    C3 = +C1+C2

A1 and C3 would both have the value 300. Now, suppose that the number in cell C2 is changed to 100. Let's step through the recalculative process. Because VisiCalc begins recalculating at the upper left corner of the worksheet, cell A1 would be evaluated first. Since the prior value of C3, 300, has not changed, A1 would retain the value 300. VisiCalc would then proceed either column by column or row by row across that worksheet until it came to cell C3. Because the value of cell C2 has changed, the value in C3 would change to 200.

Clearly, it does not make sense to have A1 and C3 contain different values when cell A1 is defined to be equal to C3. Although recalculating the worksheet again would eliminate the inequality, it would not remove the basic problem. In large and complex models, it is possible to have undetected forward references.

1-2-3's Recalculation Method

As you might expect, 1-2-3 can recalculate in a linear fashion just like VisiCalc. To do this, you override the natural default setting using /**W**orksheet **G**lobal **R**ecalculation <**C**olumn-wise or **R**ow-wise>. In fact, this method is recommended if you import a VisiCalc file that is built around either method of recalculation.

But 1-2-3 normally recalculates in what Lotus calls a *natural order*. Natural order means that all the active cells in a worksheet are inter-related, and 1-2-3 does not recalculate any given cell until the cells that it depends on have been recalculated first. Because the relationship between cells is rarely linear, the method of recalculation is not linear. Rather, recalculation occurs in a topological fashion, starting at the lowest level and working up.

$$C3$$
$$B1 \quad B3 \quad B4$$
$$A1 \quad A2 \quad A4 \quad A7 \quad A9$$

With natural recalculation, you no longer have to worry about the order of recalculation and the problem of forward references. If we re-created our forward reference example in 1-2-3 and used natural recalculation, cell C3—the most fundamental cell in the worksheet— would be evaluated before cell A1, eliminating the forward reference.

Iterative Recalculation

In most cases, it takes only one pass to recalculate a worksheet. When a worksheet contains a circular reference, however, this is not possible.

A classic example of a circular reference is the problem of trying to determine the amount of borrowing required by a firm. The thought process involved is

1. Borrowings = Assets − (Total Liabilities + Equity). Borrowings represent the difference between projected asset requirements and the sum of total projected liabilities and equity.

2. The level of equity is a function of net income and dividends.

3. Net income is a function of gross margin and interest expense.

4. Finally, interest expense and gross margin are a function of borrowings.

You can see the circular pattern. When this kind of circular reference occurs, 1-2-3 displays a CIRC indicator in the lower right corner of the screen. When you recalculate this type of worksheet using regular natural calculation, 1-2-3 will not accurately recompute all of the values. Because each value in the circular set depends, directly or indirectly, on all of the others, 1-2-3 cannot find a "toehold"; that is, 1-2-3 cannot find the most fundamental cell in the worksheet because there is no such cell.

Iterative recalculation allows 1-2-3 to overcome this problem. When 1-2-3 is in ITERATIVE mode, the worksheet will recalculate a specified number of times for each time you press the Calc (F9) key. Normally, the worksheet will recalculate only once for each time the F9 key is pressed. The default number of iterations under the ITERATION mode is 20, but you can alter this number as you see fit. If you have circular references in your worksheet, however, we suggest that you keep the number of recalculation passes high.

Iterative recalculation overcomes a circular reference because each recalculative pass through the worksheet causes the actual values of the cells to approach more closely their correct values. For example, suppose that you built a worksheet with the following set of relationships:

A3 = .05*A5
A4 = 100
A5 = A3+A4

When you first enter this formula, A3 has a value of 0, A4 equals 100, and A5 equals 100. Assume that the number of iterations is set to 5. Table 4.1 shows the values of each cell after each recalculative pass.

Table 4.1
Changing Values of Cells during Five Recalculations

Pass	Cell A3	Cell A4	Cell A5
1	5	100	105
2	5.25	100	105.25
3	5.263	100	105.263
4	5.2632	100	105.2632
5	5.26316	100	105.26316

Notice that on each pass, the difference between the prior and the current value of cells A3 and A5 becomes smaller. After only five passes, the difference is so small as to be insignificant. After 20 passes, the difference would probably be too small for 1-2-3 to recognize. At that point, the problem with the circular reference is eliminated.

Two things should be noted about iterative recalculation. First, it is possible to create a set of circular references that is too complicated for 1-2-3 to sort out in 20 passes. If this happens with one of your models, simply recalculate the worksheet *twice*, using 20 iterations each time. This process is identical to setting the iteration count to 40 (if that were possible). Second, remember that 20 calculations of a large worksheet take a long time. Be patient; control over 1-2-3 will be returned to you soon enough.

It is also possible to enter circular references that cannot be solved using this iterative approach. One symptom of this is values that quickly grow larger after each iteration.

Automatic versus Manual Recalculation

When you are working on a large worksheet that involves many formulas, it may take some time for the worksheet to recalculate. Recalculation occurs each time a new entry is made or a value is changed. One way to get around this problem is to change from the standard automatic to manual recalculation. This is done easily by executing /**W**orksheet Global **R**ecalculation, then choosing **M**anual.

With manual recalculation, you can control 1-2-3 so that it recalculates only when you press the Calc (F9) key. Manual recalculation is an advantage only with large worksheets where you are changing many values. Otherwise, 1-2-3 is fast enough that recalculation occurs almost instantly.

Setting Column Widths

One of the problems in earlier spreadsheet programs was that the widths of worksheet columns could be controlled only as a group. If you were setting up a projection of expenses for the next five years and wanted to display the full descriptions of the expense items (some of them 20 characters), you would have to set all the columns to a width of 20 characters. To avoid that situation, you would have to abbreviate or truncate the labels.

In 1-2-3, you do not have this problem. You can control separately the width of each column. You can set the first column of your projection of expenses to be 20 characters wide and the other columns to whatever width you want.

The command used to set individual column widths is /Worksheet Column Set-Width. You can set one column width at a time by either entering a number or using the ← and → cursor keys followed by Enter. The advantage of the ← and → cursor keys is that the column width actually expands and contracts each time you press a key. To get a good idea of what the width requirements are, experiment when you enter the command.

There are two things to remember about this command. First, you must locate the pointer in the proper column before you initiate the command. Otherwise, you will have to start over. Second, to reset the column width to the standard setting, you must use the /Worksheet Column Reset-Width command.

As in earlier spreadsheet programs, you can control all of the column widths at once. The command to do this in 1-2-3 is /Worksheet Global Column Set-Width (Column-width Set in Releases 1 and 1A). The standard setting for column widths is 9, but you can change this to whatever width you want for the current worksheet.

Any column width previously set by the /Worksheet Column Set-Width command will not be affected by a change in the global setting. For example, if you set the width of column A to 12 using the /Worksheet Column Set-Width command, then change all the columns in the worksheet to a width of 5 using the /Worksheet Global Column Set-Width command, every column except A will change to 5. A will remain at a width of 12 and will have to be reset to 5 with the /Worksheet Column Set-Width command.

NEW WITH R2

Hiding Columns

The /Worksheet Column Hide command allows you to suppress the display of any columns in the worksheet. Figure 4.38 shows a worksheet with columns A through G filled with numbers. Figure 4.39 shows the same worksheet after the /Worksheet Column Hide command has been used to hide columns C, D, and E.

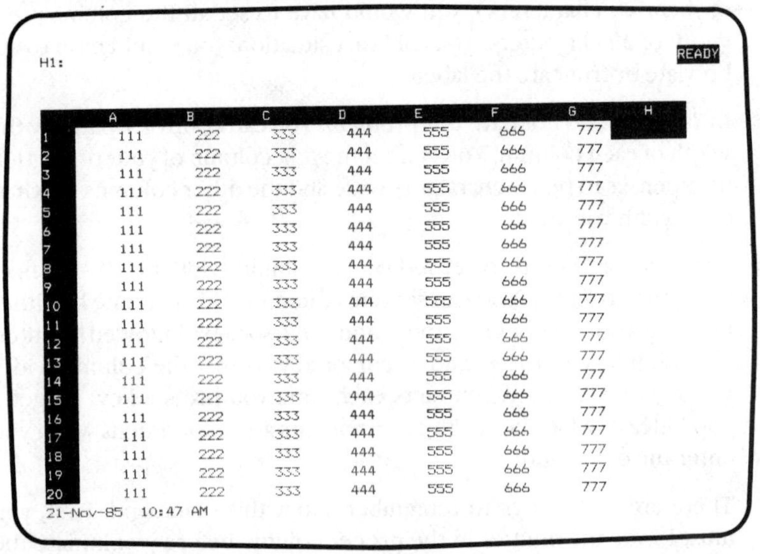
H1: READY

	A	B	C	D	E	F	G	H
1	111	222	333	444	555	666	777	
2	111	222	333	444	555	666	777	
3	111	222	333	444	555	666	777	
4	111	222	333	444	555	666	777	
5	111	222	333	444	555	666	777	
6	111	222	333	444	555	666	777	
7	111	222	333	444	555	666	777	
8	111	222	333	444	555	666	777	
9	111	222	333	444	555	666	777	
10	111	222	333	444	555	666	777	
11	111	222	333	444	555	666	777	
12	111	222	333	444	555	666	777	
13	111	222	333	444	555	666	777	
14	111	222	333	444	555	666	777	
15	111	222	333	444	555	666	777	
16	111	222	333	444	555	666	777	
17	111	222	333	444	555	666	777	
18	111	222	333	444	555	666	777	
19	111	222	333	444	555	666	777	
20	111	222	333	444	555	666	777	

21-Nov-85 10:47 AM

Fig. 4.38. Worksheet with numbers in columns A through G.

Numbers and formulas in hidden columns are still present, and cell references to cells in hidden columns continue to work properly. However, the hidden columns do not appear on the display. You can only tell that those columns are missing because of the break in the column letters at the top of the display.

When you select the /Worksheet Column Hide command, 1-2-3 prompts you for the range of columns to hide. You must invoke the command once for each range of adjacent columns that you hide.

One important use for the /Worksheet Column Hide command is to suppress display of unwanted columns when printing reports. When

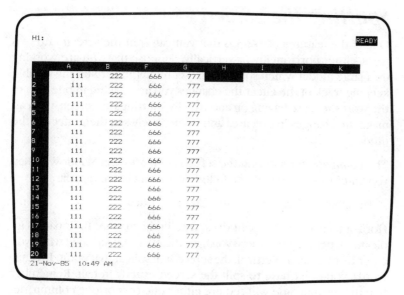

Fig. 4.39. The same worksheet with columns C, D, and E hidden.

intervening columns are hidden, a report can display data from two or more separated columns on a single page.

NEW WITH
R2

Use **/W**orksheet **C**olumn **D**isplay to redisplay hidden columns. When you select this command, all hidden columns are redisplayed with asterisks by the column letters at the top of the display. You are prompted for a range of columns to unhide.

Certain 1-2-3 commands affect only the current window when the screen has been split. For example, the **/W**orksheet **C**olumn **H**ide command can be used to hide a column in the current window without affecting the display in the other window.

Suppressing Display of Zeros

NEW WITH
R2

The **/W**orksheet **G**lobal **Z**ero command allows you to suppress the display of cells that have a numeric value of zero. This is often useful for preparing presentation reports. You can enter formulas and values for all the items in the report, including the zero items, then display the results with all the zeros removed. The **/W**orksheet **G**lobal **Z**ero command also has an option to reinstate the display of zero values.

Splitting the Screen

One of the features of 1-2-3 is that you can split the screen into two parts, either horizontally or vertically. Suppose that you are working on a large model which spans several columns and are having trouble keeping track of the effect the changes you are making in one area of the worksheet are having on another. By splitting the screen, you can make the changes in one area and immediately see their effect in the other.

The command for splitting the screen is /Worksheet Window. When you enter this command, the following menu choices appear:

Horizontal   Vertical   Sync   Unsync   Clear

Horizontal and Vertical split the screen in the manner their names indicate. Depending on where you have the cursor positioned when you enter Horizontal or Vertical, the screen will split at that point. In other words, you don't have to split the screen exactly in half. Remember that the dividing line will require either one row or one column, depending on how you split the screen.

After you split the screen using Horizontal, the cursor appears in the top window. When a Vertical division is created, the cursor appears in the left window. To jump the division between the windows, use the Window (F6) key.

The Sync and Unsync options work as a pair. In Sync screens, when you scroll one screen, the other one scrolls automatically along with it. Horizontally split screens always keep the same columns in view, and vertically split screens always keep the same rows. Sync is the standard default for 1-2-3.

Unsync screens allow you to control one screen independently of the other in all directions. In fact, you can even show the same cells in the two different windows.

With Unsync screens, you can also independently control the formats of cells in the screens. For example, you can use Unsync to display numbers on one screen and the formulas behind the numbers on another.

The Clear option removes the split window option and reverts the screen to a single window. When you use this option, the single window takes on the settings of the top or left-hand window, depending on how the screen was split.

Entering a Page-Break Character

NEW WITH
R2

The /Worksheet **P**age command inserts a blank row, and then a page-break character in the cell where the cursor was originally positioned. This command is similar to the /Worksheet Insert **R**ow command that inserts a row at the row(s) specified by the cell pointer. /Worksheet **P**age inserts a new row into the worksheet above the current location of the cell pointer. The command then places the page-break character in the cell directly above the cursor.

The page-break character is used when printing a range from the worksheet. (Printing is covered in detail in Chapter 8.) The page break is only effective when positioned at the left edge of the range being printed. When the page break is in effect, the contents of the other cells in that row within the print range are not printed.

Accessing DOS from 1-2-3

NEW WITH
R2

The /**S**ystem command gives you the ability to access other programs under the DOS operating system without leaving 1-2-3. This powerful command suspends the operation of 1-2-3 and returns you to the system prompt (A> for floppy based systems, C> for hard drive systems). When you are at the system prompt, you can execute any other programs before returning to 1-2-3 by typing *Exit* at the system prompt.

The /**S**ystem command is particularly useful for giving you access to your system's native file handling commands. For example, if you want to save your worksheet but your data disk is full, you can use the /**S**ystem command to suspend 1-2-3 processing while you initialize a new data disk using the DOS FORMAT command. After you return to 1-2-3 with Exit, you can save your worksheet to the new data disk with /**F**ile **S**ave (covered in detail in Chapter 7).

You should be aware of a few cautions about using the /**S**ystem command. First, if you have a large spreadsheet that takes up almost all of main memory, the /**S**ystem command may fail because of insufficient memory to run another program. If the /**S**ystem command fails, 1-2-3 informs you with the error message Cannot Invoke DOS, and turns on the ERROR indicator.

The second caution is that certain programs that are run from 1-2-3 using the /**S**ystem command may cause 1-2-3 to abort when you try to return with Exit. The DOS file management commands like FORMAT, COPY, DELETE, DIRECTORY, DISKCOPY, and so forth, can be invoked safely from 1-2-3, as can most business application programs.

Many so-called resident utility programs, however, will cause 1-2-3 to abort if you call one of the programs before returning to 1-2-3. Take a few minutes to experiment with the programs you may want to use with the /System command before attempting to use those commands during an important 1-2-3 session.

Freezing Titles

The /Worksheet Titles command is similar to the /Worksheet Window command. Like the /Worksheet Window command, the /Worksheet Titles command allows you to see one area of a worksheet while working on another. However, the unique function of this command is that it freezes all the cells to the left and above the current cell pointer position so that those cells cannot move off the screen.

A classic example of the advantage of this command is the task of entering the items on a pro forma Balance Sheet and Income Statement. Suppose that you are trying to set up a budget to project the level of the financial statement items month by month for the next year. Because the normal screen, without any special column widths, shows 20 rows by 7 columns, you will undoubtedly have to shift the screen so that cell A1 is no longer in the upper left corner. In fact, if you enter the month headings across row 1 and the Balance Sheet and Income Statement headings down column A, as shown in figure 4.40, you must scroll the screen several different times in order to enter all the items.

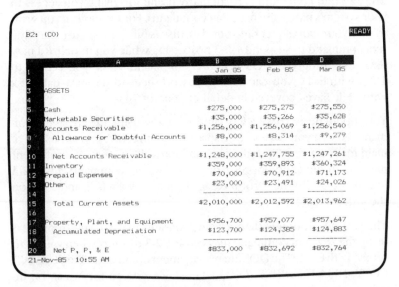

Fig. 4.40. A balance sheet worksheet.

To keep the headings in view on the screen, even when you scroll the screen, enter /wt when the cursor is in cell B2. When you enter the /wt command, the following menu items appear:

Both Horizontal Vertical Clear

If you select **H**orizontal, the rows on the screen above the cell pointer become frozen. That is, they don't move off the screen when you scroll up and down. If you select **V**ertical, the columns to the left of the cell pointer are frozen and move only when you scroll up and down (but not when you move left and right). **B**oth freezes the rows above and the columns to the left of the cell pointer. **C**lear unlocks the worksheet titles.

In our pro forma example, we have selected the **B**oth option. In this case, when you scroll right and left as well as up and down, the headings always remain in view. Figures 4.41A and 4.41B show two examples of how this works.

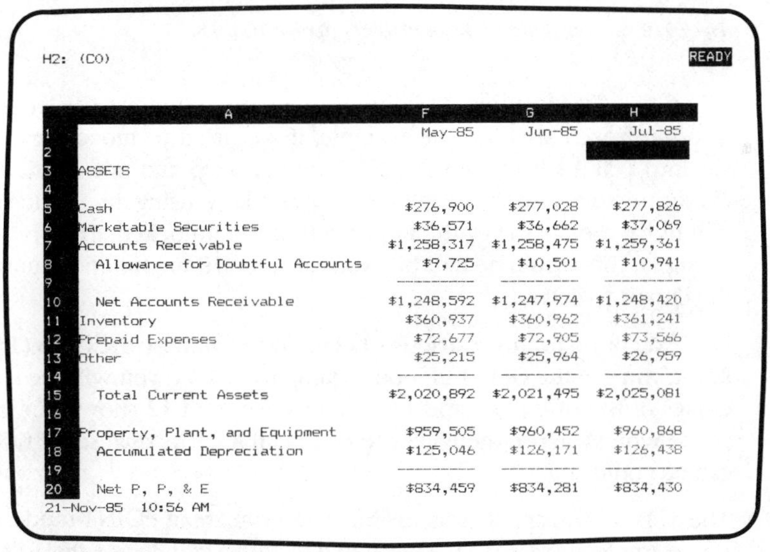

H2: (C0) READY

	A	F	G	H
1		May-85	Jun-85	Jul-85
2				
3	ASSETS			
4				
5	Cash	$276,900	$277,028	$277,826
6	Marketable Securities	$36,571	$36,662	$37,069
7	Accounts Receivable	$1,258,317	$1,258,475	$1,259,361
8	Allowance for Doubtful Accounts	$9,725	$10,501	$10,941
9		---------	---------	---------
10	Net Accounts Receivable	$1,248,592	$1,247,974	$1,248,420
11	Inventory	$360,937	$360,962	$361,241
12	Prepaid Expenses	$72,677	$72,905	$73,566
13	Other	$25,215	$25,964	$26,959
14		---------	---------	---------
15	Total Current Assets	$2,020,892	$2,021,495	$2,025,081
16				
17	Property, Plant, and Equipment	$959,505	$960,452	$960,868
18	Accumulated Depreciation	$125,046	$126,171	$126,438
19		---------	---------	---------
20	Net P, P, & E	$834,459	$834,281	$834,430

21-Nov-85 10:56 AM

Fig. 4.41A. Moving to the right in the worksheet after setting titles.

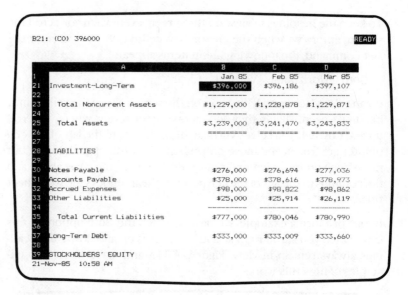

Fig. 4.41B. Moving down in the worksheet after setting titles.

When you freeze rows or columns, you cannot move the cursor into the frozen area. In our example, if you tried to move the cursor into cell A2 from cell B2, 1-2-3 would beep and not allow the cursor to move into the protected area. Similarly, using the Home key will move the cursor to the upper cell in the unlocked area. In our example, this would be cell B2. Normally, the Home function moves the cursor to cell A1.

One exception to this restriction occurs when you use the Goto (F5) key. If you use the Goto function to jump to cell A1, you will see two copies of the title rows and/or columns. Figure 4.42 shows our example when you use the F5 key to go to cell A1. The dual set of titles can be confusing.

The frozen areas are also accessible when you are in POINT mode. In our example, suppose that you wanted to define cell B6 as equal to A1. You would move the cursor to cell B6, type + to begin the formula, then use the cursor keys to point to cell A1. In this case, the cursor is allowed to move into the protected area, and 1-2-3 will not beep.

VisiCalc's method of creating worksheet titles is slightly different from 1-2-3's method. Although the two programs use almost identical command logic for the Titles command, in VisiCalc, the locked range will include the row and column where the cursor was located when the

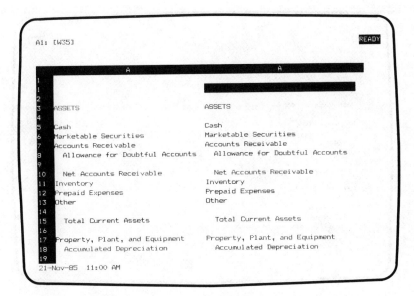

A1: [W35]   READY

```
1
1
2
3   ASSETS                        ASSETS
4
5   Cash                          Cash
6   Marketable Securities         Marketable Securities
7   Accounts Receivable           Accounts Receivable
8     Allowance for Doubtful Accounts    Allowance for Doubtful Accounts
9
10    Net Accounts Receivable          Net Accounts Receivable
11  Inventory                     Inventory
12  Prepaid Expenses              Prepaid Expenses
13  Other                         Other
14
15    Total Current Assets            Total Current Assets
16
17  Property, Plant, and Equipment    Property, Plant, and Equipment
18    Accumulated Depreciation        Accumulated Depreciation
19
21-Nov-85  11:00 AM
```

Fig. 4.42. The display after using Goto to move to cell A1.

command was executed. In our example, issuing the /**W**orksheet
Titles Both command with the cursor in cell B2 would lock both rows
1 and 2 and columns A and B. If you are a former VisiCalc user, you
should practice locking titles with 1-2-3.

Checking the Status of Global Settings

The final option on 1-2-3's main command menu, /**W**orksheet **S**tatus,
checks the status of various spreadsheet options. These options are
called global settings. Figure 4.43 shows an example of what is displayed. This command gives you an easy way to check the settings
without having to experiment to find out what the settings are.

The information in figure 4.43 indicates that the following worksheet
global settings are active:

1. **Recalculation** is **Automatic**. This is the normal default
   setting (covered in this chapter).

2. The **Global Format** is **General**. Again, this is the default
   setting (covered in Chapter 5).

```
                                                              STAT

         Available Memory:
           Conventional..... 288409 of 288464 Bytes (99%)
           Expanded......... (None)

         Math Co-processor:  (None)

         Recalculation:
           Method.......... Automatic
           Order........... Natural
           Iterations....... 1

         Circular Reference: (None)

         Cell Display:
           Format.......... (G)
           Label-Prefix.....  '
           Column-Width..... 9
           Zero Suppression. Off

         Global Protection:  Off

     21-Nov-85  11:02 AM                    CMD
```

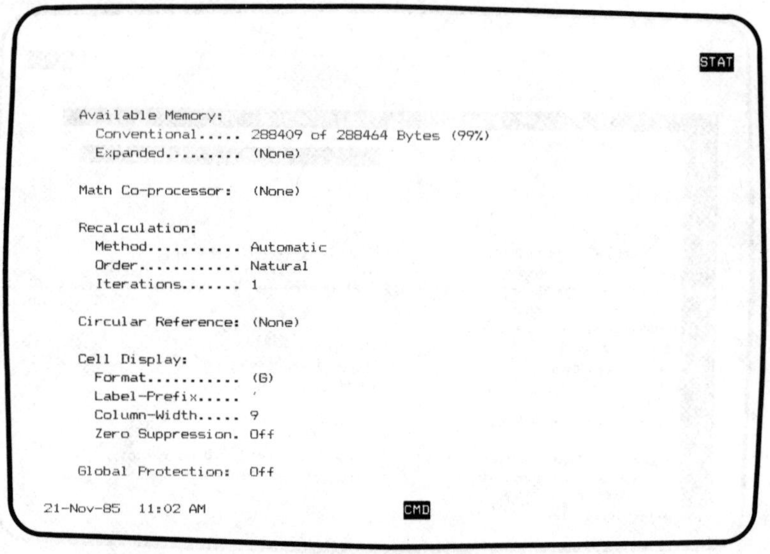

Fig. 4.43. Global settings in the worksheet.

3. The **Global Label-Prefix** is (′) for left-justification (covered in Chapter 3).

4. The **Global Column** width is nine characters (covered in this chapter).

5. **Global Protection** is off (covered in this chapter).

Conclusion

In this chapter, you learned about several of 1-2-3's most important, basic commands. Now that you have learned the fundamentals, you are ready to go on to more 1-2-3 commands. The next chapter extends the discussion by presenting 1-2-3's commands to control formats.

NEW WITH
R2

5
Formats

One of the ways that 1-2-3 surpasses earlier spreadsheet programs (including earlier releases of 1-2-3 itself) is by offering you more cell *formats* to choose from. Formats control how cell contents are displayed on the screen. 1-2-3 offers ten cell formats:

1-2-3 Formats

Fixed
Scientific
Currency
, (Comma)
General
+/- (Horizontal Bar Graph)
Percent
Date (includes Time format)
Text
Hidden

These formats primarily affect the way numeric values are displayed in a worksheet. Of the ten, only the **Text** and **Hidden** formats affect the display of labels or string values.

Many of these formats will seem familiar to those who have used other spreadsheet programs. However, you will find several subtle variations. For a complete listing of all format commands, see the 1-2-3 command-menu map included at the back of the book.

Command Roots
for Controlling Formats

The command *roots* for controlling formats are /Worksheet Global Format and /Range Format. The former controls the format of all the cells in the worksheet, and the latter controls specific ranges within the worksheet.

Generally, you use the /Worksheet Global Format command when you are just starting to enter a worksheet. You will want to choose what format the majority of cells will take. Once you have set all the cells to that format, you can use the /Range Format command to override the global format setting for specific cell ranges.

The /Range Format command has precedence over the /Worksheet Global Format command. This means that whenever you change the Global Format, all the numbers and formulas affected will change automatically unless they were previously formatted with the /Range Format command. In turn, when you format a range, the format for that range will override any already set by the /Global Format.

When a command root is entered, a common menu appears with the following entries:

> Fixed   Scientific   Currency   ,   General   +/−   Percent
> Date   Text   Hidden

General Format

General format is the only format that is common to 1-2-3 and earlier programs in a pure sense. Other formats have attributes that make them unique to 1-2-3. General format is discussed first because it is the default format for all new worksheets.

When numbers are displayed in General format, insignificant zeros to the right of the decimal point are suppressed. If numbers are too large or too small to be displayed normally, scientific notation is used. Some examples of this format for numbers are

    123.456
    5.63E+14
    −22.1
    1.9E-09

Labels are displayed as left-justified in General format. They are preceded by a single quotation mark that signals 1-2-3 to left-justify. As mentioned earlier, you can use the /Worksheet Global Label-Prefix or the /Range Label-Prefix command to change the default of left-justification.

General is the default setting for the /Worksheet Global Format. You can check the default setting by entering /Worksheet Status. (This command is explained in Chapter 4.)

When you specify General format for a range with /Range Format, the number on the command line is preceded by the indicator (G) whenever the cursor is within the formatted range. In fact, all formats specified using /Range Format display format indicators in the command line. You do not have to enter them yourself; 1-2-3 automatically provides them.

Fixed Format

1-2-3's Fixed format is similar to General format in that it does not display commas or dollar signs. The difference is that Fixed format lets you control the number of places to the right of the decimal point. When you select Fixed format, 1-2-3 prompts you for the number of decimal places you want displayed. After you have chosen a number, 1-2-3 will pad the selected cells with zeros to the right of the decimal for as many places as you indicated. Conversely, if you decide to display fewer than the number of decimal places you have entered, the number will be rounded to the specified number of places.

The following are some examples of how numbers appear in Fixed format.

In the Command Line	*In the Worksheet*
(F0)15. 1	15
(F2)1000. 2145	1000. 21
(F3)-21. 405	-21. 405
(F4)93. 1	93. 1000

You do not have to enter the format indicator (for example, F0) in the command line because 1-2-3 automatically does it for you.

This format can be useful when you want to control specifically the number of places to the right of the decimal point without the automatic removal of insignificant digits that occurs in General format. Fixed format is particularly appealing when you have columns of numbers and want all the numbers to show the same number of decimal places.

Scientific Format

Scientific format causes 1-2-3 to display numbers in exponential scientific notation. You will recall that this notation is used in the General format when numbers are too large or too small to be displayed any other way. Scientific, however, differs from General format in the way the scientific notation is controlled. With Scientific format, you control the number of decimal places and so determine the amount of precision. 1-2-3's General format controls them by default. Some examples follow:

In the Command Line	*In the Worksheet*
(S2)27. 1	2. 71E+01
(S4)453. 235	4. 5324E+02
(S1)-21	-2. 1E+01
(S0)-1	-1E+00

Currency Format

The Currency format changed significantly in the transition from earlier programs to 1-2-3.

The differences between 1-2-3 Currency format and that of other programs are that in 1-2-3 a dollar sign appears in the same cell before each entry, and commas separate hundreds from thousands, hundreds of thousands from millions, etc. Another major change is that negative values appear in parentheses ( ). Currency format also gives you the option of controlling the number of places to the right of the decimal point. This feature is helpful if you are having trouble getting values displayed because they are too large for the column width. One solution is to override the default of two places to the right of the decimal point.

If the value you want to display in Currency format is too large for the column width, a series of asterisks instead of the value will appear across the cell. In fact, this is true for all formats. The problem of space is particularly acute with this format because the dollar sign and commas take up space. The best way to handle this situation is to experiment with the formatting parameters and the column width until you get the appearance you want.

You will recall that column width is controlled through either the /Worksheet Column Set-width or /Worksheet Global Column Set-width command. The former controls specific columns in the worksheet, and the latter controls all the columns at the same time.

Numbers that appear in the command line after they are entered are preceded by the format indicator for Currency. The format indicator for Currency is C, followed by an integer to indicate the number of decimal places you have chosen, all in parentheses. The following are some examples of how numbers appear in the command line after you have entered them, and how they are displayed in the worksheet with Currency format.

In the Command Line	In the Worksheet
(C2)45	$45.00
(C2)1612.3	$1,612.30
(C3)22.805	$22.805
(C1)105.56	$105.6
(C2)-210.99	($210.99)

Cell formats are controlled with the /Worksheet Global Format or the /Range Format command, depending on how cell-specific you want the control to be, followed by Currency in this case.

Comma Format

The , (comma) format resembles Currency format, except that no dollar signs appear when the numbers are displayed, and commas separate hundreds from thousands, hundreds of thousands from millions, etc. Once the , format is chosen, you may respecify how many decimal places you would like.

This format can be particularly useful in financial statements to display all the numbers, except those at the top and bottom of columns, with commas but without dollar signs. For example, a portion of a balance sheet follows.

Cash	$1,750
Receivables	3,735
Inventories	9,200
Current Assets	$14,685

The numbers corresponding to Receivables and Inventories are displayed with the , (comma) format, and those corresponding to Cash and Current Assets are displayed with Currency format.

The +/– Format

The +/– format creates a horizontal bar graph of plus or minus signs, depending on the value of the number you enter in the cell. Asterisks are displayed if the size of the bar graph exceeds the column width. If zero is entered in a cell, a period (.) will be displayed on the graph and left-justified in the cell.

In the Command Line	In the Worksheet
(+)6	++++++
(+)-4	----
(+)0	.

Some applications use this format to mark a value in a long column of numbers. As you scan the column, the +'s and –'s will stand out, making them easier to locate (fig. 5.1).

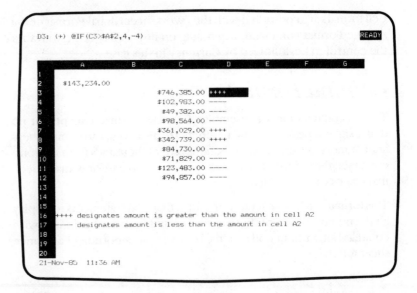

Fig. 5.1. Value of +/– format in looking at long lists of numbers.

Percent Format

The Percent format is used to display percentages with the number of decimal places controlled by you. The values displayed in the work-sheet are the result of what you enter, multiplied by 100 and followed by a percent sign.

In the Command Line	*In the Worksheet*
(PØ).12	12%
(P4)12.134	1213.4000%
(P2).5675	56.75%

One of the difficulties with this format is that it seems natural to want to enter integers instead of decimals (for example, 12 instead of .12 in the first example). 1-2-3, however, persists in its method of storing cell contents in only one way and allowing you to control only the display of the output.

Date and Time Formats

1-2-3 represents any given date internally as an integer equal to the number of days from December 31, 1899, to the given date. For example, January 1, 1900, is represented by the number 1; December 31, 2099 (which is the last date in 1-2-3's calendar), is represented by 73050. To enter a date into the worksheet, you use one of the date functions: @DATE, @DATEVALUE, or @NOW (@TODAY for Release 1 and 1A users).

1-2-3 calculates a period of hours as a fraction expressed in decimals. The calculations are based on a 24-hour clock, so-called military time. Use one of the time functions: @TIME, @TIMEVALUE, or @NOW (@TODAY for Release 1 and 1A users) to enter a time into the worksheet.

To display a date or time in its proper Date format, use either the /Range Format Date or /Worksheet Global Format Date commands. When you use the /Range Format Date command, any range that you have set using the Date format will appear in one of nine date and time formats. When you use the /Worksheet Global Format Date command, dates or times, as well as all other numbers entered in any cell in the worksheet, will be displayed in the selected date and time format.

The nine date and time formats that you can specify with the /Range Format Date and /Worksheet Global Format Date commands are shown in table 5.1.

For more information on date and time functions and formats, see Chapter 6.

Table 5.1
Date and Time Formats

Description	Example
DD-MMM-YY (Day-Month-Year)	11-Jul-85
DD-MM (Day-Month)	11-Jul
MMM-YY (Month-Year)	Jul-85
MM/DD/YY or DD/MM/YY or DD.MM.YY or YY-MM-DD (Full International Date Format)	06/11/85
MM/DD or DD/MM or DD.MM or MM-DD (Partial International Date Format)	06/11
HH:MM:SS AM/PM (Hour-Minute-Second)	11:37:43 PM
HH:MM AM/PM (Hour-Minute)	11:37 PM
HH:MM:SS or HH.MM.SS or HH,MM,SS or HHhMMmSSs (Full International Time Format—24 hour)	23:37:43
HH:MM or HH.MM or HH,MM or HHhMMm (Partial International Time Format—24 hour)	23:37

Text Format

Text format displays formulas as they are entered in the command line, not the computed values that 1-2-3 normally displays. Numbers entered using this format are displayed in the same manner used in General format.

Probably the most important application of this format is setting up Table Ranges for /Data Table commands, but another important application is debugging. Because you can display all the formulas on the screen with the Text format, finding and correcting problems are relatively easy. If the characters of your formulas exceed the cell width, you will see one less character than the column width setting. When you use this technique for debugging your model, you may have to widen the cell width to see your complete formulas.

Some examples of Text format follow:

In the Command Line	*In the Worksheet*
(T)+C4/B12	+C4/B121
(T)(A21*B4)	(A21*B4)
(T)567.6	567.6

Hidden Format

Hidden format will suppress the display of cell contents for any range that you indicate after you invoke the /Range Format Hidden command. If, instead, you want to hide all the cells in a column or range of columns, use the /Worksheet Column Hidden command, discussed in Chapter 4.

Although a cell with Hidden format will appear as a blank cell on the screen, its contents will be displayed in the control panel when you place the cursor over the cell. The hidden cell will be a part of calculations as if it weren't hidden. All formulas and values can be calculated and readjusted when values are changed. You might think that you could disguise macros in cells by allowing long labels of Alpha characters to "overwrite" hidden cells. 1-2-3, however, will not let that happen. Hidden cells will still block out long labels.

Reset Format

The /Range Format Reset command will reset the format of the indicated range to the global default setting. This command will also remove the format indicator that is displayed in the control panel when the cursor is over any cell formatted with /Range Format.

Controlling the International Formats

1-2-3 allows you to control the punctuation and currency sign displayed by Comma and Currency formats, and to control the way the date and time are displayed when you use the special international

Date and Time formats. You control these settings globally for the worksheet by using the /Worksheet Global Default Other International command.

The Punctuation option of the /Worksheet Global Default Other International command gives you a choice of eight ways to punctuate numbers and delimit function arguments. The default is the standard American convention of a period between an integer and its fractional component, commas to delimit thousands, and commas to delimit function arguments. However, should you need to change the default, seven other combinations are available for punctuating numbers.

The Currency option allows you to change the currency symbol displayed by Currency format and to specify whether that symbol is a prefix or suffix. You can enter either any character in the Lotus International Character Set or a string of characters (like "$US" or "$CAN") to be displayed.

The Date and Time options allow you to set the International Date and Time formats. You have four choices for International Date formats and four for International Time formats. The default format for dates is MM/DD/YY and, for times, HH:MM:SS.

Translating from Other File Formats

The Translate Utility does not take care of all the conventions and formats that other software products use. Common sense and caution should prevail whenever you are translating information between programs.

General Problems with 1-2-3 Formats

Despite the variety of 1-2-3's formats, you may encounter some problems in using them. First, there is no provision to left-justify or center numbers. Unlike labels, numbers can be only right-justified.

The inability to left-justify or center numbers can create an unsightly appearance when you have different-size numbers displayed in the same column. This problem eliminates some of the convenience of using the /Data Fill command for numbers used as column headers. An example of such a problem is shown in figure 5.2.

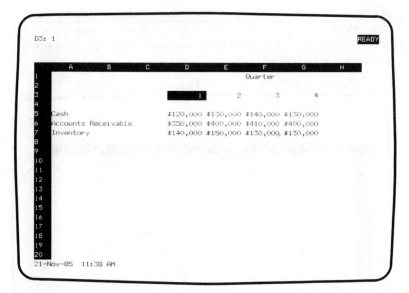

Fig. 5.2. Numbers in headings are right-justified.

The only way around this particular problem is to make the Quarter numbers labels; then you can control the alignment.

Another problem with appearance occurs when, in the same column, you center labels that are an odd number of characters long and those that are an even number of characters. The result appears to be slightly out-of-kilter because the extra character from odd-length labels is always used on the left. The following example illustrates this problem. The central characters in the cell are marked.

RAL*P*HS
SO*F*T
SH*O*ES

This problem is not unique to 1-2-3, and there is really no way around it except to try different alignments by inserting blanks or extra characters wherever possible. Because 1-2-3 can only right-justify numbers, it might be better if the program used the extra character from odd-length labels on the right instead of the left. In any case, this problem of alignment is one that you will have to learn to live with and do your best to work around.

Because the **/Range Format** and **/Worksheet Global Format** commands punctuate numeric values, 1-2-3 may display asterisks in the cell (fig. 5.3). This occurs when the requested format exceeds the number of character places available, which is determined by the column width. The solution is to widen the column to accommodate the punctuation. More information on this procedure can be found in Chapter 6 of this book.

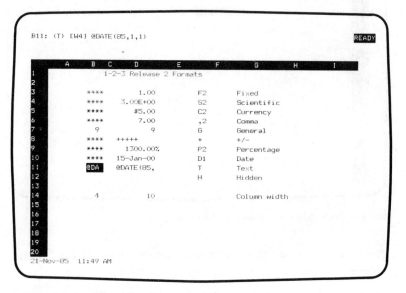

```
B11:  (T) [W4] @DATE(85,1,1)                                    READY

        A     B   C    D        E       F      G        H       I
1                    1-2-3 Release 2 Formats
2
3            ****       1.00           F2            Fixed
4            ****       3.00E+00       S2            Scientific
5            ****       $5.00          C2            Currency
6            ****       7.00           ,2            Comma
7              9          9            G             General
8            ****     +++++            +             +/-
9            ****       1300.00%       P2            Percentage
10           ****     15-Jan-00        D1            Date
11           @DA      @DATE(85,         T            Text
12                                     H             Hidden
13
14             4         10                          Column width
15
16
17
18
19
20
21-Nov-85  11:49 AM
```

Fig. 5.3. A long text label in 1-2-3.

The /Range Justify Command

1-2-3's /**R**ange Justify command is something of an orphan. This command provides 1-2-3 with the first hint of word-processing capabilities but is completely unsupported by other text-processing tools. For this reason, we think of the /**R**ange Justify command as an advanced formatting tool rather than a simple word processor.

As we have seen, 1-2-3 allows text entries to be wider than the width of the column in which they are entered. The labels will overwrite adjoining cells, unless a cell already contains text. Once the text is entered, a justify command will block the text into the space you indicate. For example, suppose that you typed the line of text shown on the 1-2-3 worksheet in figure 5.4.

Notice that this label, which was entered in cell A1, extends across the cells from A1 to F1. Using the /**R**ange Justify command, you can ask 1-2-3 to justify this text into columns A and B; A, B, and C; or A, B, C,

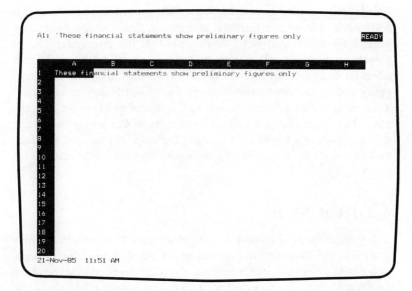

Fig. 5.4. A view of the effect of cell width on cell format.

and D. For example, you could specify that the text be blocked into three 9-character columns (A, B, and C) by issuing the command /rjA1..C1. The results are shown in figure 5.5.

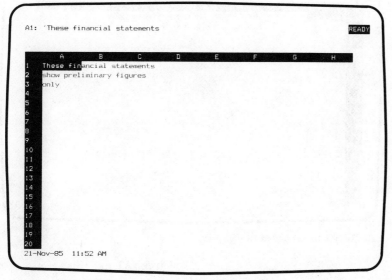

Fig. 5.5. Label after justification into columns A through C.

This function can be used to fine-tune the captions and notes that are commonly attached to financial documents. But /Range Justify has some limitations. The worst of these is that the command pushes down any entries in cells below the cell being justified. Normally this effect is not a problem, but in some cases the rearrangement can mess up a carefully constructed worksheet. For example, figure 5.6 shows a sample worksheet. Figure 5.7 shows the same sheet after the /rj command has been used on cell A1. Notice how the labels that were aligned in the first figure are no longer aligned in the second. Be careful when you use /rj—its results are sometimes hard to predict.

Conclusion

1-2-3's wide range of formats sets it apart from other spreadsheet programs. In this chapter, you learned about 1-2-3's formatting options, saw examples of the various formats, and were exposed to some of the problems you may encounter with them. You also learned about the /Range Justify command and how it works as a formatting tool.

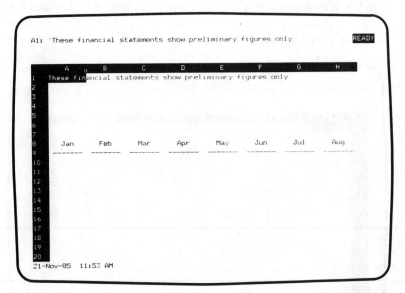

Fig. 5.6. Worksheet before /Range Justify.

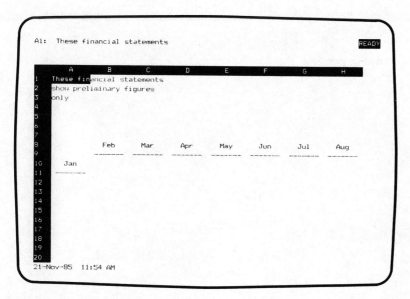

Fig. 5.7. Worksheet after /Range Justify.

6
Functions

1-2-3's set of functions (built-in mathematical formulas) performs tasks that would take much longer or could not be done at all with mathematical symbols alone, such as +, /, *, or –. Working with 1-2-3's other high-powered features, such as the database or macros, the functions help you solve an endless variety of problems. The program incorporates many functions to handle string processing (manipulating alphanumeric data), timekeeping, and a wealth of financial activities. A sophisticated lookup-table function, newly available in Release 2, is one of many functions that help manage 1-2-3's expanded worksheet capabilities.

In this chapter 1-2-3's functions are shown by application: mathematical, statistical, financial, data management, logical, special, string, date, and time.

Using 1-2-3 Functions

A 1-2-3 function is always identified by the @ symbol preceding the function's name in capital letters. So identified, these built-in formulas can be distinguished easily from all other label entries.

Although most functions can adapt flexibly to many different applications, the functions can still be categorized by purpose. The 1-2-3 functions' *arguments*, written in parentheses, specify the cell or cells in which the function will act. For example, the following function, which we will assume lies in cell B21, computes the total of a range of eight cells:

    @SUM(B12..B19)

In this function, @ signals that the entry is a function. SUM is the name of the function being used. The statement (B12..B19) is the argument (in this case, a range). This function tells 1-2-3 to compute the sum of the numbers located in cells B12, B13, B14, B15, B16, B17, B18, and B19 and display the result in cell B21.

A few functions, like @ERR and @NA, do not take an argument. These functions are discussed in detail later.

The following are examples of the variety of functions and argument types that are available in 1-2-3.

Table 6.1
Some Functions and Arguments Available in 1-2-3

@SUM(A2..H14)	Computes the sum of the numbers in the rectangular range A2 to H14
@COUNT(TOTALS)	Returns the number of nonblank cells in the range named TOTALS
@MAX(C15..H32)	Returns the maximum value in the rectangular range C15 to H32
@SUM(A2..H14,A15)	Computes the sum of the numbers in the range A2 to H14 and cell A15
@DATEVALUE(AA1)	Converts the string value in cell AA1 (such as "12/23/85") to a serial number representing the number of days since December 31, 1899
@RATE(1000,500,5)	Computes the compound growth rate for the present value of 500 to grow to a future value of 1000 over 5 periods
@NPV(.15/ 12,A1..A17)	Computes the net present value of the 18-month range A1 to A17 at the monthly rate of 1.25 percent
@LOWER ("TIMES")	Converts the string "Times" (new in Release 2) to lowercase

Like mathematical and string formulas, functions can be much more complex than those in table 6.1. For example, several functions can be combined in a single cell by having one function use other functions as its arguments. The length of an argument, however, is limited. Like formulas, functions can contain a maximum of 240 characters per cell.

Inserting two or more functions in the same cell is called "nesting" a function, as shown in figure 6.1. The @SUM function acts as one of the arguments of the @MAX function. The nested @MAX function finds the maximum of the sum of cells A1 through A4, the value of cell A5, the value of cell A6, and the value of cell A7.

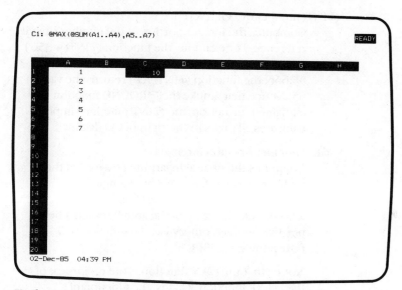

Fig. 6.1. Example of nested functions.

Mathematical Functions

1-2-3 contains several functions to perform mathematical operations. These functions include

@ABS(number or cell reference)
     Computes the absolute value of a number or cell reference. For example, the function @ABS(-4) returns the value 4, and the function @ABS(-556) returns the value 556. The function @ABS(3) returns 3. @ABS(A1) returns the absolute value of the contents of cell A1.

@EXP(number or cell reference)

Computes the value of the constant e (approximately 2.7182818) to a power specified by the number or cell reference. For example, the function @EXP(5) returns 148.41316. If cell A1 contains the value 2.75, the function @EXP(A1) returns 15.642632. If the number or cell reference is greater than 230, the function returns all asterisks (*).

@INT(number or cell reference)

Computes the integer portion of the number or cell reference. For example, the function @INT(4.356) returns the value of 4. If cell A1 contains the value 55.666, the function @INT(A1) returns the value 55. Notice that, unlike the @ROUND function explained further on, the @INT function simply truncates all digits to the right of the decimal.

@LN(number or cell reference)

Computes the natural logarithm (base e) of the number or cell reference. For example, the function @LN(17.634) returns the value 2.8698289. The value of the argument must be a positive number; otherwise, the function will return the value ERR.

Notice that the @LN function is the reciprocal of the @EXP function. That is, the function of @EXP(@LN(2)) returns the value 2, and the function @LN(@EXP(5)) returns the value 5. The value of the argument must be a positive number, or the function will return the value ERR.

@LOG(number or cell reference)

Computes the logarithm (base 10) of the number or cell reference. For example, the function @LOG(4.56) returns the value 0.658964. If cell A1 contains the value 3.555, the function @LOG(A1) returns the value 0.550839. The value of the argument must be a positive number, or the function will return the value ERR.

@SQRT(number or cell reference)
>   Computes the square root of the number or cell
>   reference. For example, the function @SQRT(5)
>   returns the value 2.236067. If cell A1 contains the
>   value 16, the function @SQRT(A1) returns the
>   value 4. The value of the argument must be a
>   positive number or the function will return the
>   value ERR.

Trigonometric Functions

1-2-3 also has a complete set of trigonometric functions. Because these functions are not normally used in financial calculations, many 1-2-3 users will never need these functions. But these functions will be invaluable to anyone using 1-2-3 to solve engineering problems. 1-2-3's trigonometric functions include

@PI
>   This function, which requires no argument, returns
>   the value of the constant pi, accurate to 15 decimal
>   places, or 3.141592653589794.

@SIN(number or cell reference)
@COS(number or cell reference)
@TAN(number or cell reference)
>   These functions compute the common
>   trigonometric functions. The value of the number
>   or cell reference is interpreted by 1-2-3 in radians
>   as an angle.

@ASIN(number or cell reference)
@ACOS(number or cell reference)
@ATAN(number or cell reference)
>   These functions compute the arc sine, arc cosine,
>   and arc tangent of the argument. The arc functions
>   are the reciprocals of the @SIN, @COS, and @TAN
>   functions. The *A* at the beginning of each function
>   is interpreted as "the angle whose." The function
>   @ASIN(1), therefore, returns "the angle whose"
>   sine is 1, or 1.570796 in radians. The function
>   @ATAN(.567) returns the value 0.515801. The
>   argument of the @ASIN and @ACOS functions
>   must have a value of between 1 and –1, or the
>   function will return the value ERR. The argument of
>   the @ATAN function can be any number.

To convert from radians to degrees, multiply the value in radians by 180/@PI. The value of @ASIN(1) in degrees is 1.570796*180/@PI, or 90 degrees.

@ATAN2(number,number)

The @ATAN2 function is similar to the @ATAN function except that @ATAN2 computes the four-quadrant arc tangent of its two arguments. For example, @ATAN2(1,1) returns the value 0.785398 (the radian equivalent of 45 degrees).

NEW WITH
R2

Special Mathematical Functions

The following mathematical built-in functions require special explanation.

@RAND	Generates random numbers
@ROUND	Rounds numbers to a given precision
@MOD	Returns the remainder (the modulus) from division

The @RAND Function

The @RAND built-in function generates random numbers between 0 and 1 with up to eight decimal places. Cells containing the @RAND function will display a different value between 0 and 1 each time the worksheet is recalculated. The following two examples (figs. 6.2 and 6.3) show worksheets filled with @RAND functions. Notice that each cell in the second worksheet has a different value from that in the first because the second worksheet was recalculated.

Random number generation can be used to generate scenarios, especially for risk analysis. One popular type of scenario generation is a Monte Carlo simulation with simulated values systematically substituted into probable models followed by a tabulation of the results. The simulation model can be set up using 1-2-3. (The Monte Carol simulation, however, is well beyond the scope of this book. For further information, see "Risk Analysis in Capital Investment,' David B. Hertz, *Harvard Business Review*, January-February, 1964, and November-December, 1979.)

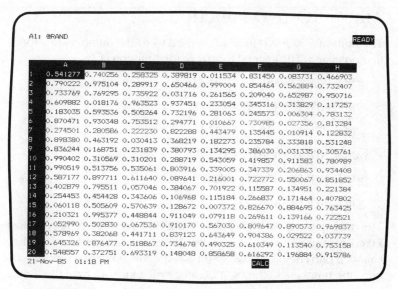

Fig. 6.2. Table of values generated by the @RAND function.

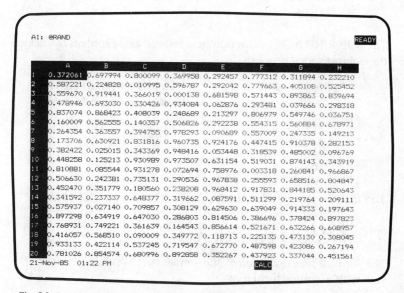

Fig. 6.3. A second table generated by the @RAND function.

The @ROUND Function

The built-in @ROUND function is used to round numbers to a specified precision. The general format of the function is

@ROUND(123.456,3) = 123.456

@ROUND(123.456,2) = 123.46

@ROUND(123.456,1) = 123.5

@ROUND(123.456,0) = 123

@ROUND(123.456,-1) = 120

@ROUND(123.456,-2) = 100

The advantage of the @ROUND function over the /Range Format
Fixed command is that you avoid the errors inherent with adding
rounded currency amounts. If you add the following two sets of numbers, the numbers in the right column will appear to have the wrong
total.

Value Stored	Value Displayed in Currency Format To Nearest Cent
123.025	$123.03
123.025	$123.03
246.05	$246.05

The @ROUND built-in function gets around this problem by making
the columns total properly.

Value Stored	Value Displayed in Currency Format To Nearest Cent
123.025	$123.03
123.025	$123.03
246.05	$246.06

The total on the right has the format @ROUND(@SUM(A1..A2),2).

The @MOD Function

The @MOD function returns the remainder (modulus) from a division with a general format of

@MOD(number,divisor)

The following examples illustrate how @MOD is used:

@MOD(7,3) = 1

@MOD(71.3,21) = 8.3

@MOD(31,0) = ERR

If you specify 0 for the divisor, 1-2-3 will issue an ERR message.

For example, the @MOD function can help you determine the number of parts left over from running equal batches of 33 items with 500 items expected as the total product demand during the course of a year. The result is five items, as in

@MOD(500,33) = 5

Statistical Functions

1-2-3 functions can also perform simple statistical analyses. These functions are used typically with an argument consisting of a range of cells. A range is a rectangular block of one or more continuous cells.

Basic Functions

1-2-3's simpler statistical functions are @SUM, @MAX, @MIN, @COUNT, and @AVG.

The @SUM Function

The @SUM(range) computes the sum of a range of entries. This is perhaps the most useful statistical function. The range is typically a partial row of a column, but a range can also be a named area or a block defined by cell coordinates. For example, if the simple worksheet in figure 6.4 were created, the function @SUM(A1..A2) would return the value of 1110, or 345 + 765. The function @SUM(A1..C1) would return the value of 1368, or 345 + 456 + 567. The function @SUM(A1..C2) would return the value 3330, the total of all of the numbers in the six-cell range. Notice that the range in this case consists of two partial rows.

You can also define the range of the @SUM function as a discontinuous set of cells. For example, the function @SUM(A1,B2,C1) returns the value 1566. This function is equivalent to the formula +A1+B2+C1. A more useful hybrid is the function @SUM(A1..B2,C1), which computes the total of the range A1 to B2 plus the value in C1, or 2787.

In figure 6.4, using @SUM is only slightly faster than using the long-hand arithmetic +A1+B1+C1. But in cases where the range is long, this function can save time.

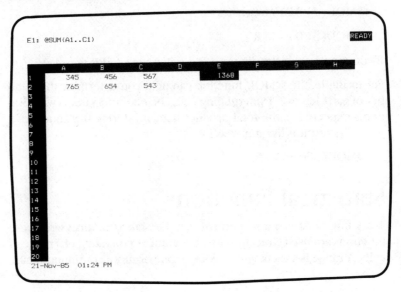

Fig. 6.4. The @SUM function.

Another advantage of the @SUM function (and other range functions as well) is that @SUM is more adaptable than a formula to changes made in the worksheet with cut-and-paste commands. For example, in figure 6.4, the function @SUM(A1..C1) is equivalent to the formula +A1+B1+C1. But if we use /wdc (for /Worksheet Delete Column) to delete column B, the worksheet would change to look like figure 6.5.

The formula has changed to +A1+ERR+B1, which returns the message ERR. The function, on the other hand, has changed to @SUM(A1..B1)and returns the correct answer, 912.

If we had gone the other way and inserted a column using /wic, what would have happened? The resulting worksheet would look like figure 6.6.

The formula would be +A1+C1+D1 and would still have the value 1368. The function is now @SUM(A1..D1). If we inserted a number in the new cell B1, the function would include that number in the new total; but the formula would not.

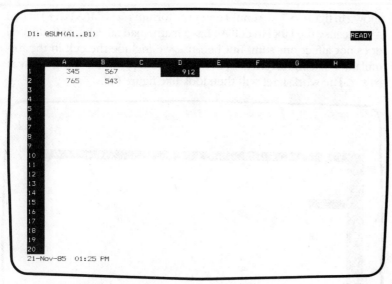

Fig. 6.5. The @SUM function after deleting column B.

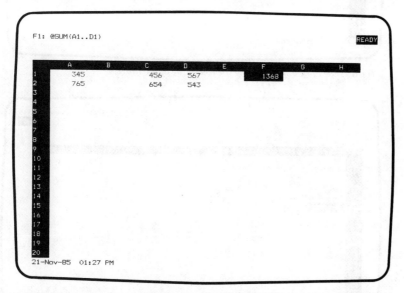

Fig. 6.6. The @SUM function after inserting a column.

This insert feature has a practical application. Whenever possible, we define a sum range to include one extra cell at the end of the function. Frequently, this can be done by including the cell that contains the underline to mark the addition in the range. For example, in the sheet

shown in figure 6.7, we could enter the formula @SUM(A1..A4) in cell
A5. Because the label in cell A4 has a mathematical value of 0, the cell
does not affect our sum. But because we include the cell in the formula, we can add an extra item in the list simply by inserting a row at
row 4. The worksheet will then look like figure 6.8.

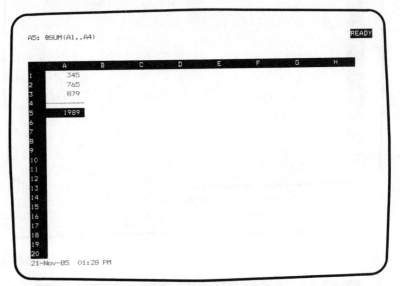

Fig. 6.7. Use of @SUM including the underline in the range.

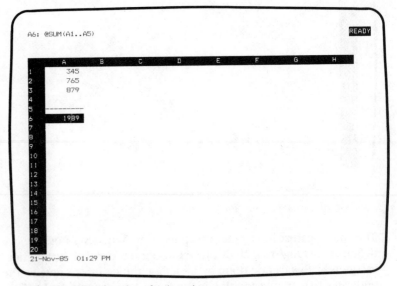

Fig. 6.8. The @SUM function after inserting a row.

The formula in cell A6 is now @SUM(A1..A5). If we insert the number 111 in cell A4, the formula will immediately pick it up and display the value 2,100 in cell A6.

The @MAX and @MIN Functions

The @MAX and @MIN functions return the maximum and minimum values in a range. As with the @SUM function, the range can be a partial row or column, a block or several partial rows and columns, a named area, or a discontinuous group of cells joined by commas. Both of these functions assign a value of 0 to labels but completely ignore empty cells. For example, in the simple worksheet in figure 6.9, the function @MAX(A1..A5) returns the value 777. The function @MIN(A1..A5) would return the value 134, and the function @MIN(A1..A6) also would return 134 because cell A6 is blank. But if the label "abcd" had been entered in cell A6, the function @MIN(A1..A6) would return the value 0.

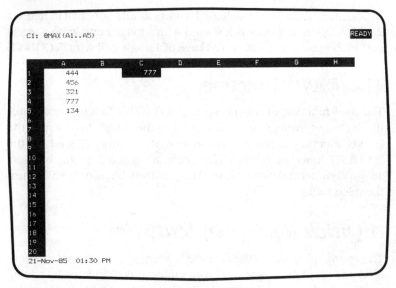

Fig. 6.9. Example of the @MAX function.

The @COUNT Function

The @COUNT function is similar to the @MAX, @MIN, and @SUM functions. @COUNT returns the count of the number of nonblank entries in a range. In figure 6.9, the function @COUNT(A1..A6) would return the value 5. If a label or number were entered in cell A6, the value of the function would be 6.

The @COUNT function works properly only when its argument is a range, even when the range is a single cell like the range A1..A1. When the argument is a single cell reference like A1, @COUNT always returns 1 regardless of the contents of the cell.

One interesting feature of the @COUNT function is the way it reacts to a single blank cell. To return a zero for a blank cell, you must use @COUNT with the @@ function discussed later in this chapter. To return a zero for the blank cell A1, for example, you would use @COUNT with @@ in the following way: enter the label A1..A1 in cell A2; then in cell A3 enter the formula

    @COUNT(@@(A2))

Because of the @@ function, 1-2-3 interprets the A2 in the formula as A1..A1. The outcome of the formula will be a 0.

Experienced Release 1 or Release 1A users should note that in Release 2, @COUNT now works as it should with a range containing a single cell. In Release 2, you can test a range of a single cell with @COUNT.

The @AVG Function

The final function in this group is @AVG. This function computes the mean, or average, of all the cells in the range. In essence, the @AVG function is similar to the @SUM function divided by the @COUNT function. Because blank cells are ignored by the function, an @AVG function that refers to a range with all blank cells will return the value ERR.

A Quick Review of Statistics

The *mean*, often called the arithmetic average, is commonly used to mark the average of a group of data values. It is calculated by adding up the values and dividing the sum by the number of values. The mean is not to be confused with the *median* or the *mode*, which are also measures of central tendency. The median is the value midway between the highest and lowest values in the group, in terms of probability. Half of the values in the group are above the median, and half are below it. The mode is the most likely value in a group of items (that is, the value you see most often).

Variance and *standard deviation* are related dispersion statistics. To calculate the variance, you subtract the mean of the numbers from each number in the group and square each result. You then add the squares and divide the total by the number of items in the group. To compute the standard deviation, you take the square root of the variance. 1-2-3's new built-in statistical functions automatically do these things for you.

What does the standard deviation tell you? As a general rule, about 68 percent of the items in a normally distributed population will fall within a range that is plus or minus one standard deviation of the mean. About 95 percent of the items fall within plus or minus two standard deviations of the mean.

To understand 1-2-3's new built-in statistical functions, you should know the difference between *population* and *sample* statistics. Population statistics are used when you know the value of all the items in a population. When the number of items, however, is large and you don't know them all (which is usually the case), you are unable to compute the population statistics. Instead, you must rely on sample statistics as estimates of the population statistics.

For more information on statistics, see *Statistical Methods*, Donald Harnett, Addison-Wesley Publishing Company, Philippines, 1982.

More Complex Statistical Functions

Two slightly more complex statistical functions offered by 1-2-3 are

@VAR(list)   Computes the population variance

@STD(list)   Computes the standard deviation of a population

A simple example that uses both functions is shown in figure 6.10. This example shows a list of salesmen and the number of items they sold during a given period. The list of the number of items sold is the population in this example. The population is used as the range for all the statistical functions.

The mean of the population (about 101) is computed using the @AVG function. The standard deviation is about 24, that means that roughly 68 percent of the salesmen sold between 77 and 125 items.

If we realistically assume that we only had a small portion of the entire population of sales figures, we can compute the *sample* statistics. This is even more realistic if we examine only one month's sales out of the

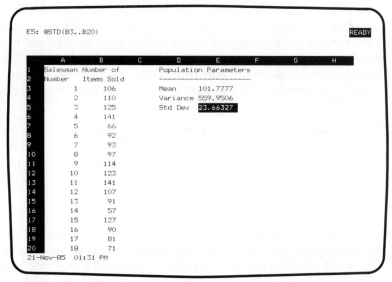

Fig. 6.10. Use of the @STD function to determine population standard deviation.

total population of all the monthly sales for a year. When we move into the realm of sample statistics, we start dealing with much more sophisticated statistical concepts.

To calculate the sample variance for the sales data used above, you multiply the population variance by n/n-1 (degrees of freedom), where n equals the number of items in the sample. The degrees of freedom tell you how much freedom you have in calculating a variance. The results of this calculation are shown in figure 6.11.

To compute the sample variance in figure 6.11, we used the built-in @COUNT function to determine the degrees of freedom:

$$\text{Sample Variance} = \frac{\text{@COUNT(list)}}{\text{(@COUNT(list)}-1\text{)*@VAR(list)}}$$

To compute the standard deviation of the sample, we took the square root of the sample variance. A convenient way to do this is to use the built-in @SQRT function:

Sample Standard Deviation = @SQRT(Sample Variance) =

$$\frac{\text{@SQRT@COUNT(list)}}{\text{(@COUNT(list)}-1\text{)*@VAR(list)}}$$

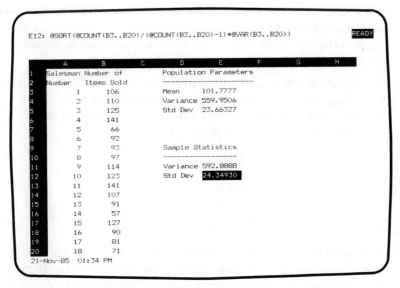

```
E12: @SQRT(@COUNT(B3..B20)/(@COUNT(B3..B20)-1)*@VAR(B3..B20))          READY

        A          B        C        D        E        F        G        H
1   Salesman  Number of              Population Parameters
2   Number    Items Sold             --------------------
3          1      106                 Mean      101.7777
4          2      110                 Variance  559.9506
5          3      125                 Std Dev   23.66327
6          4      141
7          5       66
8          6       92
9          7       93                 Sample Statistics
10         8       97                 --------------------
11         9      114                 Variance  592.8888
12        10      123                 Std Dev   24.34930
13        11      141
14        12      107
15        13       91
16        14       57
17        15      127
18        16       90
19        17       81
20        18       71
    21-Nov-85  01:34 PM
```

Fig. 6.11. Use of the @VAR function to compute sample standard deviation.

Financial Functions

1-2-3 also has several built-in financial functions that perform a variety of investment calculations. The basic financial functions, @NPV and @IRR, calculate two different measures of investment return for a series of cash flows; whereas @PV, @FV, and @PMT perform loan and annuity calculations. Release 2 also adds the financial functions @RATE, @TERM, and @CTERM to perform compound-growth calculations, and @SLN, @DDB, and @SYD to calculate depreciation by three commonly used methods.

The @NPV Function

The @NPV function computes the net present value of a stream of cash flows. As one of the most important financial concepts, computing net present value was the first financial function offered in early spreadsheet programs. The form of this function is

@NPV(Discount Rate,Range)

The discount rate is the interest rate that 1-2-3 uses to compute the net present value. The range is the stream of cash flows to be discounted. The interval between the cash flows must be constant and must agree with the period of the discount rate. For example, an annual discount rate should be used for cash flows occurring a year apart. If the cash flows occur every month, a monthly rate should be used.

The @NPV function can be used to evaluate a variety of investment opportunities. For example, suppose that you had an opportunity to buy a piece of property that would create the following stream of income in each of the next five years:

Year 1	100,000
Year 2	120,000
Year 3	130,000
Year 4	140,000
Year 5	50,000

You could create a simple worksheet to evaluate this problem, as illustrated in figure 6.12. The function @NPV(A3,A1..E1) would return the value 368075.1, the net present value of that stream at a discount rate of 15 percent. If this rate represents the rate you want to earn on the investment, and the price of the property is equal to or less than $368,075, then you could conclude that the property is probably a good investment.

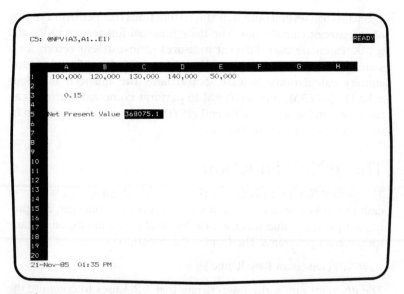

Fig. 6.12. Net present value of an income property.

Notice that we use a cell reference, A3, to enter the discount rate into the function. Because it would be just as easy to enter the formula @NPV(.15,A1..E1), you might wonder why we took the approach we did. In fact, there is no advantage to using either method until you decide to change the rate.

For example, assume that in our example you wanted to evaluate the investment using a rate of 14 percent. With the method we used, all you need to do is enter the number .14 in cell A3 and recalculate the worksheet. If the rate had been embedded in the formula, we would have to edit the cell, replace the .15 with .14 close the cell, then recalculate. If several changes were required, this operation would waste a lot of valuable time.

The @IRR Function

Internal rate of return (IRR) is the discount rate that equates the present value of expected cash outflows with the present value of expected inflows. In simpler terms, IRR is the rate of return, or profit, that an investment is expected to earn. Like the other financial calculations, IRR determines the attractiveness of an investment opportunity.

The internal rate of return function is built on an interative process in which you provide an initial ballpark estimate discount rate (actually anything between 0 and 1 will do), and 1-2-3 calculates the actual discount rate, equating the present value of the series of cash outflows with the present value of the series of inflows. Although 1-2-3's method may seem awkward, it is actually quite logical. The same method is used to calculate IRR manually.

Given the format of the equation, all the inflows and outflows must be in the same range. The general form of the @IRR function is

@IRR(estimate,range)

1-2-3 should reach convergence on a discount rate within .0000001 after a maximum of 20 iterations, or ERR is returned. Figure 6.13 shows an example of how the @IRR built-in function is used.

The internal rate of return, or profit, for the project illustrated in figure 6.13 is about 16 percent.

You may encounter some problems with the @IRR function. As indicated earlier, 1-2-3 may not converge on a value based on your initial estimate. Either the stream of cash flows does not have an internal rate

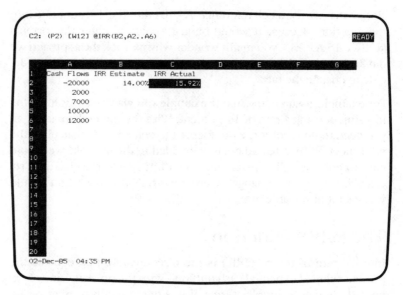

Fig. 6.13. Internal rate of return of a stream of cash flows.

of return, or your initial estimate is too far from the actual internal rate of return for 1-2-3 to converge within 20 iterations.

An extreme example of the stream of cash flow without an internal rate of return is a stream of all outflows with no inflows. Without income to cover the expenditures, no interest rate will yield a net present value of 0.

If your initial estimate is too far from the actual internal rate of return for convergence within 20 iterations, you will receive an ERR message or the return of an unreasonable value. For example, figure 6.14 shows a series of 11 cash flows, an IRR guess of .20, and an actual IRR of approximately –289 percent. Even though 1-2-3 did not reach convergence, the ERR message is not displayed.

The proper IRR for this stream of cash flows is approximately 138 percent. To get 1-2-3 to display 138 percent, your estimate must be greater than or equal to .74.

If you get an ERR message or an unreasonable value from the @IRR function, try different initial estimates to find the correct answer and double-check the result.

The mathematical character of the @IRR calculation may present another problem. If the stream of cash flows changes signs more than once, several interest rates can yield a net present value of zero. For

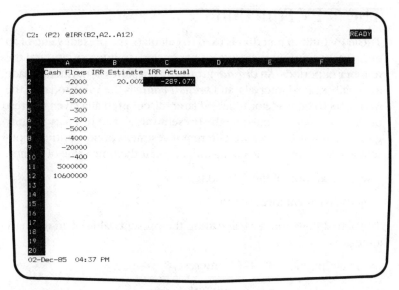

Fig. 6.14. Example of @IRR with initial estimate too far from actual internal rate of return.

example, the cash flows in figure 6.15 start out negative, then become positive, and are negative once again at the end of the stream. If the initial estimate is zero, the @IRR function converges on the value of approximately 58 percent. Both these values are valid results of the @IRR function for this stream of cash flows.

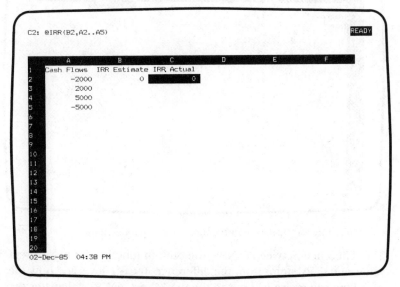

Fig. 6.15. Example of a stream of cash flows with two internal rates of return.

The @PV Function

The @PV built-in function is used to calculate the present value of an ordinary annuity given a payment per period, an interest rate, and the number of periods. An *ordinary annuity* is a series of payments made at equally spaced intervals, and *present value* is the value today of the payments to be made or received later, discounted at a given interest or discount rate. Calculating the present value of an ordinary annuity gives you a way to compare different investment opportunities or potential obligations while taking into account the time value of money.

The general form of the @PV function is

@PV(payment,interest,term)

The actual equation for calculating the present value of an ordinary annuity is

$$PV = payment * \frac{1-(1+interest)^{-n}}{interest}$$

Figure 6.16 shows an example of how the @PV built-in function is used.

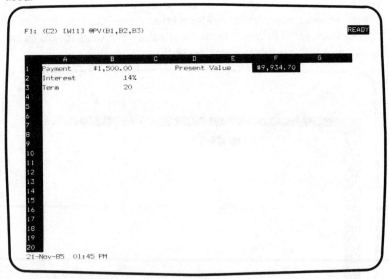

Fig. 6.16. Using @PV to determine the present value of an annuity.

The difference between @NPV, the built-in function for net present value, and @PV stems from the difference in cash flows and how the cash flow values are laid out in the worksheet. @NPV calculates the new present value of a series of flows that may or may not be equal, but that are all contained in a range of cells in the worksheet. The cash flows in the @PV function must all be equal, and the amount of the flows must be contained in a single cell or entered as a value in the @PV function.

The @FV Function

The @FV built-in function is similar in form to the @PV function, but is used to calculate the future value of an ordinary annuity. *Future value* is the value at a given day in the future of a series of payments or receipts, discounted at a given interest or discount rate. Calculating the future value of an annuity allows you to compare different investment alternatives or potential obligations. The @FV function looks like this:

@FV(payment,interest,term)

The equation for calculating the future value of an ordinary annuity is

$$FV = payment \ast \frac{(1+interest)^n - 1}{interest}$$

An example using the @FV built-in function is shown in figure 6.17.

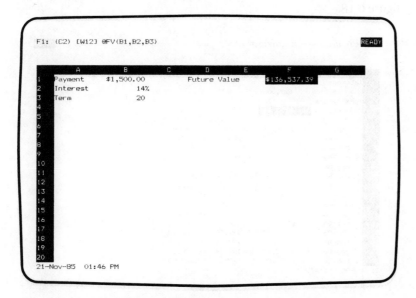

Fig. 6.17. Using @PV to determine the future value of an annuity.

1-2-3's method of computing the future value of an annuity is similar to the method of computing the present value, except that the future value equation is used.

The @PMT Function

The @PMT function calculates the mortgage payment required for a given principal, interest rate, and number of periods. The format of this function with n equalling the number of periods is

@PMT(principal,interest,n)

Again, the formula which the function represents calculates the present value of an ordinary annuity, but, rearranged, yields the period payment as the result.

$$PMT = principal * \frac{interest}{1-(1+interest)^{-n}}$$

This built-in function is a variation of the @PV built-in function discussed earlier. This function can help you build a table of mortgage rate payments similar to those in the SAMPLES.BAS program supplied with DOS. You can easily construct a table like the one shown in figure 6.18.

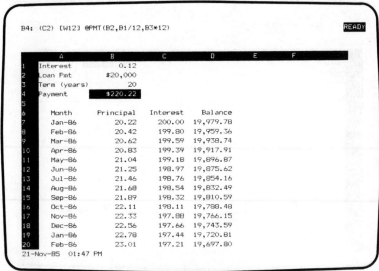

Fig. 6.18. Table of mortgage payments using @PMT.

The @RATE function

NEW WITH
R2

The @RATE function calculates the compound growth rate for an initial investment that grows to a specified future value over a specified number of periods. The rate is the periodic interest rate and not necessarily an annual rate. The format of this function, where n equals the number of periods, is

@RATE(future value,present value,n)

This function's basic formula calculates the future value of an initial investment given the interest rate and the number of periods. For the @RATE calculation, the formula is rearranged to compute the interest rate in terms of the initial investment, the future value, and the number of periods.

Interest Rate = (future value/present value)^(1/n) – 1

As an example, you could use the @RATE function to determine the yield of a zero-coupon bond that is sold at a discount of its face value. Suppose that for $350 you can purchase a zero-coupon bond with a $1,000 face value maturing in 10 years. What is the implied annual interest rate? The answer is 11.07 percent, as shown in figure 6.19.

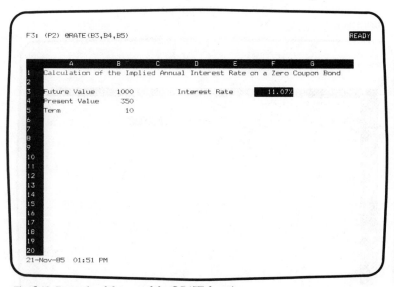

Fig. 6.19. Example of the use of the @RATE function.

The @RATE function is also useful in forecasting applications to calculate the compound growth rate between current and projected future revenues, earnings, and so on.

The @TERM Function

The @TERM function calculates the number of periods required to accumulate a specified future value by making equal payments into an interest-bearing account at the end of each period. The form of the @TERM function is

@TERM(payment,interest,future value)

The @TERM function is similar to the @FV function except that instead of finding the future value of a stream of payments over a specified period, the @TERM function finds the number of periods required to reach the given future value. The actual equation for calculating the number of periods is

$$n = \frac{@LN(1+(interest*future\ value)/payment)}{@LN(1+interest)}$$

Suppose that you want to determine the number of months required to accumulate $5,000 by making a monthly payment of $50 into an account paying 6 percent annual interest compounded monthly (.5 percent per month). Figure 6.20 shows how @TERM can help you get the answer, which is slightly more than 81 months (6 years and 9 months).

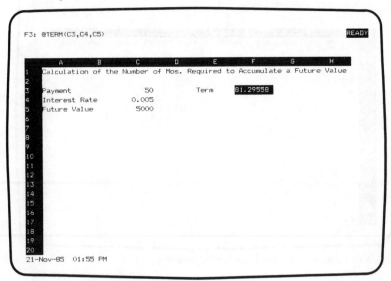

Fig. 6.20. Example of the @TERM Function.

The @CTERM Function

The @CTERM function calculates the number of periods required for an initial investment earning a specified interest rate to grow to a specified future value. Whereas @TERM calculates the number of periods needed for a series of payments to grow to a future value at a specified interest rate, the @CTERM function specifies the present value, the future value, and the interest rate, and finds the required number of periods. The form of the @CTERM function is

@CTERM(interest,future value,present value)

The actual equation used to calculate @CTERM is

$$TERM = \frac{@LN(\text{future-value}/\text{present-value})}{@LN(1+\text{interest})}$$

The @CTERM function is useful for determining the term of an investment necessary to achieve a specific future value. For example, suppose that you want to determine how many years it will take for $2,000 invested in an IRA account at 10 percent interest to grow to $10,000. Figure 6.21 shows how to use the @CTERM function to determine the answer, which is just over 16 years and 10 months.

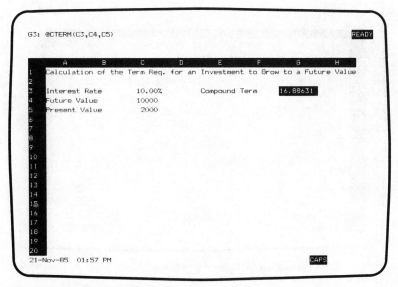

Fig. 6.21. Example of the @CTERM Function.

The @SLN, @DDB, and @SYD Functions

The @SLN, @DDB, and @SYD functions calculate depreciation by the *double-declining-balance*, *straight-line*, and *sum-of-the-years'-digits* methods, respectively.

The @SLN function calculates straight-line depreciation given the asset's cost, salvage value, and depreciable life. The form of the function is

@SLN(cost,salvage value,life)

The actual formula used to calculate @SLN is

(cost-salvage value)/life

The @SLN function conveniently calculates straight-line depreciation for an asset. For example, suppose that you have purchased a machine for $1,000 that has a useful life of 5 years and a salvage value estimated to be 10 percent of the purchase price ($100) at the end of its useful life. Figure 6.22 shows how to use the @SLN function to determine the straight-line depreciation for the machine, $180 per year.

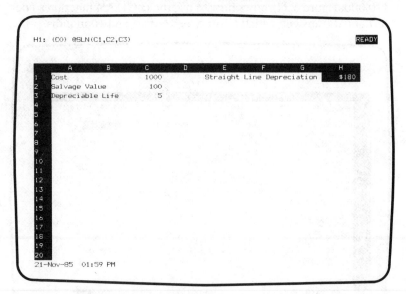

Fig. 6.22. @SLN calculates straight-line depreciation.

The @DDB function calculates depreciation using the double-declining-balance method, with depreciation ceasing when the book value reaches the salvage value. Double-declining-balance depreciation is a method of accelerating depreciation so that greater depreciation expense occurs in the earlier periods rather than the later ones. Book value in any period is the purchase price less the total depreciation in all prior periods.

NEW WITH
R2

The form of the @DDB function is

@DDB(cost,salvage value,life,period)

In general, the double-declining-balance depreciation in any period is

book value*2/n

in which book value is the book value in the period, and n is the depreciable life of the asset. 1-2-3, however, adjusts the results of this formula in later periods to ensure that total depreciation does not exceed the purchase price less the salvage value.

Figure 6.23 shows how the @DDB function can calculate depreciation on an asset purchased for $1,000, with a depreciable life of five years and an estimated salvage value of $100. In the figure, the @DDB function uses the book value formula in the first four years and adjusts for the salvage value in the fifth year.

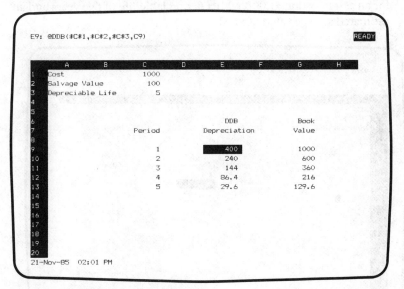

Fig. 6.23. Example of the @DDB function.

The @SYD function calculates depreciation by the sum-of-the-years'-digits method. This method also accelerates depreciation so that the earlier life of the item reflects greater depreciation than later periods.

The form of the function is

@SYD(cost,salvage value,life,period)

in which the cost is the purchase cost of the asset, the salvage value is the estimated value of the asset at the end of the depreciable life, life is the depreciable life of the asset, and period is the period for which depreciation is to be computed.

@SYD calculates depreciation with the following formula:

$$\frac{(\text{cost-salvage value})*(\text{life-period}+1)}{(\text{life}*(\text{life}+1)/2)}$$

The expression *life-period+1* in the numerator shows the life of the depreciation in the first period, decreased by 1 in each subsequent period. This reflects the declining pattern of depreciation over time. The expression in the denominator, life*(life+1)/2, is equal to the sum of the digits 1 + 2 + . . . + life. This is the origin of the name sum-of-the-years'-digits.

Figure 6.24 shows how the @SYD function can calculate depreciation for an asset costing $1,000 with a depreciable life of five years and an estimated salvage value of $100.

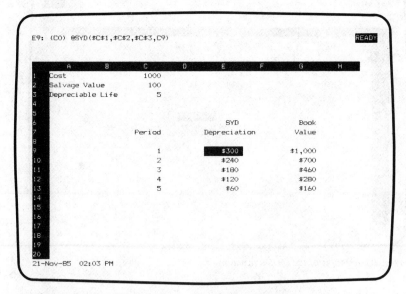

Fig. 6.24. Using the @SYD function to calculate depreciation.

Data Management Functions

1-2-3 had four simple data management functions: @CHOOSE, @VLOOKUP, @HLOOKUP, and @INDEX. These functions are called "special" functions by Lotus, but we prefer the term data management functions, because the functions retrieve data from lists and tables. These functions should not be confused with 1-2-3's database statistical functions, which operate only on databases. Those functions are explained in Chapter 11.

The @CHOOSE Function

The @CHOOSE function uses a key value provided by the user to select a number from a list. This function has the following form:

@CHOOSE(Key,Argument,Argument,. . .,Argument)

@CHOOSE displays the argument whose position in the list matches the key (with the first position corresponding to a key of 0, the second position corresponding to a key of 1, etc.). For example, the function

@CHOOSE(2,3,4,5)

returns the number 5 because 5 is in the third position in the list. If the key is changed to 0, as in

@CHOOSE(0,3,4,5)

the function will return the value 3.

The first argument (the key) in the @CHOOSE function can be a number, a formula, or a function with numeric value. The remaining arguments can have either numeric or string values. The @CHOOSE function can also be used to select formulas that will vary in different situations. For example, the percentage rate used to compute depreciation under the ARCS depreciation system varies with the useful life of the asset. Thus, an asset with a three-year life would be depreciated at a different rate in the first year of its life from that of an asset with a five-year life. A function like

@CHOOSE(ACRS class, Rate for 3-year asset, Rate for 5-year
   asset. . .)

dramatically simplifies the computation.

The @HLOOKUP and @VLOOKUP Functions

@HLOOKUP and @VLOOKUP are two variations on the basic @LOOKUP function pioneered by VisiCalc. As their names suggest, these functions "look up" a value from a table based on the value of a test variable. The forms of these functions are

@HLOOKUP (test variable, range, row offset number)

@VLOOKUP (test variable, range, column offset number)

The first argument, the test variable, can have either a numeric value or a string value. The test variable may be any valid 1-2-3 numeric or string expression (number or string formula). The test variable may also be a cell or range reference to a single cell containing the value. (Release 1 and 1A users note that you can only perform "numeric" lookups. Strings are not included.)

The second argument is a range containing at least two partial rows or columns. This range includes the entire lookup table from the top left corner of the comparison column to the bottom right corner of the last data column. A range name can be used in place of actual cell references.

The third argument, called the offset number, determines which data column should supply the data to the function. In every case, the comparison column has an offset number of zero, the first column to the right of the comparison column has an offset number of 1, and so on. The offset number must be between 0 and the maximum number of columns or rows in the lookup table. You will receive an ERR message if you try to include negative or excessive offset numbers.

To use the lookup functions, you need a lookup table in your worksheet. This table must consist of two or more adjacent partial rows or columns. An example of a numeric vertical lookup table is illustrated in figure 6.25.

What differentiates this table from a string vertical lookup table is the contents of M, the first column. (The first column in a vertical lookup table is called the comparison column.) In a numeric vertical lookup table, the comparison column must contain numbers arranged in ascending order. In a string vertical lookup table, the comparison column can contain labels in any order.

In figure 6.25 the comparison column contains the values that will be used to look up the data shown in the second and third columns

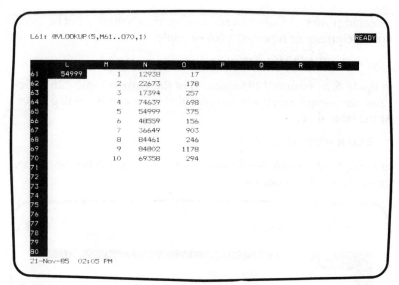

Fig. 6.25. Example of numeric lookup with @VLOOKUP.

(N and O). To access this columnar table, use the @VLOOKUP or vertical lookup function.

In this table, the function

   @VLOOKUP(5,M61..O70,1)

returns the value 54999. To get this result, 1-2-3 searches the comparison column for the largest value that is not greater than the key and returns the value in the data column with an offset number of 1 (in this case, column N). Remember that the comparison column has an offset number of 0. Column N, therefore, has an offset number of 1, and column O has an offset number of 2.

Because the lookup table searches for the largest key in the table that is not greater than the search variable and not a specific match, the function @VLOOKUP(5.5,M61..O70,1) would also return the value 54999. Similarly, a key of 100 would return 69358, the number that corresponds to the largest key in the list. If 0 is used as the key, an ERR message will appear because no key in the table is less than or equal to 0.

The data in column O also can be looked up with @VLOOKUP. For example, the function @VLOOKUP(10,M61..O70,2) would return the value 294.

Lookup tables must follow specific rules. As mentioned earlier, the comparison column values for numeric lookups must be arranged in ascending order. (In other words, a comparison value cannot be listed out of sequence or repeated.) For example,

@VLOOKUP(2,M61..O70,1)

in figure 6.26 returns 12938 instead of the correct value 22673 because the comparison values in column M are not in ascending order. At the same time,

@VLOOKUP(5,M61..O70,1)

in figure 6.27 returns 74639 instead of the correct value 54999 because the key 5 is repeated.

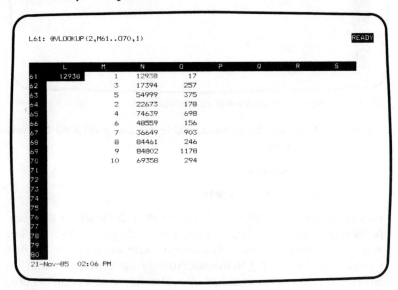

Fig. 6.26. Numeric @VLOOKUP with keys out of sequence.

Besides numeric table lookups, 1-2-3 can also perform string table lookups. Some other spreadsheet programs have had this feature for quite a while, but string table lookups were not included in Releases 1 and 1A of 1-2-3. Including string table lookups in 1-2-3 adds considerable power to the program.

NEW WITH

R2

In the new string-table-lookup facility, 1-2-3 looks for a perfect match between a value in the comparison column and the test variable. For example, in figure 6.28, 1-2-3 uses the function

@VLOOKUP("rakes",M101..O110,1)

to search for the value in column N corresponding to rakes. Notice that the string argument is enclosed in double quotation marks.

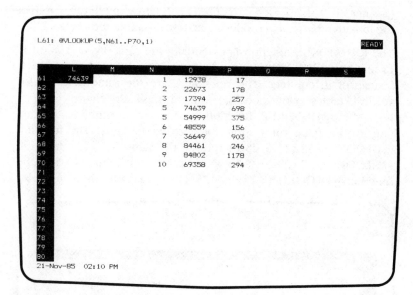

Fig. 6.27. Numeric @VLOOKUP with duplicate keys.

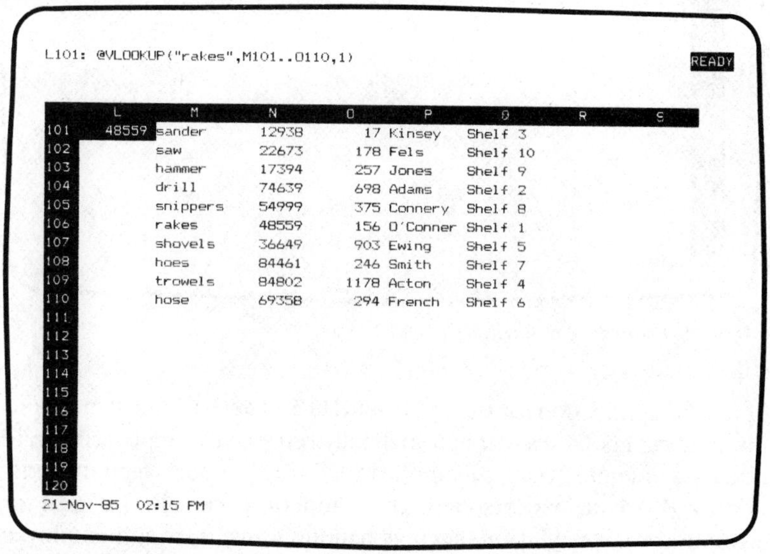

Fig. 6.28. Example of string @VLOOKUP.

If 0 is used as the offset number for the @VLOOKUP statement in figure 6.28, the value returned will be 5. This number corresponds to the
position of the matched string in the lookup range. The first entry

NEW WITH

R2

NEW WITH

R2

(sander) is 0, the second entry (saw) is 1, and so on. If the search of the lookup table fails to produce a match, the value returned is ERR.

The @HLOOKUP function is essentially the same as @VLOOKUP, except that @HLOOKUP operates on tables arranged across rows instead of in columns. The rules here are the same as those for vertical tables. Now look at the example in figure 6.29 of how the @HLOOKUP function works for a numeric lookup. (Again, the same rules apply for a string lookup). The function @HLOOKUP(5,L123..S125,1) returns the value 567. The function @HLOOKUP(8,L123..S125,1) would return the value 890, and the function @HLOOKUP(3,L123..S125,2) would return the value 765.

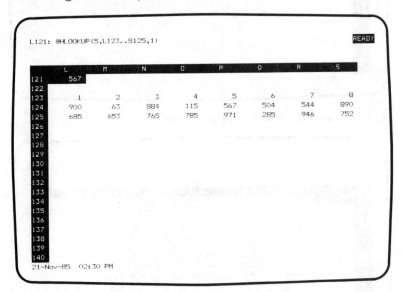

Fig. 6.29. Example of numeric @HLOOKUP.

A useful application for the @VLOOKUP and @HLOOKUP functions is creating tax tables that automatically retrieve the appropriate rate base on income. In fact, this application is the one for which the function was originally developed. These functions can also be used for simple data management, such as handling inventory and employee lists, although in 1-2-3 these functions can be performed better with the database commands.

The @INDEX Function

The last data management function, @INDEX, is similar to the table-lookup functions described earlier; however, @INDEX has some unique features. The general form of the function is

@INDEX(range,column-number,row-number)

Like the table-lookup functions, the @INDEX function works with a table of numbers. But unlike the table-lookup functions, the @INDEX function does not use a test variable and a comparison column (or row). Instead, the @INDEX function requires you to indicate the row-number and column-number of the range from which you wish to retrieve data. For example, the function

@INDEX(L142..S145,3,2)

in figure 6.30 returns the value 2625.

```
L141: @INDEX(L142..S145,3,2)                              READY

         L        M        N        O        P        Q        R        S
141   2625
142   4313     1954     8936     5886     4703     5063     8506     2849
143   7979     4245     8095     5285     9231     9431     7005     8221
144   4190     9823     1393     2625     7221     3317     4382     1035
145   6472     2651     8183     1185     7477     7681     5173     1917
146
147
148
149
150
151
152
153
154
155
156
157
158
159
160
21-Nov-85   02:31 PM
```

Fig. 6.30. Example of @INDEX function.

Notice that the number 0 corresponds to the first column, 1 corresponds to the second column, and so on. The same numbering scheme applies to rows. Using 3 for the column-number and 2 for the row-number indicates that you want an item from the fourth column, third row.

With the @INDEX function, you cannot use column and row numbers that fall outside the relevant range. Using either negative numbers or numbers too large for the range will cause 1-2-3 to return the ERR message.

The @INDEX function is useful when you know the exact position of a data item in a range of cells and wish to locate the item quickly. For instance, the @INDEX function works well for rate quotation systems. Figure 6.31 shows an example of a system for quoting full-page magazine advertising rates.

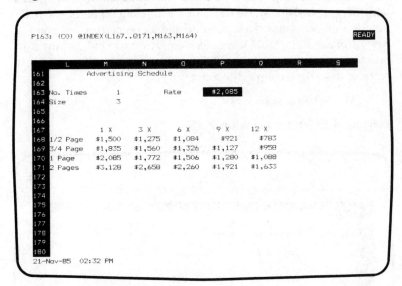

Fig. 6.31. Use of @INDEX for advertising rate quotations.

In this example, the function

@INDEX(L167..Q171,M163,M164)

returns a value of $2,085. This value corresponds to the amount in the first column and the third row of the index range. If a 6 is entered for the frequency, the ERR message will appear instead of a valid dollar amount.

Logical Functions

Like most electronic spreadsheets, 1-2-3 includes logical functions that can be considered a subset of the mathematical functions. 1-2-3 analyzes logical functions as either true or false. A logical function that is true has a numeric value of 1, but a false logical function has a numeric value of 0. The importance of a logical function's numeric value will be made clear shortly.

Logical functions are helpful because they let you build conditional tests into cells. These tests return different values, depending on whether they are true (1) or false (0). 1-2-3's primary conditional function is @IF. Several new logical functions, however, have been added in Release 2 to increase the power of the program over earlier spreadsheet programs.

Simple Operators

In many cases, conditional functions require logical operators. These operators help to determine the relationship between two or more numbers or strings. The following is a list of *simple* logical operators and their meanings:

Operator	Meaning
=	Equal
<	Less than
<=	Less than or equal to
>	Greater than
>=	Greater than or equal to
< >	Not equal

Simple logical operators have lower precedence than any mathematical operator, but they all have equal precedence within their group.

The logical operators build conditional statements that are either true (1) or false (0). For example, the statement 5<3 has the value false (0), whereas the statement 16<27 has the value true (1). 1-2-3's @IF function tests the conditional statement as either true (1) or false (0) and returns a value based on the results of the test.

Let's create a logical statement using the @IF built-in function. The general form of this function is

@IF(a,vtrue,vfalse)

where the first argument *a* is tested for true or false. If the result of the test is true (1), the function will take the value of the second argument *vtrue*. However, if the value of the first argument is false (0), the function will take the value of the third argument *vfalse*. The following are examples of logical statements that use the @IF function, followed by explanations. Veteran Release 1 and 1A users should note that Release 2 allows strings in @IF functions, whereas the earlier releases do not.

@IF(B4>=450,B5,C7)

> If the value in cell B4 is greater than or equal to 450, then use the value in cell B5. Otherwise, use the value in cell C7.

@IF(A3<A2,5,6)

> If the value in cell A3 is less than the value in cell A2, then assign the number 5. Otherwise, assign the number 6.

@IF(G9<>B7,G5/9,G7)

> If the value in cell G9 is not equal to the value in cell B7, then use the value in cell G5 divided by 9. Otherwise, use the value in cell G7.

Complex Operators

Things get more complicated when another set of logical operators is introduced: the *complex* operators.

Operator	Meaning
#NOT#	Not (logical)
#AND#	AND (logical)
#OR#	OR (logical)

The complex logical operators have lower precedence than the simple logical operators. The #AND# and #OR# have equal precedence in this group, whereas #NOT# has a precedence greater than #AND# and #OR#, but lesser than the simple logical functions.

Now that we have a complete set of logical operators, we can combine simple and complex operators to create the following @IF functions.

@IF(A1<>1#AND#G5="yes",E7,E6)

> If the numeric value in cell A1 is not equal to 1 and the string value in cell G5 is "yes," use the value in cell E7. Otherwise, use the value in cell E6.

@IF(#NOT#(Cost=50)#AND#A1=1,L10,K10)

> If the amount stored in the cell named Cost is not $50 and the value in cell A1 is equal to 1, then use the value in cell L10. Otherwise, use the value in cell K10.

1-2-3's conditional functions are quite sophisticated and can be complicated. The @IF statement can be used in a wide variety of situations to allow 1-2-3 to make decisions. Figure 6.32 is a simple example of how the @IF function can be used.

```
D6:  (C2)  @IF($C6=D$4,$B6,0)                                        READY

          A        B        C        D        E        F        G        H
 1  ================================================================================
 2  ABC Company July 1985 Expense Report
 3  ================================================================================
 4    Date    Amount   Code       1        2        3        4        5
 5    ------   ------   ------   
 6    01-Jul  $678.00            $0.00    $0.00    $0.00    $0.00    $0.00
 7    01-Jul   $52.00            $0.00    $0.00    $0.00    $0.00    $0.00
 8    01-Jul  $265.00            $0.00    $0.00    $0.00    $0.00    $0.00
 9    02-Jul  $347.00            $0.00    $0.00    $0.00    $0.00    $0.00
10    02-Jul   $13.00            $0.00    $0.00    $0.00    $0.00    $0.00
11    02-Jul   $86.00            $0.00    $0.00    $0.00    $0.00    $0.00
12    02-Jul   $90.00            $0.00    $0.00    $0.00    $0.00    $0.00
13    03-Jul  $341.00            $0.00    $0.00    $0.00    $0.00    $0.00
14    03-Jul  $255.00            $0.00    $0.00    $0.00    $0.00    $0.00
15    03-Jul  $754.00            $0.00    $0.00    $0.00    $0.00    $0.00
16    03-Jul  $324.00            $0.00    $0.00    $0.00    $0.00    $0.00
17    04-Jul  $462.00            $0.00    $0.00    $0.00    $0.00    $0.00
18    04-Jul  $142.00            $0.00    $0.00    $0.00    $0.00    $0.00
19    04-Jul  $876.00            $0.00    $0.00    $0.00    $0.00    $0.00
20    04-Jul  $354.00            $0.00    $0.00    $0.00    $0.00    $0.00
21-Nov-85   02:34 PM
```

Fig. 6.32. A worksheet to distribute costs to accounts, using @IF.

Figure 6.32 shows a simple worksheet that summarizes a company's expenditures for the month of July, 1985. Column A contains the date of each expenditure, and column B contains the amounts of the disbursements. Notice that column C has been labeled "Code" and that row 4 contains a sequence of numbers, beginning with 1 in column D and ending with 5 in column H. We'll call these numbers Accounts. Now suppose that the following formula was entered in cell E6:

@IF($C6=E$4,$B6,0)

Similarly, suppose that the formula

@IF($C6=F$4,$B6,0)

was entered in cell F6. These formulas can be translated as: If the number in cell C6 (the code) equals the number in cell E4 or cell F4 (the account), then enter the value in cell B6 here; otherwise, enter 0 here.

Suppose that similar formulas existed in all of the cells in range D6..H20. Now suppose that we enter a code for each check recorded in column A. The code for each disbursement should be a number less than six. Now, imagine that you recalculated the worksheet. The result would look like figure 6.33.

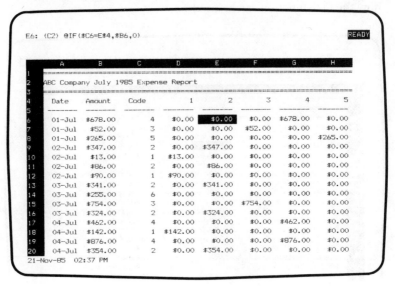

Fig. 6.33. Account distribution worksheet after recalculation.

Notice that in each cell, 1-2-3 has compared each code to the account numbers located in row 4. In the cells where the code and account match, 1-2-3 has recorded the amount of the disbursement. In all the other cells, 1-2-3 has entered a zero. This is exactly what we would expect from the conditional tests we used in these cells.

Like so many other things in 1-2-3, the best way to understand logical operators is to experiment with them. If you want more information on logical functions and more examples on how these functions are used, look for Que's book *1-2-3 for Business*. This book contains a number of practical business models that demonstrate a variety of interesting 1-2-3 techniques.

The @IF Function

Two examples of the @IF function follow:

@IF(A9< >"January",45,"wrong entry")

>   If the value in cell A9 is not the string "January", then assign the number 45. Otherwise, assign the string "wrong entry". Note that if a string value is

entered in cell A9, assign either the vtrue or the vfalse argument. However, if a number is entered in cell A9, or if the cell is left blank, 1-2-3 returns the ERR indicator. Note also that January must be entered in cell A9 as a label or a string expression without a trailing quotation mark. Keep in mind that upper- and lowercase do not matter when entering strings.

@IF(@FALSE,"ok","not ok")

This @IF statement always returns the value "not ok" because the value of the @FALSE function is 0 (false). (See the discussion of the @FALSE function for more information.) The @IF statement in this example emphasizes the numeric character of the @IF function even with seemingly nonnumeric arguments.

Notes on Strings

NEW WITH
R2

Strings have created an additional level of complexity in 1-2-3's logical functions. When you use strings in conditional functions, notice how 1-2-3 reacts to your entering numbers or leaving cells blank. The results can be quite different from similar numeric conditional tests. The cases that follow illustrate some of the differences.

In case 1, cell C1094 is left blank.

Function	Value Displayed on Screen
@IF(C1094="1","lambda","beta")	ERR
@IF(C1094=1,"lambda","beta")	beta
@IF(C1094=1#OR#C1094="1","lambda", "beta")	ERR

In case 2, cell C1094 has the numeric value 1:

Function	Value Displayed on Screen
@IF(C1094="1","lambda","beta")	ERR
@IF(C1094=1,"lambda","beta")	lambda
@IF(C1094=1#OR#C1094="1","lambda", "beta")	ERR

In case 3, cell C1094 contains the label '1 (the string "1"):

Function	Value Displayed on Screen
@IF(C1094="1","lambda","beta")	lambda
@IF(C1094=1,"lambda","beta")	ERR
@IF(C1094=1#OR#C1094="1","lambda", "beta")	ERR

Some of these results may seem illogical when you first look at them, especially the final function in case 3. You might expect that 1-2-3 would display "lambda" instead of the ERR message. These examples, however, show that you need to understand the entry in a logical function (numeric or string). To examine the type of entry you are using, look at the discussion of the @ISSTRING, @ISNUMBER, @CELL, and @CELLPOINTER functions later in this chapter.

The @N and @S Functions

The two functions, @N and @S, can help you prevent ERR messages in conditional statements.

1-2-3 ordinarily does not allow strings and numbers to be mixed in conditional statements. This prevents you from inadvertently mixing the two types of values by entering a label where a number should go, or vice versa. You, however, will often have to include a cell in a conditional statement when you do not know whether the cell will contain a string or a number.

The @N and @S functions give you a way out of this quandary. @N returns the value of a number or numeric formula found in a cell. If the cell is empty or contains a blank, @N returns the value 0. @N will always have a numeric value.

The @S function returns the string value of a cell. If the cell contains a string or a formula that evaluates to a string, then @S returns this string. If the cell contains a number or is empty, @S returns the null string. @S will always have a string value.

The forms of these functions are

@N(range)

@S(range)

The argument must be a range, not a single cell reference. For example, if cell A1 contains the number 1, the value of @N(A1) is ERR, whereas the value of @N(A1..A1) is 1. If the argument is a multicell range, @N and @S return the numeric or string value of the upper left corner of the range.

The @N and @S functions can be demonstrated by the following two conditional expressions and their results:

Function	Value Displayed on Screen
@IF(C1094=1#OR#C1094="1","lambda", "beta")	ERR
@IF(@N(C1094..C1094)=1#OR#	lambda
@S(C1094..C1094)="1","lambda", "beta")	or beta

In these expressions, the @N and @S functions allow the same cell to be tested for the numeric value 1 and the string value "1" at the same time. The @N and @S functions let 1-2-3 check whether a string or number follows a conditional statement so that the statement can work properly. 1-2-3 returns an ERR message because the condition must be a numeric value or formula that results in a numeric value even though the arguments can be strings.

Error-Trapping Functions

You may have situations where 1-2-3's error-trapping functions can help you avoid problems in your worksheets. These functions help you exercise greater control over your templates.

The @NA and @ERR Functions

If you run across a situation where you just don't know what number to put for a value, but you don't want to leave the cell blank, you can enter *NA* (for "Not Available"). 1-2-3 then will display NA in that cell and in any other cell that depends on that cell.

Another condition that you may run across, particularly when you are setting up templates for other people, is unacceptable values for cells. For example, suppose that you are developing a checkbook balancing macro where checks with values less than or equal to zero are unacceptable. One way to indicate the unacceptability of these checks is to use ERR to signal that fact. You might use the following version of the @IF built-in function:

    @IF(B9<=0,@ERR,B9)

In simple English, this statement says: If the amount in cell B9 is less than or equal to zero, then issue ERR on the screen; otherwise, use the amount. Notice that we have used the @ERR function to control the display in almost the same way that we used @NA above.

1-2-3 also uses ERR as a signal for unacceptable numbers—for example, a division by zero or mistakenly deleted cells. ERR often will show up temporarily when you are reorganizing the cells in a worksheet. If the ERR message persists, however, you may have to do some careful analysis to figure out why.

As it does for NA, 1-2-3 displays ERR in any cells that depend on a cell with an ERR value. Sometimes many cells will display ERR after only one or two small changes have been made to a worksheet. To correct the errors, you must trace back through the chain of references to find the root of the problem.

The @ISERR and @ISNA Functions

@ISERR and @ISNA relate closely to the @ERR and @NA functions. @ISERR and @ISNA, which are usually used with the @IF function, allow you to test the value in a cell for the value ERR or NA.

The @ISERR and @ISNA functions are like the logical operators we discussed earlier; they are always either true or false. The function @ISERR(A1) is false if cell A1 does not contain the value ERR, and true if cell A1 equals ERR. Similarly, the @ISNA function is true if the cell referred to contains the value NA, and false if the cell does not.

The @ISERR function is frequently used to keep ERR messages resulting from division by 0 from appearing in the worksheet. For example, at one time or another as you use 1-2-3, you will create a formula that divides a number by a cell reference, as in the formula 23/A4.

If A4 contains a value, the function will simply return the value of the division. But if A4 contains a label, a 0, or is blank, the function will return the value ERR. The @ERR will be passed along to other cells in the worksheet, creating an unnecessary mess.

Using the formula

    @IF(@ISERR(23/A4),0,23/A4)

will eliminate the ERR result. This function says: If the value of 23/A4 is ERR, then enter a 0 in this cell; otherwise, enter the value of the division 23/A4. The function essentially traps the ERR message and keeps the message off the worksheet.

@ISNA works in much the same way. For example, the formula

@IF(@ISNA(A4),0,A4)

tests cell A4 for the value of NA. If the value of A4 is NA, the formula returns a 0. Otherwise, the formula returns the value in A4. This type of formula can be used to keep an NA message from spreading throughout a worksheet.

The @TRUE and @FALSE Functions

@TRUE and @FALSE are logical functions that can be used to check for errors. Neither one of these functions requires an argument. The numeric value of @TRUE is 1, and the numeric value of @FALSE is 0. Typically, these functions are used with @IF and @CHOOSE, mainly for documentation. For example, the function

@IF(B3<30,@TRUE,@FALSE)

is exactly equivalent to @IF(B3<30,1,0). In this case, the @TRUE and @FALSE functions provide better documentation than their numeric equivalents.

The @ISSTRING and @ISNUMBER Functions

NEW WITH
R2

Before using the contents of a cell, you may want to use functions to test the cell's aspect. You may want to look at the type of cell—whether contained data is a number or a label, or whether the cell is empty. A cell's aspect also concerns the cell's address, the row and column the cell resides in, the cell's label prefix (if any), the width of the cell, and the cell's format. Depending on the characteristics of a cell's aspect, you may need to use different cell-processing methods.

Two functions that help you determine the type of value stored in a cell are @ISSTRING and @ISNUMBER. Both of these functions are most often used with the @IF function, but they can be used with other types of functions as well.

The @ISNUMBER function helps to verify whether a cell entry is a number. The general format of the function is

@ISNUMBER(argument)

If the argument is a number, the numeric value of the function is 1. If, however, the argument is a string, including the blank string " ", the numeric value of the function is 0.

As a simple example, suppose that you want to test whether the value entered in cell B3 is a number. If the value is a number, then you want to show the label "number" in the current cell; otherwise, you want to show the label "string". The function you can use is

@IF(@ISNUMBER(B3),"number","string")

With this function, you can be fairly certain that the appropriate label will appear in the current cell. Besides numbers, however, the @ISNUMBER function also gives blank cells a numeric value of one. Obviously, the function itself is incomplete because the function will assign the label "number" to the current cell if cell B3 is empty. For complete reliability, the function must be modified to handle blank cells.

You can distinguish between a number and an empty cell by using the following formula (note that cell AA3 must contain the label B3..B3):

@IF(@ISNUMBER(B3),@IF(@COUNT(@@(AA3)),"number",
    "blank"),"string")

The first step this function performs is to test whether the cell contains a number or a blank. If so, then the function uses the @COUNT function to test whether the range B3..B3 contains an entry. (Recall that @COUNT assigns a value of 0 to blank cells and a value of 1 to cells with an entry when the argument used is a range rather than a cell reference. See the discussion of the @COUNT function earlier in this chapter for more explanation.) If the cell contains an entry, the label "number" is displayed. Otherwise, the label "blank" is displayed. If the cell does not contain a number or a blank, the cell must contain a string with the "string" label displayed.

As an alternative, you may consider using the @ISSTRING function. @ISSTRING works in nearly the same way as @ISNUMBER. @ISSTRING, however, determines whether a cell entry is a string value. The general format of the command is

@ISSTRING(argument)

If the argument for the @ISSTRING function is a string, then the value of the function is 1. If the argument, however, is a number or blank, the value of the function is 0. One nice feature of @ISSTRING is that you can use this function to stop what Lotus calls the "ripple-through" effect of NA and ERR in cells that should have a string value. 1-2-3 considers both NA and ERR as numeric values.

NEW WITH
R2

Returning to the earlier example about discriminating between a number and an empty cell, you can also complete the function with the help of @ISSTRING by using the following formula (note that cell AA3 must contain the label B3..B3):

@IF(@ISSTRING(B3),"string",@IF(@COUNT(@@(AA3))>0,
"number","blank"))

The first step that this function performs is to test whether string data is present. If string data is present, then the function assigns the label "string". Otherwise, the @COUNT function is used to determine whether the range B3..B3 contains a number or is empty. If the data is a number, then the label "number" is assigned. Otherwise, the label "blank" is assigned.

@ISNUMBER provides the capability to test for a number, although the function's inability to distinguish between numbers and blank cells is its principal weakness. In many applications, however, @ISNUMBER provides sufficient testing of values, especially when you are certain that a cell is not blank. @ISSTRING provides the capability to test for a string. With the @COUNT function, @ISSTRING can distinguish blank cells from strings. The @COUNT function combined with both @ISNUMBER and @ISSTRING can help you distinguish between blank cells and numbers.

Special Functions

NEW WITH
R2

The following functions are listed together in a separate category because they provide information about cell or range content or spreadsheet location. @CELL and @CELLPOINTER are two of 1-2-3's most powerful special functions with many different options. @ROWS and @COLS lets you determine the size of a range. The function @@ lets you indirectly reference one cell with another cell within the spreadsheet.

The @CELL Function

The @CELL function is an efficient way of determining the nature of a cell. Because @CELL gives you so many different options, it is one of 1-2-3's most comprehensive functions. The general form of the @CELL function is

@CELL(string,range)

The first argument is a string value indicating a particular cell aspect to be examined. The second argument represents a cell in the range format (such as A1..A1). If you use just the single-cell format, 1-2-3 returns the ERR message. If you specify a range larger than a single cell, 1-2-3 uses the upper left corner cell for evaluation. The following examples show all the string arguments you can use with @CELL, and the results you will receive.

@CELL("address",SALES)

    If the range named SALES is C187..E187, 1-2-3 returns the absolute address $C$187. This is a convenient way of listing the upper left corner of a range's address in the worksheet. To list all the range names and their addresses, see the /Range Name Table command.

@CELL("prefix",C195..C195)

    If the cell C195 contains the label 'Chicago, 1-2-3 will return ' (indicating left alignment). If, however, cell C195 is blank, 1-2-3 will return nothing; in other words, the current cell will appear blank.

@CELL("format",A10)

    1-2-3 will return the ERR indicator because the second argument is not in the range format.

@CELL("width",B12..B12)

    1-2-3 will return the width of column B as viewed in the current window regardless of whether that width was set using the /Worksheet Column Set-width command (for the individual column) or the /Worksheet Global Column-Set-Width command (for the default column width).

The @CELLPOINTER Function

The @CELLPOINTER function is similar to the @CELL function, except that @CELLPOINTER works with the *current* cell. The current cell is the cell where the cell pointer was sitting at the time the worksheet was last recalculated. The general format of the command is

@CELLPOINTER(string)

You can use the same strings as those for the @CELL function (see page 208). For example, to determine the address of the current cell, you can enter @CELLPOINTER("address") in cell B22. If recalculation is set to automatic, the value displayed in that cell will be the absolute address $B$22. This same address will remain displayed until you recalculate the worksheet by making an entry elsewhere in the worksheet or pressing the Calc (F9) key. The address that appears in cell B22 will change to reflect the position of the cell pointer when the worksheet was recalculated. If recalculation is manual, you can change only the address by pressing the Calc key.

The @ROWS and @COLS Functions

Both @ROWS and @COLS are used to describe the dimensions of ranges. The general form of these commands is

@ROWS(range)

@COLS(range)

Suppose that you want to determine the number of columns in a range called EXPENSES and to display that value in the current cell. The function you enter is @COLS(EXPENSES). Similarly, you can enter @ROWS(EXPENSES) to display the number of rows in the range.

One rule to remember about @ROWS and @COLS is that you cannot specify a single cell as the argument unless that cell is in the range format (for example, C3..C3). Otherwise, 1-2-3 will display the ERR message.

The @@ Function

The @@(cell reference) function provides a way of indirectly referencing one cell by way of another cell. A simple example shows what the @@ function does. If cell A1 contains the label 'A2, and cell A2 contains the number 5, then the function @@(A1) returns the value 5. If the label in cell A1 is changed to 'B10, and cell B10 contains the label "hi there", the function @@(A1) now returns the string value "hi there".

The argument of the @@ function must be a cell reference to the cell containing the indirect address. Similarly, the cell referenced by the argument of the @@ function must contain a string value that evaluates to a cell reference. This cell can contain a label, a string formula, or a reference to another cell, as long as the resulting string value is a cell reference.

The @@ function is primarily useful in situations where several formulas each have the same argument, and the argument must be changed from time to time during the course of the application. 1-2-3 lets you specify the arguments of each formula through a common indirect address. Figure 6.34 shows an example of this situation.

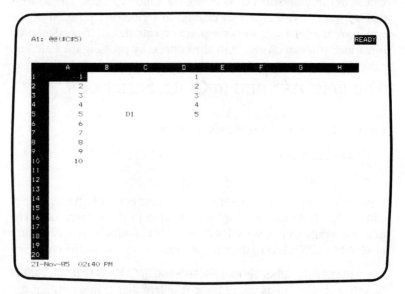

Fig. 6.34. Example of @@ function in a series of formulas.

In figure 6.34, the 10 formulas in column A all use the @@ function to reference 1 of 5 values in column D indirectly through cell C5. When you are ready to change the cell being referenced, you only have to change the label in cell C5 instead of editing all 10 formulas in column A. Figure 6.35 shows the same formulas after the indirect address has been changed from 'D1 to 'D2.

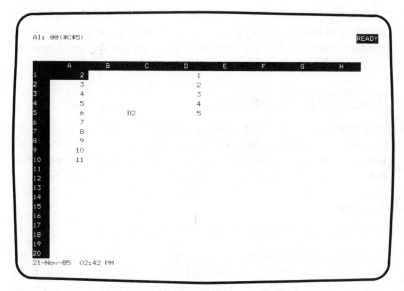

Fig. 6.35. Formulas using @@ after change of indirect reference.

String Functions

NEW WITH
R2

1-2-3 has a variety of string functions that give the user significantly more power to manipulate strings than do earlier integrated packages, including earlier releases of 1-2-3. (As Release 1A users are well aware, that version of 1-2-3 has limited power to manipulate strings, and offers no string functions whatsoever.)

Take particular care to avoid mixing data types in the new string functions now available in Release 2. For instance, some functions produce strings, whereas others produce numeric results. Be careful not to combine functions from these two different groups unless you have taken all the precautions discussed throughout this section on string functions.

The numbering scheme for positioning characters in a label is also something to watch for when using the new string functions. These positions are numbered beginning with zero and continuing to a number corresponding to the last character in the label. The following example shows the position numbers for a long label:

```
        111111111122222
01234567890123456789801234
'two chickens in every pot
```

The prefix (') before the label does not have a number because the prefix is not considered part of the label. Nor are negative position numbers allowed. The importance of position numbers will become clearer in the next section.

The @FIND Function

One of the simplest string functions is @FIND, the best function for showing how position numbers are used in strings. The @FIND function locates the starting position of one string within another string. For instance, using the string that was just illustrated, suppose that you want to find at what position the string "every" occurs in this string. The general format of @FIND is

@FIND(search string,overall string,start number)

The search string is the string you want to locate. In this example the search string is "every". The overall string is the target string to be searched. In this example, "two chickens in every pot" is the overall string. Finally, the start number is the position number in the overall string where you want to start the search. If you wish to start at position 6 and you are using the overall string located in cell B5, the function you use is

@FIND("every",B5,6)

Your result is the number 16, the position of the first (and only) occurrence of "every" in the overall string. If the search string "every" was not found in the overall string, the ERR message would be displayed.

Notice that in our example, choosing the starting number of 6 has no bearing on the outcome of the function. You could just as easily choose 0 (or any other number less than or equal to 16) for the starting position of the search string. If "every" appeared more than once in the overall string, however, the start number could locate its occurrence elsewhere. Suppose that the following overall string appears in cell B5:

'two chickens in every pot, two cars in every garage

Now suppose that you decide to locate all the occurrences of "every" in the overall string. As before, starting with the function @FIND("every",B5,0) returns a value of 16. Try changing the start number by adding 1 to the result of the original function (1 + 16 = 17). The appropriate function is now @FIND("every",B5,17). This new function returns the number 39, the starting location of the second occurrence of "every". Next, add 1 to the second result (1 + 39 = 40), and use @FIND("every",B5,40). The resulting ERR message tells you that you have found all the occurrences of the search string.

NEW WITH **R2**

Keep in mind that @FIND (like strings in general) is limited to 240 characters in a string. Another rule to remember is that any decimals in a start number will be ignored by 1-2-3.

Still another rule to remember is that any search string must be entered exactly as you wish to find it because @FIND does not perform approximate searching. In the preceding example, if you had used a search string of "Every" instead of "every", you would get the ERR message instead of a number value.

The @MID Function

NEW WITH **R2**

Whereas @FIND helps you to locate one string within another, the @MID function lets you extract one string from another. This operation is called *substringing*. The general form of the function is

@MID(string,start position,length)

The start position is a number representing the character position in the string where you wish to begin extracting characters. The length argument indicates the number of characters to extract. For example, to extract the first name from a label containing the full name "Laura Mann", use @MID("Laura Mann",0,5). This function extracts the string starting in position 0 (the first character) and continuing for a length of 5 characters.

Now suppose that you want to extract the first and last names from a column list of full names and to put those two names in a separate column. To accomplish this, use the @MID and @FIND functions together. Because you know a blank space will always separate the first and last names, @FIND can locate the position of the blank in each full name. With this value, you can then set up the functions to extract the first and last names.

If cell A1 contains the full name "Gerald Frankel", place the function

@MID(A1,0,@FIND(" ",A1,0))

in cell B1. The value of this function will appear as "Gerald" since @FIND(" ",A1,0) will return a value of 6 for the length argument. Next place the function

@MID(A1,@FIND(" ",A1,0)+1,99)

in column C. The @FIND function indicates that the start position is one character beyond the blank space. In addition, the length of the string to be extracted is 99 characters. Obviously, a length of 99 is overkill, but there is no penalty for this excess. The string that 1-2-3 extracts is "Frankel".

Now that you have seen how the @MID and @FIND functions can separate first and last names, you may want to try using these functions in a case with a name containing a middle initial.

The @LEFT and @RIGHT Functions

@LEFT and @RIGHT are special variations of the @MID function and are used to extract one string of characters from another, beginning at the leftmost and rightmost positions in the underlying string. The general formats of the functions are

@LEFT(string,length)

@RIGHT(string,length)

The length argument is the number of character positions in a string to be extracted. For example, if you want to extract the ZIP code from the string "Cincinnati, Ohio 45243", use

@RIGHT("Cincinnati, Ohio 45243",5)

@LEFT works the same way as @RIGHT except that @LEFT extracts from the beginning of a string. For instance, extract the city in our example with

@LEFT("Cincinnati, Ohio 45243",10)

(In most cases, however, use @FIND(",",0) instead of 10 for the length in the function to extract the city from the address.)

The @REPLACE Function

The @REPLACE function removes a group of characters from a string and replaces the characters with another string using the same numbering scheme as @FIND. That is, @REPLACE numbers the character positions in a string, starting with zero and continuing to the end of the string (up to a maximum of 239). The general form of the command is

@REPLACE(original string,start number,length,replacement
    string)

The start number argument indicates the position where 1-2-3 will begin removing characters in the original string. The length shows how many characters to remove, and the replacement string contains new characters to replace the removed ones. For example, suppose that the string "Now is the time for all good men" appears in cell C1, and you want to replace "men" with "people". The function to use is

@REPLACE(C1,29,3,"people")

Instead of starting at 0 and counting up the 30 positions of the start-number, you may want to use the @FIND function instead. For instance, you can enter

@REPLACE(C1,@FIND("men",C1,0),3,"people")

This example is just one of many in which combining functions can save you much time and effort.

The @LENGTH Function

The @LENGTH function simply indicates the length of your strings. The general form of the function is

@LENGTH(string)

For example, suppose that cell E9 contains the string "Credit policy". Then the value of @LENGTH(E9) is 13. If, in the same spreadsheet, cell J6 contains the string value +E9&" respondents", the value of @LENGTH(J6) is 25.

The @LENGTH function returns the value ERR as the length of numeric values or formulas, blank cells, and null strings.

The @EXACT Function

The @EXACT function compares two strings, returning a value of 1 for strings that are alike and 0 for strings that are unalike. The general form of the function is

@EXACT(string1,string2)

@EXACT's method of comparison is like the = operator in formulas except that the = operator checks for an approximate match, and the @EXACT function checks for an exact match. For example, if cell A2 holds the string "Marketing Function" and cell B2 holds the string "marketing function", the numeric value of A2 = B2 is 1 because the two strings are an approximate match. Conversely, the numeric value

NEW WITH

R2

of @EXACT(A2,B2) is 0 because the two functions are not an exact match.

Using this function, keep in mind that @EXACT cannot compare nonstring arguments. If you try to compare an A2 that is empty and a B2 with a valid string, the value of @EXACT(A2,B2) is ERR. In fact, if either argument is a nonstring value of any type (including numbers), 1-2-3 will return the ERR message. (Note that the @S function can be used to ensure that the arguments of @EXACT have string values.)

NEW WITH

R2

The @LOWER, @UPPER, and @PROPER Functions

1-2-3 offers three different functions for converting the case of a string value. First, @LOWER converts all uppercase letters in a string to low-ercase letters. For instance, if cell B3 contains the string "ALL iN GooD tiME", the value of @LOWER(B3) is "all in good time".

Second, @UPPER is nearly the opposite of @LOWER because it raises all the letters in a string to uppercase letters. For example, the value of

@UPPER("ALL iN GooD tiME")

is "ALL IN GOOD TIME".

Finally, @PROPER capitalizes the first letter in each word of a label. (Words are defined as groups of characters separated by blank spaces.) @PROPER goes on to convert the remaining letters in each word to lowercase. For example, the value of

@PROPER("when IS tHE meeTING?")

is "When Is The Meeting?"

As you might expect, none of these three functions work with non-string values. For instance, if cell E9 contains a number or a null string, 1-2-3 will return ERR for each of these functions. (Note that using the @S function will ensure that the arguments of these functions have string values.)

NEW WITH

R2

The @REPEAT Function

@REPEAT repeats strings within a cell much as the backslash (\ ) re-peats characters. But @REPEAT has some distinct advantages over the backslash. The general form of the function is

@REPEAT(string,number)

The number argument indicates the number of times you wish to repeat a string in a cell. For example, if you want to repeat the string "COGS" three times, you can enter @REPEAT("COGS",3). The resulting string will be "COGSCOGSCOGS". This string follows 1-2-3's rule for long labels. That is, the string will display beyond the right boundary of the column, provided no entry is in the cell to the right. The technique for repeating labels with \ is different from that of @REPEAT because with \, 1-2-3 will fill the column to exactly whatever the column width may be.

You can set up a function to fill a cell almost exactly by using the @CELL and @LENGTH functions. If A3 is the cell you wish to fill by repeating the string "COGS", the first step is to enter @CELL("width",A3..A3) in an out-of-the-way cell, say, K4. The next step is to enter @LENGTH("COGS") in K5, another out-of-the-way cell. The final step is to enter

   @REPEAT("COGS",K4/K5)

in cell A3. If the width of column A is 9 (the default column width), the label that appears in cell A3 is "COGSCOGS". Notice that since @REPEAT uses only the integer portion of the "number" argument, "COGS" is repeated only twice rather than 2.25 times.

The @TRIM Function

The @TRIM function can take out unwanted blank spaces from the beginning, end, or middle of a string. If more than one space occurs consecutively in the middle of a string, 1-2-3 removes all but one of the blank spaces. For instance, if the string

   "   When   in   the   course   of human events"

resides in cell A3, @TRIM(A3) will appear as

   "When in the course of human events"

Notice that the extra blank spaces have been removed. Notice also that whereas the value of @LENGTH(A3) is 40, the value of @LENGTH(@TRIM(A3)) is 34. (For trimming other characters besides blank spaces, see the @CLEAN function described later in this chapter.)

Converting Strings to Numbers and Vice Versa

Two of the most important and powerful functions that 1-2-3 offers are @STRING and @VALUE. The @STRING function can convert a number to a string, whereas @VALUE converts a string to a number.

The @STRING Function

NEW WITH
R2

The @STRING function lets you convert a number to a string so that the number can act with 1-2-3's string functions. For example, @STRING can override 1-2-3's automatic right-justification of numbers, and display a number justified to the left. The general form of the @STRING function is

@STRING(number to convert,decimal places)

1-2-3 uses the fixed-decimal format for the @STRING function. The decimal-places argument represents the number of places to be included in the string. For example, if the number-to-convert argument within cell J7 is 9.482, enter @STRING(J7,2) in the current cell. The resulting string '9.48 is displayed with left-justification, the default setting.

If the number-to-convert argument is 9.478 instead of 9.482, 1-2-3 will round the number upward to 9.48, just as 1-2-3 rounds any number displayed in the fixed-decimal format.

If you wish to create a string reflecting the number 9.482 as a percentage, the formula @STRING(J7*100,2)&"%" will produce the string "948.20%". Note that to create a string from a number in any format other than fixed decimal, you must add the additional format characters yourself.

The @VALUE Function

NEW WITH
R2

If you have been entering string data but decide that you prefer the data as numbers, use the @VALUE function. For example, suppose that you enter part numbers and their quantities in a database as labels. The information on part numbers works fine in the string format; but @VALUE will change the format of the quantity data to add different part quantities together. The general form of the function is

@VALUE(string)

If cell K11 contains a database entry for the quantity data in the string format, you can enter @VALUE(D11) in an out-of-the-way cell in the worksheet, say, Z11. If the string in cell K11 is "23", then the number displayed in cell Z11 is 23. You can now use the number in cell Z11 in any kind of numeric operation.

NEW WITH
R2

Besides converting strings in the standard number format (for example, 23.445), @VALUE can also convert strings with decimal fractions as well as numbers displayed in scientific format. For example, if cell T10 contains the string "12 31/32", @VALUE(T10) will appear as 12.96875. Even if cell T10 contains the string "12 54/32", @VALUE still will convert the string to the number 13.6875. Similarly, if a number is displayed as the string "137E+1", @VALUE will convert the string to the number 13.7.

A few rules should be remembered when you use @VALUE. Although 1-2-3 does not object to extra spaces left in a string, the program has trouble with some extra characters, such as trailing percent signs. Acceptable, however, are (1) currency signs (such as $) that precede the string and (2) brackets around negative numbers. Try experimenting with different extra characters to see how @VALUE reacts. Another point to remember is that a numeric value as an argument for @VALUE will simply return the original number value.

Functions Used with LICS

NEW WITH
R2

1-2-3 offers a few special functions for interfacing with the Lotus International Character Set (LICS), which Lotus calls "an extension of the ASCII printable character set." (Be aware that the ASCII code number for a given character may not correspond to its LICS code number.) Actually, the LICS can best be thought of as a new character set created by Lotus and superimposed on top of the ASCII character set.

The complete set of LICS characters is listed in the 1-2-3 reference manual and includes everything from the copyright sign to the lowercase *e* with the grave accent. The many characters allow you great flexibility.

The @CHAR Function

NEW WITH
R2

The @CHAR function produces the LICS equivalent of a number between 1 and 255 on screen. The general form of the function is

@CHAR(number)

1-2-3 represents a ™ sign on screen with a T. To display the trademark sign on screen, enter @CHAR(184) in a cell. What is more, a string formula can concatenate the trademark sign to a product name. For instance, enter the formula +"8080"&@CHAR(184) to produce the string "8080/T". When you print the screen display, this string prints as "8080 TM."

Keep in mind two simple rules when using @CHAR. First, if the numeric argument you are using is not between 1 and 255, 1-2-3 returns the ERR message. Second, if the argument you use is not an integer, 1-2-3 disregards the noninteger portion of the argument.

Nonprintable Characters in LICS

Be aware that not all the LICS characters are printable, nor will they always show up on the screen. More specifically, codes 1 through 31 are the problem area. But because these codes include all the characters necessary for making boxes and arrows in 1-2-3, you may want access to these characters.

You can get at these nonprintable characters with the Edit key. First, the /Data Fill command enters the numbers 1 through 31 in the range B1..B31. Then, after moving one column to the left, you enter @CHAR(B1) in cell A1 and copy that formula to the cells below. Finally, use the /Range Values command to convert the formulas in column A to the actual string values. Even though the cells in column A appear blank, you can see any one of the characters by moving the cursor to any cell in column A and pressing the Edit key. Figure 6.36 shows how the screen should appear.

Because these characters @CHAR(1) through @CHAR(31) are nonprintable, only blanks will appear if you try to print them out.

The @CODE Function

The @CODE function performs as the opposite to @CHAR. Whereas @CHAR takes a number between 0 and 255 and returns an ASCII/LICS character, @CODE examines an ASCII/LICS character and returns a number between 0 and 255. The general form of the function is

@CODE(string)

Suppose that you want to find the ASCII/LICS code number for the letter *a*. You enter @CODE("a") in a cell, and 1-2-3 returns the number 97. If you had entered @CODE("aardvark"), 1-2-3 would still re-

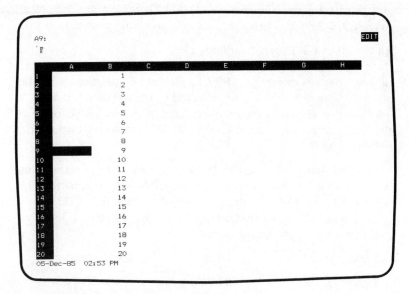

Fig. 6.36. Nonprintable characters in the LICS character set.

turn 97, the code of the first character in the string. Remember that if you specify a number as the argument for @CODE (expressed as a number and not a string), 1-2-3 returns the ERR message.

The @CLEAN Function

Sometimes when you import strings with /File Import, especially by way of a modem, the strings will contain nonprintable characters (ASCII codes below 32) interspersed throughout. The @CLEAN function removes the nonprintable characters from the strings. The general format of the function is

@CLEAN(string)

The argument of @CLEAN must be a string value or a cell reference to a cell containing a string value. 1-2-3 will not accept a cell entry containing @CLEAN with a range argument.

Date and Time Functions

One of 1-2-3's most advanced features is its ability to manipulate dates and times. This feature can be used for such things as mortgage analysis, aging of accounts receivable, and time management. (In Release 1

NEW WITH

R2

and 1A of 1-2-3, the program could handle dates but not time. With Release 2, 1-2-3 has been expanded to handle time as well.)

All aspects of 1-2-3's date-handling capability are based on 1-2-3's ability to represent any given date as a serial integer equal to the number of days from December 31, 1899, to the date in question. With this scheme, January 1, 1900, is represented by the number 1; January 2, 1900, is represented by the number 2; and so on. The maximum date that 1-2-3 can handle is December 31, 2099, represented by the serial number 73050.

1-2-3's time-handling capability is based on fractions of serial numbers. For instance, 8:00 a.m. is represented by the decimal fraction 0.333333 (or 1/3). Similarly, the decimal fraction for 10:00 p.m. is 0.916666. 1-2-3's serial numbering system allows you to devise an overall number representing both date and time.

Date	Time	Serial Number
January 3, 1900	01:00 a.m.	3.041666666
December 9, 1935	12:00 p.m.	13127.5
December 30, 1983	12:00 a.m.	30680
June 25, 1984	09:21 a.m.	30858.38958
December 31, 2099	11:00 p.m.	73050.95833

The serial numbering system also lets you manipulate dates and times just like any other number in 1-2-3. For example, after setting the beginning date for a project and adding the number of days that the project should take to the beginning date, you can determine the completion date easily. Time values are just as easy to work with. For example, you can set up a complete schedule for the day by dividing it into hour increments.

The @DATE Function

Perhaps the most commonly used date function is @DATE. This function allows you to convert a date into an integer that 1-2-3 can interpret. The form of the @DATE function is

@DATE(year number,month number,day number)

Following are examples showing how the built-in @DATE function can be used:

@DATE(55,12,30)=   20453

@DATE(12,1,1)=   4384

@DATE(C7,C8,D10)=   integer equivalent of the date
                        represented by these cells. If the cells
                        contain the values 83, 12, and 25,
                        respectively, the function will have
                        the value 30675.

The numeric arguments have certain restrictions. First, the year number must be between 0 (indicating the year 1900) and 199 (2099). Second, the month number must be between 1 and 12. Third, the day number must be one of the actual values for a given month (for example, 30 days for September and 31 days for December). Finally, 1-2-3 truncates all but the integer portion of the numeric arguments.

Once a date has been interpreted by 1-2-3 as an integer, you can use the Format command to display the date in a more recognizable way, such as 01/01/86. (More information on 1-2-3's date and time formats may be found later in this chapter and also in Chapter 5.)

The @DATEVALUE Function

@DATEVALUE is a variant of @DATE producing a serial number from the month, day, and year information that you assign the function. But unlike the numeric arguments of @DATE, a string argument is assigned to @DATEVALUE. The general form of the function is

@DATEVALUE(date string)

The date string must be in any of the available date formats: D1, D2, D3, D4, or D5. If the string conforms to one of the five date formats, 1-2-3 will display the appropriate serial integer.

Function	Date Format	Number
@DATEVALUE("26-JUN-84")	D1	30859
@DATEVALUE("26-JUN")	D2	30859
@DATEVALUE("JUN-84")	D3	30834
@DATEVALUE("6/26/84")	D4	30859
@DATEVALUE("6/26")	D5	30859

Notice that for the second and fifth date formats, 1-2-3 automatically supplied 84 as the year. You can assume that a date in 1984 was entered at the start of a day's session when DOS prompted the user for a date or as a response to the DOS date function. Notice also that for the third function, 1-2-3 defaults to the first day in June as the day value.

You may prefer to enter the date string in one of what Lotus calls the International Date formats (formats D4 and D5). The default separation character for the International Date formats is / (for example, 6/26/84), but you can use instead periods or dashes. If you plan to use something other than the default setting for the International Date formats, however, you must modify one of the configuration settings with the /Worksheet Global Default Other International Date command. You may then select the format you want.

Suppose that you have chosen the default setting for the separation character, and you want to enter the date string in the D4 (MM/DD/YY) format. If you enter @DATEVALUE("6/26/84"), 1-2-3 will display the number 30859. If you enter @DATEVALUE("6-26-84"), 1-2-3 will return the ERR message. 1-2-3 does not expect the hyphen (-) as the separation character unless you change the default settings.

The @DAY, @MONTH, and @YEAR Functions

The built-in functions of @DATE, @MONTH, and @YEAR allow you to extract parts of a date in integer form. In the example

@DAY(30284) = 29

@MONTH(30284) = 11

@YEAR(30284) = 82

the three functions, taken together, are nearly the reverse of the @DATE built-in function because these functions allow you to convert from integer format back to Gregorian format. You can use these functions for various time-related chores, such as aging accounts receivable and setting up a table for amortizing a loan.

Displaying Dates

The five date functions already discussed are extremely useful for entering dates in the worksheet in a form that 1-2-3 can understand. The results of these functions, however, are integers that don't look like dates and are therefore hard to comprehend. For example, can you figure out the dates represented by the numbers 20124 and 32988?

The /Range Format Date command allows you to display dates in five different forms. As indicated earlier, dates are represented as integers that equal the number of days that have elapsed since December 31, 1899. The date format displays these integers in one of the following five arrangements (Lotus calls them D1 through D5), depending on which one you select.

Number	Arrangement	Example
1	DD-MMM-YY	26-Jun-84
2	DD-MMM	26-Jun
3	MMM-YY	Jun-84
4	MM/DD/YY	06/26/85
5	MM/DD	06/26

Note that for all the examples shown above, the integer 30859 is displayed in the worksheet prior to formatting.

Notice, too, that the first option (D1) creates a string 9 characters long—too long to be displayed in a column with the default width of 9. In general, you will need to expand any column containing dates formatted in the DD-MMM-YY format so that the column width is 10 or more characters. Because the other date formats can be displayed in normal width columns, these formats (especially D4) can be used in place of the more detailed, but wider, DD-MMM-YY format.

The @NOW Function

NEW WITH
R2

The @NOW function returns today's date and time as an integer. The number represents the number of days since December 31, 1899, and a fraction representing the time elapsed since 12:00 a.m. yesterday. This built-in function is particularly useful for taking advantage of an IBM PC's (and an IBM compatible's) timekeeping capability. If you have a clock that automatically supplies the date and time, or if you simply enter the date and time when you are prompted by DOS at the start of the day, the @NOW function will give you access to the date and time in the current worksheet. For example, if you enter the date 6-26-85 in response to the DOS date prompt, and 16:00 to the DOS time prompt (corresponding to 4:00 p.m.), the @NOW function will have the value

   @NOW = 31224.66

Because the @NOW function is dependent on the PC DOS or MS-DOS system date and time for its value, you must always remember to enter at least the date, and preferably the date and time, in response to the operating system prompt before you enter 1-2-3. (If you want to modify the operating system date and time during a session, see the discussion on the /System command in Chapter 4 for using DOS commands from within 1-2-3.)

Users of Release 1A of 1-2-3 may recognize @NOW as being similar to the @TODAY function. The only difference between the two functions is that @NOW includes the time as well as the date. Although @TODAY function is not available in Release 2, Release 1A spreadsheets using @TODAY still work because Release 2 automatically translates @TODAY to @NOW as it reads in the worksheet. Release 2 users can use the @INT(@NOW) to reproduce the @TODAY function.

The @Time Function

NEW WITH
R2

As mentioned earlier, 1-2-3 expresses time in fractions of serial numbers between 0 and 1. For example, .5 is equal to twelve hours (or 12:00 p.m.). In addition, 1-2-3 works on military time; 10:00 p.m. in normal time is 22:00 in military time. 1-2-3's timekeeping system may seem a little awkward at first, but you will soon grow used to it. Here are some general guidelines to help you:

1 hour =	0.0416666
1 minute =	0.0006944
1 second =	0.0000115

The built-in @TIME function arrives at a serial number for a specified time of day. The general form of the function is

@TIME(hour number,minute number,second number)

The following are examples of how the @TIME built-in function is used:

@TIME(3,12,30) =	0.133680
@TIME(23,0,0) =	0.958333
@TIME(C7,C8,D10) =	integer equivalent of the time represented by these cells. If the cells contain the values 23, 12, and 59, respectively, the function would have the value 0.967349.

The numeric arguments have certain restrictions. First, the hour number must be between 0 and 23. Second, both the minute number and second number must be between 0 and 59. Finally, 1-2-3 truncates all but the integer portion of the numeric arguments.

Once a time has been interpreted by 1-2-3 as a fraction of a serial number, you can use the /Range Format command to display the time in a more recognizable way (for example, 10:42 p.m.). 1-2-3's time formats are discussed later in this chapter.

The @TIMEVALUE Function

NEW WITH
R2

Just like @DATEVALUE and @DATE, @TIMEVALUE is a variant of @TIME. Like @TIME, @TIMEVALUE produces a serial number from the hour, minute, and second information you give to the function. But unlike @TIME's numeric arguments, @TIMEVALUE uses string arguments. The general form of the function is

@TIMEVALUE(time string)

The time string must appear in one of the four time formats: T1, T2, T3, or T4. If the string conforms to one of the time formats, 1-2-3 will display the appropriate serial number fraction. (If you then format the cell, 1-2-3 will display the appropriate time of day.)

Function	Time Format	Number
@TIMEVALUE("12:30:59 pm")	D6	0.521516203
@TIMEVALUE("12:30 pm")	D7	0.520833333
@TIMEVALUE("13:30:30")	D8	0.562847222
@TIMEVALUE("13:30")	D9	0.5625

Notice that the time used for the first format is 12:30 p.m. and 59 seconds. The time used for the third format is 1:30 p.m. and 30 seconds.

The first two time formats, D6 and D7, accept times from 12:00 a.m. to 11:59 a.m., and from 12:00 p.m. to 11:59 p.m. The second two time formats, called International Time formats by Lotus, accept military time from 00:00 (12 a.m.) to 23:59 (11:59 p.m.). The separator character for the International Time formats defaults to a colon (:), but you can change this by using the /Worksheet Global Default Other International Time command.

The @SECOND, @MINUTE, and @HOUR Functions

The built-in @SECOND, @MINUTE, and @HOUR functions allow you to extract different units of time from a numeric time fraction. In the example

@SECOND(31412.4432) = 12

@MINUTE(31412.4432) = 38

@HOUR(31412.4432) = 10

notice that the argument includes both an integer and a decimal portion. Although the integer portion is important for date functions, it is disregarded for time functions. You can use these functions for various time-related chores, the most important of which is developing a time schedule.

Displaying Times

You have now seen all of 1-2-3's time functions, but the resulting serial number fractions do not look familiar as expressions of time. The /Range Format Date Time command allows you to display times in a more recognizable format. Lotus offers the following four different formats, called D6 through D9:

Number	*Arrangement*	*Example*
D6	HH:MM:SS a.m./p.m.	11:51:22 p.m.
D7	HH:MM a.m./p.m.	11:51 p.m.
D8	HH:MM:SS (24 hours)	23:51:22
D9	HH:MM (24 hours)	23:51

Note that for all these examples, the fractional number displayed in the worksheet prior to formatting is 0.994.

The first option (D6) creates a string of 11 characters that requires a column width of 12 in order to display the time in this format. For this reason, and because you may rarely use seconds, the D7 format is more useful for most people. Of course, you may find another of the four formats better suited to your needs.

General Comments on Date and Time Arithmetic

1-2-3's date and time arithmetic capabilities actually incorporate both a set of functions and a set of formats. Don't be confused by this mix. The functions, like @DATEVALUE, enter dates or times in the worksheet; the formats display these functions in an understandable form. Although the format can be used without the function, or the function without the format, the two tools are better used together.

In most cases date and time arithmetic will require simply subtracting one number from another. By subtracting, you can easily determine the number of days between dates, or hours between times. For example, subtracting @DATE(84,7,31) from @DATE(84,8,15) results in the value 15 (days). Similarly, subtracting @TIME(10,4,31) from @TIME(12,54,54) results in a value of 0.11832175 (2 hours, 50 minutes, and 23 seconds.) To 1-2-3 these problems are as simple as subtracting the serial number for

@DATE(84,7,31)+@TIME(10,4,31)(30894.4198)

from the serial number for

@DATE(84,8,15)+@TIME(12,54,54)(30909.5381)

You can even determine the number of minutes, hours, weeks, and years between two serial numbers by dividing the difference by an appropriate number. If you need only a rough idea, you can use the banker's convention of 7 days in a week, 30 days in a month, and 360 days in a year. If you want to be more exact, you can use the @MOD function for remainders. You can even build in odd-numbered months and leap years. 1-2-3's date keeping and timekeeping capabilities will allow you to simplify analysis or make the analysis as sophisticated as you like.

You will find December 31, 1899, as the starting date for date and time arithmetic a good choice. The selection of an ending date is more important. The date has to be far enough in the future to allow you to perform long-term analysis. The choice of December 31, 2099, seems to work just fine.

As mentioned earlier, besides using date and time functions in arithmetic calculations, you can also use them in logical expressions, such as @IF(@DATE(84,15,05)>B2,C3,D4). In simple English this statement says: If the serial number equivalent to May 15, 1984, is greater than the value in cell B2, then assign the value in cell C3 to the current cell; otherwise, use the value in D4. This kind of test can be used to help keep track of investment portfolios or time performance.

7
File Operations

The ability to store, retrieve, and delete files to and from disks is common to all spreadsheet programs. What makes 1-2-3 unique is its scale in performing these functions. Lotus lists the disk requirements for the program as either "two double-sided disk drives or one double-sided disk drive and a hard disk." Clearly, the program can function with less than these requirements (one double-sided disk drive is enough to squeak by), but this is not what Lotus had in mind. 1-2-3 was written for users who intend to mix and match many large files that will be moved in and out of storage quite frequently.

A complete listing of all file-operation commands can be found in the 1-2-3 menu map included at the back of this book.

A General Description of 1-2-3 Files

1-2-3 file names can be up to eight characters long with a three-character extension. The three basic rules for file names are

1. File names may include the characters A through Z, 0 through 9, and the underscore (_). Depending on your system, you may be able to use other special characters, but 1-2-3 will definitely not accept the characters < > , *. Although 1-2-3 separates the file name from the three-letter extension, it does not accept the . (period) within the file name. For example, 1-2-3 will not accept the file name SALES1.1.TXT

2. File names may not contain blanks.

3. Lowercase letters are automatically converted to uppercase in file names.

Although you determine the eight-character name, 1-2-3 creates the extension automatically according to the type of file you are handling. The three possible file extensions are

.WK1 For worksheet files

.PRN For print files

.PIC For graph files

NEW WITH

R2

Experienced 1-2-3 users should note that Release 2 uses .WK1 as a file extension for worksheets rather than .WKS, used in previous releases. This difference allows 1-2-3 to distinguish between worksheets written by different releases and to prevent previous 1-2-3 releases from loading worksheets written by Release 2.

Release 2 will easily read your older worksheets with .WKS extensions, but will write them as new files with .WK1 extensions when the worksheet is saved. If you want to run .WK1 files with earlier versions of 1-2-3, you will need to use the Translate utility, discussed later in this chapter.

NEW WITH

R2

In addition to creating files with the .WK1, .PRN, and .PIC extensions, 1-2-3 Release 2 lets you supply your own extension. To create a file name with your extension, enter the file name according to the rules listed above, enter a period, and then add an extension of one to three characters. Please note that any file name with your own extension will not be displayed in the lists of .WK1, .PIC, or .PRN files. The /File Retrieve command, for example, will retrieve all .WK1 files but not files with your special extensions. To retrieve your special file, type the file name after the Name of file to retrieve: B:\ prompt.

If you would like to see a list of your own files, the /File List Other command will list all files including .WK1, .PRN, .PIC, with your own extended files. Although not fail-safe, creating file names with your own extensions can provide a level of security for those files to which you want to limit user access. Additional ways of limiting access to files are provided by Release 2's password system, described in the next section on simple storage and retrieval.

Keep in mind that only one worksheet exists in a file, and that you can work on a worksheet only when it is in main memory.

Simple Storage and Retrieval

The basic file functions of storing and retrieving entire files are easy to perform in 1-2-3. The /File Save command allows you to save an entire worksheet in a file on disk.

When you enter this command, 1-2-3 will try to help you by supplying a list of the current worksheet files on the disk. You can either point to one of the entries or enter a new file name. To enter a new file name, you must use the rules previously expressed. 1-2-3 Release 2 will automatically supply a .WK1 extension, as shown in figure 7.1.

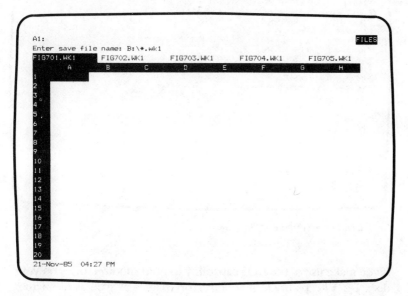

Fig. 7.1. File name list during /File Save.

The /File Save command makes an exact copy of the current worksheet, including all of the formats, range names, and settings you have specified.

To call a file back into main memory from disk, use the /File Retrieve command. Again, 1-2-3 will display a list of all the file names currently on disk.

Whenever you have to choose a file name, 1-2-3 helps you with the file commands by displaying a list of the files on the current drive and directory. If the file name you want is in the list, you can select it by pointing. Otherwise, you can type in the file name you want.

You can get a full screen display of the file names by pressing the Name key (F3) when 1-2-3 is displaying a list of file names. For example, if you are at the display in figure 7.1 and press the Name key, you get the full screen display of names shown in figure 7.2. You will also see the date, time of creation, and file size in bytes of each file highlighted by the cursor.

```
A1:                                                                         FILES
Enter save file name: B:\*.wk1
            FIG701.WK1     11/19/85        12:04            1438
FIG701.WK1      FIG702.WK1     FIG703.WK1     FIG704.WK1     FIG705.WK1
FIG706.WK1      FIG707.WK1     FIG801.WK1     FIG802.WK1     FIG803.WK1
FIG804.WK1      FIG806A.WK1    FIG806B.WK1    FIG901.WK1     FIG902.WK1
FIG903.WK1      FIG904.WK1     FIG905.WK1     FIG906.WK1     FIG907.WK1
FIG908.WK1      FIG909.WK1     FIG910.WK1     FIG911.WK1     FIG912.WK1
FIG913.WK1      FIG914.WK1     FIG915.WK1     FIG916.WK1     FIG917.WK1
FIG918.WK1      FIG919.WK1     FIG920.WK1     FIG921.WK1     FIG922.WK1
FIG923.WK1      FIG924.WK1     FIG925.WK1     FIG927.WK1     FIG928.WK1
FIG929.WK1      FIG930.WK1     FIG931.WK1     FIG932.WK1     FIG933.WK1
FIG934.WK1      FIG935.WK1     FIG936.WK1     FIG937.WK1     TEST01.WK1
TEST02.WK1      TESTME.WK1




21-Nov-85   04:28 PM
```

Fig. 7.2. Full screen display of file names.

If you make use of the DOS capability to hold subdirectories on your disk, 1-2-3 keeps track of subdirectory names as well as file names (especially relevant for hard disk users). These names are displayed in the current directory with the subdirectories distinguished from files by the backslash (\ ) after the subdirectory name.

If you point to a subdirectory name and press Enter during a 1-2-3 file command, 1-2-3 switches to that subdirectory and displays a list of its files. You then can specify a file name in that subdirectory.

If you want to access a file on a different drive or in a directory that is not a subdirectory of the current directory, press the Esc key to erase the current drive and directory specification. Then enter the specification for the drive and directory you want. Also, in all the 1-2-3 file commands except /Worksheet Global Default Directory, the default pathname appears on the control panel in EDIT mode so that you can edit the file specification just like any label entry.

Some valid file names, drive, and directory specifications are

B:\SAMPLE1.WK1   Worksheet file on drive B:

C:\123\   Worksheet file in subdirectory
SAMPLE1.WK1   123 on Drive C:

C:\123\DATA\   List of all .PIC files in subdirectory DATA
*.PIC   of subdirectory 123 on Drive C:. 1-2-3
                   displays the list and waits for you to select
                   a specific file name.

A:*.*   List of all files on Drive A:. 1-2-3 displays all
                   file names and waits for you to select a
                   specific file name.

If you want to find out more about DOS pathnames and subdirectories, you can consult *PC DOS User's Guide* or *MS-DOS User's Guide,* both by Chris DeVoney, QUE Corporation, 1984. See also Chris DeVoney's *Using PC DOS Version 3*, Que Corporation, 1986.

Password Protection

NEW WITH
R2

Release 2 lets you protect your files with its password protection system. You can create a password with the /File Save command so that your file can be retrieved with only the exact password.

To create a password, begin by selecting the /File Save command. At the Enter save file name: B:*.wk1 prompt, type the file name, leave a space, then type *p*. After pressing Enter, a password prompt will appear; type your password and press Enter again. 1-2-3 will then ask you to Verify password; type the password once more. Any difference between the first and second passwords will result in nonacceptance.

If you enter your password correctly, the worksheet will appear. However, if you enter the password incorrectly, the words Incorrect password will appear in the lower left corner of the screen, and the mode indicator will flash ERROR. Press Esc to return to a blank worksheet.

1-2-3 will accept any LICS character up to 15 characters long for a password. You need to be careful, however, because 1-2-3 will accept the password only in the exact uppercase or lowercase letters you entered. If, for example, you entered the code pdfund as your password, 1-2-3 would not retrieve the file if you typed *PDfund* or *PDFUND* or

NEW WITH

R2

any combination of uppercase and lowercase letters. Be sure not to forget your password.

You can delete a password by retrieving the file with the password you want to delete. Then, when you are ready to save the file, select the /File Save command. When the

```
Enter save file name: B:\*.wk1[PASSWORD PROTECTED]
```

prompt appears, press the backspace key to erase [PASSWORD PRO-TECTED]. Proceed with the /File Save operation, and 1-2-3 will save the file without the password.

To change a password, complete the first three steps for deleting the password name. After you have deleted [PASSWORD PROTECTED], press the space bar, type *p*, and press Enter. At this point, 1-2-3 will prompt you for a new password and ask you to verify it. Once you have completed these steps and saved the file, the new password will be stored.

Partial Loads and Saves

There will be times when you want to store only part of a worksheet (a range of cells, for instance) in a separate file on disk. For example, you may want to extract outlays from an expense report or revenues from an income statement. One of the best uses for a partial storage is breaking up worksheet files that are too large to be stored on a single disk.

With the /File Xtract command, you can save part of the worksheet file, either the formulas existing in a range of cells or the current values of the formulas in the range, depending on the option you select. Both options create a worksheet file that can be reloaded into 1-2-3 with the /File Retrieve command. If you decide to save only the current values, however, the resulting worksheet file will contain numbers but no formulas. Selecting the formula option creates a file with all of the formulas intact.

The /File Xtract command also requires that you specify the portion of the worksheet you want to save. The range to be saved can be as small as a cell or as large as the entire worksheet.

When the Values option is used with the /File Xtract command, you can "lock" the current values in a worksheet. To lock the values, issue the command and select the Values option. Next, specify the entire worksheet as the range to extract. This will save the current values stored in the worksheet. You can think of this as taking a snapshot of the current worksheet. The new values-only file can be reloaded into the worksheet and printed or graphed.

Another function that you will want to perform is making copies of certain ranges of cells from other worksheets and placing them into strategic spots in the current worksheet. For example, if you work for a large firm, you may want to combine several divisions' balance sheets and income statements in one all-encompassing worksheet.

A simple technique for accomplishing this kind of consolidation is to start with and keep a copy of an "empty master." You will always have an empty master ready when it is time to perform a consolidation. When you start with an empty master, you can copy the first divisional worksheet onto the master, leaving the original copy of the divisional worksheet untouched.

Copying a range of cells can be helpful also when you want to combine quarterly data into a yearly statement. Again, the formats must be compatible, and you will benefit by keeping an empty master.

The command used to combine data in the preceding examples is /File Combine. This command gives you the following menu options:

Copy
To pull in an entire worksheet or a named range and have the new contents write over the corresponding cells in the existing worksheet. Cells in the worksheet that correspond to empty cells in the file or range being combined are not affected. (There is an important distinction here between empty cells and cells containing a blank in the combine file.)

Add
Pulls in the values from an entire worksheet or a named range and adds these values to the corresponding cells in the current worksheet. The Add command affects only cells in the worksheet that are blank or contain numeric values. Cells containing formulas or labels are unchanged. Cells in the file being combined that contain labels or string formulas are not added.

Subtract
Pulls in an entire worksheet or a named range and subtracts the values from the corresponding cells in the current worksheet. When an existing cell is empty, the incoming value is subtracted from zero. Like Add, cells containing formulas or labels in

the current worksheet are unaffected, and cells from the worksheet being combined that contain labels or string formulas are not subtracted.

The specified worksheet or named range is combined into the current worksheet, with the current position of the cursor as the upper right corner of the combine range. For example, if the cursor is at cell A1, the specified worksheet or named range will be combined into the current worksheet, starting at cell A1. If the cursor is at cell AA100, the worksheet or range will be combined into the current worksheet, starting at cell AA100.

In the Copy command, if the worksheet or named range cells being combined contain formulas, the cell references in those formulas are adjusted relative to the cursor location where the worksheet or range is combined, including absolute cell references. After the combining is completed, the absolute cell references in cells that were combined into the current worksheet behave normally when you copy or move those cells.

Figures 7.3, 7.4, 7.5, and 7.6 show examples of the Copy and Add options. Figure 7.3 shows a worksheet that we created and stored on disk. Figure 7.4 shows a similar worksheet that is stored in 1-2-3's memory. Figure 7.5 shows the results of combining these two worksheets, using the Copy option with the cursor in A1. Figure 7.6 shows the results of combining these two worksheets with the Add option with the cursor in A1. The Subtract option is so much like the Add option that we did not include it here.

These three options are useful in combining worksheets. The /File Combine Add command is especially helpful because the command can be used to consolidate one worksheet with another. For example, /fca could be used by a business with several divisions to consolidate the income statements for each division into a company-wide statement.

Deleting Files

When you save files to disk, you may sometimes find that the disk is full. To let you know, 1-2-3 flashes the message Disk full in the lower left corner of the screen. You can then either swap disks or delete one or more of the current files occupying space on the disk.

There are two ways to delete stored files in 1-2-3. The first way is the /File Erase command. When you enter /fe, a menu prompt will ask

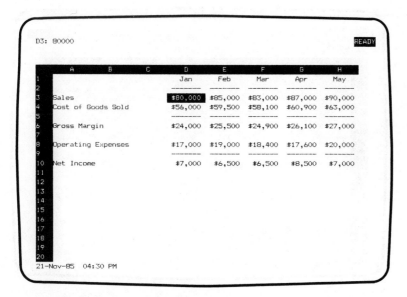

Fig. 7.3. Worksheet for /File Combine.

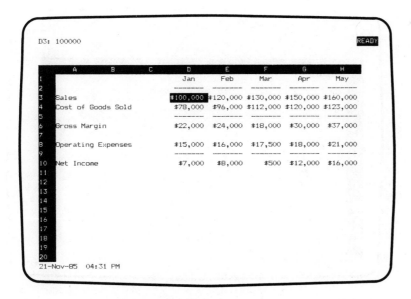

Fig. 7.4. Another worksheet for /File Combine.

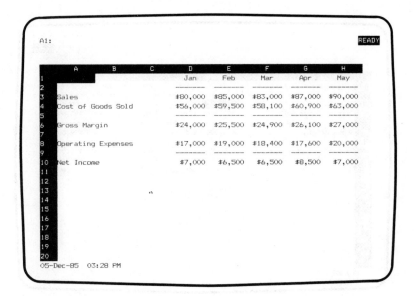

Fig. 7.5. Worksheet after /File Combine Copy.

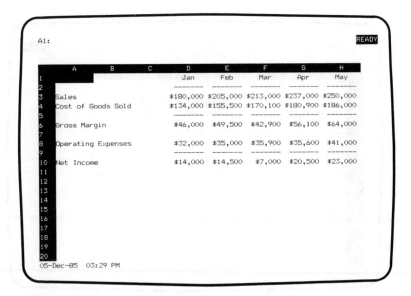

Fig. 7.6. Worksheet after /File Combine Add.

whether you want to erase a **Worksheet**, **Print**, **Graph**, or **Other** file. According to your choice (**W**, **P** or **G**), 1-2-3 will show you only .WK1 (created in Release 2) or .WKS (if created in 1 or 1A) files, .PRN files, or .PIC files, respectively. If you choose **Other**, 1-2-3 will list all files. You can point to the file you want erased, or type its name and press Enter.

Certain wildcard characters can be used with this command to display all the files of a certain type that are to be deleted. These are the same wildcard characters used for DOS and other commands throughout 1-2-3, and should look familiar.

* Matches the remaining characters of a file name. B* matches BOB, BARNEY, BOQUIST, etc.

? Matches all characters in a single position in a file name. B?RD matches BARD, BIRD, and BYRD, but not BURT.

A word of warning: Be careful when you use the /**File Erase** command. Once a file is deleted, the file cannot be recovered by conventional means. Always check and doublecheck that you really want to delete a file before you do so.

Another way to delete files is to use the /**System** command (discussed in Chapter 4) and the DOS DEL command. This method has the advantage of placing the full power of DOS at your command, but the disadvantage of requiring more time to suspend 1-2-3 execution, perform the DOS command, and return to 1-2-3.

SuperCalc users will recall that the command to format a single cell in SuperCalc is /fe. Because this same command in 1-2-3 begins the process of erasing a file, think twice before using the command to format a cell. There is a confirmation step to the /fe command in 1-2-3, but be careful.

NEW WITH
R2

Specifying a Drive

The /**Worksheet** **Global** **Default** **Directory** setting is normally drive B. This means that B is the active disk drive for storing and retrieving files. There may be times, however, when you will want to override this setting temporarily (for example, when drive B malfunctions, but you want to continue using 1-2-3). The /**File** **Directory** command lets you specify another drive for the duration of the current session.

Listing the Different Files

1-2-3 can list all the names of a certain type of file on the active drive and directory with the /File List command. The choices for file types are

Worksheet   Print   Graph   Other

Worksheet, Print, and **Graph** list the three types of 1-2-3 data files. The fourth choice, **Other,** lists all files of all types on the current drive and directory.

Which drive is the active drive depends on the /Worksheet Global Default Directory setting and whether that setting has been over-ridden by the /File Directory command. Normally, the active drive in a floppy disk system is drive B. A list of worksheet files might look like figure 7.7.

```
A1:                                                                    FILES
Name of files to list: B:\*.wk?
            FIG701.WK1      11/19/85       12:04          1438
FIG701.WK1      FIG702.WK1      FIG703.WK1      FIG704.WK1      FIG705.WK1
FIG706.WK1      FIG707.WK1      FIG801.WK1      FIG802.WK1      FIG803.WK1
FIG804.WK1      FIG806A.WK1     FIG806B.WK1     FIG901.WK1      FIG902.WK1
FIG903.WK1      FIG904.WK1      FIG905.WK1      FIG906.WK1      FIG907.WK1
FIG908.WK1      FIG909.WK1      FIG910.WK1      FIG911.WK1      FIG912.WK1
FIG913.WK1      FIG914.WK1      FIG915.WK1      FIG916.WK1      FIG917.WK1
FIG918.WK1      FIG919.WK1      FIG920.WK1      FIG921.WK1      FIG922.WK1
FIG923.WK1      FIG924.WK1      FIG925.WK1      FIG927.WK1      FIG928.WK1
FIG929.WK1      FIG930.WK1      FIG931.WK1      FIG932.WK1      FIG933.WK1
FIG934.WK1      FIG935.WK1      FIG936.WK1      FIG937.WK1      TEST01.WK1
TEST02.WK1      TESTME.WK1      TESTME.WKS


21-Nov-85   04:42 PM
```

Fig. 7.7. A list of 1-2-3 files with /File List.

Transferring Files

One thing to be applauded is Lotus's creation of different commands for interfacing 1-2-3 with outside programs, specifically the /File Import and /Print File Options Other Unformatted commands and the

Translation Utility. Although the kinds of files that can be transferred with these techniques are limited, this is only a minor setback because most files can be converted to the proper format one way or another. The following methods work well and with a few small exceptions are easy to use.

If you are an applications developer, Lotus provides you with an additional method of handling external files with 1-2-3's sequential file macro commands (see Chapter 12).

Transferring Files with /File Import

The /File Import command is used to copy standard ASCII files to specific locations in the current worksheet. .PRN (print) files are one example of standard ASCII text files created to print after the current 1-2-3 session. (.PRN files and their uses are covered in Chapter 8.) Other standard ASCII files include those produced by different word-processing and BASIC programs.

In the early versions of 1-2-3, the /File Import command was used to import records from dBASE to 1-2-3. In Release 2, dBASE files can be translated with the Translation Utility.

Transferring Standard ASCII Files

A standard ASCII text file with any extension can be transferred. Before you begin /File Import, position the cursor at the cell where you want the upper left corner of the imported file to be located. You then invoke the /File Import command with either Text or Numbers. These two options have quite different effects on the worksheet.

The Text designation causes 1-2-3 to create a separate left-justified label in the first cell of a new row for each line of imported text. In other words, everything in a line gets placed in just one worksheet cell that Lotus calls a "long label." By using the /Range Justify command on the newly created list of long labels, you can rearrange the list down a series of consecutive rows. (For more information on /Range Justify, see the "Text Processing" section of Chapter 5.)

Alternatively, the /Data Parse command can split up the contents of the long labels into separate cells based on a specified pattern. This method is useful for importing data from tabular reports you want to use in the spreadsheet.

In contrast to the Text option, where numbers are treated as text, the Numbers option treats numbers as numbers. The rules here are that only text enclosed in double quotation marks is valid, and that each valid item in a line must be placed in its own cell within a row.

Be aware that when the file items are imported into the worksheet, everything in the space they will occupy will be written over regardless of whether the Text or Numbers option is selected for /File Import. Be sure that there isn't anything important in the affected range of cells.

Transferring Files with the Translate Utility

The Translate Utility is used to import files from VisiCalc (in either VC or DIF format) and dBASE II or III into 1-2-3, and to export 1-2-3 files in DIF, dBASE II, and dBASE III formats. This feature provides good communication with VisiCalc and dBASE. The Translate Utility also provides translation capabilities between all of Lotus's products, allowing free interchange of worksheets between 1-2-3 Release 2 and Symphony, Jazz, and earlier releases of 1-2-3.

You can use the Translate Utility to import your VisiCalc files. From our experience, the transfer works well, with only a few minor hitches. If you are an advanced user, you may also want to export your 1-2-3 worksheet files in DIF format for use with other programs that can accept data in DIF format. Many presentation graphics packages accept data in DIF format. The Translate Utility allows you to take advantage of the more advanced statistical and plotting capabilities of these programs.

Transferring Records between dBASE and 1-2-3

NEW WITH
R2

Aside from the obvious advantage of 1-2-3's spreadsheet capability, the primary reason to transfer dBASE II or dBASE III records to or from 1-2-3 is that 1-2-3 has much faster and more easily implemented data sorting and querying capabilities. If a database is large, only a portion of it can be imported because of 1-2-3's limitation on worksheet size. For small to medium-sized files that will be sorted and accessed frequently (such as address lists, telephone numbers, personnel files, etc.), there is a real advantage to using 1-2-3 over dBASE II and dBASE III.

Lotus has put the Translate Utility to work in both directions. You can load a dBASE II or dBASE III database into 1-2-3, process the database, and then write the database back into dBASE to use with dBASE procedures and reports. Why would you want to do this? As you may already know, although dBASE is particularly good at finding and processing records one at a time, 1-2-3 is best at making changes to whole sets of records, using full-screen editing techniques; formulas; and block copy, move, insert, and delete commands. An experienced dBASE application developer may find these dBASE translation capabilities the most exciting part of 1-2-3 Release 2.

Translating from dBASE to 1-2-3

To translate a dBASE file to 1-2-3, you enter the Translate Utility and specify that you are translating from dBASE II or dBASE III to 1-2-3. Then you enter the drive, subdirectory or subdirectories, and file name of subdirectories, and file name of the 1-2-3 worksheet to be created from the dBASE data file (see fig. 7.8). The Translate Utility then quickly performs the translation.

NEW WITH
R2

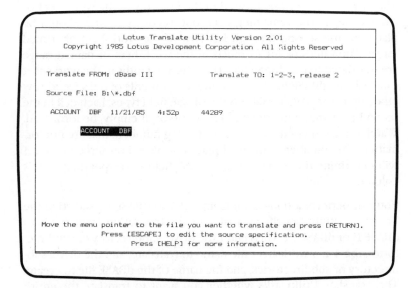

```
                Lotus Translate Utility   Version 2.01
        Copyright 1985 Lotus Development Corporation  All Rights Reserved


   Translate FROM: dBase III              Translate TO: 1-2-3, release 2

   Source File: B:\*.dbf

     ACCOUNT  DBF  11/21/85   4:52p     44289

          ACCOUNT   DBF







   Move the menu pointer to the file you want to translate and press [RETURN].
             Press [ESCAPE] to edit the source specification.
                   Press [HELP] for more information.
```

Fig. 7.8. Translating from dBASE III.

The translation is performed on dBASE records in the actual order they appear in the file; and only the first 8,191 records are translated. If you want the dBASE records from a file larger than 8,191 records or in some other order, you must sort or extract the records into another dBASE file before using the 1-2-3 Translate Utility.

The translation result is a 1-2-3 worksheet with one column for each field in the dBASE file. The first row of the worksheet holds the dBASE field names with column widths set to the widths of the dBASE fields. All the rows after the first row contain the data read from the dBASE file, one record per row, with the cells formatted according to the dBASE field specification. A dBASE character field changes to a 1-2-3 label, a dBASE numeric field translates to a number in fixed format, and a dBASE date field becomes a 1-2-3 date.

Translating from 1-2-3 to dBASE

NEW WITH

R2

You can translate an entire worksheet or just a named range in a worksheet to a dBASE II or III file. To translate a worksheet or named range to a dBASE file, the worksheet must be in a specific format, corresponding closely to the way a dBASE file is translated to a 1-2-3 worksheet.

The field names must be located in the first row of the worksheet or named range. The remaining data, one record per row, should be placed in the second through last row of the worksheet or named range. The values of any formulas in the worksheet or named range are translated to the dBASE file. The column widths in the worksheet establish the dBASE field widths; and the contents of the second row (the first row of data) establish the dBASE field types. Each cell in the second row, therefore, must hold a value or, if empty, be formatted. Watch out for second-row cells containing numbers that are not formatted. The number of decimal places displayed on screen in 1-2-3 will determine the format of the dBASE field corresponding to this column.

You can perform a translation from 1-2-3 to dBASE by selecting the Translate Utility, specifying that you are translating from 1-2-3 to dBASE II or dBASE III. Then enter the drive, subdirectory or subdirectories, the 1-2-3 worksheet file name to translate, and the drive, subdirectory or subdirectories, and file name of the dBASE file to create. The Translate Utility asks whether you want to translate the entire worksheet or just a named range, then quickly performs the translation. The Translate Utility does not build or update dBASE index files, so you must enter dBASE and rebuild any indexes after the translation is completed.

Lotus's Translate Utility offers a strong link between 1-2-3 worksheets and dBASE data files. A wish list for a perfect link would include direct links between the 1-2-3 worksheet and dBASE files by way of 1-2-3 commands. Ideally, these commands would allow you to create, index, and manipulate data in dBASE-formatted data files directly from within the 1-2-3 worksheet.

Conclusion

1-2-3's file commands allow you to perform the basic operations of saving, retrieving, and deleting entire files. Although all other spreadsheet programs also perform these operations, 1-2-3 has even more to offer. You can store and retrieve parts of files, produce a list of all the files currently on a disk, and even transfer files from other programs, such as VisiCalc and dBASE. All the file operations are effective and easy to use.

Conclusion

8

Printing Reports

1-2-3 gives you far more control over printing reports than earlier spreadsheet programs. With 1-2-3, you can set options to write directly to the printer from within the program, create a print file to be printed outside the program, print headers and footers that include the date and page numbers, print column or row headings on every page of a report, etc. With just a little investment of set-up time, you will discover many different print options to meet your needs. Of course, the 1-2-3 system defaults should prove sufficient in most cases.

The best way to describe the print options and functions is to show how two different kinds of reports might be printed. The first report, the "Meatloaf Consumption Report," is simple. We are more interested in the figures on the nationwide meatloaf consumption projected over the next 12 months than in the format of the printed page. The only special care we will take printing this report is to print all 12 months on one standard 8 1/2-by-11-inch page. Figure 8.1 shows a portion of this report.

The second report is much more complex and multifaceted. Our "Bank Loan Report" contains several pages of financial schedules with comments interjected throughout the report. In addition, this document goes to the Loan Officer at the bank, so the report must make a good impression with attractively printed features such as headers, footers, and so on. Figure 8.2 shows a portion of this report.

When and How To Print

Your first choice is whether to print your file now or later. If you are working without a printer on your system, you may not know how to

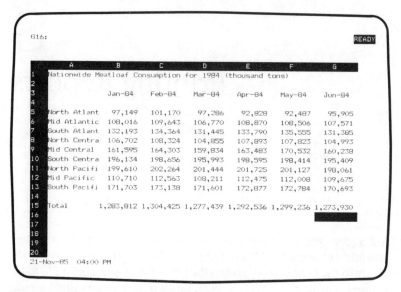

Fig. 8.1. The Meatloaf Consumption Worksheet.

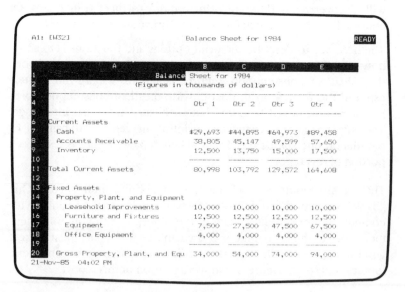

Fig. 8.2. A portion of the Bank Loan Worksheet.

control the different print options such as margins, character size, etc. If you have a printer but want to wait to print, you can set up a file to be printed when the 1-2-3 session is over. The **/Print Printer** command takes you directly to the printer in the current 1-2-3 session; whereas the /**Print File** command stores output in a file to be printed later with the DOS TYPE command or a special printing routine. The /**Print Printer** and /**Print File** commands are the basis or "root" of all other print commands.

Files created with the /**Print File** command root have a .PRN file name extension. Portions of .PRN files can be called back into 1-2-3 from disk and entered into specific locations in a worksheet with the /**File Import** command. Importing .PRN files is not as straightforward as it sounds, however. (Chapter 7 provides more information on importing .PRN files.)

Suppose that you want an immediate printout of the Meatloaf Consumption Report on the dot-matrix printer currently attached to your system, or that you want to wait to print the Bank Loan Report on a letter-quality printer after all of the related financial schedules are collected. In either case, you must begin by accessing the /**Print** menu.

The /Print Menu

The /**Print** menu appears after you choose /**Print Printer** or /**Print File** with the following choices:

   Range Line Page Options Clear Align Go Quit

Whenever you perform one of these functions, the menu returns you to the **Print** menu. Be careful not to press the Enter key again at this point, unless you want the same function to be executed a second time. It is particularly disconcerting to return from printing the worksheet with the **Go** option only to press Enter again accidentally and print the file a second time. If this occurs, press Ctrl-Break to stop the print. The **Print** menu is an example of a "sticky" menu because you can leave the menu only by selecting the **Quit** option or pressing the Esc key.

The technique of selecting **Quit** immediately after **Go** is handy. This technique will place the command in the keyboard buffer and execute the command after control is regained from the printing process.

Designating a Print Range

A preliminary step in printing any report is specifying the range of cells to be printed. The command used to designate a range is /**Print File Range**. Multiple ranges (as those in the Bank Loan Report) corresponding to different schedules and notes must be designated and printed one at a time.

Because we chose the /Print File command root for the Bank Loan Report, the ranges will be appended one after another in the file. 1-2-3 lets you control the format of each range that is written. This is helpful when you want to control the printing of each schedule. Each time a range is designated and print options are changed, you must enter Go from the /Print File menu to send the range to the print file. Go is also required to send a range to the printer.

If, on the other hand, you are printing a large range like that of the Meatloaf Consumption Report, you will want to use the special function keys, PgUp, PgDn, End, to designate ranges. One particularly useful sequence for pointing to a print range, when the range is the entire sheet, is End followed by Home. This sequence is a special GOTO command to locate the cursor at the lowest rightmost cell in the worksheet—what Lotus calls the end of the "active area." This saves your having to move the cursor down manually or remember the appropriate cell address for a GoTo (F5).

Setting Print Options

Aside from designating print ranges, the only other printing-reports task that requires explanation is setting print options. Several print options will be designated for the Bank Loan Report, whereas only a few options will be used for the Meatloaf Consumption Report (to get everything on one page).

By selecting Options from the Print menu, you can choose from the following selections:

Header   Footer   Margins   Borders   Setup   Pg-Length
   Other   Quit

Setting Headers and Footers

For the Bank Loan Report, the next step after a print range is designated is to set the Header and Footer options. These options allow you to specify up to 240 characters of text in each of three positions—left, center, and right—in the header and footer. In reality, however, you should use only enough text to fit on the printed page.

Although all extra features of the text could be entered manually, 1-2-3 offers special characters to control page numbers, the current date, and text placement in the header and footer lines. These special characters are

\#   Automatically prints page numbers starting with 1

@   Automatically includes the current date in the
form 29-Jun-84. Use the date you entered when you
loaded DOS—that is, the current date.

| Headers and footers have three separate segments:
left-justified, centered, and right-justified. Use
this character to separate one segment from
another.

Figure 8.6, at the end of this chapter, shows how the **Header** and **Footer** options are set up with these special characters for the Bank Loan Report.

Keep in mind two important notes about headers and footers. First, 1-2-3 always places two blank lines below the header and two above the footer line. This happens even when you do not specify a header or footer, and, on an 11-inch page, limits the maximum number of lines to 60 out of 66 (at 6 lines per inch). Second, if you use the special character # for page numbers and you want to print a report a second time before you leave the **Print** menu, you must **Clear** the **Print** Options and respecify them before the second printing. (See the "Clearing Print Options" section later in this chapter.) Otherwise, the page counter will pick up where it left off.

Setting Margins

Now that the headers and footers are set, the next logical step is to set the margins of the two reports. The **Margins** option overrides the /Worksheet **Global Default** settings for the top, bottom, left, and right margins of the page. The /Worksheet **Global Default** margin settings from the edge of the paper are

Left	4
Right	76
Top	2
Bottom	2

The /**Print**<**Printer** or **File**>**Options Margins** command lets you override these settings temporarily for printing both the Meatloaf Consumption and Bank Loan Reports. An added note: The /**Worksheet**

Global Default Printer command lets you change the default margins and other printer settings permanently. Be sure to use the /Worksheet Global Default Update command to make your changes permanent.

For the Meatloaf Consumption Report, you will want everything on an 8 1/2-by-11-inch page. But the 11 active columns of data in the worksheet combine to form a total worksheet width of 131 characters. The only way to fit everything on one page is to use compressed print on a dot-matrix printer. Compressed print provides up to 136 characters on a line; and, with 0 characters for the left margin and a worksheet width of 131, you will stay just within the limit of 136. The right margin should be set at 136, and a Setup string should be sent to the printer. (See the discussion of Setup later in this chapter.)

An alternative to the compressed print would be to use the original defaults of a left margin of 0 and a right margin of 80. You could let the printer print up to 80 columns on one page, using pica or elite type, then continue on to the next page with the rest of the report. This solution is not ideal because the report is broken into two parts.

For the Bank Loan Report, the top and bottom margins are set at 5 for the "Balance Sheet for 1984" schedule, the first schedule to be printed in the report. This margin setting is the distance from the top of the page to the header and from the bottom of the page to the footer and should give us a good appearance.

The left margin is set at 4 for this report, and the right margin at 76. You may have to try several different combinations to get the setup you want.

Repeating Headers on Multipage Printouts

One of 1-2-3's special features lets you print column and/or row headings on a multipage printout, such as the Bank Loan Report. For example, if you want to print a comparative income statement with several columns of monthly figures that carry over to more than one page, you can have the row headings that usually occur in the first column of the first page (Sales, Gross Margin, etc.) repeated on each page. The /Print<Printer or File>Options Borders Columns command repeats the row headings.

You can also print nonadjacent rows with the Borders Rows option. To show how this option works, suppose you want to separate assets from liabilities when you print the Balance Sheet for the Bank Loan

Report. To print the assets, you would first issue the /**Print File Options Borders Rows** command and use A1..A5 as the ROWS range. This range corresponds to the main captions on the Balance Sheet. Next, you would specify A6..A31 as the print range. Notice that this range does not include the main captions. If you include the main captions in the print range, they would be printed twice on the page. To print the liabilities portion with the main captions, leave the **Borders Rows** range as it is and specify A33..E50 as the print range. Figure 8.3 shows the liabilities portion of the Balance Sheet with the repeated headings.

```
                      Balance Sheet for 1984
                  (Figures in thousands of dollars)
---------------------------------------------------------------------
                              Qtr 1     Qtr 2     Qtr 3     Qtr 4
                            ---------------------------------------------
Current Liabilities
  Accounts Payable          $18,750   $20,625   $22,500   $26,250
  Notes Payable                       20,000    40,000    60,000
  Income Taxes Payable        4,065     6,321     7,632     9,805
                            --------  --------  --------  --------
Total Current Liabilities     22,815    46,946    70,132    96,055

Noncurrent Liabilities
  Long-Term Debt             20,000    18,000    16,000    14,000
                            --------  --------  --------  --------
Total Liabilities            42,815    64,946    86,132   110,055

Common Stock, $1.00 Par Value 50,000   50,000    50,000    50,000

Retained Earnings            16,394    35,357    58,251    87,664
                            --------  --------  --------  --------
Total Liabilities and Equity $109,209 $150,303 $194,383 $247,719
                            ========  ========  ========  ========
```

Fig. 8.3. Liabilities portion of the Balance Sheet.

There are two things to watch for when you use the **Borders** option. First, you should not go to the /**Print<Printer** or **File>Options Borders<Rows or Columns>** function in the command menu unless you actually want borders to be printed. If you go there by accident, the cell pointed to by the cell pointer will be entered for either **Rows** or **Columns**, depending on which one you selected. If this happens, you can enter /**Print<Printer** or **File>Options Clear Borders** to remove the selection.

The second thing to watch out for is the possible duplication of the first column on the first page. When you repeat column headers, you usually want the first column of the first page to be printed on subsequent pages. However, if you specify that column as the border before you print the first page, you will get double first columns on the first page. To use this command properly, print a range corresponding to the first page without specifying a border, then specify the first column of the first page as the border for subsequent pages.

The Borders option is not used in printing the Meatloaf Consumption Report because everything is on one page. The Columns feature is convenient, however, for some of the reports and schedules in the Bank Loan Report, where repetition of the row headings is necessary from one page to another.

Another method of printing nonadjacent columns together in a report is to use the /Worksheet Column Hide command to suppress the display of the intervening columns. The hidden columns will also not be printed.

Sending a Setup String to the Printer

Another print option that we use in our report examples is 1-2-3's ability to pass a setup string to the printer. This option controls the compressed printing for the Meatloaf Consumption Report.

The Setup option sends a string of up to 39 characters to the printer. The string is sent every time you enter Go from the Print menu.

All printers are different, so you will have to look carefully at the manual to see what is required for your printer. The string is made up of backslashes (\ ) followed by the three-digit decimal equivalent of special characters in ASCII code. For example, to initiate compressed print on an Epson dot-matrix printer, you would use the string \015. It will be used in printing the Meatloaf Consumption Report. You must do the actual translating of the appropriate ASCII codes into 1-2-3's \nnn format yourself, using the "Printer Control Codes" appendix in the back of the *1-2-3 Manual*.

Like the other printing Options commands, the Setup string is a temporary override of a /Worksheet Global Default setting. (For a more detailed description of this option, go to the *1-2-3 Manual* with your printer manual in hand and experiment.) If you don't expect to use your printer's special features and just want regular printing, then don't worry about this command.

Remember that if you are using compressed print, you should change the right margin to get the full 136 characters. Otherwise, you may not get all of the columns to print on one page.

Printer Control within the Worksheet

1-2-3 also gives you the ability to embed within the worksheet printer-control strings that will take effect when the cell containing the printer commands is printed. The /Worksheet Page command inserts a new row followed by a page-break command above the cursor (see the next section).

Another, more general, method of embedding printer-control strings in the worksheet is to enter into a cell a label consisting of two vertical bars (||) followed by the desired printer-command string. (These printer-command strings are the same as the printer-setup string.) Do not place a label prefix before the first vertical bar.

Suppose, for example, that you want to switch from normal text to enhanced text to emphasize a portion of your printout. You can do this on an Epson or compatible printer by placing the string *||\027E* in the first cell of the row before the rows to be enhanced, and *||\027F* in the first cell in the row after the last row to be enhanced.

Both methods of placing printer controls in the worksheet require that the cell with the printer control must be the leftmost cell in the partial row within the range being printed to keep from printing the printer-control string as a label. Also, because nothing else in the row containing the printer-control string will be printed, place any printer-control strings in blank rows within your print range.

Setting the Page Length

The /Worksheet Global Default for the number of lines printed on one page is 66. You can change this number temporarily to any number between 20 and 100 with the *Page-Length* option. This option is useful when you use special forms, paper, or type sizes. Because we are using standard 8 1/2-by-11-inch paper for both reports, however, we will let this option default to 66 in both cases.

Release 2's /Worksheet Page command enables you to enter your own page breaks within the worksheet and, therefore, control where you want to begin printing a new page. To enter a page break, first move the cursor to column A and then to one row below where you want the page break to occur. Next, select the /Worksheet Page command and press Enter. 1-2-3 will insert a new blank row containing a page break symbol (::) in column A. Any data in the row containing the page break symbol will not be printed.

Two procedures can help you avoid problems when you use the /Worksheet Page command.

1. Enter page break symbols right before you print or create a print file.

2. Delete page break symbols right after printing or creating a print file.

To erase a page break symbol, use the /Range Erase command. /Worksheet Delete Row will then delete the blank row created by the /Worksheet Page command. If you use /Worksheet Delete Row, remember that all data within the row will be erased along with the page break symbol.

When you use the /Worksheet Page command, keep in mind the following effects of using the command with the /Print Printer Options Page-Length command. The /Worksheet Page command does not override the /Print Printer Options Page-Length command whenever the page-length setting is less than the number of rows between the beginning of a print range and a page break, or rows between page breaks. If, for example, you enter a page break in row 72 and your /Print Printer Options Page-Length is 65, a new page will begin in both places. On the other hand, /Worksheet Page will override the Page-Length command whenever the page-length setting is greater than the number of rows between the beginning of a print range and page break symbol or between page break symbols.

The /Worksheet Page command will also override the command for suppressing page breaks—the /Print Printer Options Other Unformatted command. Therefore, even when you have selected this command, new pages will begin wherever a page break symbol is located in column A.

Printing Cell Formulas

Another advantage that 1-2-3 has over earlier spreadsheet programs is that you can print cell contents in more than one way. For our two reports, the contents will be printed just as they are displayed on the screen, but we will also print a one-line-per-cell listing of the cell formulas for the Bank Loan Report.

The command /Print<Printer or File>Options Other controls the way cell formulas are printed. The choices that you are given when you enter this command are

As-Displayed   Cell-Formulas   Formatted   Unformatted

The Cell-Formulas option is used to create the one-line-per-cell listing of the contents of a worksheet. Although this option is often very convenient for debugging, it is used here to document the cell formulas in the Bank Loan Report, in case the Loan Officer asks us a tough question about how we got our numbers. Figure 8.4 shows the Cell-Formulas listing of the Bank Loan Report.

The As-Displayed option works with Cell-Formulas to reverse the Cell-Formulas option. It returns to printing the format on the screen.

The other two options, Formatted and Unformatted, work together. The Unformatted option suppresses page breaks, headers, and footers. This option is also used to create /Print Files for input to programs independent of 1-2-3, such as print routines, database management systems, or word-processing programs. The Formatted option returns things to normal. (These commands will not be used in printing our two reports.)

Clearing Print Options

If we wanted to print our two reports together one after the other, we would need a way to clear the different print options and settings between printing the reports. The Clear option on the Print menu allows you to eliminate all, or just a portion, of the print options that you chose earlier. The choices displayed are

    All   Range   Borders   Format

You can clear every print option, including the print range, by selecting All, or you can be more specific by using the other choices.

Range	Removes the previous print range specification
Borders	Cancels Columns and Rows specified as borders
Format	Clears out Margins, Page-Length, and Setup string settings. Everything that is Cleared returns to the default setting. This option is very useful when you make mistakes or want to print reports with different formats one after the other.

Controlling the Printer

1-2-3 gives you a great deal of control over the printer from within the program itself. In fact, you get so much control that you hardly ever have to touch the printer, except to turn it on just before printing a report and to turn it off when you are done.

This feature will be used to great advantage in printing the Bank Loan Report shown in figure 8.4. Between some of the different schedules and text to print for this report, we will need to space down several lines. The /**Print Printer Line** command makes the printer skip a line each time the command is entered. This command will be used several times in a row to skip between some of our schedules.

We will often need to skip to a new page. The command to do this is /**Print Printer Page**. Like the **Line** command, the **Page** command causes the printer to skip to a new page each time you enter the command. When **Page** is used at the end of a printing session, the footer will be printed on the last page. If you **Quit** from the /**Print** menu before issuing the **Page** command, you won't get the last footer.

Finally, when we start printing the report, we will need a way to signal to the printer where the top of the page is. The command used to align the page is /**Print Printer Align**. Again, this command saves you from having to touch the printer control buttons.

The **Go** command must be entered from the **Print** menu to start the printer. (This command also allows you to send a range to a /**Print File**.)

If you want to interrupt the printing of a report in midstream, simply hold down the Ctrl key and simultaneously press the Break key. It may take some time for the print buffer to clear, depending on its size, but the print menu will appear almost immediately. In the meantime, you can perform another menu function.

Now that you understand how to set print options, let's take a look, first of all, at the commands that were used to do the printing. The commands used to print the Meatloaf Consumption Report were

/**Print Printer Range** A1..M15
        Options Margins Right 136~
             Setup \015~
             Quit
    Go
    Quit

```
A1: [W32] '                    Balance Sheet for 1984
A2: [W32] '              (Figures in thousands of dollars)
A3: [W32] \-
B3: \-
C3: \-
D3: \-
E3: \-                                B20: @SUM(B15..B19)
B4: ^Qtr 1                            C20: @SUM(C15..C19)
C4: ^Qtr 2                            D20: @SUM(D15..D19)
D4: ^Qtr 3                            E20: @SUM(E15..E19)
E4: ^Qtr 4                            A21: [W32] '   Accumulated Depreciation
A5: [W32] \-                          B21: 6700
B5: \-                                C21: 8400
C5: \-                                D21: 10100
D5: \-                                E21: 11800
E5: \-                                B22: "--------
A6: [W32] 'Current Assets            C22: "--------
A7: [W32] '  Cash                    D22: "--------
B7: (C0) 29693                        E22: "--------
C7: (C0) 44895                        A23: [W32] '   Net P, P, and E
D7: (C0) 64973                        B23: +B20-B21
E7: (C0) 89458                        C23: +C20-C21
A8: [W32] '   Accounts Receivable    D23: +D20-D21
B8: 38805                             E23: +E20-E21
C8: 45147                             A25: [W32] '   Deposits
D8: 49599                             B25: 611
E8: 57650                             C25: 611
A9: [W32] '    Inventory             D25: 611
B9: 12500                             E25: 611
C9: 13750                             A26: [W32] '   Other
D9: 15000                             B26: 300
E9: 17500                             C26: 300
B10: "--------                        D26: 300
C10: "--------                        E26: 300
D10: "--------                        B27: "--------
E10: "--------                        C27: "--------
A11: [W32] 'Total Current Assets     D27: "--------
B11: @SUM(B7..B10)                    E27: "--------
C11: @SUM(C7..C10)                    A28: [W32] 'Total Fixed Assets
D11: @SUM(D7..D10)                    B28: +B26+B25+B23
E11: @SUM(E7..E10)                    C28: +C26+C25+C23
A13: [W32] 'Fixed Assets             D28: +D26+D25+D23
A14: [W32] '  P, P, and E            E28: +E26+E25+E23
A15: [W32] '     Leasehold Improvements  A30: [W32] 'Total Assets
B15: 10000                            B30: (C0) +B28+B11
C15: 10000                            C30: (C0) +C28+C11
D15: 10000                            D30: (C0) +D28+D11
E15: 10000                            E30: (C0) +E28+E11
A16: [W32] '     Furniture and Fixtures  B31: "=======
B16: 12500                            C31: "=======
C16: 12500                            D31: "=======
D16: 12500                            E31: "=======
E16: 12500                            A33: [W32] 'Current Liabilities
A17: [W32] '     Equipment           A34: [W32] '  Accounts Payable
B17: 7500                             B34: (C0) 18750
C17: 27500                            C34: (C0) 20625
D17: 47500                            D34: (C0) 22500
E17: 67500                            E34: (C0) 26250
A18: [W32] '     Office Equipment    A35: [W32] '   Notes Payable
B18: 4000                             C35: 20000
C18: 4000                             D35: 40000
D18: 4000                             E35: 60000
E18: 4000                             A36: [W32] '   Income Taxes Payable
B19: "--------                        B36: 4065
C19: "--------                        C36: 6321
D19: "--------                        D36: 7632
E19: "--------                        E36: 9805
A20: [W32] '  Gross P, P, and E      B37: "--------
```

```
C37:  "--------              A45: [W32] 'Common Stock, $1.00 Par Value
D37:  "--------              B45: 50000
E37:  "--------              C45: 50000
A38: [W32] 'Total Current Liabilities   D45: 50000
B38: @SUM(B33..B37)          E45: 50000
C38: @SUM(C33..C37)          A47: [W32] 'Retained Earnings
D38: @SUM(D33..D37)          B47: +B30-B43-B45
E38: @SUM(E33..E37)          C47: +C30-C43-C45
A40: [W32] 'Noncurrent Liabilities   D47: +D30-D43-D45
A41: [W32] '  Long-Term Debt      E47: +E30-E43-E45
B41: 20000                   B48: "--------
C41: 18000                   C48: "--------
D41: 16000                   D48: "--------
E41: 14000                   E48: "--------
B42:  "--------              A49: [W32] 'Total Liabilities and Equity
C42:  "--------              B49: (C0) +B47+B45+B43
D42:  "--------              C49: (C0) +C47+C45+C43
E42:  "--------              D49: (C0) +D47+D45+D43
A43: [W32] 'Total Liabilities   E49: (C0) +E47+E45+E43
B43: +B41+B38                B50: "========
C43: +C41+C38                C50: "========
D43: +D41+D38                D50: "========
E43: +E41+E38                E50: "========
```

Fig. 8.4. Cell formula listing of the Bank Loan Report.

The commands used to print the first schedule in the Bank Loan Report were

/Print Printer Range A1..E50~

        Options Header | Oltuna Manufacturing Company | @~

                Footer | Page #~

                Margins Top 5~

                Margins Bottom 5~

                Margins Left 4~

                Margins Right 76~

                Setup \027@~

                Quit

      Go

      Quit

Second, let's take a look at the actual reports as they appear when printed (see figs. 8.5A and 8.5B). The entire Meatloaf Consumption Report and the first page of the Bank Loan Report are shown.

Nationwide Meatloaf Consumption for 1982 (thousand tons)

	Jan-82	Feb-82	Mar-82	Apr-82	May-82	Jun-82	Jul-82	Aug-82	Sep-82	Oct-82	Nov-82	Dec-82
North Atlant	97,149	101,170	97,286	92,828	92,487	95,905	100,817	96,878	91,245	90,668	95,305	100,708
Mid Atlantic	108,016	109,643	106,770	108,870	108,506	107,571	109,316	105,167	107,825	107,022	105,767	108,464
South Atlant	132,193	134,364	131,445	133,790	135,555	131,385	133,315	130,887	132,475	135,524	131,107	131,607
North Centra	106,702	108,324	104,855	107,893	107,823	104,993	106,696	103,959	107,747	106,317	104,717	106,563
Mid Central	161,595	164,303	159,834	163,483	170,532	160,238	162,598	158,757	163,406	168,778	159,532	162,132
South Centra	196,134	198,656	195,993	198,595	198,414	195,409	196,920	195,820	197,906	198,025	193,700	195,091
North Pacifi	199,610	202,264	201,444	201,725	201,127	198,061	201,726	200,604	200,530	199,497	197,819	200,327
Mid Pacific	110,710	112,563	108,211	112,475	112,008	109,675	112,386	106,346	111,219	111,842	109,426	112,160
South Pacifi	171,703	173,138	171,601	172,877	172,784	170,693	171,385	169,821	171,307	172,541	169,363	170,508
Total	1,283,812	1,304,425	1,277,439	1,292,536	1,299,236	1,273,930	1,295,159	1,268,239	1,283,660	1,290,214	1,266,736	1,287,560

Fig. 8.5A. The Meatloaf Consumption Report.

Ol Tuna Manufacturing Company   21-Nov-85

Balance Sheet for 1984
(Figures in thousands of dollars)

	Qtr 1	Qtr 2	Qtr 3	Qtr 4
Current Assets				
Cash	$29,693	$44,895	$64,973	$89,458
Accounts Receivable	38,805	45,147	49,599	57,650
Inventory	12,500	13,750	15,000	17,500
Total Current Assets	80,998	103,792	129,572	164,608
Fixed Assets				
P, P, and E				
Leasehold Improvements	10,000	10,000	10,000	10,000
Furniture and Fixtures	12,500	12,500	12,500	12,500
Equipment	7,500	27,500	47,500	67,500
Office Equipment	4,000	4,000	4,000	4,000
Gross P, P, and E	34,000	54,000	74,000	94,000
Accumulated Depreciation	6,700	8,400	10,100	11,800
Net P, P, and E	27,300	45,600	63,900	82,200
Deposits	611	611	611	611
Other	300	300	300	300
Total Fixed Assets	28,211	46,511	64,811	83,111
Total Assets	$109,209	$150,303	$194,383	$247,719
Current Liabilities				
Accounts Payable	$18,750	$20,625	$22,500	$26,250
Notes Payable		20,000	40,000	60,000
Income Taxes Payable	4,065	6,321	7,632	9,805
Total Current Liabilities	22,815	46,946	70,132	96,055
Noncurrent Liabilities				
Long-Term Debt	20,000	18,000	16,000	14,000
Total Liabilities	42,815	64,946	86,132	110,055
Common Stock, $1.00 Par Value	50,000	50,000	50,000	50,000
Retained Earnings	16,394	35,357	58,251	87,664
Total Liabilities and Equity	$109,209	$150,303	$194,383	$247,719

Fig. 8.5B. The first page of the Bank Loan Report.

9
Creating and
Displaying Graphs

A picture tells me at a glance what it takes dozens of pages of a book to expound.

—Turgenev

Next to the spreadsheet, graphics is the most-used element of 1-2-3. The integration of graphics with 1-2-3's exceptional spreadsheet is a major step forward in the development of analysis software.

1-2-3's graphics are designed for quick and easy implementation. Because they are an integral part of the entire program, data can be represented graphically with almost no effort. There is no need to transfer data from one program to another to create a graph. Instead, you issue two simple commands, and—presto!—the graph is drawn. 1-2-3 also offers a number of graphics options that allow titles, labels, and legends to be inserted in the graph. A listing of all the graph creation and display commands can be found in the 1-2-3 menu map included in the back of this book.

Although 1-2-3 has a good set of basic graphics commands and adds a few bells and whistles, it does not offer the power or flexibility of some of the dedicated graphics programs. In other words, some graphics programs are more comprehensive than 1-2-3, just as some data management programs are more comprehensive than 1-2-3. But because 1-2-3's graphics are an integrated part of an entire management system, they offer far more than most stand-alone systems.

Since 1-2-3's introduction, several major computer magazines have carried articles that compared 1-2-3's graphics with stand-alone graphics packages. 1-2-3 has been rated favorably against, and sometimes even as outperforming, many of these packages. 1-2-3's graphics score highest in their ease of use and immediacy; data is taken directly from the spreadsheet and graphed. 1-2-3's graphics score lowest in their scope and variability; the program offers limited display options and graph types (what can be called "business" graphs).

If you require graphics principally for analysis and internal business use rather than for formal presentations, 1-2-3 may have all the power you will ever need.

The /Graph Command

In 1-2-3, graphs are created and formatted through the /Graph command, which is one of the commands on 1-2-3's main menu. When you type /G, the following menu will appear in the control panel:

Type XABCDEF Reset View Save Options Name Quit

1-2-3 offers five basic types of graphs:

Line
Bar
XY
Stacked-Bar
Pie

Types of Graphs
Bar Graphs

Suppose that you want to create a simple worksheet containing data about steel production in the Western countries in 1979, as shown in figure 9.1. You can create many interesting graphs that will help make this data more understandable. For example, you can make a simple bar graph to illustrate the data on U.S. steel production alone. This graph is illustrated in figure 9.2.

Making a Simple Bar Graph

Bar graphs are used to compare different sets of data. Typically, a bar graph consists of vertical bars that show value by height. To create a bar graph, first type /G to enter the /Graphics command. At this point, the Graph menu will appear in the control panel.

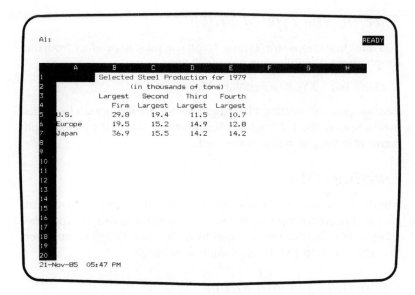

Fig. 9.1. Selected Steel Production data for 1979.

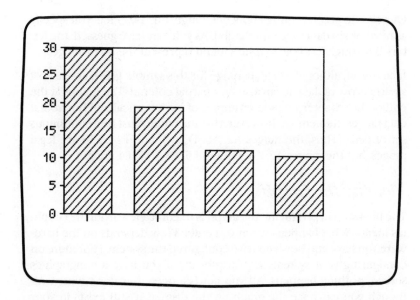

Fig. 9.2. Bar graph representing 1979 U.S. Steel Production by Producer worksheet.

Selecting the Type of Graph

You must first choose the Type of graph you want to produce from the Graph menu. The following menu will appear:

Line   Bar   XY   Stacked-Bar   Pie

Because you are creating a bar graph, select the **Bar** option from this menu. Notice that 1-2-3 automatically returns you to the main Graph menu after the graph type is selected.

Entering Data

Now that you have told 1-2-3 what type of graph to create, you must give the program some data to use in creating the graph. This process is begun by selecting the **A** option from the main Graph menu. After this option is selected, 1-2-3 prompts for a range.

Choosing the Data Range

As usual, the range can be defined with cell references or a range name. In this case, we used the coordinates B5..E5. Remember that this reference can be entered either by actually typing the cell coordinates from the keyboard or by using 1-2-3's POINT mode.

Our simple graph requires only one range, but 1-2-3 lets you specify as many as six data ranges per graph. As you may have guessed, the letters B through F on the graphics menu represent the other ranges.

In addition, although the data range for this sample graph consists of a partial row of data, it can also be a partial column. The graphs at the end of this chapter include examples of both vertical and horizontal data ranges. Remember, however, that the range must be a continuous set of cells. Thus, the ranges A2..A6, D3..F3, and F14..F30 are legal ranges, but the ranges A2, A4, D7 and E5, E8, F17, L4 are not.

Viewing the Graph

The final step in producing the graph is to enter View from the Graphics menu. What happens when you enter View depends on the hardware you have and how you have configured the system. (For more on configuring your system, see Chapter 2.) If you have a nongraphics screen, nothing happens. All you get is a beep, but don't worry. Although you can't see the graph on the display, it still exists in your computer's memory. The graph can be saved and printed later with the PrintGraph program.

If you have a graphics card and either a monochrome or color screen, you should see the bar graph displayed on the screen after you enter View. If you have a Hercules Graphics Card for your monochrome display, the graph will appear on that display. Notice that in both of these cases, the graph replaces the worksheet on the screen. You can return to the worksheet by pressing any key.

Finally, if you are fortunate enough to have both a graphics monitor and a monochrome display, the bar graph will appear on the graphics monitor when you select View. The worksheet will remain in view on the monochrome display. If your graphics monitor can display color, you can format the graph to take advantage of that capability.

Redrawing the Graph

The most exciting feature of 1-2-3's graphics capabilities is its redrawing capability. Suppose that you want to update the data in figure 9.2 to reflect a change in size of the fourth largest producer in the United States. Figure 9.3 shows the updated spreadsheet.

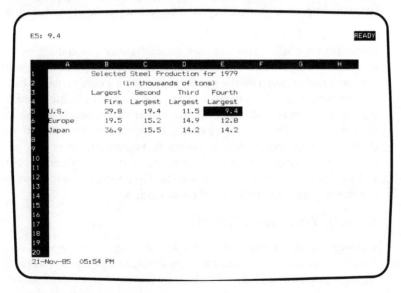

Fig. 9.3. Revised steel production data.

Now suppose that you want to graph this new data. You can do this in one of two ways. First, you can use the graphics command /Graph View to redraw the graph. But 1-2-3 offers an easier method.

A quick way of redrawing the graph is to press the F10 (Graph) key while you are in READY mode. Graph F10 is the equivalent of View, but saves your having to go through the Graph menu. (The F10 key does not work while you are in a graph menu.)

The F10 key makes 1-2-3's graphics mode different from any other program. Because you can redraw a graph immediately after making a change to the spreadsheet, you can perform "what if" analysis that includes graphics. To understand the importance of this, think about the process of creating graphics with the stand-alone graphics packages. Data must be transferred by way of an intermediate file between graphics package and the program that generates the data. It is not practical, therefore, to display graphically the result of each change in the data. Instead, the stand-alone graphics package commonly is used to graph only the finished product. Although this strategy is useful, it cannot produce graphs reflecting immediate changes in the data.

In 1-2-3, graphics can be an integral part of "what if" analysis. You can use graphics extensively while you fine-tune projections, budgets, or other projects. You'll be amazed at how graphics can help you understand the impact of changes in your data on the results of your models.

The F10 key has another use. If you have a color graphics card and a monochrome display, you may have noticed that graphs remain on the screen after they are defined until you redraw them, replace them with another graph, or turn off the system. This makes it easy to glance back and forth between the worksheet and your graph. On single-monitor systems this is not possible because the graph and the worksheet share the same space. Thanks to the F10 key, however, you don't have to re-define the graph completely to review it. You simply press F10, and the graph will appear again in place of the worksheet. When the F10 and Esc keys are used as toggles, you can flip back and forth between the two displays. Figure 9.4 displays this graph.

Adding Titles and Labels

Although our description of 1-2-3's graphics capability appears very attractive, we need more tools for actually building graphs. To create the graph, we must add titles, labels, and a variety of other information. The next sections will show you how to make these additions.

You will probably want to enter titles for the overall graph and for the x- and y-axes. This is done through the /Graph Options Titles menu. It gives you the following choices:

First   Second   X-Axis   Y-Axis

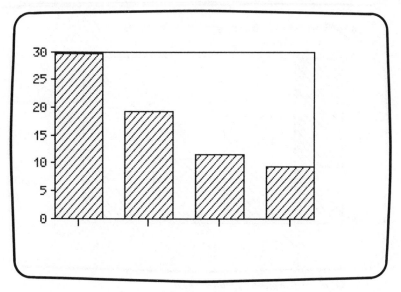

Fig. 9.4. Bar graph representing revised U.S. Steel Production.

We used **X**-Axis and **Y**-Axis to enter the labels "Firm Size" and "Thousand Tons Produced," respectively. For example, to enter the x-axis label, we selected the **X**-Axis option and simply typed the title ("Firm Size") we wanted for the x-axis of the graph. The y-axis label was similarly specified.

The graph titles at the top of figure 9.5 were entered using the **First** and **Second** options. First was used for the main title ("Selected Steel Production for 1979"), and Second was used for the subtitle below it ("in thousands of tons").

These titles are usually entered by typing the title from the keyboard. In this case, however, we used the special backslash (\ ) feature made available to this and other /Graph Options commands for entering the contents of cells instead of typing in text. To use the contents of a cell for legend text, place a backslash (\ ) before the actual cell address when 1-2-3 asks you for a title. We entered \B1 for **First** and \C2 for **Second**. The same technique can be used to enter x- and y-axis titles and legends.

A range name can also be used to create a title or label. To do this, you enter the range name, instead of the cell references, after the backslash. The title must be 39 characters or less.

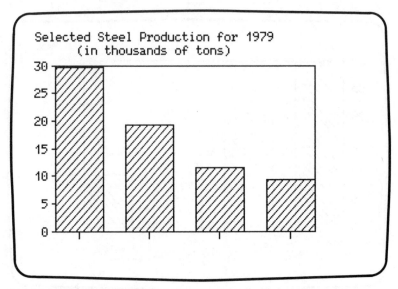

Fig. 9.5. Steel production graph with titles added.

If you are working along on your computer, did you notice that after you entered a title, the options menu appeared and not the title menu? For some reason, 1-2-3 skips up two menu levels after you enter a title. To enter another title, you have to press Enter to return to the title menu, then select the option (**First**, **Second**, **X**-Axis, **Y**-Axis) for the title you want to create. It would be much simpler if the title selection menu remained active after a title was entered.

You should be aware of two things about the way 1-2-3 displays titles. First, notice that 1-2-3 automatically centered the **First** and **Second** graph titles when displaying the graph, irrespective of the label prefixes used in the worksheet. 1-2-3 will always do this.

Second, you will see that the **First** and **Second** titles appear similar in size and intensity on the screen. 1-2-3 will always display the titles this way on the screen. The PrintGraph program, however, includes options that allow you to alter either title or both titles when you print the graph. (This facility is explained in the next chapter.)

Another enhancement you may want to make to your graph is to add labels along the x-axis to define the data items you are plotting. Figure 9.6 shows our basic graphs with x-axis labels added.

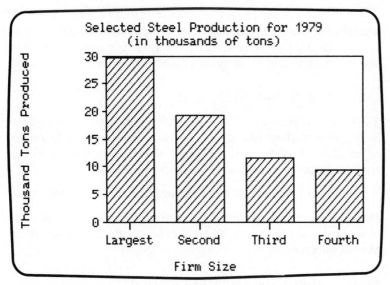

Fig. 9.6. Steel production graph with x-axis labels.

These labels are entered by selecting **X** from the **/G**raph menu, then pointing to the range of labels in the worksheet. In this example, the labels are located in the range B3..E3 in figure 9.3. We used 1-2-3's POINT mode to simplify the process of identifying the limits of the range. 1-2-3 uses the contents of the cells in the indicated range as X labels. Notice that 1-2-3 automatically centers the X labels.

Setting Scale Limits

As we create graphs, we limit the amount of data to be shown. If one axis indicates the time covered by the activity on the graph, the beginning of the activity rests at one end of the scale and the ending of the activity extends to the other end of the same scale. 1-2-3 lets us set our scales either automatically or manually.

Automatic Scale Settings

When we created our graph for the first time, 1-2-3 automatically set the scale (lower limit and upper limit) of the y-axis to fit our data. This adjustment is extremely convenient. 1-2-3 is designed to use a scale that shows all the data points in as much of the screen as possible. If 1-2-3 did not automatically set the scale in this way, creating graphs would be much more cumbersome.

Sometimes you will want to change the scale that 1-2-3 has chosen for a graph. For example, you may want to focus attention on a certain range of values, such as those surrounding a target goal. Alternatively, you may want to create a series of graphs that all have the same scale.

Overriding the Automatic Scale

1-2-3's automatic scale can be overriden with the **Graph Options Scale**. Once you have issued this command, you are given the choice of rescaling either the x-axis or the y-axis. Once you have made a selection, you are presented with the following menu:

Automatic   Manual   Lower   Upper   Format   Indicator   Quit

Manual is used to override 1-2-3's automatic scaling, whereas **Automatic** is used to reinstate it. The other choices are options under the **Manual** selection.

Organization of the Manual Command

The organization of this command departs slightly from 1-2-3's normal command logic. If the **Manual** command followed the standard form, the options **Lower** and **Format** would be contained in a menu one level below the **Manual** or **Automatic** choice. This break with the usual logic was made to avoid adding a sixth level of commands to the program.

The **Lower** and **Upper** selections are used to set the scale limits when **Manual** has been chosen. Figure 9.7 shows how this function works. This figure is a graph using the same data as that in figure 9.6, except that we have changed the scale to have an upper limit of 50 and a lower limit of –50.

Formatting Numbers

The **Format** option allows you to change the way the numbers on the x- and y-axes are displayed. The alternatives under this option are the same as those for the /**Range** Format and /**Worksheet Global** Format commands. You can specify that the numbers be displayed with a fixed number of digits, with an embedded "$" or comma, or as a percentage with an appended "%" sign. For example, figure 9.8 shows the same graph as in figure 9.7, except that the scale has been assigned the **Fixed 2** format.

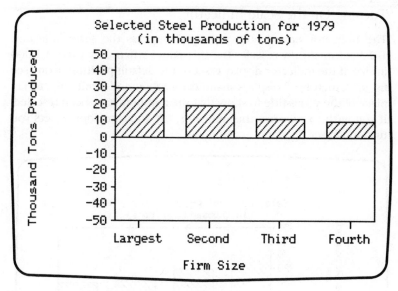

Fig. 9.7. Steel production graph with manual scale.

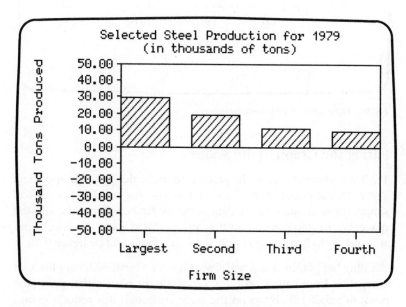

Fig. 9.8. Steel production graph with scale formatted (F2).

Turning Off the Scale Indicator

The Indicator option allows you to suppress the scale indicator. 1-2-3 automatically rescales the axis values when they exceed 1,000 in size. If the indicator display is set to the default position of on (see fig. 9.9), then 1-2-3 displays an indicator (thousands, millions, etc.) in place of the y-axis title to show that the numbers have been rescaled. If you wish to suppress this indicator, the Indicator option lets you turn it off (see fig. 9.8).

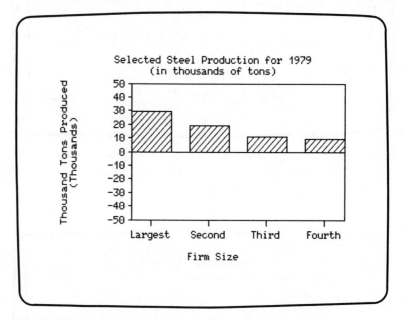

Fig. 9.9. The scale indicator turned on.

Fitting the Graph to the Scales

1-2-3 will always try to fit the graph into the scales you have specified. If you set the upper limit of a scale too low, the resulting graph will simply show as much of the data as can be squeezed into the allotted space. For example, if you set the upper limit at 5 and the lower limit at 0 and try to graph our sample data, the result will be figure 9.10.

Building bar graphs, 1-2-3 will always ignore a positive Lower limit, or a negative Upper limit on the y-axis scale, to ensure that zero (the point of origin) is always on the scale. Although this reduction may seem to reduce the flexibility of 1-2-3's graphics mode, it is, in fact, a valuable feature. Graphs that do not display points of origin can be mis-

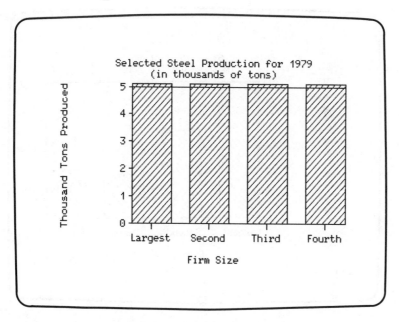

Fig. 9.10. Steel production graph with manual upper limit of 5.

leading. 1-2-3 deals with this problem by not allowing such graphs to be created.

The **S**cale option from the **/G**raph **O**ptions menu will not let you vary the spacing of the tick marks on the y-axis. This program automatically places ticks at generally well-spaced intervals along the y-axis.

Other Scale Options

Several other options may be selected for formatting a graph. They are best applied to other types of graphs and will, therefore, be demonstrated later. For now, we are finished with the sample graph we created. Figure 9.11 shows our original graph with all of its formatting options.

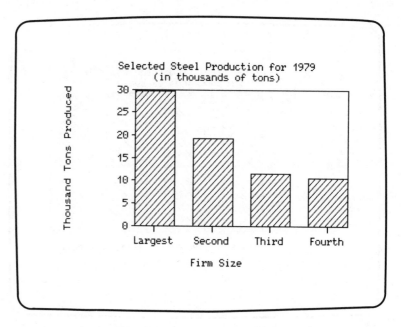

Fig. 9.11. Original steel production graph (data from fig. 9.1).

Saving and Recalling Graph Settings

Only one graph at a time can be the "current" graph. Before you can build a new graph, you must store the old one.

By issuing the /**Graph Name Create** command, you can instruct 1-2-3 to remember the parameters used to define the current graph. With this command, you can create a graph name of up to 14 characters to represent the current graph. All of the information relating to this graph—the data range settings, the graph titles, axis titles, etc.—will be saved under this name. When you save the 1-2-3 worksheet, the graph name will also be saved.

You can recall a named graph at any time by issuing the /**Graph Name Use** command. When this command is issued, 1-2-3 presents a list of all the graph names stored in the current worksheet. You can select the graph names stored in the current worksheet. You can select the graph you want to plot either by typing the name from the keyboard or by pointing to the name on the list. The /**Graph Name Use** command will retrieve the graph settings of the named graph and automatically redraw it.

This command is the only way a graph can be stored for later recall and display. If you don't name a graph, and either delete the graph or change the specifications, there is no way to replot it without re-specifying the settings. If you forget to save the settings under a graph name before you exit, the /gnu command is of no use to you. Similarly, if you fail to save the current worksheet after you name a series of graphs in that worksheet, the names will be lost. *Be careful!* This is an all-too-common mistake.

It is not unusual to create several different graphs for a single work-sheet. The /Graph Name Create and /Graph Name Use commands make it easy to create and use a number of graphs. For example, the settings for the various simple and stacked-bar graphs used in the "Selected Western Steel Production" examples are stored under different graph names in the same worksheet file. The /Graph Name Create and Use commands allow us to define, recall, and draw each graph without reentering its settings.

The /Graph Name Use command can also be used to recall a number of graphs in rapid sequence, creating what is, in effect, a slide show of 1-2-3 graphics. This feature can be used effectively in presentations to display a large number of graphs with a minimal number of keystrokes.

Deleting Graphs

To delete a single graph name from the worksheet, you use the /Graph Name Delete command. As with the /Graph Name Create command, 1-2-3 will prompt you with a list of all the graph names in the current sheet. You can either point to the name you want to delete, or type the name from the keyboard. If you choose not to delete any graphs, simply press Esc three times in succession (or Ctrl-Break) to return to READY mode.

To delete *all* the graph names, issue the /Graph Name Reset command. This command automatically deletes all the graph names in the current worksheet. *Be Careful!* When the name of a graph is deleted, the parameters for the graph are deleted also. It cannot be plotted again without being completely respecified. There is no "Yes/No" confirmation step in the /Graph Name Reset command, so once you press the R for reset, the graphs are gone.

Saving Graphs for Printing

As mentioned previously, the main 1-2-3 program does not have the capability to print graphs. The PrintGraph program must be used to print graphics. Before a graph can be printed with PrintGraph, however, the graph must be saved with the /Graph Save command. This command saves to a graph file the current graph, along with all of the formatting options you have selected. All graph files have the extension .PIC.

Once you have created a .PIC file, you can no longer access it from the main 1-2-3 menu. It is accessible from only the PrintGraph program. If you want to re-create the graph on the screen from within 1-2-3, you must save your graph settings under a name in the worksheet file.

Resetting the Current Graph

Suppose that you have named your first graph and want to begin work on a new one. The first thing to do is remove all the information related to the first graph from 1-2-3's active memory. This can be done by issuing the /Graph Reset command.

After this command is selected, the following menu appears:

   Graph   X   A   B   C   D   E   F   Quit

One of the options on this menu, Graph, lets you reset all of 1-2-3's graph parameters. If you do not want to use any of the old parameters in your new graph, this is the option you should select.

If, on the other hand, your new graph shares some parameters with the old graph, you can delete only part of the information relating to the old graph. For example, you can reset the parameters on one or more ranges by choosing options A through F. The X option resets the X labels.

Because the next example builds directly on the data from our first graph, we do not want to reset any of the settings we have defined.

Creating a More Complex Bar Graph

Before going on to discuss colors, data labels, and various other commands and features, we should first increase the complexity of the bar graph in figure 9.11 to aid further explanations. We can build a more complex graph by including the data for European and Japanese steel production alongside the data for the United States.

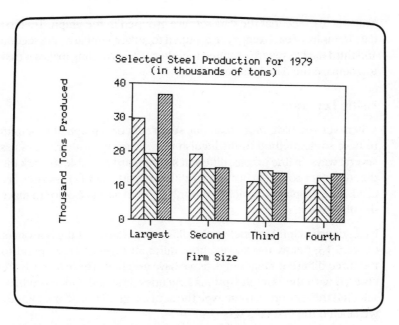

Fig. 9.12. Steel production graph with three countries' data.

Adding More Data Ranges

The first thing that must be done in creating the new graph is to inform 1-2-3 that this new graph will include two additional data ranges. To do this, we enter the Graph menu by selecting /**Graph**. Because we've already created one data range, the next set of data will go into the B range. To enter the data range, we select the **B** option from the menu (either by pointing with the cursor or by pressing B) and tell 1-2-3 that the data is located in the range C2..C5. Similarly, to enter the third data set, we would select the **C** option and indicate the location of the data: D2..D5. We are now ready to draw the graph, so we enter **View** because we are in MENU mode.

Notice the different crosshatch patterns within the bars this time. We had only one pattern of crosshatches in the first graph we drew, because we had only one set of data. Because the graph in figure 9.12 has several sets of data, we have several contrasting sets of crosshatches. Cross-hatching makes it easy to distinguish between the different sets of data graphed in black and white. 1-2-3 automatically controls the crosshatches.

You will also see that the data sets are grouped in the graph. The first data items from each range are grouped together; similarly, the second and third data items are grouped together. This grouping makes it easy to compare the data in each data set.

Using Legends

Whenever you have more than one set of data on a graph, it is helpful to have some method to distinguish one set from another. 1-2-3 has several ways. In line graphs, different symbols are available to mark the different data points. In bar graphs, different patterns of crosshatch are used. If the display is a color monitor, 1-2-3 can also use color to make the distinction.

Legends are helpful in labeling the different patterns. At the bottom of figure 9.13, below the x-axis, three different legends correspond to the three different ranges of data we have graphed. These legends are entered with the /Graph Options Legends command. Once you have selected this option, you can type the actual legend text. For example, we labeled the first data set "U.S."

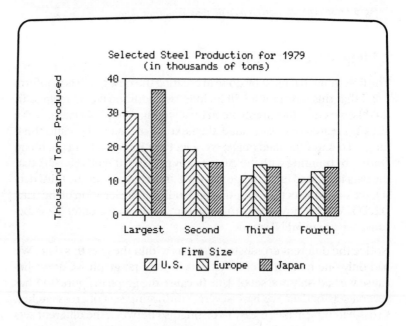

Fig. 9.13. Steel production graph with legend added.

Like titles, labels can be entered with \ and a cell reference or a range name, instead of by typing the label. For example, we put \A5 for /**Graph O**ptions **Legend A**, \A6 for **B**, and so on.

Displaying the Graph in Color

If you have a color monitor, you can instruct 1-2-3 to display graphics in color. This is one of the nicest features of the program. 1-2-3 can display graphics in three colors: white, red, and blue. These are not to be confused with the larger selection of colors the program can actually use for printing graphs if you have the appropriate printer. (Printing graphs and the additional colors available are covered in the next chapter.)

To display the graph from figure 9.12 in color, you would select **Color** from the /**Graph O**ptions menu. The bars and lines for each data range and the legend blocks take on the following colors:

A	White
B	Red
C	Blue
D	White
E	Red
F	Blue

NEW WITH
R2

The list of colors is obviously limited. In complex graphs, different data ranges displayed in the same color can be easily confused. In fact, this color restriction is probably one of the biggest limitations of 1-2-3's Graphics mode.

This restriction is eased, however, by the PrintGraph program's ability to add color to your graphs when they are printed or plotted. The colors in PrintGraph are completely independent of the colors you assign with the **Color** option of 1-2-3. Even graphs that are saved with no colors can be printed in color with PrintGraph.

The /**Graph O**ptions **B&W** command switches the graphics display from color to black and white.

Stacked-Bar Graphs

A slight variation on the basic bar graph is the stacked-bar graph. Stacked-bar graphs are frequently used to compare different sets of data while showing the components and total of each data set. In these graphs, the totals are created by stacking the component data items one on another. In figure 9.14, you can see the total tonnage for the four largest steel producers in the United States, Europe, and Japan.

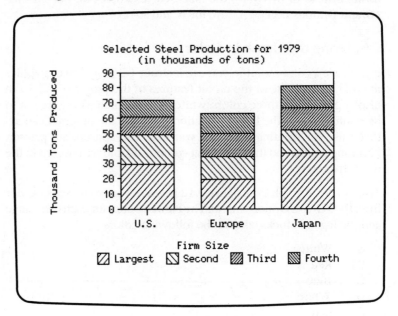

Fig. 9.14. Stacked-bar graph of Steel Production worksheet.

This graph was created in much the same way as our second graph. To select the graph type, you issue the command **/Graph Type Stack Bar**. There are four data ranges for this graph. You select the first by choosing the **A** option and indicating the data range B5..B7. In a similar manner, you set the second, or B range, to C5..C7. The other data ranges are selected by choosing the **C** and **D** options.

As usual, the **View** command draws the graph. Notice that we've already added legends, x-axis labels, and titles to this graph. They were added just as they were in the simpler examples.

For example, the First and Second titles in figure 9.14 are the same as those in our earlier examples. The X and Y titles, however, are different. They were entered by selecting the **X** and **Y** options and typing the title.

The legends in figure 9.14 were created by selecting the **Legend** option from the **/Graph Options** menu and specifying the range B3..E3. Notice that these legends are the same as the X labels in our earlier examples.

The X labels in figure 9.14 are the same as the legends in the earlier graphs. These labels were entered by selecting the **X** option from the main graph menu and indicating the range A5..A7.

Line Graphs

The third type of graph offered by 1-2-3 is a line graph. Line graphs are particularly useful for showing time-series data, but they are by no means restricted to this use. Consider the following data on "Interest Rate Movements for February, 1983," shown in figure 9.15.

```
A1:  'Interest Movements for February 1983                    READY

         A         B         C         D       E       F       G
1    Interest Movements for February 1983
2
3      Date            Fed Funds Rate   LIBOR
4    02-Feb-83                   8.13    9.56
5    04-Feb-83                   8.31    9.50
6    07-Feb-83                   8.53    9.50
7    09-Feb-83                   8.63    9.38
8    11-Feb-83                   8.38    9.31
9    14-Feb-83                   8.56    9.25
10   16-Feb-83                   8.42    9.25
11   18-Feb-83                   8.31    9.13
12   22-Feb-83                   8.38    9.13
13   23-Feb-83                   6.38    9.06
14   25-Feb-83                   8.19    9.13
15   28-Feb-83                   8.63    8.88
16
17
18
19
20
21-Nov-85   06:36 PM
```

Fig. 9.15. Interest rate data.

This data was taken from *The Wall Street Journal* and reflects the Federal Funds Rate and the London Interbank Offering Rate (LIBOR) for the indicated dates.

Making a Line Graph

To create a line graph of the Federal Funds Rate plotted against time, we first select the **Line** option from the /**Graph Type** menu. Next, we select the **A** option and enter the range C4..C15 as the **A** range. As always, the graph is drawn with the **View** option. Figure 9.16 illustrates this line graph.

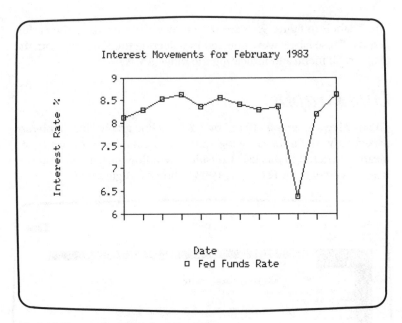

Fig. 9.16. Line graph of the Federal Funds Rate.

Once again, notice that we've added titles to this graph. This was done by selecting the **T**itles option from the **O**ptions menu and entering the titles shown for **F**irst, **S**econd, **X**, and **Y** selections.

Notice also that our line graph has no x-axis labels. Our next step is to enter the range of dates in column A as the X range. As with the bar graph, we enter X labels by selecting the X option from the main graphics menu. In this example, we want to use the information in column A as X labels, so we enter the range A4..A15.

If this graph is redrawn (by stepping back to the main Graph menu and typing View), figure 9.17 shows that using the entire set of labels in column A causes a problem. There is simply not enough room on the graph to display all of the labels without overlapping. This can happen any time you select a large number of X labels, as in this case, or if the the X labels are unusually long.

The /**G**raph **O**ption **S**cale **S**kip command makes it possible to "skip" every n^{th} X label when the graph is displayed. After you type the command, 1-2-3 will prompt you for the skipping factor. In most cases, skipping every other label will be sufficient to clean up the graph. This is done by specifying a factor of 2. On some graphs, however, it may

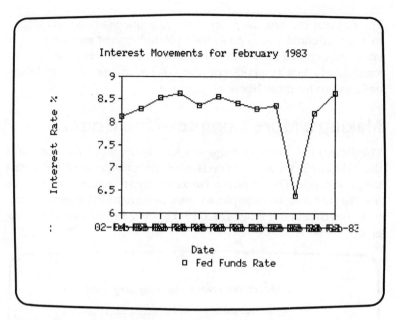

Fig. 9.17. Interest rate graph with X Labels.

be necessary to choose a much larger factor. 1-2-3 has the ability to skip as many as 8,192 X labels. Figure 9.18 shows the line graph with an x-axis skipping factor of 2.

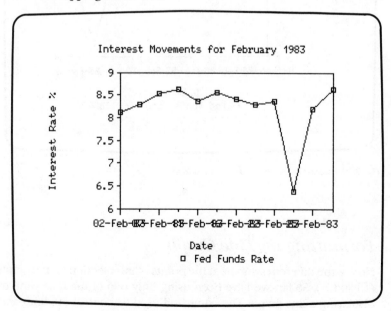

Fig. 9.18. Interest graph with skip set to 2.

The fact that the date labels are ordered sequentially doesn't matter to 1-2-3. It could just as easily have plotted against any other set of labels. Notice that cells containing date functions were used for the x-axis labels. As with all titles or labels, 1-2-3 can use numbers, labels, or functions for these labels.

Making a More Complex Line Graph

The data set we've created suggests a second line graph that compares the variations in the Federal Funds rate to the changes in LIBOR across the same period. This graph is really a simple extension of the previous one. To continue the example, we must first create a **B** range that captures the data in the range D4..D15. Figure 9.19 illustrates our new graph.

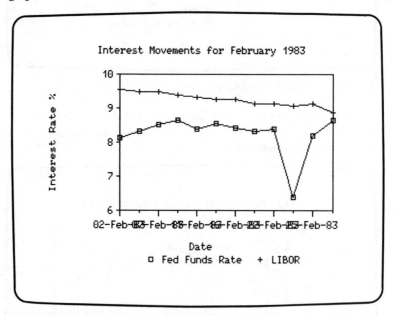

Fig. 9.19. Interest graph with LIBOR rate added.

Formatting the Line Graph

Notice the different symbols at the points of intersection on the graph (□ and +). So far, we have been using only two of the four ways of displaying a line graph. The command used to control the lines and symbols at the points of intersection on a line graph is /Graph Options Format. This command has the following menu:

Graph   A   B   C   D   E   F   Quit

By choosing **Graph**, you can format all lines. By selecting one of the other options, you format only the corresponding line. After you make a selection, the following menu appears:

Lines   Symbols   Both   Neither

Lines

Lines signals 1-2-3 to connect the different data points with only a straight line and no symbols. Figure 9.20 shows the graph from figure 9.19 with the graph format set to lines only.

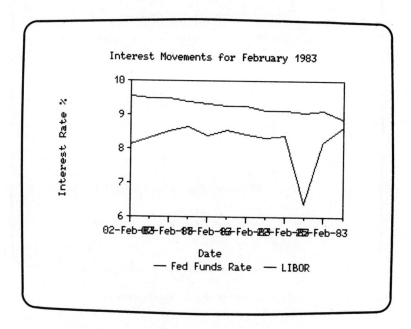

Fig. 9.20. Interest rate graph with format set to Lines.

Symbols

The **S**ymbols option tells 1-2-3 to leave out the straight lines and use different graphic symbols for each of up to six data ranges. The symbols used are

A	□	D	△
B	+	E	×
C	◇	F	▽

Figure 9.21 shows the graph with Federal Fund set to lines, and LIBOR set to symbols. Although the symbols format can be used with line graphs, it is more commonly used with XY plots.

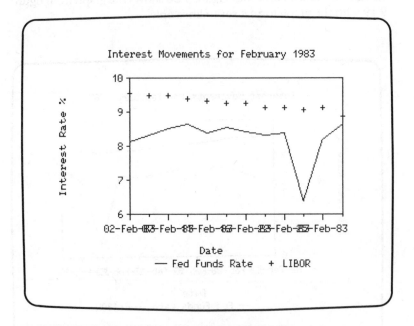

Fig. 9.21. Interest rate graph with LIBOR format set to symbols.

Both Lines and Symbols

The third choice in the menu is **B**oth. This is actually the default used in figures 9.18 and 9.19 to get both lines and symbols. Because it is difficult to tell one data set from another without using both lines and symbols, in most cases **B**oth is the preferred option.

Neither Lines nor Symbols

The final choice on this menu, **Neither**, suppresses both lines and symbols. You may wonder how points of intersection can be shown if neither lines nor symbols appear on the graph. The answer is through **Data Labels**.

Using Data Labels

1-2-3's **Data Label** command places *data* as labels from the worksheet into a graph. These labels can be placed in the graph in the vicinity of the data points on the graph. The **Data Label** option is a part of the **Graph Options** menu. After this selection is made, the following menu appears:

A   B   C   D   E   F   Quit

Notice that the options here correspond to the data ranges options: one set of data labels for each set of data. In general, you will want to use the same coordinates to define the data labels and the data range. For example, in our sample graph, the data labels for data range A are entered by entering the label range B5..I5. 1-2-3 then presents the option of placing the data label above or below the data point, centered on the data point, or to the left or the right.

The data labels can be numbers, values, or text. All data labels are converted to labels before they are placed in the worksheet. In most cases, you will want to use numbers as data labels. If you use text, be sure to keep the strings short to avoid cluttering the graph.

Data labels can be used in a line graph that includes lines and symbols, as well as one that contains no lines or symbols to mark the data points. If you are not using lines or symbols (on a line graph), you will probably want to center the data labels on the data points. Otherwise, you'll want to choose one of the other options to avoid cluttering the graph.

Figure 9.22 shows our first sample line graph (with only one data set) with data labels, but without data symbols or lines. Of course, data labels can also be used in graphs with symbols and lines. In fact, in line graphs with multiple data sets, lines or symbols are required to differentiate the various data sets. Otherwise, the graph will look like a jumble of numbers. Figure 9.23 shows our second line graph (with two data sets) with data labels. Notice that legends are meaningless when they appear in a line graph without lines or symbols.

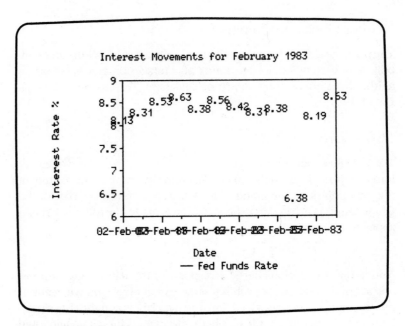

Fig. 9.22. Interest rate graph with data labels.

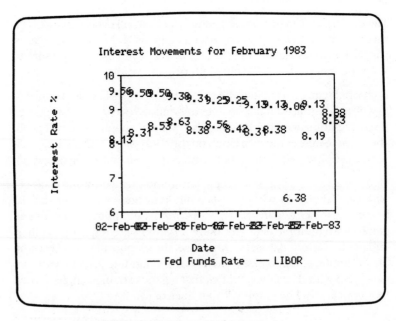

Fig. 9.23. Graph with two interest rates using data labels.

Data labels work also with bar graphs. In bar graphs, the labels are centered above each bar. As is true for line graphs, the data labels can help to identify the numeric value of each data point.

Sometimes it is easy to get confused about the difference between the x-axis titles, the X labels, and the data labels. An x-axis title usually describes the units of measurement used on the x axis (like dollars or years). X labels distinguish the different data points (for example, 1981 and 1982 data) in a graph. Data labels describe individual data items.

Using Grids

1-2-3 offers one more option for formatting graphs: grids. This option allows a grid to be interposed on a 1-2-3 graph. The command to create this grid is /Graph Options Grid. The submenu under this command offers the following options:

Horizontal   Vertical   Both   Clear

The first option creates a horizontal grid over the graph. As you would expect, the second option creates a vertical grid. The third option, Both, causes both types of grids to be displayed. This option is illustrated in figure 9.24. The last option, Clear removes any grid from the current graph.

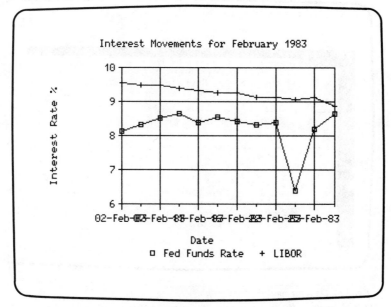

Fig. 9.24. Interest rate graph with a grid.

Although grids can be useful, they also can clutter the graph unnecessarily. You may find that using data labels works better than grids for many applications.

Pie Graphs

Another graph provided by 1-2-3 is the simple pie graph. Pie graphs can show relationships in a single set of data items. Each data item becomes a slice of the pie. The sum of the slices represents the entire pie.

In many ways, a pie graph is the simplest of 1-2-3's graphs. Only one data range can be represented by a pie graph, so only the /Graph A option is needed to define a pie. Because a pie graph has no axes, the x- and y-axis titles cannot be used. Similarly, grids, scales, and data labels are not used with pie graphs.

One convenient way to show the advantages of a pie graph, as well as its limitations, is to add some additional data to figure 9.1. The additional data is shown in figure 9.25. As you can see, the new data is simply the names of the four largest steel producers in the United States, Europe, and Japan.

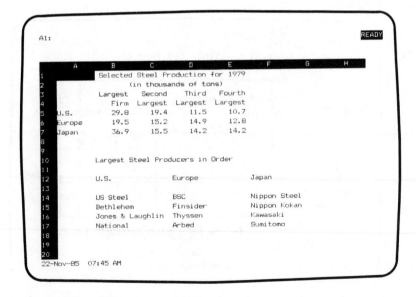

Fig. 9.25. Data for relative share graph.

To create the pie graph shown in figure 9.26 we first selected the **Pie** option from the **Type** menu. Next, we entered B5..E5 for the A range. Because pie graphs do not have an x- or y-axis, 1-2-3 adopts the convention of using the X labels as the captions for the slices of the pie. Here B14..B17 is designated as the X label range. Figure 9.26 shows the resulting graph.

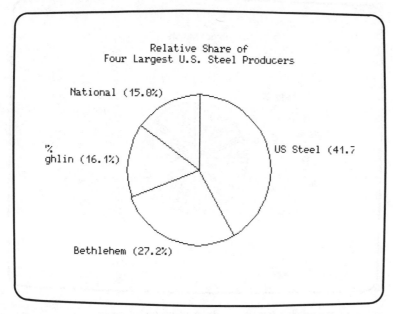

Fig. 9.26. A relative share graph (pie graph).

You should notice two things about this pie graph: the number of slices in the pie, and the percentages next to the labels. The number of slices in the pie corresponds to the number of data items in the A range—in this case, four. The most important limitation on the number of data items used in a pie graph is that too many labels will crowd each other. Each situation is different, but you might try collecting some of the smallest slices in an "Other" category if you have many small data items.

The percentages next to the labels in the pie graph are calculated and automatically placed there by 1-2-3. This process is consistent with the purpose of a pie graph, which is to show the relationship of each data item to the whole. It would be nice, however, if there were a way to display the value of each data item in the graph next to the percentage.

Pie Graph Crosshatches

The basic pie graph of figure 9.26 can be enhanced by the addition of shading or color. 1-2-3 provides eight different shading patterns for monochrome display or eight different colors for a color display. Figure 9.27 shows the pie graph shading codes.

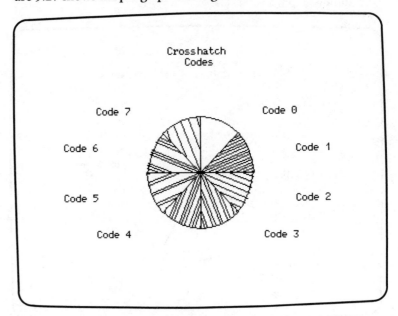

Fig. 9.27. The crosshatch shading codes available for pie graphs.

You indicate the shadings or colors for each pie wedge, using the B range. The B range can be any range of your worksheet that is the same size as the A range. Enter a number between 1 and 7 in each cell in the B range to indicate the desired shading of the corresponding wedge. The codes 0 and 8 indicate an unshaded wedge. Figure 9.28 shows the Relative Share Graph with shadings.

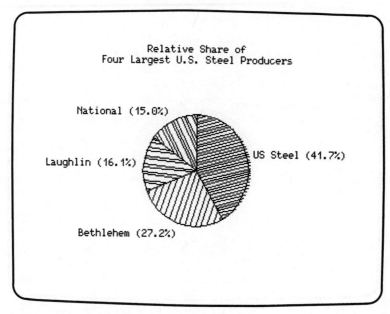

Fig. 9.28. Pie graph (Relative Share graph) with shadings.

Exploded Pie Graphs

Exploded pie graphs let you emphasize one or more slices in a pie graph. By adding a value of 100 to the normal B-range value for shading, you can have 1-2-3 set a slice apart from the others. You can explode any or all of the wedges in a pie graph. The result of adding 100 to the shading code for U.S. Steel in the Relative Share graph is shown in figure 9.29.

XY Graphs

The XY graph is the final type of graph offered by 1-2-3. An XY graph is sometimes called a scatter plot. What sets this type of graph apart from the others mentioned so far is that, in an XY graph, two or more different data items from the same data range can share the same X value. If you think about it for a moment, you'll realize that this is not possible with a line graph. Rather than showing time-series data, XY graphs illustrate the relationships between different attributes of data items, like age and income or educational achievements and salary.

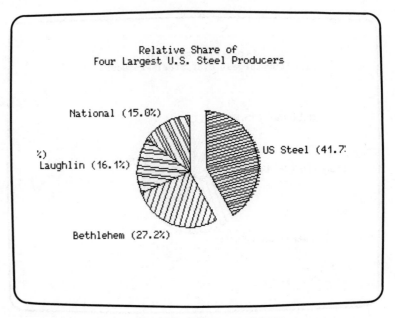

Fig. 9.29. Pie graph (Relative Share graph) with exploded wedge.

In an XY graph, the X labels become more than simple labels on the graph. They are, in fact, the x-axis scale. This means that an XY graph requires a minimum of two pieces of information: an X range and an A range.

In every other respect, an XY plot is similar to a line graph. In fact, a line graph can be thought of as a specialized type of XY graph. For an example of an XY graph, look at the data in figure 9.30 and the sample graph we've created in figure 9.31.

Notice that we've added titles, X labels, and a grid to this graph. We've set the format to show only symbols instead of both lines and symbols. This was done by selecting the **F**ormat option from the **O**ptions menu and specifying the **S**ymbols alternative. Typically, XY graphs are formatted to display only symbols instead of symbols and lines. You can display the symbols, however, using any format you wish. If you format an XY graph to include lines between the data points, be sure that at least one of the data sets is sorted in either ascending or descending order. Otherwise, the lines that connect the data points will cross one another, making the graph difficult to read.

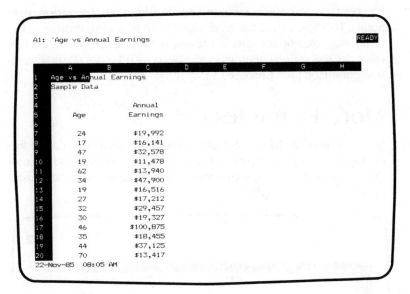

Fig. 9.30. Earnings versus age data.

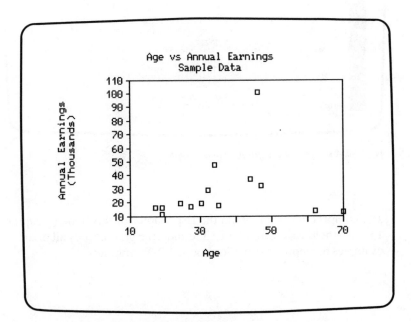

Fig. 9.31. XY plot of earnings versus age data.

Frequently, scatter plots include a line in addition to the various data points. This line, called the *regression line*, is an approximation of the trend suggested by the data in the graph. You can create such a line using the regression coefficient calculated with 1-2-3's **/Data Regres-sion** command (see Chapter 11).

More Examples

Now that all of the basic 1-2-3 graph types have been covered, the following six examples illustrate each type of graph, along with the commands that were used to create them. Figure 9.32 shows the data used to create the sample graphs.

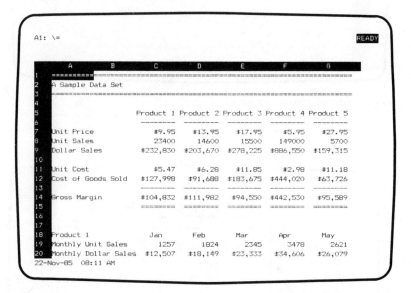

Fig. 9.32. A sample data set for the sample graphs.

The comprehensive model in the last chapter of this book (Chapter 13) also includes examples of a line and a pie graph. Study all of these examples for more information about 1-2-3's graphics.

The commands required to produce the first example, shown in figure 9.33, follow.

/Graph Type Bar
  A C8..G8~
  X C5..G5~
  Options Scale Skip 2~
     Title First A Sample Graph~
     Title Second Comparative Unit Sales~
     Title X-Axis Product~
     Title Y-Axis Units~
     Quit
  View

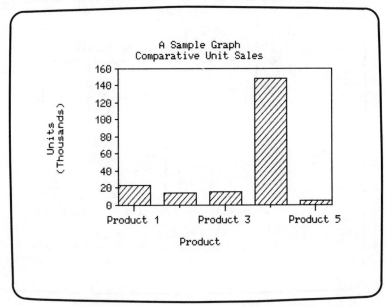

Fig. 9.33. A sample graph.

The commands required to produce the second example, shown in figure 9.34, follow.

/Graph Type Stacked Bar
      A C12..G12~
      B C14..G14~
      X C5..G5~
      Options Scale Skip 2~
            Title First A Sample Graph~
            Title Second Components of Total Dollar Sales~
            Title X-Axis Product~
            Title Y-Axis Dollars~
            Legend A Cost of Goods Sold~
            Legend B Gross Margin~
            Quit
    View

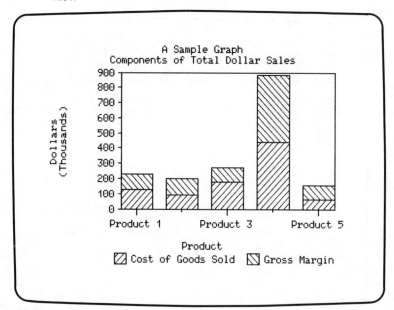

Fig. 9.34. A sample graph.

The commands required to produce the third example, shown in figure 9.35, follow.

/Graph Type Bar
      A C7..G7~
      B C11..G11~
      X C5..G5~
      Options Scale Skip 2~
            Title First A Sample Graph~
            Title Second Unit Price To Unit Cost~
            Title X-Axis Product~
            Title Y-Axis Dollars~
            Legend A Unit Price~
            Legend B Unit Cost~
            Quit
     View

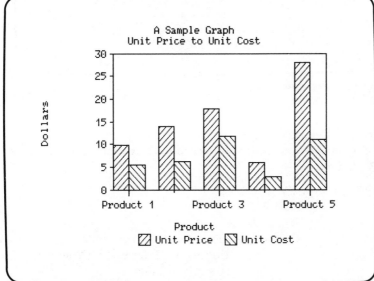

Fig. 9.35. A sample graph.

The commands required to produce the fourth example, shown in figure 9.36, follow.

/Graph Type Pie
      A C9..G9~
      X C5..G5~
      Options Title First A Sample Graph~
            Title Second Contribution to Total
               Revenue~
            Quit
     View

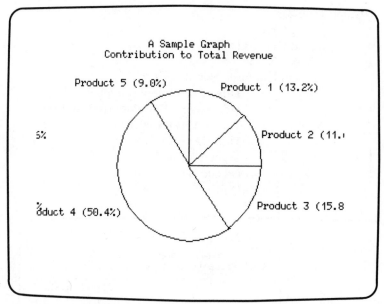

Fig. 9.36. A sample graph.

The commands required to produce the fifth example, shown in figure 9.37, follow.

    /Graph Type XY

              A C7..G7~

              X C8..G8~

              Options Title First A Sample Graph~

                        Title Second Price vs. Unit Volume~

                        Title X-Axis Units~

                        Title Y-Axis Price~

                        Legend A Unit Price~

                        Format Graph Symbols Quit

                        Quit

              View

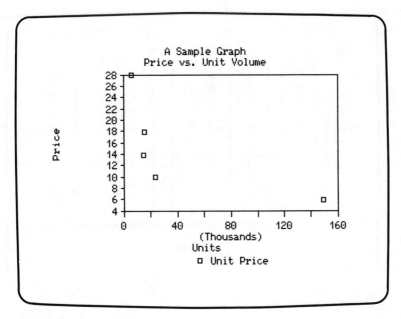

Fig. 9.37. A sample graph.

The commands required to produce the sixth example, shown in figure 9.38, follow.

/Graph Type Line
        A C20..N20~
        X C18..N18~
        Options Title First A Sample Graph~
                Title Second Product 1
                    Monthly Dollar Sales~
                Title X-Axis Month~
                Title Y-Axis Dollars~
                Grid Both
                Format Graph Both Quit
                Quit
        View

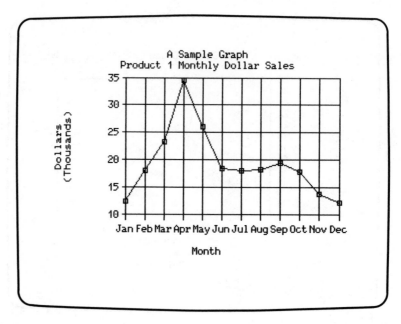

Fig. 9.38. A sample graph.

10
Printing Graphs

Printing graphs is different from creating and displaying them, because the main 1-2-3 program cannot print graphics. To print a graph, you must first save it to a graph file and then exit 1-2-3 to the PrintGraph program through the Lotus Access System. Finally, you select the file and set the options for printing.

This may seem rather complicated, but Lotus wanted the main program to be of reasonable size. By making the PrintGraph program separate, Lotus was able to decrease the total size of the main program. A great deal of interactive capability, however, was removed from printing graphs.

The trade-off, however, is not severe. The menus and command structure of the PrintGraph program are similar to the main 1-2-3 program. (See the back of this book for a command menu map picturing all of 1-2-3's commands.) As a further help, the PrintGraph program is written for batch processing. This means that the program can print more than one graph at a time. (In this chapter, however, we will print only one graph at a time.)

Because of its "independence," PrintGraph has many special features that are not available in the main program. These features include the ability to produce high-resolution output on special printers and plotters, enlargements and reductions, rotations, and several additional colors and font types.

Accessing the PrintGraph Program

Both 1-2-3 and the PrintGraph program are accessed through the Lotus Access System. You will probably use PrintGraph most often immediately after a 1-2-3 session. Before quitting 1-2-3, save your graph file with the /Graph Save command (see Chapter 9.) After entering the /Quit command, instead of exiting from the Access System to DOS, use the system to access the PrintGraph program. Once you reach the Lotus Access System, enter *p* or point to the PrintGraph selection and press Enter. If you are using 1-2-3 on a floppy disk system, remove the 1-2-3 system disk, put the PrintGraph disk in its place, and press Enter once more.

If you have sufficient RAM, 1-2-3 will allow you to use PrintGraph after you issue the /System command. You will not have to reload 1-2-3 after leaving PrintGraph; by typing *exit* after the system prompt, you can go directly back into 1-2-3. Be careful, though. Always save your worksheet before using PrintGraph.

To use this technique, check how much RAM is available by using the /Worksheet Status command. With approximately 150K left (a conservative estimate), you should be able to run PrintGraph and 1-2-3 together without overwriting your worksheet. You may, however, require more RAM to print several graphs at one time. After leaving 1-2-3 (using the /System command) enter *pgraph* from the system prompt. If you are using a driver set other than the default 1-2-3 set, you must enter *pgraph* plus the driver-set name (for example, *Pgraph hp*). At this point, you will move into PrintGraph.

Starting at DOS, you can go into PrintGraph directly or go through the Lotus Access System. To go into the program directly, simply type and enter *pgraph* after the operating system prompt. To go through the Lotus Access System, type and enter *lotus*.

Configuring PrintGraph

To configure PrintGraph, you must first choose the appropriate driver set when the program is installed (see Chapter 2). The graphics devices you can use as you run PrintGraph depend entirely on the devices selected during installation. You can run PrintGraph only if your graphics devices have been selected previously.

You can select more than one graphics device during installation. For example, if you have an HP plotter and an Epson FX-80 printer, you can select both as graphics output devices. If your printer or plotter, however, is not on the list of 1-2-3-supported graphics devices, you may want to check with Lotus to see whether a device driver has been released for your equipment.

After entering PrintGraph, you need to indicate your particular hardware setup as well as where your graphs and fonts are stored. Figure 10.1 shows an example of the PrintGraph screen after you have selected and saved to a .CNF (configuration) file the type of printer you will be using.

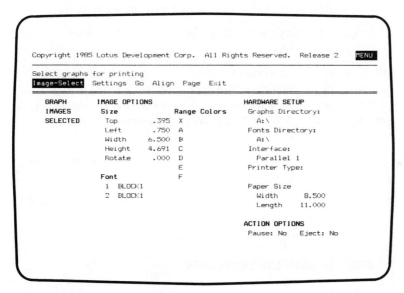

Fig. 10.1. The PrintGraph Main Menu.

Notice that HP 7475A appears below the Printer Type: message on the right side of the screen. Once you have selected your printer type, PrintGraph automatically activates your HP plotter as you enter the program. You will never need to change this setting unless you install an additional or different graphics device.

Printer Selection

To choose a printer from among the graphics printer drivers you selected during installation, select **S**ettings from among the PrintGraph main menu choices:

Image-Select   Settings   Go   Align   Page   Exit

After you have selected **S**ettings, the following menu choices will appear:

Image   Hardware   Action   Save   Reset   Quit

Selecting **H**ardware tells PrintGraph you wish to change the hardware setting. Finally, select **P**rinter from the following menu items:

Graphs-Directory   Fonts-Directory   Interface   Printer
   Size-Paper   Quit

After you have chosen **P**rinter, a menu of the graphics devices that you selected during installation will appear on the screen (see fig. 10.2). If you did not, however, choose a graphics printer during the installation procedure, 1-2-3 will indicate that you must edit the driver set and add a graphics printer selection to the driver.

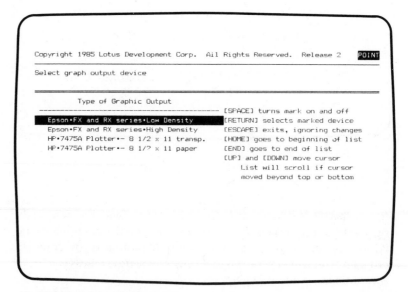

Fig. 10.2. The printer selection menu.

To change to the Epson, just move the cursor to the appropriate line and press the space bar. This action makes the change and marks the selected printer with a # symbol. When you press Enter, PrintGraph will return to the main PrintGraph Hardware Settings sheet.

Graph and Font Directories

When you configure PrintGraph to your hardware, you must also indicate the directories for the graph and font files with Graphs-Directory and Fonts-Directory. Because PrintGraph normally resides in drive A on a two floppy disk system, A:\ is the default for finding the graph and font files. If you have a hard disk and have stored all the PrintGraph files in a directory, you will need to change this default setting. (On systems with two floppy disk drives, change the graph directory to B:\ )

The Interface Option

The Interface option of the Hardware menu specifies either a parallel or a serial interface card for your system. You are given eight choices:

1. A parallel interface—the default.

2. A serial interface (RS-232-C-compatible)—optional. You must specify a baud rate (see below).

3. A second parallel interface—optional.

4. A second serial interface (RS-232-C-compatible)— optional. You must specify a baud rate (see below).

5. DOS Device LPT1:

6. DOS Device LPT2:

7. DOS Device LPT3:

8. DOS Device LPT4:

NEW WITH
R2

The first four settings specify printers physically connected to your system. The rest indicate logical devices that your printing system can connect to the appropriate physical device. The logical device options are generally used to connect printers over a local-area network.

If you specify a serial interface, you need to select a *baud* rate, which determines the speed at which data is transferred. Because each printer has its own requirements, you will need to consult your printer's manual for the appropriate rate. Many printers will accept more than one baud rate, so a general guideline is to choose the fastest baud rate that the printer will accept without corrupting the data. The available baud rates appear in table 10.1.

Table 10.1 Baud Rates per Setting	
Setting	*Baud rate*
1	110
2	150
3	300
4	600
5	1,200
6	2,400
7	4,800
8	9,600
9	19,200

The Size-Paper Option

The Size-Paper option lets you tell PrintGraph the length and width of the paper. The default is a length of 11 inches and a width of 8 inches. On a wide carriage printer, you may want to set the width to 14 inches and use the manual size option to incorporate the entire 11-by-14-inch page.

Configurations to Save and Reset

To save the hardware settings, select Save from the Settings menu. The saved settings can be used in subsequent PrintGraph sessions. The settings are saved in a file called PGRAPH.CNF that is read each time PrintGraph is loaded. You will probably not want to change hardware settings unless you change your hardware.

Another option in the Settings menu, **Reset**, provides a function almost the opposite from Save. **Reset** cancels all the Settings made during the current session and returns to the options that were present when PrintGraph was loaded or the options Saved during the current session, whichever occurred last.

The Image Settings

Besides hardware configuration settings, other settings can affect the way graphs appear on the printed page. These Image settings apply to all the graphs printed in a batch. All the Image settings are saved when you update the .CNF file. If you want different Image settings for different graphs, you must select and print the graphs one at a time.

To specify the Image settings, select Image from the Settings menu. The following choices are then displayed:

   Size   Font   Range-Colors   Quit

Adjusting Graph Size and Orientation

The Size option in the Image menu lets you adjust the sizes of graphs and decide where they will be printed on a page. This Image option also allows you to rotate the axes by as much as 90 degrees. The menu for the Size option gives you the following menu choices:

   Full   Half   Manual   Quit

Full means that the graph will occupy an entire page; and Half, that the graph will take up a half page. Whatever the paper size, PrintGraph assumes an 8 1/2-by-11-inch page. PrintGraph automatically handles all the spacing and margins for both these choices unless you specify Manual.

The following choices appear for Manual:

   Top   Left   Width   Height   Rotation   Quit

Top, Left, Width, and Height adjust the respective margins. Rotation adjusts the number of counterclockwise degrees of rotation. You must choose a number between 0 and 90. On the one extreme, 0 will not cause any rotation, and the x-axis will appear on the page as it normally does. At the other extreme, a full 90 degrees of rotation will shift the x-axis to a vertical position.

Interestingly enough, if you choose the Full option, 1-2-3 will print graphs rotated 90 degrees. The x-axis of a bar graph will run along the long edge of an 8 1/2-by-11-inch page. If you choose the Half option, 1-2-3 considers the degree of rotation 0, and the x-axis of a bar graph will run along the short edge of a sheet of paper so that you can get two graphs on a single page.

You will need to experiment to get the results you want from **Rotation**. The default settings for **Height** and **Width** when **Half** is selected are 6.500 and 4.691. This setting gives an aspect ratio of approximately 1 (x-axis) to 1.385 (y-axis). If you change the aspect ratio, distortion can, and often will, occur when PrintGraph fits a rotated graph into the specified height and width. Distortion in bar and line graphs is usually not a problem. Distorted pie graphs, however, probably will look like ellipses instead of pies. When you change the settings for height and width, the best policy to avoid distortion is to maintain the 1 to 1.385 aspect ratio.

Choosing Fonts

1-2-3 allows you to print in different character types (fonts). (This includes printing with a dot-matrix printer.) The **Font** option lets you choose from among 11 different character types. Figure 10.3 shows a printout of the type fonts available. The number after the font name indicates the density—how dark the printed character will be. The fonts followed by a 2 are identical to the fonts with the same names followed by a 1, but the number-2 fonts are darker.

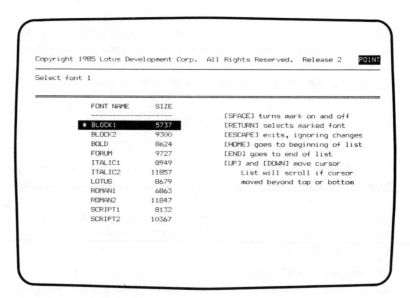

Fig. 10.3. Fonts available in PrintGraph.

You can even set the first line of text, the graph title, in one font and the remaining lines of text in another. If you specify only one font, it will be used for all the text in the graph.

An example is the exploded pie chart of the steel companies' relative shares from Chapter 9; a dark *Italic* typeface is used for the first graph title, and a lighter *Italic* for the other lines. To get these fonts, you specify ITALIC1 for Font 1 (the first line of the title line). If another font had not been chosen for Font 2, it would have automatically taken on the same value as Font 1. Once the fonts are specified, ITALIC2 appears in the settings sheet for Font 1, and ITALIC1 for Font 2. (See fig. 10.4.)

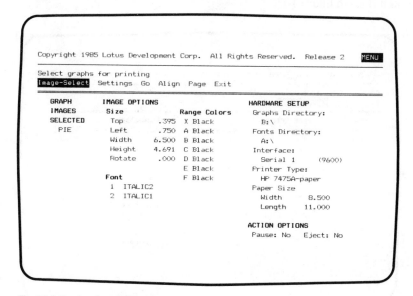

Fig. 10.4. Fonts selected for pie graph.

Choosing Colors

If you have a color printing device, select the **Range-Colors** from the **Image** menu. This option sets the colors for printing or plotting different parts of graphs. If the device you are using does not support color graphics (most printers do not), you will of course, not have this choice.

PrintGraph assigns a default color of black to every data range and to the grid, axes, and scales. However, the program can handle nine other colors: red, green, blue, orange, lime, gold, turquoise, violet, and brown. You may assign any of these colors to any data range, or you may assign the same color to more than one data range.

When you select **Range-Colors**, PrintGraph asks you to assign colors to the data ranges in your graphs. Each time you specify a range name (X and A through F), Printgraph will display a list of colors from which you can choose. The colors you use in PrintGraph do not have to be the same colors you use in the main 1-2-3 program. In fact, you don't have to have a color monitor to print color graphs, but you do need a printer with a color capability to print color graphs.

After you have assigned colors to the graph ranges, the screen will look as it does in figure 10.5.

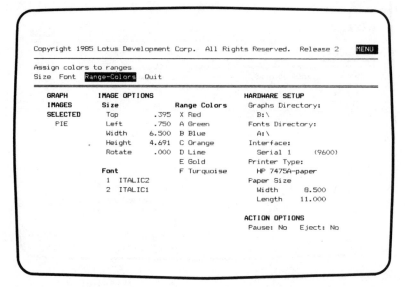

Fig. 10.5. Selecting Range-colors.

You may save the color settings by means of the **Save** option from the **Settings** menu. This choice saves color settings (and all other image and hardware settings) to PGRAPH.CNF so that the settings will be available for the next PrintGraph session.

Selection of Files for Printing

After you have configured PrintGraph, you can return to the main PrintGraph menu and choose **Image-Select**. After you use PrintGraph the first time, **Image-Select** will probably be the first step every time you use the program. This option gives you a list of all the .PIC files on the current **Graphs-Directory**. A typical list of graph files is shown in figure 10.6.

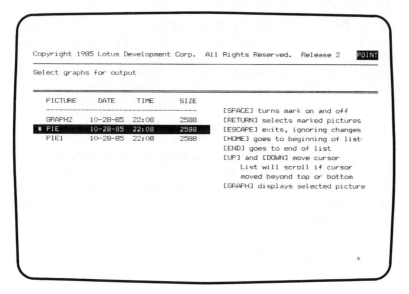

```
Copyright 1985 Lotus Development Corp.  All Rights Reserved.  Release 2   POINT

Select graphs for output


   PICTURE    DATE     TIME    SIZE
   ---------------------------------------        [SPACE] turns mark on and off
   GRAPH2    10-28-85  22:08   2588               [RETURN] selects marked pictures
 # PIE       10-28-85  22:08   2588               [ESCAPE] exits, ignoring changes
   PIE1      10-28-85  22:08   2588               [HOME] goes to beginning of list·
                                                  [END] goes to end of list
                                                  [UP] and [DOWN] move cursor
                                                      List will scroll if cursor
                                                      moved beyond top or bottom
                                                  [GRAPH] displays selected picture
```

Fig. 10.6. A graph selection menu.

The directions for selecting files are on the right side of the display. To select a graph file to print, use the up- and down-arrow keys to position the cursor at the appropriate entry; then press the space bar. PrintGraph will place a # next to the graph name in order to indicate that the graph has been selected for printing. Finally, press Enter to get back to the main PrintGraph menu.

You can select as many graphs as you wish before you press Enter. A # will appear next to each graph you select. To view a graph on the screen before selecting it for printing, press Graph (F10). The graphs in PrintGraph will differ slightly from those in 1-2-3 because of PrintGraph's special type fonts.

Printing Graphs in Batch Mode

The way you print graphs in batch mode will depend on your particular graphics device. For instance, if you have a graphics device that accepts only single sheets of paper, such as the HP 7475A plotter, you can configure PrintGraph to run unattended except when you have to load a new piece of paper. Many graphics devices, such as the HP plotter, are smart enough to know when you have room to print the next graph. If you do have room, the device will print. Otherwise, it will pause for you to load another piece of paper.

If, on the other hand, you have a graphics device that accepts continuous-form paper, such as the IBM Color Graphics Printer, you can have graphs printed continuously and unattended. You simply elect not to have the printer pause between graphs. (Set **Pause** to **No** as discussed below.)

Individual Print Options

If your configuration settings are inappropriate for one of your graphs, you can easily override them. For example, suppose you want to change the **Size** settings. You simply call up the **Size** menu and choose the settings you need. These new settings remain in effect until you change them or exit from the program.

Pause and Eject Options

Another **Settings** menu selection is **Action**, which controls the interval between graphs when you are printing in batch mode. The two choices for **Action** are **Pause** and **Eject**. **Pause** makes the printer pause between graphs so that you can change settings, and **Eject** controls whether the printer stops for you to change paper. Your choices of these options depend on how many graphs you are printing and what size they are. For example, if you are printing several full-size graphs on a dot-matrix printer, you probably want the **Eject** option set so that the paper advances automatically between graphs.

Align and Advance Options

The **Align** selection in the main PrintGraph menu sets the program's built-in, top-of-page marker. When you choose the **Align** option, PrintGraph assumes that the paper is correctly aligned in the printer, with the top of the form in the right place. PrintGraph then inserts a form feed at the end of every page, using the page-length information you provided when installing the graphics device.

Note: Many printers have controls that allow you to scroll the paper up and down one line at a time. PrintGraph does not recognize these controls. If, for example, you scroll the paper up three lines without realigning, PrintGraph will be three spaces off when the next form-feed command is issued.

Page selection advances the paper one page at a time. This useful option advances continuous-form paper to help you remove the printed output at the end of a printing session.

The Finished Product

To print a graph, you must select **G**o from the main PrintGraph menu. PrintGraph should begin to print. If you have several graphs, you may as well go have lunch while you wait because PrintGraph's high-resolution printing takes a long time. Printing the graph shown in figure 10.7 in full size on a Toshiba 1340 printer took about four minutes.

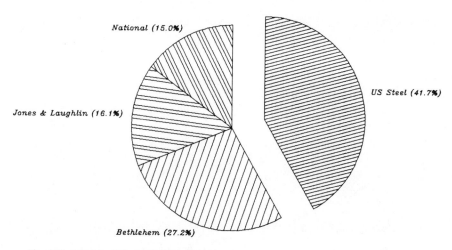

Fig. 10.7. A finished pie graph of steel shares.

Exiting from PrintGraph

Exiting from PrintGraph is similar to exiting from 1-2-3. You simply choose **E**xit from the main PrintGraph menu. After you select **E**xit, you will be returned to the Lotus Access System or to DOS, depending on how you entered PrintGraph. If you entered from DOS (started with the 1-2-3 /System command), type *exit* and press Enter. You will be returned to the 1-2-3 worksheet.

11
Data Management

In addition to the electronic spreadsheet and business graphics, 1-2-3 has a third element: data management. Lotus calls this feature *database management* but has redefined the term. In the past, the term *database management* described the management of data on disk. Because of the greater memory (RAM) capacity of the IBM PC, however, the entire 1-2-3 database resides in the spreadsheet within main memory. There are both advantages and disadvantages to this approach.

The advantages of having the database in RAM are speed, ease of use, and ease of access. The speed results from a reduction in the time required to manipulate the database in RAM. By doing all the work inside the spreadsheet, 1-2-3 saves the time required for input and output to disk. 1-2-3's extremely fast database manager does most of its operations in the blink of an eye.

The ease of use is a result of integrating data management with other spreadsheet functions and commands. The database function meshes well with 1-2-3's other functions, including graphing and text processing. The commands for adding, modifying, and deleting items in a database are the same ones you have already seen for manipulating cells or groups of cells within a worksheet. (To locate commands quickly, refer to the 1-2-3 command menu map at the back of this book.) Specific commands for manipulating the database are consistent with all the other spreadsheet commands.

Finally, Lotus Development Corporation has made the entire database visible within the spreadsheet. Other databases hide on disk everything except the items you have specified. In 1-2-3, however, you can clearly see all the items in the database by scrolling through the worksheet. The database therefore is easier to understand and use.

The major disadvantage of Lotus's approach is the limitation it imposes on the size of the database. The maximum number of records you can have in any database is just under 8,200. The number of records you can have in a particular database is a function of the amount of memory each record requires both in the computer and on disk. If your computer has 640K of memory, you can store about 1,000 400-byte records or 8,000 50-byte records. For large databases, you need to extend the memory capacity beyond 640K. A database of 8,000 500-byte records requires the maximum four megabytes of extended memory (see Chapter 3 for further discussion of extended memory). A database of 8,000 500-byte records will also take up four megabytes on disk.

Because of these limitations, 1-2-3 works best with "personal" databases—small to medium-sized databases that fit easily in RAM. Lists of telephone numbers, addresses, checks, etc., are all well suited to this kind of database application.

1-2-3's file-translation capabilities let dBASE users take advantage of 1-2-3's data commands. With ease, the dBASE user can pull all or part of a dBASE database into 1-2-3; process it with the 1-2-3 data commands; and, if necessary, use the Translate Utility to write the information in dBASE format back to disk.

All the commands in this chapter share the same /Data command root. Some of them, however, are not actually database commands, but more properly belong to the spreadsheet application. The /Data Fill, /Data Table, /Data Distribution, /Data Matrix, and /Data Regression commands all fit into this category. They are covered in their own sections at the end of this chapter.

What Is a Database?

A database is a collection of information. In its simplest form, a database is merely a list. The list might contain any kind of information, from addresses to tax-deductible expenditures.

In 1-2-3, the word *database* means a range of cells that spans at least one column and more than one row. This definition, however, does not distinguish between a database and any other range of cells. Because a database is actually a list, its manner of organization sets it apart from ordinary cells. Just as a list must be organized to be useful, a database must be organized to permit access to the information it contains.

Remember nonetheless that in 1-2-3 a database is similar to any other group of cells. This knowledge will help you as you learn about the different /Data commands that are covered in this chapter. There are many instances in which you can use these database commands in what you might consider "nondatabase" applications.

As mentioned before, an important aspect of a database is the way it is organized. The manner of organization depends on what is in the database. To understand the organization of a database, you need to know a few terms.

First, databases are made up of *records*. Each record corresponds to an item in a list. For example, if you list all the things you have to do next week and list beside each item the day of the week by which you hope to have the item completed, then each item and associated day of the week correspond to a record in a database.

Records are made up of *fields*. One field of the list in figure 11.1 contains the name of a task, and the other field contains the day planned for completion of the task. The term *field* can also refer collectively to all fields in a database that contain the same kind of information. For example, the term *field* can be used in reference to all of the entries in figure 11.1 that list things to be done.

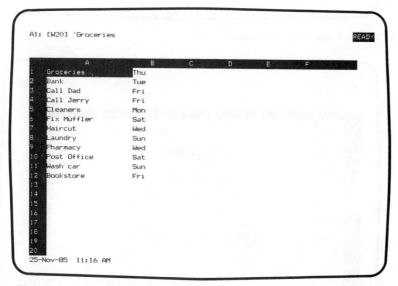

Fig. 11.1. A simple to-do list.

1-2-3 has its own definitions for records and fields. A *record* is a row of cells within a database, and a *field* is a single cell (cell A5, for instance) within a record (or row). For example, in the Addresses database, figure 11.2A, the third record includes all cell contents in the row beginning with "Cotter, James F." (row 5). In the Deductible Expenses database, figure 11.2B, the Amount field for the Secretarial Help record contains $150.00 (cell C4).

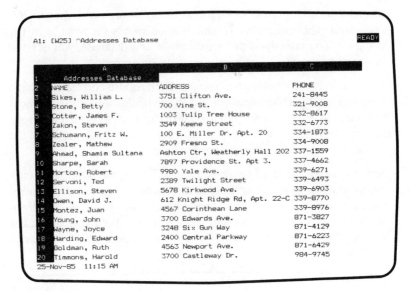

Fig. 11.2A. The Addresses Database.

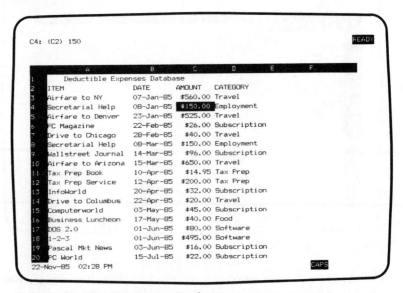

Fig. 11.2B. The Deductible Expenses Database.

Notice that the labels at the top of the columns are *field names*. Field names may be necessary for some database manipulations.

What Can You Do with a Database?

The mailing list shown in figure 11.3 is an example of a very simple 1-2-3 database. If this were your own database, what would you use it for? You might want to *sort* it by last name to help you find an address. You might want to sort also the items by ZIP code to create mailing labels for mailing items at the special bulk mailing rates for sorted mail.

```
F2: [W6] '46209                                              READY

          A          B         C                  D          E      F
 1  LAST        FIRST     STREET ADDRESS       CITY        STATE ZIP
 2  Harrington  James     12345 Arlington Lane Covington   KY    46209
 3  Thomas      Brian     18499 Central Park Ave New York  NY    12945
 4  Leugers     Karen     21 Hill St. Apt. 34  San Francisco CA  34892
 5  Englert     Michael   224 Orange St.       Buffalo     NY    13427
 6  Smith       Margaret  2341 Kyles Lane      Hoboken     NJ    08125
 7  Pryor       Aaron     2345 Milford St.     Cincinnati  OH    45209
 8  Cleary      Esther    238 Higgins St. Apt. 14 Spokane  WA    89042
 9  Wright      Ned       31238 Carolina St.   Kettering   OH    43289
10  Saunders    Ronald    3124 Keystone Ave.   Indianapolis IN   46250
11  McGruder    Mary      3214 Park Lane Apt. 32 Raleigh   NC    23459
12  Simpson     Jeremy    3509 Ludlow Ave.     Newport     KY    43892
13  Wolf        Barbara   3890 Arnold Ave.     Dallas      TX    57820
14  Rooney      Kevin     3910 Atwater Ave. Apt. 3 Providence RI 02912
15  Franks      Mike      4284 Knight Circle   Rochester   NY    09025
16  Sorrenson   Sarah     432 Keys Crescent    Bloomington IN    47401
17  Holland     Earl      4983 Drake Rd.       Cincinnati  OH    45243
18  Tuke        Samuel    9038 Greenup St.     Seekonk     RI    02915
19  Malvern     Thomas    939 Dime Circle      Nashville   TN    47341
20  Yeager      Patrick   4237 Mariemont Ave.  Eugene      OR    57869
25-Nov-85  10:08 AM
```

Fig. 11.3. The Mailing List database.

Besides sorting the list, you might want to *query* it for a name or group of names. For example, you could search for the address for a particular person, or select all the people in the database that live in the state of New York.

Sorting and querying are the main methods used in 1-2-3 to extract information from a database. Both of these methods have one or more special /**Data** commands associated with them.

Creating a Database

A database looks like any other list in a 1-2-3 worksheet. In fact, you enter data into cells in the same way that you do for all applications.

To create a database, first find an out-of-the-way area of the worksheet that will not be needed for anything else. The area you choose should be large enough to accommodate the number of records you plan to enter in the current session as well as in the future. The number of records you intend to add in the future may be difficult to gauge. In many cases, you are safe entering the database at the foot of the active area of the worksheet, where you will have room for expansion.

After you have selected the appropriate area of the worksheet for the database, enter the field names across a single row. The field names must be labels, even if they are the numeric labels "1," "2," etc. You can use more than one row for the field names, but 1-2-3 processes only the values that appear in the bottom row. Keep in mind that all field names should be unique; any repetition of names "confuses" 1-2-3 when you search or sort the database.

After the field names are entered, enter the records in the database. To enter the first record, move the cursor to the row directly below the field-name row; do not leave any blank rows if you plan to search values in the database. You can then enter data across the row in the normal manner.

Enabling you to enter database information just as you enter other worksheet data is one of 1-2-3's simplest, yet most elegant, features. This consistency is one reason why manipulating database information is so much easier in 1-2-3 than in specialty database programs, such as dBASE III.

In those other programs, the length and type of each field must be specified in great detail before data is entered. These specifications actually tell the program how to store the values on disk. As you will recall from Chapter 2, the 1-2-3 program internally controls the way that data is stored on disk. You control the format for display purposes only. Recall that 1-2-3 offers the Format and Column-width options for controlling the way cells are displayed on the screen.

Modifying a Database

The first thing you will want to know after you have created a database is how to change it. To add and delete records in a database, use the same commands for inserting and deleting rows that you use for any other application in 1-2-3. Because records correspond to rows, you begin inserting a record with the /Worksheet Insert Row command. (This command was used earlier to insert blank rows in a worksheet.) You then fill in the various fields in the rows with the appropriate data. Figure 11.4 shows an example of inserting a record in the middle of a database.

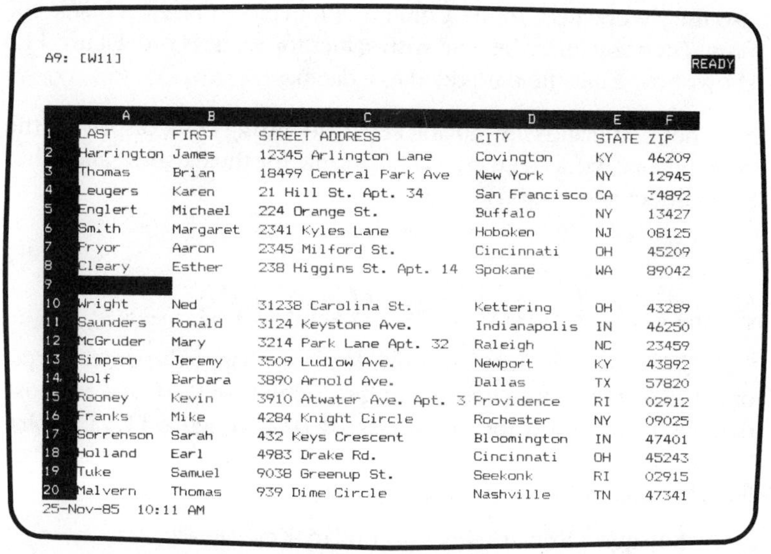

Fig. 11.4A. Making space for a new entry in the Mailing List database.

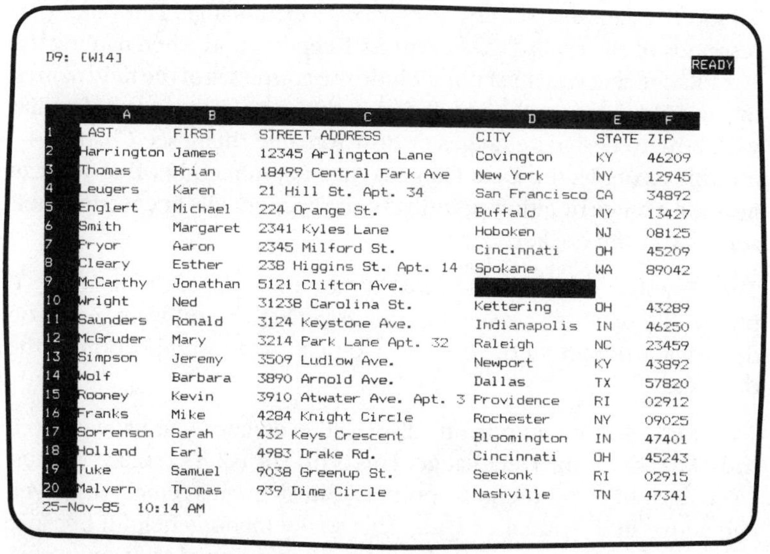

Fig. 11.4B. Mailing List with new entry in progress.

To delete records, move your cell pointer to the row or rows that you wish to delete and use the /Worksheet Delete Row command.

Modifying fields in a database is really the same as modifying the contents of cells in any other application. As shown in Chapter 3, you modify cell contents by either retyping the cell entry or using the F2 (Edit) key and editing the entry. To add a new field to a database, you use the /Worksheet Insert Column command to insert a blank column. Then you fill in the field with values for each record. Figure 11.5 shows how a new field is added to a database.

All other commands for moving cells, formatting cells, displaying the contents of a worksheet, etc., are the same for the database and other spreadsheet applications.

Sorting Database Records

1-2-3's data management capability lets you change the order of records by sorting them according to the contents of the fields. Suppose that you want to sort the Addresses database in figure 11.3 in alphabetical order by last name. The command to sort the records, /Data Sort, has the following command menu:

Data-Range   Primary-Key   Secondary-Key   Reset
   Go   Quit

To sort the database, start by designating a Data-Range. This range corresponds to the records to be sorted. Keep in mind when naming the Data-Range that you must not include the addresses of the field names, or the field names will be included in the sort. (If you are unfamiliar with how to designate ranges or how to name them, see Chapter 4.) For this example, the Data-Range is A2..F20. Remember that you can indicate a range by either pointing to the proper cells or entering their addresses from the keyboard.

The Data-Range does not necessarily have to be the entire database. If part of the database already has the organization you want, or if you don't want to sort all the records, you can sort just a portion of the database.

The /Data Sort menu remains displayed even after you have entered the addresses of the Data-Range. This is one of 1-2-3's "sticky" menus. (The /Print Printer menu is another.) Sticky menus remain displayed and active until you enter Quit. This sticky menu is helpful because you don't have to enter /Data Sort at the beginning of each command.

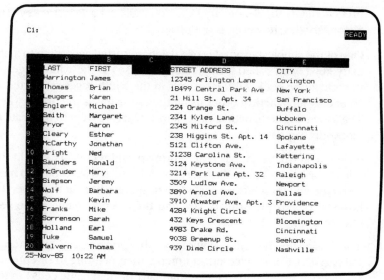

Fig. 11.5A. New column in the Mailing List database.

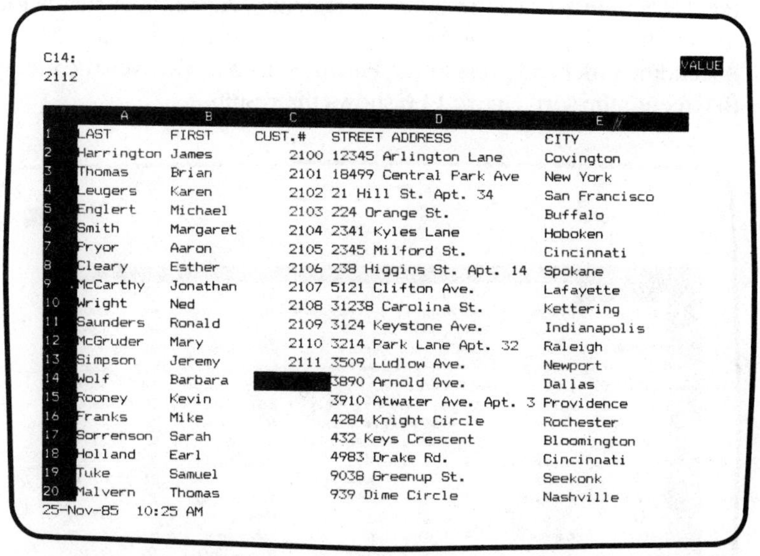

Fig. 11.5B. New column with data entered.

After choosing the **Data-Range**, you must specify the keys for the sort. *Keys* are the fields to which you attach the highest precedence when the database is sorted. The field with the highest precedence is the **Primary-Key**, and the field with the next highest precedence is the Secondary-Key. You must set a Primary-Key. The Secondary-Key, however, is optional.

One of the simplest examples of a database sorted according to a primary key (often called a single-key database) is the white pages of the telephone book. All the records in the white pages are sorted in ascending alphabetical order using the last name as the primary key. This ascending alphabetical-order sort is what we want to re-create in our Addresses database.

A double-key database has both a primary and secondary key. In the telephone book's Yellow Pages, records are sorted according to business type and then further sorted by business name. In this case, the business type is the primary key, and the business name is the secondary key.

You designate the name column as the primary key by entering Primary-Key from the command menu, then pointing to or entering the address of any entry (including blank or field-name cells) in the column containing the primary-key field. In the Addresses database example, you point to cell A1 as the Primary-Key and press Enter. 1-2-3 then asks you to enter "Sort order (A or D)." *A* stands for Ascending and *D* for Descending. For this example, you choose Ascending order and press Enter. Finally, you enter Go from the menu to execute the sort. Figure 11.6 shows the results.

```
A1: [W11] 'LAST                                                    READY

        A          B          C                   D            E      F
1   LAST       FIRST      STREET ADDRESS          CITY         STATE  ZIP
2   Cleary     Esther     238 Higgins St. Apt. 14 Spokane      WA     89042
3   Englert    Michael    224 Orange St.          Buffalo      NY     13427
4   Franks     Mike       4284 Knight Circle      Rochester    NY     09025
5   Harrington James      12345 Arlington Lane    Covington    KY     46209
6   Holland    Earl       4983 Drake Rd.          Cincinnati   OH     45243
7   Leugers    Karen      21 Hill St. Apt. 34     San Francisco CA    34892
8   Malvern    Thomas     939 Dime Circle         Nashville    TN     47341
9   McGruder   Mary       3214 Park Lane Apt. 32  Raleigh      NC     23459
10  Pryor      Aaron      2345 Milford St.        Cincinnati   OH     45209
11  Rooney     Kevin      3910 Atwater Ave. Apt. 3 Providence  RI     02912
12  Saunders   Ronald     3124 Keystone Ave.      Indianapolis IN     46250
13  Simpson    Jeremy     3509 Ludlow Ave.        Newport      KY     43892
14  Smith      Margaret   2341 Kyles Lane         Hoboken      NJ     08125
15  Sorrenson  Sarah      432 Keys Crescent       Bloomington  IN     47401
16  Thomas     Brian      18499 Central Park Ave  New York     NY     12945
17  Tuke       Samuel     9038 Greenup St.        Seekonk      RI     02915
18  Wolf       Barbara    3890 Arnold Ave.        Dallas       TX     57820
19  Wright     Ned        31238 Kitty Hawk St.    Kettering    OH     43289
20  Yeager     Patrick    4237 Mariemont Ave.     Eugene       OR     57869
25-Nov-85   10:30 AM
```

Fig. 11.6. Mailing List after sorting by name.

The speed of the sort is surprising. It takes only a split second for this example and only slightly longer for much larger databases. Again, the main reason for the speed is that the database resides in RAM.

As an example of a double-key database, we will use the Deductible Expenses database (see fig. 11.7A). Our goal is to sort the database alphabetically by category, and by date within each category.

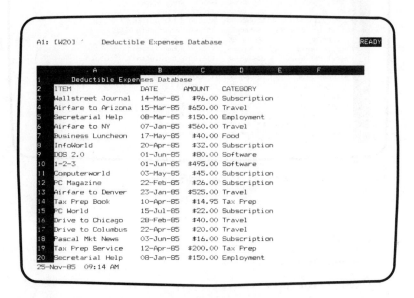

Fig. 11.7A. Deductible Expenses Database before sorting.

To enter the parameters for the sort, we begin by designating A3..D20 as the Data-Range. For the Primary-Key, we enter the address of any entry in the Category column and A for ascending. For the Secondary-Key, we use the address of any entry in the Date column and again enter A for ascending. Finally, we enter Go. Figure 11.7B shows the results.

The order in which the records appear after the sort depends on the ASCII numbers of the contents of the primary and secondary keys. For this reason, you do not want to include blank rows past the end of the database when you designate the Data-Range. Because blanks have precedence over all the characters in a sort, these blank rows will appear at the top of your sorted database.

By using the Install program, you can determine the order of precedence that 1-2-3 uses for sorting text strings. The three choices are:

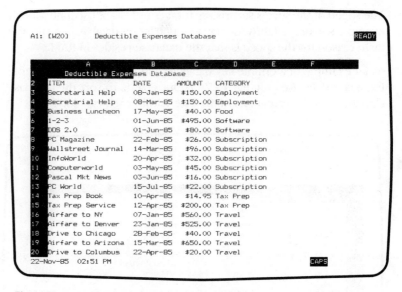

Fig. 11.7B. Deductible Expenses Database after sorting.

NEW WITH

R2

1. ASCII

2. Numbers First

3. Numbers Last

The default sort order is Numbers First. The ASCII and Numbers First options both sort in the following order:

Blank spaces

Special Characters (!, #, $, etc.)

Numeric Characters

Alpha Characters

Special Compose Characters

NEW WITH

R2

The Special Compose Characters are a function of the Compose Key (Alt-F1) and are used to create special international characters.

The only difference between the ASCII and Numbers First options is that in the ASCII sequence, uppercase is sorted before lowercase; in the Numbers First sequence, the case of characters is ignored. The Numbers Last sequence is like Numbers First except that numeric characters come after all alpha characters.

Another rule is that text-string cell entries precede number cell entries. For example, the text-string cell entry "George" precedes the number cell entry 456. Also, formulas are evaluated first for their numeric result and then sorted as numbers. For example, @DATE (80,1,1) is sorted according to its numeric equivalent (29221).

To understand the order of precedence that 1-2-3 uses in sorting, try a simple experiment. Start by making various text, number, and formula entries in a column of cells. Then sort the range of cells you have created and see what happens. Performing a simple experiment like this will help you avoid making mistakes later.

Remember that sorting is not reserved for databases alone. Any list of adjacent rows can be sorted on primary and secondary keys, even though the list may not look like a database in the strictest sense. You might recall from the discussion of lookup tables in Chapter 6, for example, that the items in a table must be arranged in ascending order prior to executing a lookup. Figure 11.8 shows how to sort a lookup table in ascending order.

Another general comment about sorting records in a database is that it is often hard to reconstruct the original order of the records after you have sorted them. If you think that you may want to restore records to their original order, take a simple precaution before sorting: add an additional field containing a number that signifies the original order of the records to the database. If the database contains many records, you may want to use the /Data Fill command to put the numbers in this field.

If you forget this precautionary step and have sorted the database into an order that you simply cannot live with, you can always get the original database back from the disk. The /File Retrieve command will bring the original version into the spreadsheet again, replacing the improperly sorted database. You can reclaim the original version in this way until you have Saved an updated version of the database.

Be sure to save the database before sorting so that you will be able to retrieve the original if you need it. If you save the sorted database under a different name, the original remains available on disk in case the sorted database should turn out to be unusable.

The Reset command is another option on the /Data Sort menu. This command clears the settings for keys and Data-Range that were previously specified in the /Data Sort settings. This is a convenient option if you want to change the settings for sorting items in another area of the worksheet.

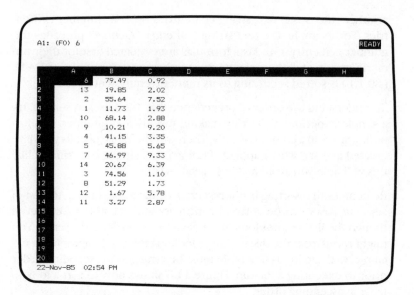

Fig. 11.8A. Data for a Lookup table.

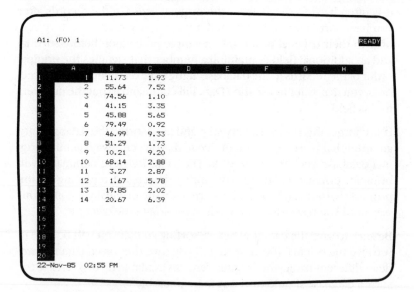

Fig. 11.8B. Lookup table after sorting.

Searching for Records

In addition to sorting a database, 1-2-3's /Data commands let you search for records and then edit, extract, or delete the records you find. These commands also let you find specific records individually or in groups. For example, with 1-2-3 you can find in a telephone-number database the records of all customers who have a certain Area Code; then you can update the information in that group (fig. 11.9). Another use of the **Data** commands would be to extract from a checking-account database the names of all people to whom checks for more than $100.00 were written. Still another example is to purge from an overdue-accounts database the records of all accounts that have been paid.

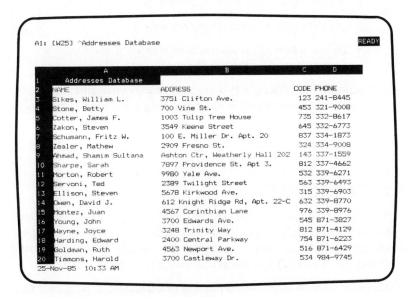

Fig. 11.9. Address and Phone Number database.

We want to locate the cursor at all the records that have an Area Code of 812. The command used to perform the search is /**Data Query.** (*Query* is just another word for *search.*)

/**Data Query** is actually the host command for a series of subcommands.

Find   Moves down through a database locating the cursor at records that match given criteria. You may enter or change data in the records as you move the cursor through them.

Extract   Creates copies in a specified area of the worksheet
            of all or some of the fields in certain records that
            match given criteria

Unique   Similar to extract, but recognizes that some of the
            records in the database may be copies. Includes
            only unique records

Delete   Deletes all the records in a database that match
            given criteria and shifts the remaining records to fill
            in the gaps that are left

In our first example, the Find option is used. Before we can execute
the command, however, we must do three things:

1. Set the input range to be searched

2. Set the criteria for searching records

3. Define where the output will be written in the worksheet
   (not required for Find or Delete)

Accordingly, the /Data Query command requires that three ranges be
specified: the Input range, the Criterion range, and the Output range.

Input Range

The Input range for the /Data Query command is the range of records
you want to search. In our Area Code example, the Input range includes the field names as well as the records of the entire database
(the range A2..D20), but this is not always the case.

You may want to search just a portion of a database, especially if that
database is already well organized. For example, suppose that you had
already sorted a database according to check number and wanted to
find all the checks for more than $150.00 that were written prior to
check number 300. You would have to specify as the Input range only
the area of the database that includes checks with numbers 300 and
below.

The Input range for the Area Code example is similar to the Data-
Range that might be specified for a /Data Sort operation. The field
names *must*, however, be included in the input range, whereas they
cannot be included in the Sort Data-Range. Again, the Input range for
our Area Code example is A2..D20, as shown in figure 11.10.

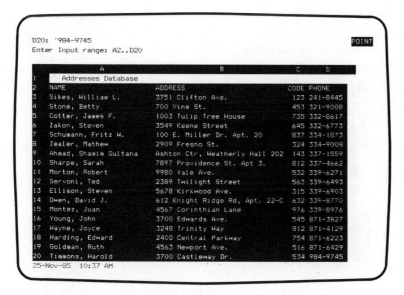

```
D20: '984-9745                                                    POINT
Enter Input range: A2..D20

            A                    B                    C    D
1    Addresses Database
2  NAME                 ADDRESS                       CODE PHONE
3  Sikes, William L.    3751 Clifton Ave.             123  241-8445
4  Stone, Betty         700 Vine St.                  453  321-9008
5  Cotter, James F.     1003 Tulip Tree House         735  332-8617
6  Zakon, Steven        3549 Keene Street             645  332-6773
7  Schumann, Fritz W.   100 E. Miller Dr. Apt. 20     837  334-1873
8  Zealer, Mathew       2909 Fresno St.               324  334-9008
9  Ahmad, Shamim Sultana Ashton Ctr, Weatherly Hall 202 143 337-1559
10 Sharpe, Sarah        7897 Providence St. Apt 3.    812  337-4662
11 Morton, Robert       9980 Yale Ave.                532  339-6271
12 Servoni, Ted         2389 Twilight Street          563  339-6493
13 Ellison, Steven      5678 Kirkwood Ave.            315  339-6903
14 Owen, David J.       612 Knight Ridge Rd, Apt. 22-C 632 339-8770
15 Montez, Juan         4567 Corinthian Lane          976  339-8976
16 Young, John          3700 Edwards Ave.             545  871-3827
17 Wayne, Joyce         3248 Trinity Way              812  871-4129
18 Harding, Edward      2400 Central Parkway          754  871-6223
19 Goldman, Ruth        4563 Newport Ave.             516  871-6429
20 Timmons, Harold      3700 Castleway Dr.            534  984-9745
25-Nov-85  10:37 AM
```

Fig. 11.10. An Input range for an Area Code query.

Criterion Range

The Criterion range includes information specifying the search criteria. Because we want to find all records with an Area Code equal to 812, our search criterion is 812. We need to find a way to express this in terms that 1-2-3 can understand. Figure 11.11 shows the Criterion range for our Area example.

This Criterion range conforms to the general 1-2-3 rules for ranges. A Criterion range can have a maximum width of 32 columns although the length is two or more rows; the first row must contain the field names of the search criteria. The rows below the unique field names contain the criteria themselves.

You can use numbers, labels, or formulas as criteria. In figure 11.11, the position of the number 812 below the field name "Code" in the Criterion range is an example of these criteria. With numbers and labels, the criteria must be positioned directly below the field name to which they correspond in the Criterion range. In figure 11.11, the Criterion range is F2..F3. Be aware that the field names of the Input range and of the Criterion range must match exactly. The Criterion range should be placed in an out-of-the-way spot; in this instance, it is placed beside the Input range.

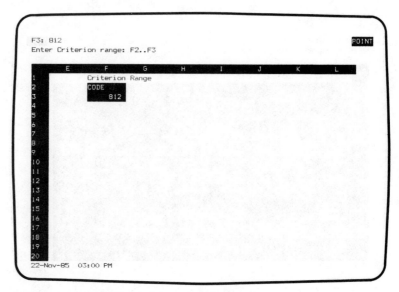

Fig. 11.11. Criterion range for an Area Code query.

The last range usually required for a /Data Query command is the Output range. An Output range, however, is not required in a Find operation because we are simply searching through the Input range. If, though, we needed to extract a copy of the Input range, based on our criteria, we would need to specify an Output range.

Figure 11.12 shows what happens after you specify all the appropriate ranges and finally select Find from the /Data Query command menu.

Notice that the cursor appears on the first record that conforms to our search criterion. By using the ↓ cursor key, we can position the cursor at the next record conforming to the criterion, as shown in figure 11.13.

The ↓ and ↑ cursor keys let you position the cursor to the next and previous records that conform to the search criteria set out in the Criterion range. The Home and End keys can be used to position the cursor on the first and last records in the database, even if those records do not fit the search criteria. Notice that the mode indicator changes from READY to FIND during the search. To end the Find operation and return to the Data Query menu, press either Return or Esc.

In previous releases of 1-2-3, it was not possible to edit the data in a record while in FIND mode. However, Release 2 lets you edit and

```
A10: [W25] 'Sharpe, Sarah                                                FIND

            A                       B                       C    D
 1      Addresses Database
 2  NAME                    ADDRESS                         CODE PHONE
 3  Sikes, William L.       3751 Clifton Ave.               123 241-8445
 4  Stone, Betty            700 Vine St.                    453 321-9008
 5  Cotter, James F.        1003 Tulip Tree House           735 332-8617
 6  Zakon, Steven           3549 Keene Street               645 332-6773
 7  Schumann, Fritz W.      100 E. Miller Dr. Apt. 20       837 334-1873
 8  Zealer, Mathew          2909 Fresno St.                 324 334-9008
 9  Ahmad, Shamim Sultana   Ashton Ctr, Weatherly Hall 202  143 337-1559
10  Sharpe, Sarah           7897 Providence St. Apt 3.      812 337-4662
11  Morton, Robert          9980 Yale Ave.                  532 339-6271
12  Servoni, Ted            2389 Twilight Street            563 339-6493
13  Ellisrn, Steven         5678 Kirkwood Ave.              315 339-6903
14  Owen, David J.          612 Knight Ridge Rd, Apt. 22-C  632 339-8770
15  Montez, Juan            4567 Corinthian Lane            976 339-8976
16  Young, John             3700 Edwards Ave.               545 871-3827
17  Wayne, Joyce            3248 Trinity Way                812 871-4129
18  Harding, Edward         2400 Central Parkway            754 871-6223
19  Goldman, Ruth           4563 Newport Ave.               516 871-6429
20  Timmons, Harold         3700 Castleway Dr.              534 984-9745
25-Nov-85  10:43 AM
```

Fig. 11.12. First record found in Area Code query.

```
A17: [W25] 'Wayne, Joyce                                                 FIND

            A                       B                       C    D
 1      Addresses Database
 2  NAME                    ADDRESS                         CODE PHONE
 3  Sikes, William L.       3751 Clifton Ave.               123 241-8445
 4  Stone, Betty            700 Vine St.                    453 321-9008
 5  Cotter, James F.        1003 Tulip Tree House           735 332-8617
 6  Zakon, Steven           3549 Keene Street               645 332-6773
 7  Schumann, Fritz W.      100 E. Miller Dr. Apt. 20       837 334-1873
 8  Zealer, Mathew          2909 Fresno St.                 324 334-9008
 9  Ahmad, Shamim Sultana   Ashton Ctr, Weatherly Hall 202  143 337-1559
10  Sharpe, Sarah           7897 Providence St. Apt 3.      812 337-4662
11  Morton, Robert          9980 Yale Ave.                  532 339-6271
12  Servoni, Ted            2389 Twilight Street            563 339-6493
13  Ellison, Steven         5678 Kirkwood Ave.              315 339-6903
14  Owen, David J.          612 Knight Ridge Rd, Apt. 22-C  632 339-8770
15  Montez, Juan            4567 Corinthian Lane            976 339-8976
16  Young, John             3700 Edwards Ave.               545 871-3827
17  Wayne, Joyce            3248 Trinity Way                812 871-4129
18  Harding, Edward         2400 Central Parkway            754 871-6223
19  Goldman, Ruth           4563 Newport Ave.               516 871-6429
20  Timmons, Harold         3700 Castleway Dr.              534 984-9745
25-Nov-85  10:45 AM
```

Fig. 11.13. Next record with Area Code 812.

change data as soon as 1-2-3 finds the record you're searching for. To
edit data, use the ← and → cursor keys to move the cursor to different
fields in the current record, then enter new values or use the Edit key
to update the current values in the field. One caution: if you change

the record so that it no longer satisfies the Find criteria and then move away from that record, you cannot use the ↓ or ↑ key to return to the record during the Find operation.

More Complicated Criterion Ranges

Figure 11.14 shows an example of a slightly more complicated Criterion range. It is used with a different database, which stores checking-account records.

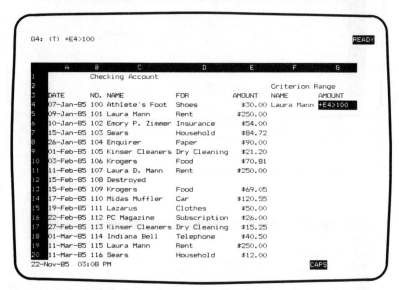

Fig. 11.14. Checking account query with compound criteria.

Notice the label "Laura Mann" below the field name "Name" and the formula +E4>100 below the field name "Amount" in figure 11.14. (This formula is displayed in Text format.) The formula in combination with the "Name" indicates a search for all the checks (with amounts beginning in E4) made out to Laura Mann for an amount greater than $100.00.

You should notice also that the formula is written with a relative address referring to the first row of the database. This is the way all Criterion range formulas should be written. If you want to refer to values outside the Input range, however, you must use absolute addressing. Figure 11.15 shows how relative and absolute addressing are used in the Criterion range. Notice that the address $B$1 is used to refer to the number 812 in cell B1.

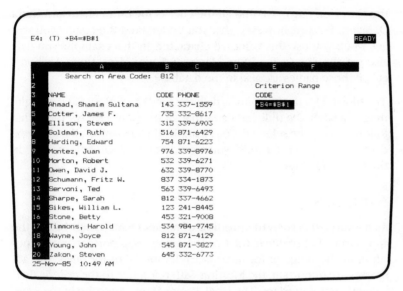

Fig. 11.15. Formula criterion with relative and absolute references.

Wildcards

Referring again to figure 11.14, notice that at least one of the checks in the database was made out to Laura *D*. Mann. We will not get a match with our Criterion range if we don't have a way of handling this discrepancy.

1-2-3 has some special "wildcard" provisions for matching labels. The characters ?, *, and ~ have special meaning when used in the Criterion range. The ? character instructs 1-2-3 to accept any character in that specific position. For example, if we want to see all the checks written for insurance in figure 11.14 and we know that the word "insurance" may or may not have been capitalized, we can enter *?nsurance* below "For" in the Criterion range. Use of the wildcard ensures that we find all the checks for insurance whether the name is entered as "Insurance" or "insurance."

Note that if the sort order is Numeric First (the default) or Numeric Last, 1-2-3 ignores case in /Data Query searches. Use the ? technique only if you have set the sort order to ASCII, using the Advanced Options menu of the Install program, or if you cannot remember the character in a name (Brian or Bryan, for instance).

The * character tells 1-2-3 to accept any and all characters that follow. In the example in figure 11.14, if we enter Laura* below "Name" in the Criterion range, we find all the checks for Laura Mann and Laura D. Mann. Be sure, however, that you understand the results you will get when you use this wildcard character. In this example, you may also get the checks for Laura Manfredi, Laura Mars, Laura Anybody, etc., if those names are also in the database.

The tilde (~) is the last wildcard character. When placed at the beginning of a label, the tilde indicates that all the values *except* those that follow it are to be selected. For example, if you wanted all checks except those written for food, you would enter *~Food* below "For" in the Criterion range.

Formulas

As mentioned earlier, the position of numbers and labels below the appropriate field name in the Criterion range is important, but the position in the range of formulas is irrelevant. With formulas, the addresses are important; the location with reference to the criteria field names is not important. The label "Laura Mann" must be in the same column as "Name" in figure 11.14 to get the desired results. In contrast, if we wanted all checks written for amounts over \$100.00, regardless of to whom they were written, we could enter the criterion in either cell F4 or cell G4:

Example 1		*Example 2*	
Name	Amount	Name	Amount
+E4>100			+E4>100

Compound Criteria

When more than one criterion is used in the second line of the Criterion range, you are giving explicit directions for the results you want. In the previous example, if you place both "Laura Mann" and "+E4>100" on the same line, you are saying that you want to search for checks made out to Laura Mann *and* that were written for amounts over \$100.00. If you add a third line to the Criterion range and move the formula down to the third line, as shown in the following examples, you indicate that you want either checks made out to Laura Mann *or* checks written for over \$100.00. The two Criterion ranges are completely different and will give different results.

Example 1		*Example 2*	
Name	Amount	Name	Amount
Laura Mann	+E4>100	Laura Mann	+E4>100

If these two Criterion ranges were used for sorting the database in figure 11.14, the Criterion range on the left (Example 1) would select check numbers 101, 107, and 115, and the Criterion range on the right (Example 2) would select numbers 101, 107, 110, and 115.

Remember two simple rules: Criteria placed on the same row have the effect of a logical AND. Criteria placed on different rows have the effect of a logical OR. You can make many different kinds of Criterion ranges by combining ANDs and ORs.

For example, the Criterion range below solves the problem of having some checks made out to Laura Mann and others to Laura D. Mann. This criterion definition allows us to get both. The criteria state specifically that we want all the checks made out to Laura Mann AND written for over $100.00 OR those made out to Laura D. Mann AND written for over $100.00.

Name	Amount
Laura Mann	+E4>100
Laura D. Mann	+E4>100

Complex Criteria

Criterion ranges can become complex when you combine complicated formulas with AND and OR criteria. Consider the following example, which selects records for parts from two different suppliers whose prices have increased more than 12 percent from 1984 to 1985.

Supplier	Price
J & L	(Price85>(Price84*1.12))
Bearings Inc.	(Price85>(Price84*1.12))

Notice that in this Criterion range, Price84 and Price85 are range names assigned to the cell addresses of the prices for 1984 and 1985 for the first record in the database. You can assign the field names easily to the cell addresses of the corresponding fields in the first record in the database, using the /Range Name Label Down command (see Chapter 4).

Remembering that you can create a Criterion range containing as many as 32 different fields, look at the Criterion range in figure 11.16, which uses six fields. This Criterion range could be used to select specific stocks from a database that includes one week's data from all the stocks on the American and New York Stock Exchanges.

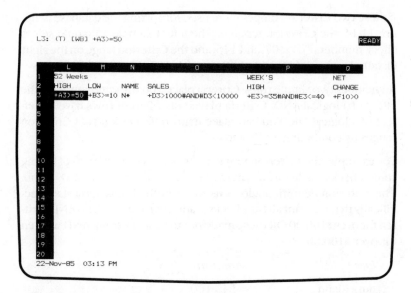

Fig. 11.16. A complex Criterion range for a stock query.

This Criterion range selects (from a database listing stock activities of the past 52 weeks) those stocks that had a high greater than or equal to 50 and a low greater than or equal to 10, a name beginning with "N," sales between 1,000 and 10,000 shares in the last week, a high value between 35 and 40 in the last week, and a positive net change in the last week. As you can see, selection criteria can be made quite complex when necessary.

The best way to become comfortable with Criterion ranges is to experiment with them.

Output Range

The results of a /Data Query are sometimes written to a special area of the worksheet called the Output range. All you need to specify for the Output range is a single row containing the names of the fields that you want copied. You can specify a larger area for the Output range, but all 1-2-3 actually needs is the field names.

If you specify just the row containing the field names as the Output range, 1-2-3 uses all rows beneath the Output range, overwriting any information stored in that area. If you specify a multirow Output range, however, 1-2-3 will not disturb cells outside the specified range. But if you specify a multirow Output range and more records meet the criteria than there are rows in the Output range, an error will occur.

As in the Criterion range, field names for the Output range must match exactly those for the Input range. As you create these ranges (Criterion or Output) use the /Copy command to copy the names to the place where you will create the ranges.

Figure 11.17 shows the output range for our previous example, which extracted all the checks written to Laura Mann for over $100.00. Now we have chosen Extract from the /Data Query menu. Figure 11.18 shows the results.

As you can see, the Extract operation copies (leaving data intact in the Input range) all records conforming to the selection criteria to the area below the field names. In figure 11.17, the Output range F8..I8 was specified.

The advantage of the Extract option is that you can use it to perform detailed analysis on a database. Extract can help you pull a *subset* of data from one or more records in a database and perform special processing on the subset. For example, by setting up the proper Criterion range, you can use a formula to ask the question, "For what have we written checks for over $1,000.00?" The results are shown in figure 11.19.

Fig. 11.17. Output range for checks to Laura Mann.

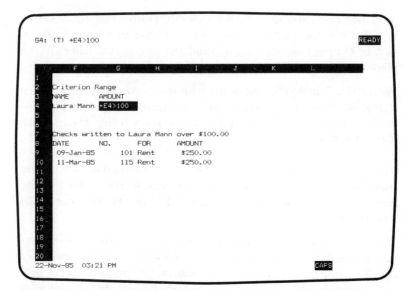

Fig. 11.18. Result of a /Data Query Extract.

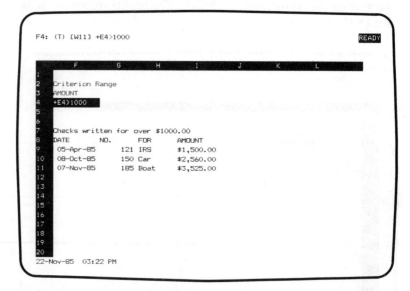

Fig. 11.19. Results of /Data Query Extract for checks for over $1,000.

Once you have extracted the appropriate records, you can analyze them further by setting up new Criterion and Output ranges. For example, you could ask the question, "Of those checks mentioned above, which ones were written in the last 15 days?" Figure 11.20 shows the answer.

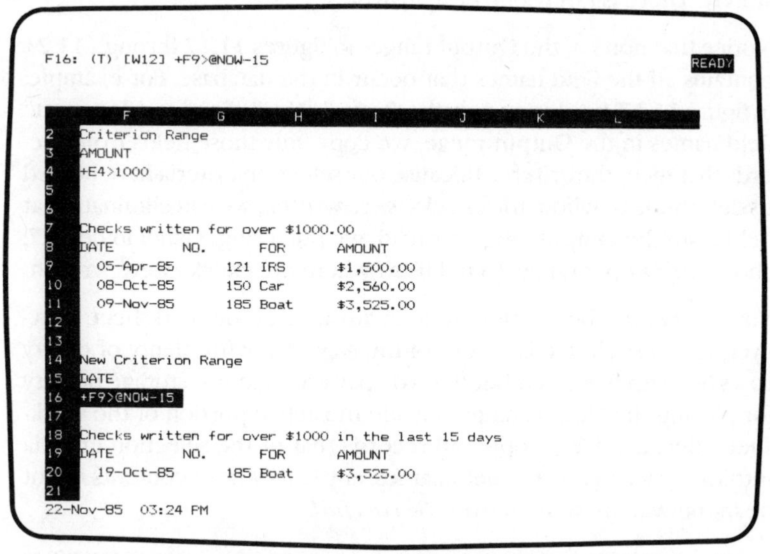

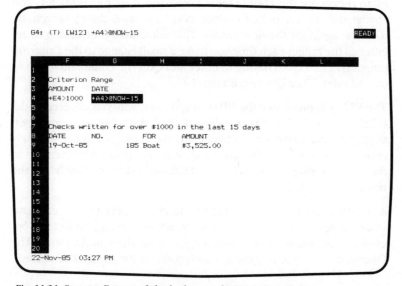

Fig. 11.20. Second Extract of checks for over $1,000 in last 15 days.

We could have achieved the same results in figure 11.20 by performing a single /Data Query operation and combining the selection criteria from the two Criterion ranges, as shown in figure 11.21.

Fig. 11.21. One-step Extract of checks for over $1,000 in last 15 days.

Depending on the size limitations you face and your personal preferences, you can either combine the selection criteria or use them separately. There is rarely one best answer.

Notice that none of the **Output** ranges in figures 11.17 through 11.21 contains all the field names that occur in the database. For example, in figure 11.17, by placing only the "Date," "No.," "For," and "Amount" field names in the **Output** range, we copy only those fields from records that meet the criteria. Because our selection criteria have helped us determine to whom the checks were written, we can eliminate that field from the **Output** range. Instead, we put a single label in cell A7, above the **Output** range, to tell us to whom the checks were written.

You can set up the **Output** range in any area of the worksheet; however, the best choice is an out-of-the-way area with plenty of empty rows beneath it. Remember that you pay only a minor storage penalty for placing the **Output** range outside the active portion of the worksheet. Because 1-2-3 copies all records that fit the selection criteria into the space below the field names, any cells whose contents might be in the way are written over. *Be careful!*

A convenient way to execute a search a second time, or as many times as you like, is to use the F7 (Query) key. 1-2-3 remembers the latest **Input, Criterion,** and **Output** ranges, and if you have not substantially modified them (for instance, adding a third row of criteria for evaluation, yet not specifying it through /**Data Query Criterion**) you can use F7 to reexecute the /**Data Query** command. This capability lets you change the criteria in the **Criterion** range and immediately search the database again for the new values. This eliminates your having to re-enter all the ranges each time you make a small change to the **Criterion** range. You also avoid having to enter and **Quit** the command menu to execute the /**Data Query** command.

The F7 key is much like the F10 (Graph) key, which is covered in detail in Chapter 9. F10 lets you draw a graph with the latest graph settings. You can make small changes to the settings and immediately review their effect. In the same way, you can make small changes to the range settings for searching a database and immediately see the results by pressing F7.

As mentioned earlier, the maximum number of records you can have in a database is about 8,200. But if you are performing an **Extract** operation, you will require additional space for the **Output** range. The **Output** range could require as much room as the original database.

If you plan to perform an **Extract**, consider the requirements of the **Output range** and how they might limit the kind of **Extraction** you can perform. With fairly small databases, this is not a problem. The larger a database gets, however, the more you should keep a careful eye on the amount of RAM available. A frequent check of the /Worksheet Status will tell you how much RAM is left and allow you to gauge what kinds of **Extract** operations are possible given the available RAM.

If you are planning a large database that you will be extracting records from, you may have to invest in more memory to complete the application. (See the discussion at the beginning of this chapter about memory requirements for databases.)

Other Types of Searches

Another type of search, which can be performed with a variation of the /Data Query command, selects all the *unique* records in a database. This option can copy all unique records from a database to a separate part of the worksheet. Another, more popular, way to use the option is to focus on specific fields in a database. Suppose, for example, that you want a listing of all the companies represented in your customer database. Suppose further that your customer database is organized in the manner shown in figure 11.22: all the records have a "Name" field and a "Company" field.

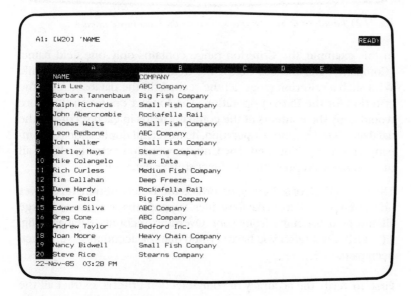

Fig. 11.22. Customer database.

As you can see, several companies are represented more than once in the database. To avoid copying duplicate records to the Output range, we use the Unique option. The Unique option is set up like the Extract option, but the results can be quite different. Figure 11.23 shows how the Extract and Unique options work on the same Criterion range (J2..J3).

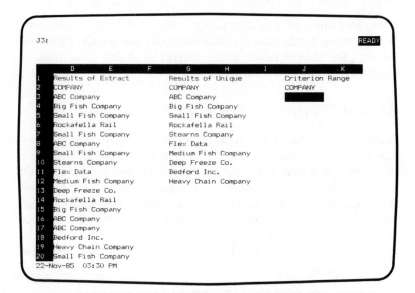

Fig. 11.23. Results of Extract Unique options on the Customer database.

In this example, the Criterion range contains only one field name, "Company," and the cell below the field name has been left blank. With such a criterion range, all the records in the database meet the criterion for the Extract operation. The Extract operation therefore would copy the contents of the company fields in each record in the database. For the Unique operation, however, all duplications of company names are eliminated. The Unique operation extracts a list of all the companies represented in the customer database.

The last method of searching records is the Delete option. It removes unwanted records from database files. Suppose that you want to purge all the paid accounts from your Overdue Accounts database (fig. 11.24), but only after you have verified that the accounts have, in fact, been paid.

First, to verify the accuracy of your selection criteria, extract all the records that have been paid. To accomplish this, use the Extract func-

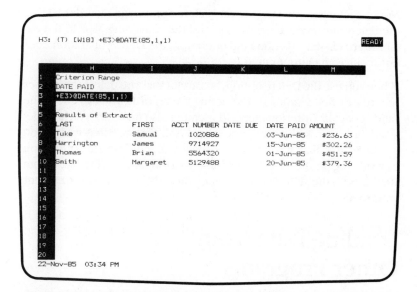

```
A1: [W12] 'Overdue Accounts Database                                    READY

        A           B          C        D         E         F
1   Overdue Accounts Database
2   LAST        FIRST      ACCT NUMBER  DUE DATE  DATE PAID  AMOUNT
3   Tuke        Samuel      1020886  20-Dec-84  03-Jun-85   $236.63
4   McGruder    Mary        4253520  21-Dec-84              $740.23
5   Wright      Orville     4211820  29-Dec-84              $339.85
6   Harrington  James       9714927  30-Dec-84  15-Jun-85   $302.26
7   Saunders    Ronald      1338822  02-Jan-85              $691.14
8   Englert     Michael     4638409  08-Jan-85              $289.88
9   Cleary      Esther      6178812  09-Jan-85              $376.12
10  Simpson     Jeremy      7993805  18-Jan-85              $844.28
11  Holland     Earl        7089077  20-Jan-85              $717.78
12  Sorrenson   Sarah       1173073  29-Jan-85              $519.48
13  Thomas      Brian       5564320  01-Feb-85  01-Jun-85   $451.59
14  Pryor       Aaron       7456362  04-Feb-85              $247.49
15  Leugers     Karen       4114529  10-Feb-85              $931.06
16  Wolf        Barbara     4587979  12-Feb-85              $627.93
17  Mansfield   James       7949146  18-Feb-85               208.98
18  Rooney      Kevin       4699322  19-Feb-85              $238.84
19  Smith       Margaret    5129488  20-Feb-85  20-Jun-85   $379.36
20  Malvern     Thomas      1020886  20-Feb-85              $857.10
25-Nov-85  10:53 AM
```

Fig. 11.24. Overdue Accounts database.

tion with the **Criterion** definitions shown in figure 11.25. The figure also shows the results of the **Extraction**.

```
H3: (T) [W18] +E3>@DATE(85,1,1)                                        READY

        H           I          J        K        L        M
1   Criterion Range
2   DATE PAID
3   +E3>@DATE(85,1,1)
4
5   Results of Extract
6   LAST        FIRST      ACCT NUMBER DATE DUE  DATE PAID AMOUNT
7   Tuke        Samual      1020886             03-Jun-85  $236.63
8   Harrington  James       9714927             15-Jun-85  $302.26
9   Thomas      Brian       5564320             01-Jun-85  $451.59
10  Smith       Margaret    5129488             20-Jun-85  $379.36
11
12
13
14
15
16
17
18
19
20
22-Nov-85  03:34 PM
```

Fig. 11.25. Extract to verify paid-up accounts before deletion.

After performing the **Extract** operation and reviewing the results shown in figure 11.25, use the same **Criterion** range for the **Delete** operation. The results appear in figure 11.26.

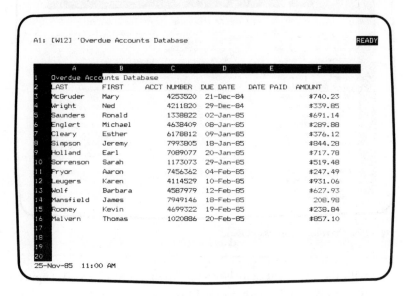

Fig. 11.26. Overdue Accounts Database after deletion of paid-up accounts.

Notice that when you execute the **Delete** option, the records meeting the deletion criteria are removed, and the remaining gaps in the database are closed. Like the **Find** operation, the **Delete** operation does not require an **Output** range.

When you use the **Delete** option, be careful that you delete the proper records. By first **Finding** or **Extracting** the records, you can check the validity of your **Criterion** range. Remember also that once you have deleted the records, they are gone from RAM. You may first want to do a **/File Save** so that, if you make a mistake using the **Delete** option, you can still regain the original database by bringing the file back from storage with the **/File Retrieve** command and writing over the current worksheet.

Loading Data from Other Programs

1-2-3 is commonly used to build spreadsheets and databases in which all the data is typed in from scratch. Most of the businesses now adopting 1-2-3, however, already have a considerable amount of data stored on other computer systems; retyping all that data into 1-2-3 would be expensive and wasteful. Although you may want to use 1-2-3 to analyze data from your accounting system, for example, the analysis may not be worth doing if all the accounting data has to be retyped. Retyping will cost you time and money and leave your program vulnerable to typing errors.

Lotus has provided several means of importing data from other programs into 1-2-3. First, the Translate Utility will translate data from VisiCalc, DIF, dBASE II, and dBASE III files directly into 1-2-3 spreadsheet format, allowing the translated data to be /File Retrieved or /File Combined into the current worksheet. (The Translate Utility is covered in Chapter 7.) If your data is in one of these formats, your problem is solved.

Second, the /File Import command provides a way of reading into a 1-2-3 spreadsheet data stored on disk as a text file. Any special "Numeric" formatted data can be read directly into a range of spreadsheet cells. Other data can be stored as long labels in a single column (one row of the report per cell) to be decoded into the appropriate data values or fields with 1-2-3's @ functions or the /Data Parse command.

Finally, some macro commands allow you to read and write an ASCII sequential file directly from within 1-2-3 macros. These macro commands are discussed in detail in Chapter 12.

NEW WITH

R2

Loading Data from ASCII Report Files

Most business software packages can store files on disk in the same format as reports sent to the printer. These "print image" files are the basis for 1-2-3's most widely used method of loading data from external programs, the /File Import command.

The /File Import command (discussed in Chapter 7) gives you a general-purpose method for loading data from other programs into 1-2-3. This method works with data written to a disk as plain text (a print image) by another program. Plain text, here, is ASCII text (character for character.) If you indicate that the data to be imported is "Numeric", 1-2-3 will interpret each data value as it is read in and place each number in its own cell. The numeric data file, however, must be in a special format with all nonnumeric data delimited by quotes (").

Some, but not all, business computer programs can write data in this special format.

If you specify that the data is "Text" rather than "Numbers," 1-2-3 reads the file into a column in the worksheet. Each line in the file is entered as a long label in a cell. Although this method does not require any special formatting of the file, the data is not ready to use in the form in which it is loaded into the worksheet. You can use 1-2-3's string functions to extract the desired values from the long labels, but the /Data Parse command can accomplish the same thing more easily.

NEW WITH

R2

Using /Data Parse

The /Data Parse command is a flexible means of extracting numeric or string data from a column of long labels. In general, the command converts a column of long labels into one or more columns of labels or numbers from a pattern you specify in the Format-Line.

For example, suppose that you have just Imported the data in figure 11.27 and you want to convert it to a 1-2-3 database. (This data was generated by printing figure 11.26 to disk.) To invoke /Data Parse, place the cursor on the first cell in the column to be parsed and select the /Data Parse command from the main menu. The following menu will appear:

Format-Line   Input-Column   Output-Range   Reset
   Go   Quit

Input-Column selects the range that you want parsed. The Format-Line command specifies the pattern or patterns for splitting up the long labels into numbers and labels. Output-Range specifies the upper left corner of a block of cells that will hold the parsed data. The Reset command resets any previously specified Input-Column and Output-Range. The Go command performs the parse based on the specified Input-Column, Format-Line(s), and Output-Range.

To parse the data in figure 11.27, you perform the following operations. First, move the cursor to the first row in the worksheet containing the data you want to parse. If, for example, you want to split the long labels containing names, account numbers, due dates, date paid, and amount, move the cursor to cell A3. Then select /Data Parse Format-Line. When you press Enter after selecting Format-Line, 1-2-3 will insert a format line above the row where you have positioned the cursor. After 1-2-3 has created a format line, you can edit it by selecting Format-line a second time and then selecting Edit.

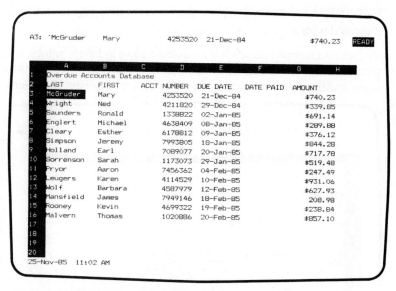

Fig. 11.27. Data entered into the worksheet with /File Import Text.

If your file contains titles and column headings as well as data, or if the data is in more than one format, you will need to create a format line for each kind of line you want to convert. To create more than one format line, you must exit from the /Data Parse command and reposition the cursor before creating the next format line. Figure 11.28 shows the data of figure 11.27 with two format lines added. One format line decodes the database names, and the other format line decodes the database records.

To complete the /Data Parse operation for multiple format lines, you use the /Data Parse Input-Range command to create an input range and the /Data Parse Output-Range command to create an output range. The input range is the column of labels you want to parse—column A in our example. The output range is the worksheet range in which you want the parsed data to be entered. The output range can be an area outside the original column of labels or an area including the original column of labels. Figure 11.29 shows the result of using the /Data Parse command with the format lines shown in figure 11.28, the range A2..A18 in figure 11.28 as the input column, and cell I2 in figure 11.29 as the Output Range. Notice that the formats (Currency, Date) were not carried to the Output range.

The first format line in figure 11.28 reads the column titles, using the Label format. Each label field in the format line consists of an *L* fol-

NEW WITH

R2

NEW WITH
R2

lowed by *greater-than* signs (>). The spaces separating the fields are indicated with asterisks (✳).

The second format line reads the database rows as labels, values, and dates. The value-field indicators consist of a *V* followed by greater-than signs, and the date fields consist of a *D* followed by greater-than signs.

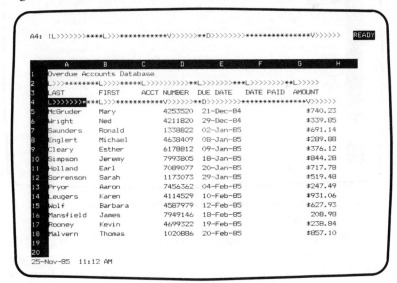

Fig. 11.28. Long labels with format lines for /Data Parse.

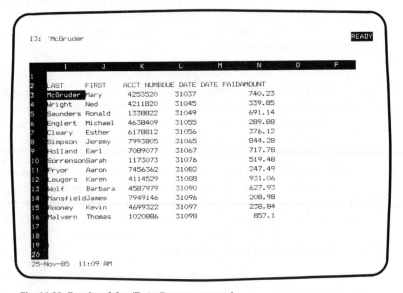

Fig. 11.29. Results of the /Data Parse command.

Cautions on Using /Data Parse

If a value in the column being parsed continues beyond the end of the field marked by the >'s, 1-2-3 keeps parsing the data until a blank is encountered or the value runs into the next field in the format line. If you are parsing labels, be sure to make the field widths in the format line wide enough so that you don't lose data because of blanks. If you are parsing values, the field widths are less critical.

To get a feel for this important command, you should experiment on small amounts of data. Once you understand how the /Data Parse command operates, you will find 1-2-3 applicable in many more situations than you thought possible.

Database Statistical Functions

1-2-3's database statistical functions are similar to the spreadsheet statistical functions but have been modified to manipulate database fields. These functions are another unique feature of 1-2-3.

Like the standard statistical functions, the database statistical functions perform in one simple statement calculations that would otherwise require several statements. This efficiency and ease of application make these excellent tools. They include:

@DCOUNT	Gives the number of items in a list
@DSUM	Sums the values of all the items in a list
@DMIN	Gives the minimum of all the items in a list
@DMAX	Gives the maximum of all the items in a list
@DSTD	Gives the standard deviation of all the items in a list
@DVAR	Gives the variance of all the items in a list
@DAVG	Gives the arithmetic mean of all the items in a list

The general form of these functions is

@DFUN(Input range, Offset, Criterion range)

The Input and Criterion ranges are the same as those used by the /Data Query command. The Input range specifies the database or part of a database to be scanned, and the Criterion range specifies which records are to be selected. The Offset indicates which field to select from the database records; the Offset value must be either zero or a positive integer. A value of zero indicates the first column, a one indicates the second column, and so on.

Now we present an example that uses the database statistical functions. The example involves computing the mean, variance, and standard deviation of the average interest rates offered by money market funds for a given week. If you are unfamiliar with the concepts of mean, variance, and standard deviation, they are covered in Chapter 6. At this point, we assume that you know what these terms mean, and we simply show you how to use them for database applications.

Figure 11.30 shows the Money Market Returns database and the results of the various database functions. Notice that the functions to find the maximum and minimum rates of return are also included.

The functions and their ranges are:

Count	@DCOUNT(A3..B20,1,D13..D14)
Mean	@DAVG(A3..B20,1,D13..D14)
Variance	@DVAR(A3..B20,1,D13..D14)
Std. Dev.	@DSTD(A3..B20,1,D13..D14)
Maximum	@DMAX(A3..B20,1,D13..D14)
Minimum	@DMIN(A3..B20,1,D13..D14)

Figure 11.30 shows that the week's mean return for 17 different money market funds works out to an annual percentage rate of 7.7 (cell E4) with a variance of .057 (cell E5). This result means that about 68 percent of the money market funds return between 7.46 and 7.94 percent annually.

One Std. Dev. below mean = 7.7 – .238 = 7.46

One Std. Dev. above mean = 7.7 + .238 = 7.94

The result of the @DMIN function (cell E8) shows that Summit Cash Reserves returns the lowest rate at 7.3 percent. This value is almost two standard deviations below the mean. That figure—two standard deviations below the mean—is computed as follows:

Two Std. Devs. below mean = 7.7 – (2 x .238) = 7.22

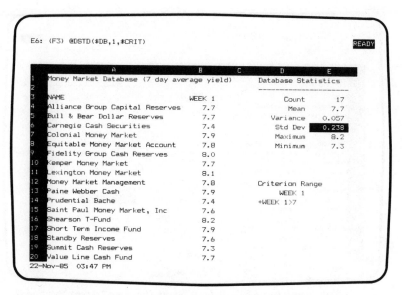

```
E6: (F3) @DSTD($DB,1,$CRIT)                                    READY

              A               B      C       D         E
1  Money Market Database (7 day average yield)   Database Statistics
2
3  NAME                     WEEK 1              Count      17
4  Alliance Group Capital Reserves    7.7       Mean      7.7
5  Bull & Bear Dollar Reserves        7.7     Variance   0.057
6  Carnegie Cash Securities           7.4      Std Dev   0.238
7  Colonial Money Market              7.9      Maximum    8.2
8  Equitable Money Market Account     7.8      Minimum    7.3
9  Fidelity Group Cash Reserves       8.0
10 Kemper Money Market                7.7
11 Lexington Money Market             8.1
12 Money Market Management            7.8     Criterion Range
13 Paine Webber Cash                  7.9         WEEK 1
14 Prudential Bache                   7.4     +WEEK 1>7
15 Saint Paul Money Market, Inc       7.6
16 Shearson T-Fund                    8.2
17 Short Term Income Fund             7.9
18 Standby Reserves                   7.6
19 Summit Cash Reserves               7.3
20 Value Line Cash Fund               7.7
22-Nov-85  03:47 PM
```

Fig. 11.30. Analysis of Money Market Fund Returns, using database statistical functions.

Because approximately 95 percent of the population falls within plus or minus two standard deviations of the mean, Summit Cash Reserves is close to being in the lowest 2.5 percent of the population of money market funds for that week; 5 percent is divided by 2 because the population is assumed to be normal. (See Chapter 6 for a further discussion of how to interpret the statistical functions.)

Conversely, the Shearson T-Fund returns 8.2 percent, the highest rate. The @DMAX function has determined the highest rate (cell B16) to be just over two standard deviations above the mean, the highest 2.5 percent of the population.

By setting up the proper criteria, you can analyze any portion of the database that you wish. Now, how do the statistics change if funds returning less than 7.5 percent are excluded from the statistics? Figure 11.31 gives the answer.

Obviously, the database statistical functions can tell you a great deal about the database as a whole and about how to interpret the values contained in it. If you add several more weeks' data to the database, as shown in figure 11.32, the database statistical functions can also be used to analyze all or part of the larger database.

```
D14: (T) [W13] +WEEK 1>=7.5                                    READY

              A              B        C        D          E
1  Money Market Database (7 day average yield)  Database Statistics
2                                              --------------------
3  NAME                      WEEK 1                   Count      14
4  Alliance Group Capital Reserves   7.7             Mean      7.8
5  Bull & Bear Dollar Reserves       7.7             Variance  0.031
6  Carnegie Cash Securities          7.4             Std Dev   0.175
7  Colonial Money Market             7.9             Maximum   8.2
8  Equitable Money Market Account    7.8             Minimum   7.6
9  Fidelity Group Cash Reserves      8.0
10 Kemper Money Market               7.7
11 Lexington Money Market            8.1
12 Money Market Management           7.8             Criterion Range
13 Paine Webber Cash                 7.9             WEEK 1
14 Prudential Bache                  7.4             +WEEK 1>=7.5
15 Saint Paul Money Market, Inc      7.6
16 Shearson T-Fund                   8.2
17 Short Term Income Fund            7.9
18 Standby Reserves                  7.6
19 Summit Cash Reserves              7.3
20 Value Line Cash Fund              7.7
22-Nov-85   03:50 PM
```

Fig. 11.31. Money Fund analysis with funds earning less than 7.5 percent excluded.

```
J3: @DCOUNT($DB,3,$CRIT)                                       READY

        D        E        F        G        H        I        J        K
1                                                    Database Statistics
2                                                    --------------------
3   WEEK 3   WEEK 4   WEEK 5   WEEK 6                 Count        17
4    7.9      7.9       8        8                    Mean        7.9
5    7.8      7.8      7.8      7.9                    Variance    0.058
6    7.5      7.5      7.6      7.6                    Std Dev     0.240
7    7.9       8        8        8                    Maximum     8.3
8    7.9       8        8       8.1                   Minimum     7.4
9    8.1      8.2      8.2      8.3
10   7.8      7.8      7.8      7.9
11   8.2      8.3      8.3      8.3
12   7.9       8        8        8                    Criterion Range
13    8        8       8.1      8.1                   WEEK 3
14   7.5      7.6      7.7      7.7                    +WEEK 3>
15   7.7      7.7      7.8      7.8
16   8.3      8.3      8.4      8.4
17   8.1      8.2      8.2      8.2
18   7.8      7.8      7.9      7.9
19   7.4      7.4      7.5      7.6
20   7.7      7.7      7.8      7.9
22-Nov-85   04:02 PM                                 CALC
```

Fig. 11.32. Additional Money Fund data.

You can use all the methods you have seen so far to interpret the statistics in figure 11.32. The Input, Offset, and Criterion ranges used for the data from the third week of our example are as follows:

Input range	A3..G20
Offset	3 (for the fourth column)
Criterion range	I13..I14

From this information, you can determine how the formulas have been set up for each week. The Criterion range displayed in figure 11.32 (I13..I14) shows the criteria used to select the values for the third week.

Table Building

The table-building function has the same **Data** command root as all the other commands covered in this chapter. Table building is an extended version of the "what if" process. In fact, you could duplicate the functions performed by the table-building feature by performing repeated "what if" analyses. Doing so would take a prohibitive amount of time, however. Table building automates the "what if" process so that you can make a thorough analysis with a minimal amount of effort. The **/Data Table** command is the host command for the table-building function, which makes 1-2-3 a superior program for performing "what if" analyses.

Table building automates the "what if" process through iteration: 1-2-3 takes sets of values and substitutes them one at a time for existing values in the worksheet. You provide the values for substitution and tell 1-2-3 where to substitute them. The program automatically records the results.

This procedure may sound mysterious, but it is actually simple; 1-2-3 does most of the work internally. All you have to know is how to set up the appropriate ranges; 1-2-3 takes care of the rest.

Although the **/Data Table** command may take some time to learn, you will find it one of the most powerful commands in 1-2-3. In fact, the strength of this command rivals similar commands in more sophisticated mainframe decision-support systems. When you consider the command's strength with its ease of implementation, the **Data Table** command is an excellent feature of 1-2-3.

The purpose of the **/Data Table** command is to structure the "what if" analysis. The command lets you build a table of input values that the program substitutes one at a time into your model. 1-2-3 then records the results in the table next to the input values.

A very simple example is to build a table of interest rates and determine their effect on the monthly payments of a 30-year mortgage, as shown in figure 11.33.

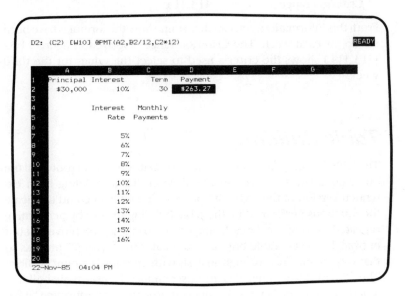

Fig. 11.33. Worksheet for monthly payment analysis.

By using the /**Data T**able **1** command, you can have 1-2-3 substitute in appropriate input cells the interest rates you have entered in a column. After calculating the results, 1-2-3 lists the monthly payments in the column next to the interest rates.

Before entering the /**Data T**able **1** command, you enter the interest-rate values in a column. (To enter those values, we used the /**D**ata Fill command, which is covered in the next section.) Cells B7..B18 hold the interest rates. The next step is to enter either the appropriate formula for calculating the results or the cell address from which to draw those results. This entry goes next to the column of interest rates and one row above the first entry.

We entered +D2 in cell C6, as shown in figure 11.34, but we could have entered in C6 the formula for computing the value. The formula in cell D2 is @PMT(A2, B2/12,C2*12). +D2 appears because the /**R**ange Format **T**ext command was issued for cell C6, causing the formula rather than the value to be displayed.

After we issue the /**Data T**able **1** command, 1-2-3 prompts us to indicate an "Input Cell." This is the cell in which all the values in the

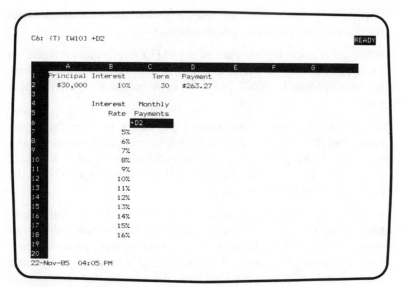

```
C6:  (T)  [W10]  +D2                                          READY

          A          B          C          D        E       F       G
1   Principal  Interest       Term    Payment
2    $30,000        10%         30    $263.27
3
4              Interest    Monthly
5                  Rate   Payments
6                          +D2
7                    5%
8                    6%
9                    7%
10                   8%
11                   9%
12                  10%
13                  11%
14                  12%
15                  13%
16                  14%
17                  15%
18                  16%
19
20
22-Nov-85   04:05 PM
```

Fig. 11.34A. Worksheet before using the /Data Table 1 command.

```
C6:  (T)  [W10]  +D2                                          READY

          A          B          C          D        E       F       G
1   Principal  Interest       Term    Payment
2    $30,000        10%         30    $263.27
3
4              Interest    Monthly
5                  Rate   Payments
6                          +D2
7                    5%   $161.05
8                    6%   $179.87
9                    7%   $199.59
10                   8%   $220.13
11                   9%   $241.39
12                  10%   $263.27
13                  11%   $285.70
14                  12%   $308.58
15                  13%   $331.86
16                  14%   $355.46
17                  15%   $379.33
18                  16%   $403.43
19
20
22-Nov-85   04:06 PM
```

Fig. 11.34B. Worksheet after using the /Data Table 1 command.

column of interest rates are entered. In this example, we enter *B2*. Then the program prompts us to enter a "Table Range," a range of cells that includes the column of interest rates and the column where the results are to appear. The entry here is B6..C18. Notice that this range specification includes the formulas row.

While 1-2-3 calculates the results, the WAIT mode indicator flashes in the upper right corner of the screen. When the calculation is finished, the sign changes to READY. Now the table contains all the payment values.

If you would like to try some other input values, you can change the values and then press the F8 (Table) key to recalculate the table automatically. Pressing F8 causes 1-2-3 to recalculate the table automatically, using the command parameters that you have specified in the previous /Data Table command.

A more complicated example (fig. 11.35) uses the /Data Table 2 command, which requires two input variables instead of one. Using more variables increases the breadth of the sensitivity analyses we can perform. This example is designed to show the effects of changes in order quantity and order point on total cost. We are after that combination of order point and order quantity that minimizes "Cumulative Costs to Date" at the end of a 12-month period.

The lower left portion of figure 11.35 shows the result of using the /Data Table 1 command to calculate the effect of different order quantities on cost. The /Data Table 2 command creates a much more extensive table, as shown in the lower right portion of the figure. This table shows the effect on cost of order point and order quantity. The result is a more complete analysis. This is the advantage of the /Data Table 2 command.

To use the /Data Table 2 command, you enter the values for Variable 2 (order quantity, in this example) in the row just above the first entry of Variable 1 (order point). In our example, these values begin in cell F21. Notice also that you enter +M12, the address of the formula for "Cost to Date," in the row directly above the first entry of Variable 1, cell E21 in our example. Again, the Text format is used, so that the cell displays +M12.

When you issue the /Data Table 2 command, 1-2-3 calls for a "Table Range" and Input Cells for Variables 1 and 2. You enter the following information for these parameters:

> Table Range E21..K47
>
> Input Cell Variable 1 B16
>
> Input Cell Variable 2 B15

	A	B	C	D	E	F	G	H	I	J	K	L	M
1	Month	Jan	Feb	Mar	Apr	May	Jun	Jul	Aug	Sep	Oct	Nov	Dec
2	---
3	Beginning Inventory	43	15	39	28	10	38	18	45	21	11	39	20
4	Past Demand for Month	28	16	11	18	12	20	13	24	10	12	19	22
5	Ending Inventory	15	-1	28	10	-2	18	5	21	11	-1	20	-2
6	Quantity Ordered	0	40	0	0	40	0	40	0	0	40	0	40
7	Setup Costs ($10 per order)	$0.00	$10.00	$0.00	$0.00	$10.00	$0.00	$10.00	$0.00	$0.00	$10.00	$0.00	$10.00
8	Inventory Costs ($.2/unit)	$3.00	$0.00	$5.60	$2.00	$0.00	$3.60	$1.00	$4.20	$2.20	$0.00	$4.00	$0.00
9	Shortage Costs ($1/unit)	$0.00	$1.00	$0.00	$0.00	$2.00	$0.00	$0.00	$0.00	$0.00	$1.00	$0.00	$2.00
10	Total Costs for Month	$3.00	$11.00	$5.60	$2.00	$12.00	$3.60	$11.00	$4.20	$2.20	$11.00	$4.00	$12.00
11	Cum Cost From Last Month	$0.00	$3.00	$14.00	$19.60	$21.60	$33.60	$37.20	$48.20	$52.40	$54.60	$65.60	$69.60
12	Cumulative Costs to Date	$3.00	$14.00	$19.60	$21.60	$33.60	$37.20	$48.20	$52.40	$54.60	$65.60	$69.60	$81.60
13	
14	
15	Order Quantity Input Cell	40
16	Order Point Input Cell	8
17	

		Order	Cumulative								
18											
19	DATA TABLE 1 -->	Quant	Cost		DATA TABLE 2 -->		Order Quantity				
20		-----	-----			--
21			+N13		+N13		38	39	40	41	42	43 Average
22		25	$104.00		1	$91.20	$103.80	$96.40	$96.00	$93.20	$91.60	$95.37
23		26	$109.60		2	$91.20	$103.80	$96.40	$93.80	$93.20	$91.60	$95.00
24		27	$106.40		3	$91.20	$86.40	$96.40	$93.80	$93.20	$91.60	$92.10
25		28	$98.00		4	$91.20	$86.40	$96.40	$93.80	$93.20	$91.60	$92.10
26		29	$99.60		5	$90.40	$86.40	$81.60	$93.80	$84.80	$91.60	$88.10
27		30	$102.40		6	$90.40	$86.40	$81.60	$93.80	$94.80	$91.60	$89.77
28		31	$95.20		7	$90.40	$86.40	$81.60	$81.60	$94.80	$91.60	$87.73
29		32	$91.60		8	$93.20	$89.40	$81.60	$81.60	$94.80	$87.00	$87.93
30		33	$94.60	0	9	$93.20	$93.60	$81.60	$81.60	$85.20	$87.00	$87.03
31		34	$95.60	r	10	$93.20	$93.60	$87.20	$81.60	$85.20	$97.00	$89.63
32		35	$86.60	d	11	$93.20	$93.60	$94.00	$88.60	$85.20	$90.00	$90.77
33		36	$88.80	e	12	$88.80	$93.60	$94.00	$88.60	$93.60	$90.00	$91.43
34		37	$84.60	r	13	$88.80	$93.60	$94.00	$88.60	$93.60	$98.60	$92.87
35		38	$93.20		14	$96.40	$93.60	$94.00	$96.80	$93.60	$98.60	$95.50
36		39	$93.60	P	15	$110.40	$100.20	$100.80	$100.80	$100.80	$106.00	$103.67
37		40	$81.60	o	16	$110.40	$108.60	$100.80	$103.80	$100.80	$106.00	$105.07
38		41	$81.60	i	17	$110.40	$108.60	$106.80	$103.80	$109.20	$106.00	$106.47
39		42	$85.20	n	18	$110.40	$116.40	$108.80	$103.80	$109.20	$106.00	$109.10
40		43	$87.00	t	19	$110.40	$116.40	$108.80	$103.80	$109.20	$106.00	$109.10
41		44	$90.00		20	$110.40	$116.40	$114.40	$112.00	$109.20	$114.60	$112.83
42		45	$88.40		21	$110.40	$116.40	$122.40	$112.00	$109.20	$114.60	$114.17
43		46	$86.80		22	$110.40	$116.40	$122.40	$112.00	$117.60	$114.60	$115.57
44		47	$86.40		23	$110.40	$116.40	$122.40	$112.00	$117.60	$114.60	$115.57
45		48	$88.40		24	$110.40	$116.40	$122.40	$128.40	$117.60	$123.20	$119.73
46		49	$90.40		25	$110.40	$116.40	$122.40	$128.40	$117.60	$123.20	$119.73
47		50	$98.00		26	$118.00	$116.40	$122.40	$128.40	$117.60	$123.20	$121.00

Fig. 11.35. Inventory Analysis with the /Data Table command.

After you enter this information, 1-2-3 begins building the table of results. Although you may have to wait awhile for the /Data Table 2 command to work, the results will be well worth your time. The table in figure 11.35 took about two minutes to calculate on an IBM PC. To duplicate manually what 1-2-3 does would take much longer. If you plan to use the /Data Table command often, you may want to invest in an 8087 or 80287 coprocessor for your computer. (See Chapter 3 for more information.)

Note that we find no one correct answer concerning the effect of changes in order quantity and order point on total cost. Our limited analysis, however, shows that on average an order point of about 9 and an order quantity of about 41 are best.

The advantage of the /Data Table command is that it allows you to perform extensive sensitivity analyses and display the results in a tabular format. You can perform analyses that you might not otherwise perform, given the time required. The power you gain from combining this command with macros and special database statistical functions can be great.

Filling Ranges with Numbers

The command for filling ranges is /**Data Fill**. /**Data Fill** is useful when combined with the other database commands mentioned earlier in this chapter, especially /**Data Table** and /**Data Sort**.

/**Data Fill** fills a range of cells with series of numbers that increase or decrease by a specified increment or decrement. For an example of the use of /**Data Fill**, look at the year numbers used as titles in the sales forecast shown in figure 11.36.

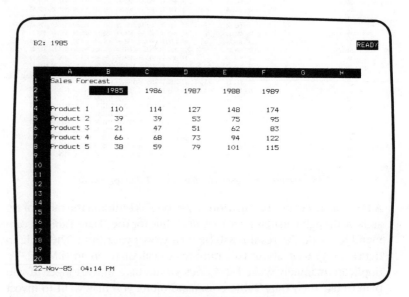

Fig. 11.36. Entering year numbers with the /Data Fill command.

When you issue the /**Data Fill** command, 1-2-3 first prompts you for the starting number of the series. The program then asks for the step (or incremental) value to be added to the previous value. Finally, 1-2-3 prompts you for the ending value.

To enter a sequence of year numbers for a five-year forecast beginning in 1985, begin by specifying the range of cells to be filled. For this example, we chose B2..F2 and then entered the beginning value, 1985.

The incremental or step value in this example is one. The ending value is 1989 for a five-year forecast.

One disadvantage of the /Data Fill command for year numbers is that you can't center or left-justify the numbers after you have created them. As numbers, they will always be right-justified. If you like your year numbers centered or left-justified, you should type them in as labels instead.

The /Data Fill command can also work with the /Data Table command to build a list of interest rates, as shown in figure 11.33. In that figure, the column of interest rate values was entered with the /Data Fill command. We specified B7..B18 for the range of cells to be filled, .05 for the starting value, and .01 for the step value. For the ending value, we let 1-2-3 default to 8,192, which is far beyond the ending value we actually needed. The /Data Fill command, however, fills only the specified range and doesn't fill cells beyond the end of the range.

The /Data Fill command is useful in conjunction with /Data Sort. Suppose that you're going to /Data Sort a database, and you want to be able to restore the records to their original order if you make a mistake in sorting them. All you need to do is add a field to the database and use /Data Fill to fill the field with consecutive numbers. Then you can sort your database. If you find that the results of the sort are unacceptable, you simply sort the database on the new field in order to return the database to its original order. Figure 11.37 shows an example before and after a /Data Sort.

In our examples, we have always used regular numbers for the beginning, incremental, and ending values, but we can also use formulas and commands. If we want to fill a range of cells with incrementing dates, after the range has been set, we can use the @DATE function to set the start value, for example @DATE(85,6,1). We can use also a cell formula, such as +E4, for the incremental value. In this case, E4 may contain the increment 7 so that there can be increments of one week at a time. We can enter the stop value @DATE(85,10,1), for example; or, if the stop date is in a cell, we can give that cell address as the stop value. 1-2-3 allows many different combinations of commands.

Frequency Distributions

The command for creating frequency distributions in 1-2-3 is the /Data Distribution command. A *frequency distribution* describes the relationship between a set of classes and the frequency of occurrence of members of each class. A list of consumers with their product

```
D2: (C2) 33                                              READY

        A              B         C        D       E       F
1  COMPANY             GROUP   SHARES   PRICE SORT FIELD
2  Boeheed             air       100   $33.00           13
3  Union Allied        chem      100   $61.00           15
4  Mututal of Pawtucket ins      100   $56.00           10
5  Rockafella Rail     tran      100   $44.13            4
6  Rubberstone         rub       200   $23.00            9
7  Bear and Bull, Inc. fin       200   $30.75            3
8  Texagulf            oil       200   $77.00           16
9  Cable Communications tele     200   $56.75            5
10 PetroChem Inc.      oil       200   $61.00            6
11 Soregums            liq       300   $41.38           11
12 Pan World           tran      300   $47.88           14
13 Brute Force Cybernetics tech  400   $11.50            1
14 Roncomart           ret       400   $31.00            8
15 Steak and Snail     food      500   $12.00            7
16 Acme Inc.           tech      500   $16.25            2
17 Zaymart             ret       600   $19.25           12
18
19
20
22-Nov-85  04:16 PM
```

Fig. 11.37A. Stocks database sorted by number of shares.

```
D2: (C2) 11.5                                            READY

        A              B         C        D       E       F
1  COMPANY             GROUP   SHARES   PRICE SORT FIELD
2  Brute Force Cybernetics tech  400   $11.50            1
3  Acme Inc.           tech      500   $16.25            2
4  Bear and Bull, Inc. fin       200   $30.75            3
5  Rockafella Rail     tran      100   $44.13            4
6  Cable Communications tele     200   $56.75            5
7  PetroChem Inc.      oil       200   $61.00            6
8  Steak and Snail     food      500   $12.00            7
9  Roncomart           ret       400   $31.00            8
10 Rubberstone         rub       200   $23.00            9
11 Mututal of Pawtucket ins      100   $56.00           10
12 Soregums            liq       300   $41.38           11
13 Zaymart             ret       600   $19.25           12
14 Boeheed             air       100   $33.00           13
15 Pan World           tran      300   $47.88           14
16 Union Allied        chem      100   $61.00           15
17 Texagulf            oil       200   $77.00           16
18
19
20
22-Nov-85  04:18 PM
```

Fig. 11.37B. Stocks database returned to original order.

preferences (fig. 11.38) illustrates use of the /Data Distribution command to produce a frequency distribution.

To use the /Data Distribution command, you first specify a "Values" range, which corresponds to the range of "Taste Preference" numbers

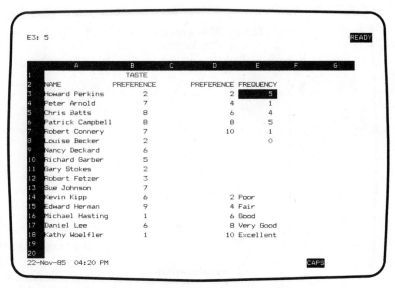

	A	B	C	D	E	F	G
		TASTE					
2	NAME	PREFERENCE		PREFERENCE	FREQUENCY		
3	Howard Perkins	2		2	5		
4	Peter Arnold	7		4	1		
5	Chris Batts	8		6	4		
6	Patrick Campbell	8		8	5		
7	Robert Connery	7		10	1		
8	Louise Becker	2			0		
9	Nancy Deckard	6					
10	Richard Garber	5					
11	Gary Stokes	2					
12	Robert Fetzer	3					
13	Sue Johnson	7					
14	Kevin Kipp	6		2 Poor			
15	Edward Herman	9		4 Fair			
16	Michael Hasting	1		6 Good			
17	Daniel Lee	6		8 Very Good			
18	Kathy Woelfler	1		10 Excellent			

E3: 5   READY

22-Nov-85 04:20 PM   CAPS

Fig. 11.38. Analysis of Taste Preference data using /Data Distribution.

in this example. After specifying B3..B18 for the values range, you set up the range of intervals at D3..D7, in what 1-2-3 calls the *Bin* range. If you have evenly spaced intervals, the /Data Fill command can be used to enter the values for the Bin range. If the intervals were not evenly spaced, you could not use the /Data Fill command to fill the range.

When you specify these ranges and enter the /Data Distribution command, 1-2-3 creates the "Results" column (E3..E8) to the right of the Bin range (D3..D7). The Results column, which shows the frequency distribution, is always in the column segment to the right of the Bin range and extends one row farther down.

The values in the Results column represent the frequency of distribution of the numbers in the Values range for each interval. The first interval in the Bin range is for values greater than zero and less than or equal to two; the second, for values greater than two and less than or equal to four, etc. The last value in the Results column, in cell E8 just below the corresponding column segment, shows the frequency of left-over numbers (that is, the frequency of numbers that don't fit into an interval classification).

The /Data Distribution command can help you create understandable results from a series of numbers. The results are easily graphed, as shown in figure 11.39.

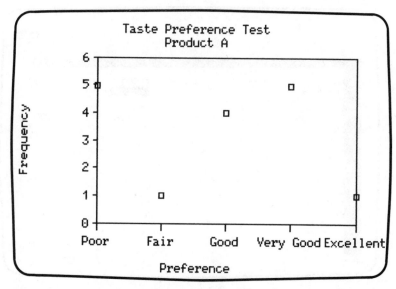

Fig. 11.39. Graph of results from the /Data Distribution command.

A manufacturer looking at this graph would probably start looking for another product or start trying to improve the taste of the current product.

The /Data Regression Command

The /**Data** **Regression** command gives you a free multiple-regression analysis package within 1-2-3. Most people will probably never use this advanced feature. But if you need to use it, 1-2-3 saves you the cost and inconvenience of buying a stand-alone statistical package for performing a regression analysis.

Use /**Data** **Regression** when you want to determine the relationship between one set of values (the dependent variable) and one or more other sets of values (the independent variables). Regression analysis has a number of uses in a business setting, including relating sales to price, promotions, and other market factors; relating stock prices to earnings and interest rates; and relating production costs to production levels.

Think of linear regression as a way of determining the "best" line through a series of data points. Multiple regression does this for several variables simultaneously, determining the "best" line relating the dependent variable to the set of independent variables. As an example, we will use the Annual Earnings versus Age data from Chapter 9. Figure 11.40 shows the data and figure 11.41 shows the data plotted as an XY graph.

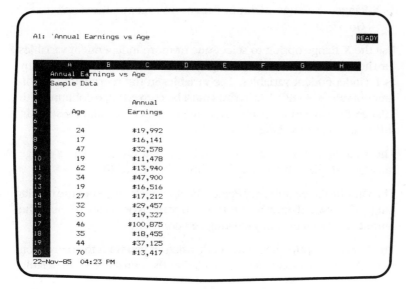

Fig. 11.40. Annual Earnings versus Age data.

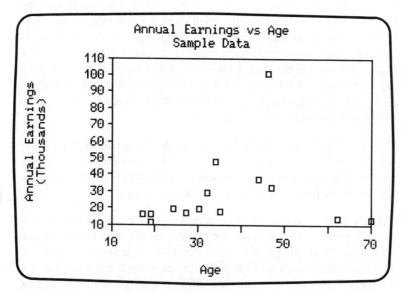

Fig. 11.41. XY graph of Annual Earnings versus Age.

NEW WITH

R2

The /**Data Regression** command can simultaneously determine how to draw a line through these data points and how well the line fits the data. When you invoke the command, the following menu appears:

X-Range   Y-Range   Output-Range   Intercept   Reset
   Go   Quit

Use the **X-Range** option to select one or more independent variables for the regression. The /**Data Regression** command can use as many as 16 independent variables. The variables in the regression are columns of values, so any data in rows must be converted to columns with /**Range Transpose** before the /**Data Regression** command is issued. In this example, the X-Range is A7..A20.

The **Y-Range** option specifies the independent variable. The **Y-Range** must be a single column; we therefore select C7..C20.

The **Output-Range** option specifies the upper left corner of the results range. This should be an unused section of the worksheet, because the output is written over any existing cell contents.

The **Intercept** option lets you specify whether you want the regression to calculate a constant value. Calculating the constant is the default, but it may be necessary in some applications to exclude a constant.

Figure 11.42 shows the results of using the /**Data Regression** command in the Annual Earnings versus Age example. The results include the value of the constant and the coefficient of the single independent variable that we specified with the **X-Range** option. The results also include a number of regression statistics that describe how well the regression line fits the data. In this case, the R-Squared value and the standard errors of the constant and the regression coefficient all indicate that the regression line does not explain much of the variation in the dependent variable.

The new data in column D is the computed regression line. These values consist of the constant plus the coefficient of the independent variable times its value in each row of the data. This line can be plotted against the original data, as shown in figure 11.43.

Looking at the Annual Earnings versus Age plot, you notice that income appears to rise with age until about age 50; then income begins to decline. You can use the /**Data Regression** command to fit a line that describes such a relationship between Annual Earnings and Age. In figure 11.44, we have added a column of data in column B containing the square of the age in column A. To include this new column in the regression, specify the range A7..B20 for the **X-Range** and recal-

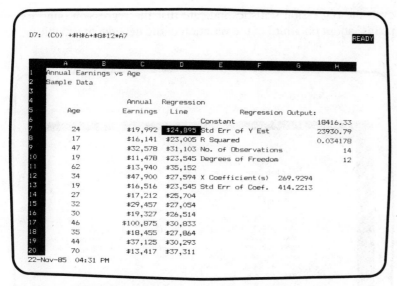

Fig. 11.42. Results of /Data Regression on Annual Earnings versus Age data.

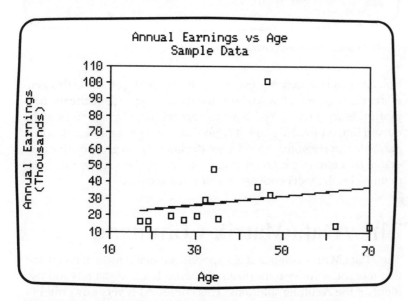

Fig. 11.43. Plot of Annual Earnings versus Age data, with regression line.

culate the regression. Note that the regression statistics are much improved over the regression of Annual Earnings versus Age. This means that the new line fits the data more closely than the old one. (How-

NEW WITH

R2

ever, the regression statistics indicate that the regression only "explains" about one-third of the variation of the dependent variable.)

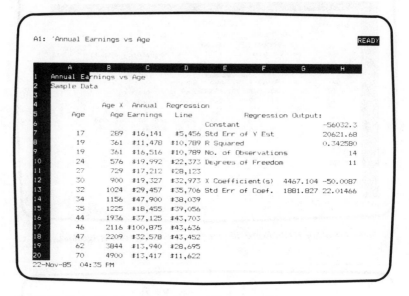

Fig. 11.44. Annual Earnings versus Age and the square of Age.

You must add the new regression coefficient to the equation that generates the regression line, and sort the data by age, to generate the new plot in figure 11.45. (You have to sort the data by age to plot the curved line on the XY graph.) Note that the regression line is now a parabola that rises until age 45, then declines. The regression line generated by a multiple regression may or may not be a straight line, depending on the independent variables that are used.

The /Data Matrix Command

The /Data Matrix command is a specialized mathematical command that lets you solve systems of simultaneous linear equations and manipulate the resulting solutions. This command is very powerful but has limited application in a business setting. If you are using 1-2-3 for certain types of economic analysis or for scientific or engineering calculations, you may find this command valuable.

The /Data Matrix command has a menu with two options: Invert and Multiply. The Invert option lets you invert a nonsingular square matrix

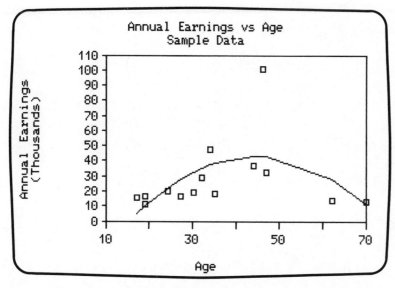

Fig. 11.45. Plot of Annual Earnings versus Age, with revised regression line.

of up to 90 rows and columns. Just select the **Invert** option and highlight the range you want to invert. Then select an output range to hold the inverted solution matrix. You can place the output range anywhere in the worksheet, including on top of the matrix you are inverting.

The time required to invert a matrix is proportional to the cube of the number of rows and columns. A 10-by-10 matrix takes about 6 seconds, and a 90-by-90 matrix takes almost one hour on an IBM PC with no numeric coprocessor. If you are going to use 1-2-3 to invert matrices, you may want to invest in an 8087 or 80287 coprocessor for your computer (see Chapter 3).

The **Multiply** option allows you to multiply two rectangular matrices together, in accordance with the rules of matrix algebra. The number of columns in the first matrix must equal the number of rows in the second matrix. The result matrix has the same number of rows as the first matrix, and the same number of columns as the second.

When you select /**Data Matrix Multiply**, 1-2-3 prompts you for three ranges: the first matrix, the second matrix, and the output range. Multiply is very fast compared to **Invert**, but may still take some time if you multiply large matrices.

NEW WITH
R2

12
Macros and
Command Language

Macros are one of the most exciting capabilities of 1-2-3. In their most basic form, 1-2-3 macros are simply collections of keystrokes that can be called up with a single, two-keystroke command. A sequence of keystrokes that includes special macro commands, as well as ordinary 1-2-3 keyboard commands, becomes a simple program written in the 1-2-3 macro command language. At their most sophisticated level, 1-2-3 macro commands can be used as a full-fledged programming language that can be used to develop custom business applications.

When 1-2-3 was introduced in 1983, its keyboard macros were one of the most innovative parts of the program. Although other spreadsheet programs such as VisiCalc and SuperCalc offered a limited degree of programmability through external command files, none came close to the power and ease of use of 1-2-3 macros. After the introduction of 1-2-3, other spreadsheet programs appeared on the market, with macro capabilities similar to those in the original version of 1-2-3.

In 1984 Lotus introduced Symphony, an integrated software package with a powerful new macro Command Language that surpassed that of 1-2-3. Ashton-Tate and other software publishers have introduced similar integrated packages that offer a comparable degree of programmability.

The most recent version of 1-2-3, Release 2, offers all the improvements made in macros since 1983 and is compatible with most macros written for Releases 1 and 1A. The Release 2 macros incorporate Symphony's macro Command Language and the full set of 1-2-3 Release 1A macro commands. The result is a state-of-the-art macro command

NEW WITH
R2

language: easy to use for automating repetitive 1-2-3 keystrokes, yet powerful enough to perform almost any conceivable task that can be handled by 1-2-3. Some of the macros discussed in this chapter can be rewritten for 1-2-3 Release 1A. To make the conversion, refer to table 12.4 at the end of the chapter.

The *1-2-3 Reference Manual* devotes 58 pages to macros and is a valuable reference for the macro commands. However, there is much that the manual does not discuss. In a more tutorial approach, this chapter first discusses the concept of a 1-2-3 macro and gives you an overview of 1-2-3's macro commands. Examples of simple macros that can perform useful functions in your worksheets are broken into two categories: *typing alternatives* and simple macros that use the command language. The macro command reference at the end of the chapter expands upon the *1-2-3 Reference Manual* by providing you with examples of how to use each command and notes on any tricks and traps associated with each macro command.

What Is a Macro?

Before releasing 1-2-3 to the general public in 1983, Lotus decided to describe macros as *typing alternatives*. This name, later de-emphasized in favor of the term *macros* or *macro command language,* describes the basic nature of macros.

The Typing Alternative

In its most basic form, a macro is simply a collection of keystrokes. These keystrokes can be commands or simple text and numeric entries. Macros provide an alternative to typing data and commands from the keyboard—hence the name "typing alternative." A macro can be used instead of the keyboard to issue commands or to enter data into the 1-2-3 worksheet.

Simple Programs Using Macro Commands

A macro can be much more than just a simple collection of keystrokes. Several special 1-2-3 macro commands can be used only within macros. These commands do such things as accept input from the keyboard during a macro, perform conditional tests similar to those of the IF-THEN command of the BASIC language, perform a sequence of commands repeatedly in a manner similar to that of the BASIC language's FOR-NEXT looping command, and create user-defined command menus. Simple macros that include these macro commands are more than typing alternatives. Such macros give you added control and flexibility in the use of your 1-2-3 worksheets. (The macros used in the comprehensive model in Chapter 13 fall into this category.)

Application Development with Macros

NEW WITH
R2

Application developers can use the macro command language as a full-featured programming language to develop custom worksheets for specific business applications. The macro command language contains all the elements necessary to develop sophisticated programs that control the worksheet and eliminate the need for the user of an application to understand 1-2-3. *1-2-3 Financial Macros,* a book published by Que Corporation, contains examples of this type of macro. To help you get started, though, many examples of *typing alternative* macros and simple programs using the command language are included in the following sections.

The Complexity of Macros

The 1-2-3 novice may want to avoid macros until he or she is fairly comfortable with 1-2-3 in general. But you do not need to know everything about 1-2-3 before you begin to use macros. This chapter contains a number of macros that you can use right away.

Even if you are new to 1-2-3, there is no reason why you can't begin to experiment with macros immediately.

If you have experience with BASIC or another programming language, the macros will be easier to learn and use. But even the advanced programmer will find some obstacles with 1-2-3's macros. First, macros can be difficult to debug. However, the single-step feature that allows the macro to be executed one step at a time helps to alleviate this problem.

One thing we don't explain in this chapter is programming theory. If you are interested in building highly complex 1-2-3 macros, we suggest that you take some time to learn programming theory. A number of excellent books on this subject are available at your local bookstore.

NEW WITH
R2

One problem with previous releases of 1-2-3 was that the macros did not have enough commands and functions to be considered a full programming language. This was frustrating to experienced programmers if they tried to use macros to create a true 1-2-3 program. This problem has been eliminated with Release 2. A host of new macro commands make the Release 2 macro language a powerful programming language that can be used to automate simple tasks or to program sophisticated applications.

The best macros are simple macros. Most users are better off using macros to automate simple, repetitive tasks. If you want to create a sophisticated program with 1-2-3, do what you would normally do before writing a program in any other language: plan it carefully and be prepared to spend a lot of time coding and debugging.

The Elements of Macros

A macro is nothing more than a specially named *text cell.* All macros are created by entering the keystrokes (or representatives of those strokes) to be stored into a worksheet cell. For example, suppose that you want to create a very simple *typing alternative* macro that will format the current cell to appear in the currency format with no decimal places. The macro would look like this:

```
'/rfc0~~
```

You would enter this macro into the worksheet in exactly the same way that you would any other label: by typing a label prefix, followed by the characters in the label. The label prefix informs 1-2-3 that what follows should be treated as a label. If this prefix were not used, 1-2-3 would automatically interpret the next character, /, as a command to be executed immediately instead of stored in the cell. Any of the three 1-2-3 label prefixes (', ", or \) would work equally well. (We chose ' because we're used to seeing labels aligned at the left edge of the cells.)

All macros that begin with a nontext character (/, \, +, –, or any number) must be started with a label prefix. Otherwise 1-2-3 will interpret the characters that follow as numbers or commands.

The next four characters represent the command used to create the desired format. If you think about it, /rfc is simply shorthand for **/R**ange **F**ormat **C**urrency. The 0 informs 1-2-3 that we want no digits to be displayed to the right of the decimal. If you were entering this command from the keyboard, you would type the *0* in response to a prompt. In the macro, the 0 is simply assumed by 1-2-3.

At the end of the macro are two characters called *tildes*. When used in a macro, the tilde represents the Enter key. In this case, the two tildes signal that the Enter key should be pressed twice. Think about this for a moment. If you were entering this command from the keyboard, you would have to press Enter twice: after supplying the 0 for the number of decimals, and again to signal that the format applied to the current cell. If you have your 1-2-3 program handy, try this procedure to see what we mean.

1-2-3 uses symbols like the ~ to stand for other keystrokes as well. For example, look at the following macro:

```
'/rfc0~. {END}{RIGHT}~
```

This macro is similar to the one we just looked at, except that the command here causes the cursor to move. This command can be used to format an entire row instead of just one cell.

Once again, notice the ' at the beginning of the macro and the ~ symbol at the end. Notice also the phrase {END}{RIGHT} in the macro. The {END} in this phrase stands for the End key on the keyboard. The {RIGHT} represents the right-arrow key. This phrase has the same effect in the macro as these two keys would have if they were typed in sequence from the keyboard. The cursor would move to the next boundary between blank and nonblank cells in the row.

Symbols like these are used to represent all of the special keys on the IBM PC keyboard. In every case, the name of the function key (that is, RIGHT for the right arrow, or CALC for function key F9) is enclosed in braces. For example, {UP} represents the up-arrow key, the symbol {END} stands for the End key, and {GRAPH} represents the F10 graph key. Release 2 also uses braces to enclose macro command keywords. Command keywords will be discussed later in this chapter. If you enclose in braces a phrase that is not a key name or a command keyword, 1-2-3 will return the error message

NEW WITH
R2

```
Unrecognized key Range name {...}(A1)
```

where {...} represents the invalid key name and (A1) says the error occurred in cell A1. Another special key representation is {?}, which is similar to BASIC's INPUT command. When 1-2-3 encounters a {?} in a macro, the program pauses and waits for the user to enter some data from the keyboard. Data, once entered, is stored in the current cell.

Table 12.1 shows the complete list of special key representations.

Table 12.1.
Special Key Representations in Macros

Function Keys

{EDIT}	Edits contents of current cell (same as F2)
{NAME}	Displays list of range names in the current worksheet (same as F3)
{ABS}	Converts relative reference to absolute (same as F4)
{GOTO}	Jumps cursor to cell coordinates (same as F5)
{WINDOW}	Moves the cursor to the other side of a split screen (same as F6)
{QUERY}	Repeats most recent query operation (same as F7)
{TABLE}	Repeats most recent table operation (same as F8)
{CALC}	Recalculates worksheet (same as F9)
{GRAPH}	Redraws current graph (same as F10)

Cursor-Movement Keys

{UP}	Moves cursor up one row
{DOWN}	Moves cursor down one row
{LEFT}	Moves cursor left one column
{RIGHT}	Moves cursor right one column
{BIGLEFT}	Moves cursor left one screen
{BIGRIGHT}	Moves cursor right one screen
{PGUP}	Moves cursor up 20 rows
{PGDN}	Moves cursor down 20 rows
{HOME}	Moves cursor to cell A1

{END}	Used with {UP}, {DOWN}, {LEFT}, or {RIGHT} to move cursor to next boundary between blank and nonblank cells in the indicated direction. Used with {HOME} to move cursor to lower right corner of the defined worksheet.
Editing Keys	
{DELETE} or {DEL}	Used with {EDIT} to delete a single character from a cell definition
{INSERT}	Toggles the editor between insert and overtype modes
{ESCAPE} or {ESC}	Esc key
{BACKSPACE} or {BS}	Backspace key
Special Keys	
{?}	Causes macro to pause and wait for input from keyboard. Macro resumes execution after the user strikes Enter.
~	Enter key
{~}	Causes tilde to appear as ~
b\b\b\ and B\ B\B\	Causes braces to appear as b\ and B\

Function Key Grammar

To specify more than one use of a special key, you can include repetition factors inside the braces of a special-key phrase. For example, you can use the following statements:

NEW WITH
R2

{PGUP 3}	Press the PgUp key three times in a row.
{RIGHT JUMP}	Press the right-arrow key the number of times indicated by the value in the cell called JUMP.

Macro Commands

1-2-3 has a set of special macro commands. They are also called *invisible* commands because they cannot be issued from the keyboard, but only from within a macro. 1-2-3's macro command set is similar to the commands offered by most higher level programming languages, such as BASIC.

Macro Command Overview

NEW WITH
R2

In Release 2, Lotus has significantly upgraded 1-2-3's macro commands by combining almost all of the Symphony Command Language with 1-2-3's original macro commands. The result is a powerful new set of macro commands that offers most of the features of a full-featured programming language. This set of commands includes the original special commands from Release 1A plus a set from Symphony's Command Language. You will find that, in many cases, commands from the command language parallel those originally in Release 1A, performing the same functions.

Think of the Release 1A macro commands as an invisible addition to the 1-2-3 command menus. These commands, which start with /x, have the same format as such other 1-2-3 commands as /fsNAME~ (/**F**ile **S**ave name). The same /x commands contained in Release 2 allow you to run, unchanged, macros that were developed for Releases 1 and 1A of 1-2-3.

The Symphony Command Language commands are also an invisible addition to 1-2-3's command set because you can invoke them only from within a macro. Their format is similar to that of special key names like {RIGHT}, and the commands take arguments in much the same way that the @ functions do. Take, for example, the command {BLANK SALES}. This command tells 1-2-3 to erase the range SALES. The command's format includes the command keyword—BLANK—and the argument SALES.

All Release 2 macro commands can be divided into groups with similar functions: commands for logical operations; commands for branching and subroutines; those for accepting input from the keyboard; those for storing and deleting data; commands for opening, reading, and writing sequential data files; and, finally, maintenance-oriented commands.

Macro commands for logical operations include: the /xi and IF commands that test the value of an expression and, based on the result, conditionally execute macro commands; the command ONERROR that automatically branches to a specified cell if an error condition occurs; and the FOR command that provides a looping capability similar to that of FOR-NEXT loops in BASIC.

Macro commands for branching and subroutines include: the branching commands /xg and BRANCH; the indirect branch command DISPATCH; the menu commands /xm, MENUBRANCH, and MENUCALL; the subroutine call commands /xc and {routine}; a RESTART command to break out of subroutine execution; and the commands RETURN and /xr that return from a subroutine.

Macro commands to accept input from the keyboard include (in addition to the special key function {?} and the interactive mode input commands from 1-2-3's own menu): the GET command, which reads a single character from the keyboard; the /xl and GETLABEL commands, which accept string input; the /xn and GETNUMBER commands, which accept numeric input; and the LOOK command, which reads a character from the keyboard buffer without pausing for keyboard input.

There are several *macro commands for storing and deleting data* in the worksheet. The storing commands LET, PUT, and CONTENTS allow you to copy or combine data into specified cells without disturbing the cursor's current location. The BLANK command is an alternative to /**R**ange **E**rase for erasing cells from a macro.

Lotus even includes *macro commands to allow you to open, read, and write sequential data files* in much the same way you would work with files in a programming language like BASIC. The file macro commands allow 1-2-3 to work directly with data files produced by such non-1-2-3 applications as a general ledger package or a payroll package. These sequential file macro commands are intended primarily for sophisticated macro applications. To use this new capability, you will need programming experience as well as an understanding of the internal formats of data files that you want to use in your worksheet.

The eleven commands in the catch-all group of *maintenance-oriented commands* are useful in various ways. The WINDOWSOFF and PANELOFF commands are particularly useful for reducing the execution time of large, complex macros by shutting off what goes to the display. WINDOWSON and PANELON allow execution to be displayed again.

As mentioned earlier, the 1-2-3 Release 2 macro command language combines features of Release 1A's macro capabilities and of Sym-

NEW WITH
R2

phony's Command Language. You may have noticed several duplicate 1-2-3 macro commands. Although the duplication primarily allows macros written for earlier releases of 1-2-3 to run unchanged in Release 2, certain Release 1A commands have useful features that are not duplicated in the new commands. These features are noted in the command descriptions at the end of this chapter.

Creating, Using, and Debugging Macros

When you start to use macros in your worksheets, keep several considerations in mind. Developing a macro involves careful planning. You begin by defining which actions you want that macro to perform; then you determine the sequence of keystrokes necessary to accomplish those actions. After planning your macro, you face the problem of where to put it; you'll want your macros out of the way, but easily accessible from your main work area. You'll want to document your macro when you enter it so that you'll still understand what it does if, after three months, you decide to change it. After entering a macro, you need to name it so that you can execute it. And, if you're like us, your macro probably won't work right the first time and will need "debugging." The following sections of this chapter deal with these considerations.

Planning Your Macro

As discussed previously, a macro can be thought of as a substitute for keyboard commands. This is particularly true for the simpler macros that do not involve extensive use of macro commands, but it also applies to more complex macros.

Because a macro is a substitute for keystrokes, the best way to plan a macro is to step through the series of instructions you intend to include in the macro from the keyboard, one keystroke at a time. Do this before you start creating the macro. Take notes about each step as you go, then translate the keystrokes that you've written down into a macro that conforms to the syntax rules.

The keystroke approach usually works well for simple macros. Stepping through an operation at the keyboard, and adding macro commands necessary for looping or conditional branching, is an easy way to build simple macros.

For more complex macros, the best approach is to break a large macro into smaller macros that execute in series. Each small macro performs one simple operation; the series of simple operations together perform the desired application.

This approach starts with an application's results. What is the application supposed to do or to produce? What form must the results take? If you start with the desired results and work backward, you lower the risk of producing the wrong results with your application.

Next, consider input. What data is needed? What data is available, and in what form? How much work is involved in going from the data to the results?

Finally, look at the process. How do you analyze available data and, using 1-2-3, produce the desired results? How can necessary calculations be divided into a series of tasks, each of which a simple macro can perform?

This "divide and conquer" method of breaking a complex task into simpler pieces is the key to successful development of complex worksheets, whether or not they include macros. Although this method entails initial work, as you analyze and plan your macros, less work is required by the time your application functions properly.

Where To Put the Macro

In most cases, you will want to place your macros outside the area that will be occupied by your main model. This will help to keep you from accidentally overwriting a macro as you create your model.

We frequently put macros in column AA in our models. We selected this column for several reasons. First, our models rarely require more than 26 columns, so we don't have to worry about overwriting the macros area with the model. Second, column AA is close enough to the origin that the macros area can easily be reached with the Tab key.

There is no rule that says you must place your macros in the same place in every model. In models that you'll use more than once, you'll want to place the macros wherever it is most convenient. In small models, you may want to put your macros in column I, which lies just off the home screen when all of the columns have a width of 9.

We typically apply the range name MACROS to the area of our sheet that contains the macros. This allows us to get at the macros quickly with the GOTO command and the range name MACROS.

Experienced 1-2-3 users should note that, because Lotus has re-worked the way that 1-2-3 uses memory, placing your macros outside the basic rectangle which contains your model no longer consumes large amounts of memory. However, placing macros outside the normal rectangle will cause the End Home key sequence to place the cursor at the right corner of the overall spreadsheet, including the macro area, instead of at the lower right corner of the model. This makes the End Home key sequence less useful.

Documenting Your Macros

Professional programmers usually write programs that are *self-documented*, or *internally documented*. This means that the program contains comments that help to explain each step in it. In BASIC, these comments are in REM (for REMark) statements. For example, in the following program, the REM statements explain the action taken by the other statements.

```
10 REM This program adds two numbers
20 REM Enter first number
30 INPUT A
40 REM Enter second number
50 INPUT B
60 REM Add numbers together
70 C=A+B
80 REM Display Result
90 Print C
```

It is also possible to document your 1-2-3 macros. The best way to do this is to place the comments next to the macro steps in the column to the right of the macro. For example, in the simple macro in figure 12.1, the macro name is in column AA, the macro itself is in column AB, and the comments are in column AC.

Including comments in your macros will make them far easier to use. Comments are especially useful when you have created complex macros that are important to the overall design of the worksheet. Suppose that you have created a complex macro but have not looked at it for a month. Then, you decide you want to modify the macro. Without built-in comments, you might have a difficult time remembering what each step of the macro does.

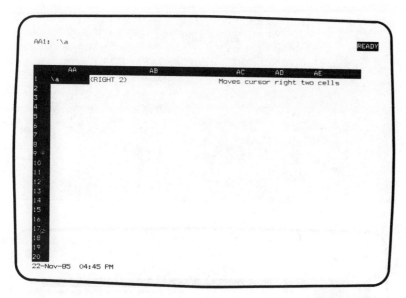

Fig. 12.1. Suggested macro layout.

Naming Macros

A macro that has been entered in the worksheet as a label (or a series of labels) must be given a name. Ranges containing macros are assigned names just like every other range. The only difference is that the name you assign to a macro which you will invoke directly from the keyboard must meet certain special conditions: it must be only one character, it must be an alphabetic character (or 0), and it must be preceded by a backslash (\ ).

You can assign any legal range name to a macro that will be either used only as a subroutine or called with a BRANCH statement from another macro. Table 12.2 shows several macro names that can be invoked from the keyboard, and others that can be invoked only by other macros.

For example, suppose that you had just built the macro shown in figure 12.2.

Now you need to name this macro so that you can invoke it from the keyboard. Although you could give the macro any one-letter name, it is always a good idea to choose a name that in some way describes the macro. Obviously, it is difficult to create descriptive one-letter names. In this case, for example, you could choose the name \d (for dollar)

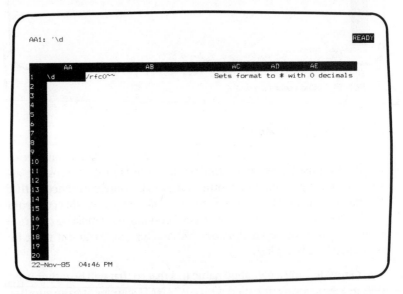

Table 12.2	
Invoked from Keyboard	*Invoked Only from Macros*
\a	\ABC
\b	ABC
\0	\?
	\1

Fig. 12.2. Naming a macro.

or \f (for format). Probably the best name for this macro would be \$, but because the symbol $ is not a letter, \$ is not a legal macro name.

Suppose that we decided to name the macro \d. To assign the name, we would issue the command /**R**ange **N**ame **C**reate. Next, we would type the name we had selected—\d—and press the Enter key. Finally, 1-2-3 would prompt us for the range to name. If the cursor were currently on cell AB1, we could simply press Enter to assign the name to the cell. Otherwise, we would move the cursor to the desired cell or type the cell coordinates from the keyboard.

Some macros require more than one row in the spreadsheet. For example, look at the simple two-row macro in figure 12.3.

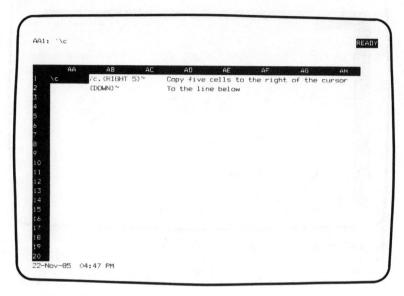

Fig. 12.3. Simple two-row macro.

To name this macro, we need to assign a name to only the first cell in the range that contains the macro. In this case, we would assign the name \c to cell AB1. There is no reason, however, why a name cannot be assigned to the entire range AB1..AB2.

1-2-3's /Range Name command is remarkably flexible. For example, one cell can be part of several different named ranges.

There is another variation on the /Range Name Labels command that can be very useful when you want to name a macro. The Right option of this command (found in the /Range Name Labels menu) allows you to name a range, using the contents of the cell immediately to its left. For example, suppose that you had created the macro in figure 12.4.

With your cell pointer on cell AA1, you can name your macro by using the /Range Name Labels Right command, which would assign the name \a to the range AB1.

The /Range Name Labels command can be used in a variety of ways. If you are documenting your macros properly, you will already have the names in the sheet; therefore, using the Labels option is a simple and convenient way to name the macros.

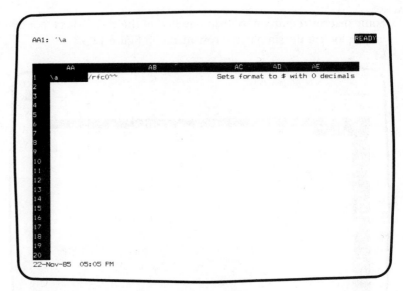

Fig. 12.4. Naming a macro with /Range Name Labels.

If you import macros from an external library file, you can use the **Labels** command to create quickly names for the imported macros. In fact, one of the macros in this chapter automatically imports a worksheet file and names all of the macros in the file.

Executing Macros

All macros except those named \0 (which are executed automatically when their file is retrieved) are executed, or invoked, by pressing the Alt key, followed by the letter name of the macro. For example, if the macro we wanted to use were named \a, we would invoke it by pressing Alt-a. The \ symbol in the name is a representation of the Alt key.

As soon as the command is issued, the macro starts to run. If there are no bugs or special instructions built into the macro, it will continue to run until it is finished. You will be amazed at its speed. The commands are issued faster than you can see them.

Many macro keystrokes or commands can be stored in a single cell. Some that are especially long or include special commands must be split into two or more cells, like the example shown in figure 12.3. This is no problem. When 1-2-3 starts executing a macro, the program continues in the first cell until all the keystrokes stored there are used. 1-2-3 then moves down one cell to continue execution. If the cell below is blank, the program stops. If that cell contains more macro commands, however, 1-2-3 will continue reading down the column until it reaches the first blank cell.

Automatic Macros

As mentioned earlier, 1-2-3 offers an exciting macro feature called *automatic macro execution*. This technique allows the user to create a special macro that will automatically execute when the sheet is loaded. This macro is created just like any other macro. The only difference is in its name. The macro that you want to execute automatically must have the name \0.

An even more powerful feature of 1-2-3 is its ability to load a model automatically into the 1-2-3 worksheet. When 1-2-3 loads, it automatically searches the current disk drive for a special worksheet file named AUTO123.WK1. If this file is on the disk, 1-2-3 will automatically load it into the worksheet. If the file contains a macro named \0, the macro will automatically execute.

You can use these features of 1-2-3 to create completely self-contained programs in the 1-2-3 worksheet. Pressing the Alt key is not required to start the macro in this case. When combined with menus and the other useful macro commands, the automatic execution feature makes macros a remarkably user-friendly tool.

Note one thing about the automatic macro: it cannot be executed by the Alt-0 key combination. If you need to be able to execute the macro from the keyboard, however, there is no reason why the macro you've named \0 could not also have another name, such as \a. One macro then becomes, in effect, two: one that executes automatically, and one that can be executed from the keyboard.

There can be only one automatic macro in each worksheet. However, this macro can be as large as you want and can include as many steps as you wish. It can include also subroutine calls that access other macros in the sheet.

Common Errors

Like all computer programs, macros are literal creatures. They have no ability to discern an error in the code. For example, you will recognize immediately that {GOTI} is a misspelling of {GOTO}. But a macro cannot do this. It will try to interpret the misspelled word and, being unable to, will deliver an error message.

This means that you must be extremely careful when you build your macros so that they have no errors. Even misplaced spaces and tildes can cause difficulty for 1-2-3. No matter how careful you are, however, some errors are going to slip through.

The biggest problem most beginners have with macros is forgetting to represent all of the required Enter keystrokes in the macros. This can lead to some dismaying results. For example, the missing ~ after the {RIGHT 5} in the macro in figure 12.5 will cause the {DOWN} command to be included in the definition of the FROM range of the /Copy command, instead of defining the TO range. The result of running this macro is shown in figure 12.6. As you can see, the /Copy command in the macro stopped in the middle of its execution because of the missing keystroke (tilde).

Another big problem with 1-2-3 macros is that the cell references included in macros are always absolute. They do not change when, for example, cells are moved about or deleted from the sheet. For example, this simple macro erases the contents of cell A6:

'/re~A6~

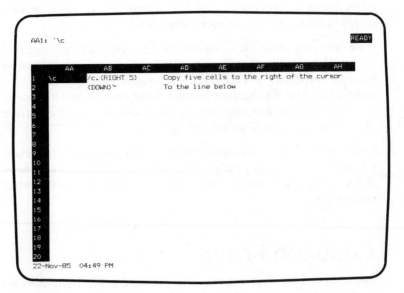

Fig. 12.5. Macro with missing ~.

```
AA1: '\c                                                        POINT
Enter range to copy TO: AA1

        AA        AB        AC        AD        AE        AF        AG        AH
1   \c            /c.{RIGHT 5}        Copy five cells to the right of the cursor
2                 {DOWN}~             To the line below
3
4
5
6
7
8
9
10
11
12
13
14
15
16
17
18
19
20
22-Nov-85  04:51 PM
```

Fig. 12.6. Result of running the macro with missing ~.

But suppose that we move the contents of the macro so that it now
lies one cell to the right. This would be done by pressing the /Move
command, pressing Enter, pressing the right-arrow key, and pressing
Enter once more. Because we still want to blank the same contents
from the sheet, we might expect our macro to say

   ' /re~B6~

If you try this example, however, you will see that the macro has *not*
changed.

If you think about it for a second, this makes perfect sense. A macro is
nothing but a label. You wouldn't expect other labels to change when
the sheet is changed. For example, if you created the label

   ' A15A15A15A15

you wouldn't expect it to change to

   ' C15C15C15C15

if you inserted two columns in the sheet to the left of column A.
Macros are no different.

The absolute nature of cell references within macros is a strong argument in favor of using range names. Because a range name remains
associated with the same range even if the range is moved, range

names within macros (and other formulas) will follow the cells to which they apply, eliminating the kind of problem we saw above.

Debugging a Macro

Almost no program works perfectly the first time. In nearly every case, there are errors that will cause the program to malfunction. Programmers call these problems *bugs* and the process of eliminating them *debugging the program.*

Like programs written in other programming languages, 1-2-3 macros usually need to be debugged before they can be used. Both Release 1A and Release 2 have an extremely useful tool that helps make debugging much simpler: the Step function. When 1-2-3 is in STEP mode, all macros are executed one step at a time. 1-2-3 literally pauses between each keystroke stored in the macro. This means that the user can follow along step by step with the macro as it executes.

Let's step through the buggy macro we developed in the previous section. The macro in figure 12.5 was supposed to copy the contents of five cells to the next line. If we attempted to run this macro, we would see the screen in figure 12.6. There is no indication in figure 12.6 that the line below has been included in the FROM range. All you know is that the macro ends with the program waiting for you to specify the TO range.

Once an error is discovered, you must first get out of the macro and into READY mode by pressing Esc one or more times. When the mode indicator says READY, you can start debugging the macro.

If we assume that we don't know what the problem is with the macro, our next step is to enter STEP mode and rerun the macro. To invoke the single-step mode, press Alt-F1 (Release 1A) or Alt-F2 (Release 2). When you do this, the mode indicator will change to the message STEP. This message will change to SST as soon as you execute the Alt-C macro. In execution after the command, the macro will move forward only one step at a time. After each step, the macro will pause and wait for you to type any keystroke before going on. Although any key can be used, we prefer using the space bar to step through a macro.

As you step through the macro, which was executed with the cursor in cell AA5, you will see each command appear in the control panel. In our example, just before the error occurs, the control panel would look like figure 12.7.

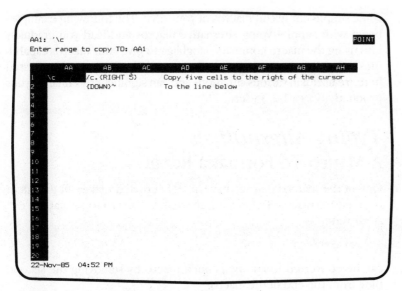

Fig. 12.7. At this point, the macro is not performing as was intended.

Thanks to single-step mode, when the error occurs, it is easy to pinpoint the location in the macro. Once the error is identified, you can exit STEP mode by pressing Alt-F2 again. Then, abort the macro by pressing Esc one or more times.

Editing the Macro

You are now ready to repair the error. Fixing an error in a macro is as simple as editing the cell that contains the erroneous code. You don't need to rewrite the cell. You need only to change the element in error.

In our example, we would first move the cursor to cell AB1, then press F2 to enter EDIT mode. Because the error is a missing ~, fixing the macro is easy. Just type ~ and press Enter to exit from EDIT mode.

Although editing complex macros can be tougher than editing a simple one like this one, the concept is exactly the same. Just use 1-2-3's cell editor (F2) to correct the cell that contains the error.

Creating Simple Macros and Using the Command Language

Now that you have been introduced to the elements of macros and to some of the considerations in using macros, it's time for you to create some simple but useful macros of your own. The following examples begin with simple typing alternative macros and lead you gradually into using the macro command language to give your macros capabilities beyond those of a simple typing alternative. The macros discussed here are useful in various situations and can significantly enhance your productivity as a 1-2-3 user.

Typing Alternatives
A Macro To Format a Range

One of the macros that we have already created makes an excellent open-ended macro. The "typing alternative" macro to format the cell as currency,

    ' /rfc0~~

can be converted to an open-ended macro by removing the second tilde from the end of the macro,

    ' /rfc0~

This macro works precisely like its closed brother, except that here the macro does not complete the formatting command. Instead, it ends, leaving the command open and waiting for a range to be provided. You would enter the range from the keyboard and then press Enter.

This feature can be very useful. For example, in many worksheets, you want some cells formatted as dollars and others as integers. In one case, you may have only one cell to format. In another, you want to format a whole row. This macro can be used in either situation. For example, if you want to format only one cell, you can place the cursor on the cell to be formatted and execute the macro. When the macro is finished, you can press Enter to complete the command. This applies the format to the current cell. On the other hand, if you want to format an entire row, you can use the arrow keys to POINT to the range to be formatted after the macro is completed.

Open-ended macros frequently specify every part of the command except the range to which the command applies. The range is provided from the keyboard.

In effect, the open-ended macro allows you to apply a format or a command to any range of the sheet you wish. Many of the /**R**ange commands can be simplified by condensing them into open-ended macros.

A Macro To Erase a Range

For example, the following macro:

```
'/re
```

starts the /**R**ange **E**rase command but stops prior to assigning the range for the command. The range is supplied from the keyboard. This macro becomes a quick way to erase any portion of the worksheet.

The Indent Macro

Here's an easy macro that you will be able to use all the time. If you've been spreadsheeting for any time at all, you've probably had occasions where you've created a row or column of labels, then decided to change the justification of those labels. For example, you may have created a column of row headers in column A that looks something like figure 12.8, and later decided to indent each label one character. Indenting a single label is not difficult. You simply edit the cell by pressing the F2 key, moving the cursor to the far left of the cell by pressing the Home key, positioning the cursor one character to the right by pressing →, then typing a space. Finally, you press Enter to end the edit. Repeating this process 20 times, however, can be tedious. The macro in figure 12.9 will do the same job and repeat it until you give a command to stop the macro. Figure 12.10 shows the results of the macro.

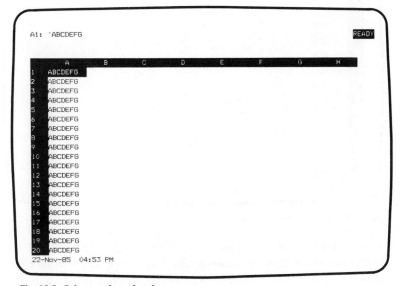

Fig. 12.8. Column of row headers.

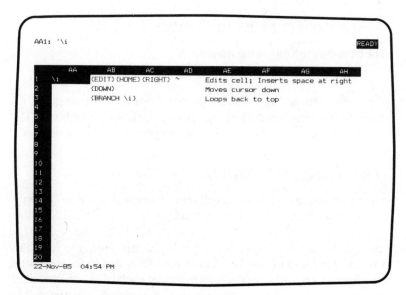

Fig. 12.9. Macro to insert a space in a column of row headers.

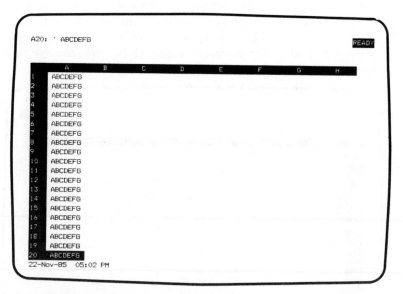

Fig. 12.10. Row headers after running the macro.

To indent all the labels in column A, you move the cursor to cell A1 and invoke our macro by pressing Alt-i. The cursor will start moving down the column, indenting each label one space. If you look at the first line of our macro carefully, you will see that it simply "macroizes" the edit process discussed in the previous paragraph. Line two of the macro moves the cursor down one row.

The statement in line three tells the macro to continue processing at the cell named \i. If you remember that this macro is named \i, you'll realize that line three is telling the macro to start over again. This kind of device is called a *loop* in programming jargon. This loop will cause the program to continue running until you stop it manually.

Once all the labels are indented, you stop the macro. The simplest way to do this is to press Ctrl-Break. The Ctrl-Break keys can always be used to stop a macro (unless you have included a BREAKOFF command) but are not a very elegant way of doing it.

A variation on this macro centers a set of column headers. This macro is illustrated in figure 12.11. To understand how it works, suppose that you built the worksheet shown in figure 12.12. You now want to center the column headers in row 2. To do this, you move the cursor to cell D2 and invoke our macro by pressing Alt-c. The labels will be centered immediately in each of the columns, as shown in figure 12.13.

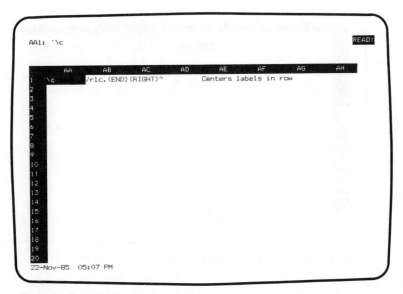

Fig. 12.11. Centering macro.

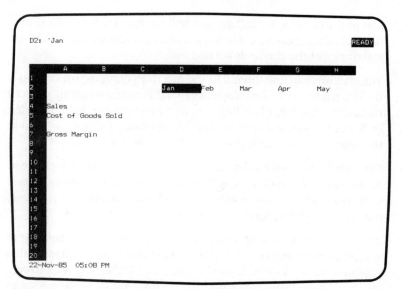

Fig. 12.12. Range before centering macro is run.

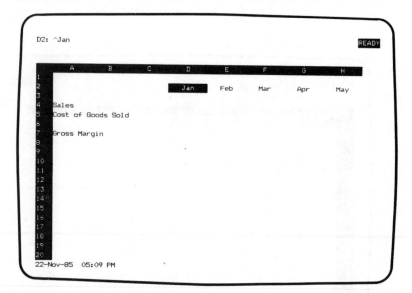

Fig. 12.13. Range after centering macro is run.

This macro points out another valuable use for macros: *editing* the worksheet. At times, we have created complex macros that added and deleted rows or columns throughout the worksheet. Editing macros is most useful when the editing task must be performed repeatedly. In this case, try to create a macro that will perform the job automatically.

A Simple Pointing Macro

One of the most useful types of macros is a pointing macro. For example,

    '+{RIGHT 3}+{DOWN 2}~

inserts a formula in the current cell that is equal to the cell three cells to the right plus two cells below. If we start in cell C17, the formula would be

    +F17+C19

Notice that this macro includes nothing but mathematical symbols and cursor-key representations.

Entering Text with Macros

Although normally you enter the Macro utility from 1-2-3's READY mode, you can also invoke a macro from MENU mode or while you are entering a label or formula into the sheet. These alternatives allow you to create macros that enter commonly used phrases into the worksheet. For example, suppose the word "expense" will occur a number of times in a given sheet. The word will sometimes occur by itself or in combination with other words, as in "sales expense" and "office expense."

You can create a macro that enters the word "expense" in the current cell. The macro would look like this:

    ' expense

Notice that an extra space appears at the beginning of the macro. This space separates the word "expense" from any other word in the cell when the macro is invoked. You will also notice that this is an open-ended macro. Other words can be appended in the cell after the word "expense."

Suppose that you are defining cell A55 as containing the label "expense—miscellaneous". First, invoke the macro to enter the label "expense" into the cell. Next, simply complete the phrase from the keyboard. The completed cell will look like this:

    ' expense—miscellaneous

NEW WITH

R2

Press Enter to close out the cell. To enter the label "Telephone expense (Local)", type *Telephone*, execute the macro, and follow the macro with "(Local)" before pressing Enter.

This kind of macro can save time when you set up a large worksheet. You should create a number of "common word" macros to use when you want to enter labels throughout the sheet.

A Macro To Create Headers

The simple macro in figure 12.14 can be used to create a row of column headers in the worksheet. Each cell contains the abbreviation of the name of a month.

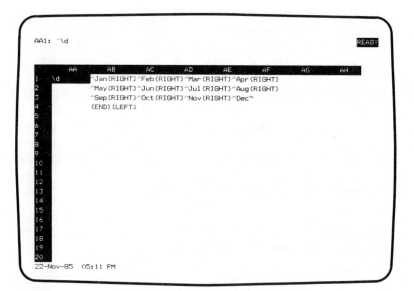

Fig. 12.14. Macro to enter abbreviated months as centered column heads.

Essentially, this macro scrolls across a row, inserting the name of one month in each cell before moving on. Notice the use of {RIGHT} to stand for the right-arrow key (→).

Dating the Worksheet

Thanks to 1-2-3's built-in date functions (@TODAY in Release 1A), you can date your worksheets with the @NOW function. The obvious way to date a sheet is to enter the @NOW function in an appropriate cell. But there is a problem with dating a worksheet this way. When the sheet is reloaded into memory after being saved, the program will automatically recalculate, changing the date before you view it and defeating the purpose of dating the sheet in the first place.

There is a macro solution to this problem. The simple macro in figure 12.15 automatically dates the sheet and ensures that the current date remains in the sheet.

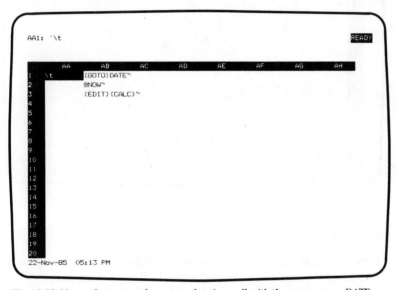

Fig. 12.15. Macro that enters the system date in a cell with the range name DATE.

This macro assumes that the range name DATE has been assigned to a single cell somewhere in the sheet. The macro goes to the range with the name DATE and inserts the value of @NOW there. The cell DATE can be formatted in any way you choose for the best display of the date.

The third line is our old friend, the formula-to-value conversion macro. This line converts the contents of the DATE cell from the @NOW function to the actual numeric value of the @NOW function. This conversion keeps the date from being updated automatically the next time the sheet is loaded.

The one problem with this macro is that it doesn't automatically return you to the point from which you started. Instead, the macro leaves the cursor on the DATE cell. This can be remedied, however, with the use of /rncHERE in a help macro. (See figure 12.34 and the accompanying discussion below.)

There is, however, an even simpler way to enter the date in a cell, using the LET command. The macro is illustrated in figure 12.16.

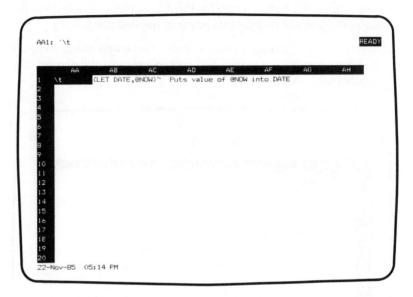

Fig. 12.16. Macro to enter the date using LET.

This macro uses the power of the LET command to enter the *value* of the @NOW function in the cell named DATE. Notice that the LET command enters into the cell the value of the function, and not the function itself, bypassing the need for our {EDIT}{CALC} macro.

Another way to perform this task is illustrated by the macro in figure 12.17, which does essentially the same thing as the LET command, except that the @NOW function must be entered manually in response to the prompt Enter today's date. The /GETNUMBER command inserts the value of the function, and not the function itself, in the indicated cell.

Both of these macros have the advantage of not moving the cursor. Thus they can be used at any time to date the sheet without repositioning the cursor.

A Macro To Name Macros

Although using the /**R**ange **N**ame **L**abel command is a convenient way to name macros, we can speed up the process by creating a macro that

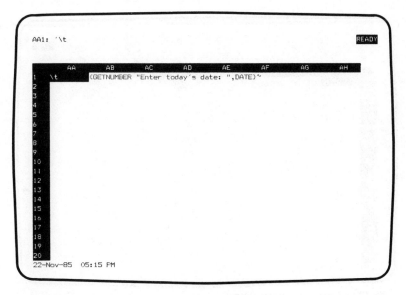

Fig. 12.17. Macro to enter the date using GETNUMBER.

automatically names another. This macro condenses the /**R**ange **N**ame command into a single keystroke:

```
'/rnlr~
```

Before you execute this macro, you must move the cursor to the cell that contains the *name* of the macro you want to name. For example, in the worksheet in figure 12.18, you would move the cursor to cell AA1 before issuing the command. After the macro is complete, the name \w would be assigned to cell AB1.

Creating a standard macro area in your worksheet will make the naming macro even simpler to use. For example, suppose that you decide to store your macros always in column AB. This means that the name for the macros will lie in column AA. You could then modify our range-naming macro to look like figure 12.19.

This macro names every cell in column AB with the cell references found in column AA. If you use this macro, however, make sure that there is no "garbage" in column AA, but only true macro names. Otherwise, the wrong names will be assigned to the macros in column AB.

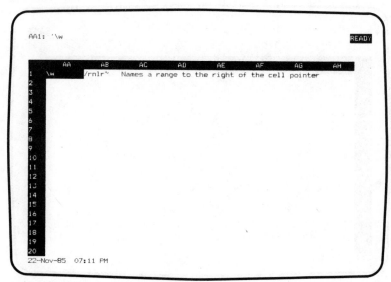

Fig. 12.18. Using the naming macro.

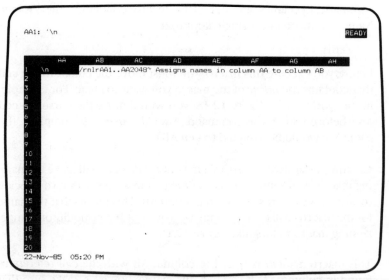

Fig. 12.19. Modified macro-naming macro.

Creating a Macro Library

Once you have become comfortable with macros and have developed
a few that you find yourself using repeatedly, you will want to develop

what we call a *macro library*. A macro library is a worksheet that contains several macros. It typically also includes the name labels associated with each macro and any internal documentation you have written.

If you decide to create a macro library, you will need the simple macro below. This macro loads into memory a set of macros that you have on disk and names each macro in the set. For example, suppose that you have a macro library which contains the following macros:

```
\a      /rfc0~~
\b      /re.
```

and that this library is stored on disk in a worksheet file called LIBRARY.WK1. Now suppose that you are creating a new model and want to include the library in the model. The macro in figure 12.20 will do the trick.

Fig. 12.20. Macro to load macro library.

This macro performs two operations. First, it moves the cursor to cell AA1; then it loads the file LIBRARY.WK1. The macros will be loaded into cells AA1 and AA3.

We can now combine this macro with the one in figure 12.20 to create the macro shown in figure 12.21.

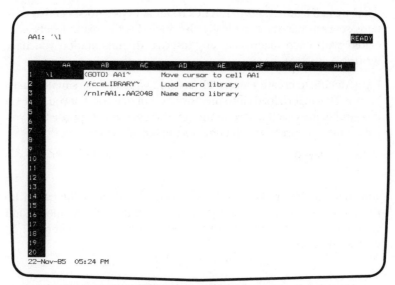

Fig. 12.21. Macro to load and name macro library.

This macro will load and name the macro library. (Although columns AA and AB are used here, you can use any range you want to store your macros.)

Using the Numeric Keypad

Many 1-2-3 users (and those of other IBM PC-based programs) lament the use of the numeric keypad for both entering numeric data and moving the cursor. Because the keypad serves double duty, it really cannot be used to enter a series of numeric data. This is especially irritating to those trained in the use of a 10-key adding machine. For example, suppose that you want to enter the following data into the worksheet:

> 123
> 234
> 345

Simple enough, right? But, to use the numeric keypad to enter the numbers into the sheet, you would have to go through the process shown in table 12.3.

Obviously, the time spent toggling back and forth between cursor movement and numeric entry would eliminate any benefit that could be gained by using the keypad to enter numbers.

Table 12.3.
Manual Steps for Using Numeric Keypad

Function	Keystroke
Position cursor on cell B1	{GOTO}B1
Convert keypad to numeric entry	{NUM}
Enter first number	123
Convert keypad to cursor movement	{NUM}
Move down one cell	{DOWN}
Convert keypad to numeric entry	{NUM}
Enter second number	234
Convert keypad to cursor movement	{NUM}
Move down one cell	{DOWN}
Convert keypad to numeric entry	{NUM}
Enter last number	345
Convert keypad to cursor movement	{NUM}

However, you can build a macro that will automatically move the cursor each time you press the Enter key. The macro illustrated in figure 12.22 will let you use the keypad to enter numbers while you move down a column or across a row.

This macro illustrates several interesting techniques. First, it prompts the user to enter some information (in this case, the number 123) in the current cell. Notice that while 1-2-3 waits for you to type in information, the mode indicator in the upper right corner of the screen reads READY, and the bottom of the screen reads CMD. These prompts remind you that a macro is under way and that 1-2-3 expects you to do something.

After data is entered, the macro automatically moves down one cell. The next line of the macro shows the BRANCH command at work. This line tells the macro to go to the cell named \k, and continue processing there. Because the macro itself is named \k, the BRANCH command forces the macro to repeat itself.

NEW WITH

R2

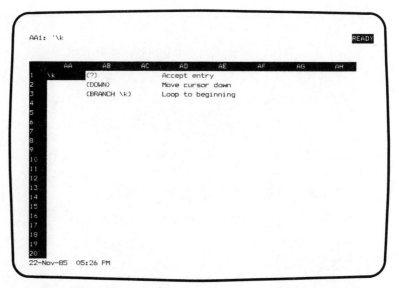

```
AA1:  '\k                                                          READY

            AA       AB       AC       AD      AE       AF      AG      AH
     1   \k        {?}                Accept entry
     2             {DOWN}             Move cursor down
     3             {BRANCH \k}        Loop to beginning
     4
     5
     6
     7
     8
     9
    10
    11
    12
    13
    14
    15
    16
    17
    18
    19
    20
    22-Nov-85   05:26 PM
```

Fig. 12.22. Simple numeric keypad macro.

When the macro starts repeating, it prompts for a second number—in this case, 234. It then moves down one cell and repeats the process. It will continue to repeat until you press Ctrl-Break to halt execution. Ctrl-Break can always be used to stop the execution of a macro. Notice that, after you press Ctrl-Break, the mode indicator returns to its normal READY status.

NEW WITH R2

Be sure that you understand the difference between 1-2-3's GOTO command and the BRANCH macro command. The GOTO command is used to move the cursor to any location on the worksheet. The BRANCH command, on the other hand, simply directs the flow of a macro.

Enhancements on the Basic Macro

We can enhance this basic macro in many interesting ways. First, we could change the middle line so that the cursor moves up, or to the left or right after each entry. You will probably find that two of these (the down variation we've demonstrated and the one that moves right after each input) will be sufficient for your needs.

The basic macro we've designed is practical but somewhat inelegant. For example, while the macro is waiting for a number, it does not provide a prompt to the user about what is expected. This can be changed by substituting a /xn command for the simple {?} function. (The /xn command is explained later in this chapter.) The macro would look like figure 12.23.

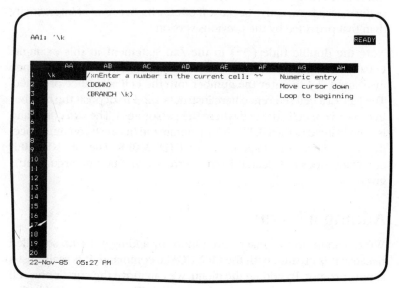

Fig. 12.23. Enhanced keypad macro.

When this macro runs, it begins by prompting the user for data, as shown in figure 12.24.

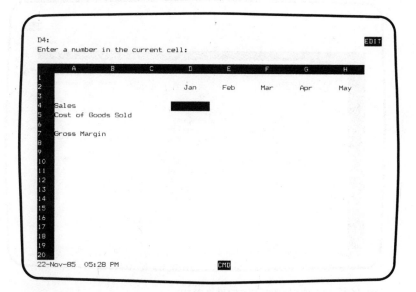

Fig. 12.24. Example of using the keypad macro.

After the number is entered, it will appear in the current cell (in this case, D4). As in the simpler example, when you press the Enter key the cursor moves down one cell, and the macro repeats. This version of the macro is attractive because it offers a higher level of interactivity than that provided by the previous version.

Note the double tilde ($\sim\sim$) in the /xn statement in this example. Usually a cell reference appears after the first tilde. The cell reference instructs 1-2-3 to enter the number into the cell reference provided. The lack of a cell reference here instructs 1-2-3 to deposit the number in the current cell (the cell where the cursor lies). The /xn command is used instead of the GETNUMBER command because you must specify a cell address or range name in GETNUMBER. The GETNUMBER command does not default to the current cell when no argument is given.

NEW WITH
R2

Adding a Menu

NEW WITH
R2

We can soup up this macro even more by adding a *menu*, so called because it is created with the MENUCALL command. It is really just a simple prompt. By adding the menu, we can move the cursor one cell in any direction after we enter the number. The macro looks like figure 12.25.

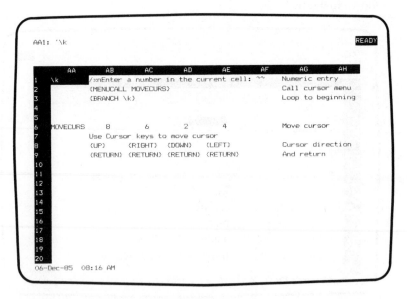

Fig. 12.25. Numeric keypad macro with menu.

Because this macro is fairly complex, let's go through it one step at a time. The macro begins, just like the previous one, by prompting the user to enter a number. After the number is entered, however, the macro gives control over 1-2-3 to a menu, which begins in cell AB6. The statement {MENUCALL MOVECURS} translates as: Begin processing the menu located at cell MOVECURS(AB6).

NEW WITH

R2

Notice that the menu located in cells AB6 through AE9 is generally similar to the sample menu we illustrated earlier. The main difference is that the menu includes just one cell of explanatory text below the basic menu line. We could have included more lines, but they were not needed in this example.

When 1-2-3 begins processing the menu, the screen looks like figure 12.26.

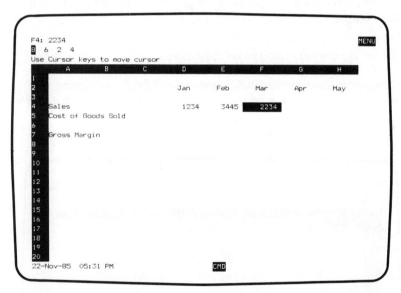

Fig. 12.26. Use of the numeric keypad macro with menu.

You may be puzzled by the choices offered by this menu. At first, it doesn't seem to make sense. Notice, however, that the numbers 8, 6, 2, and 4 correspond to the up-, right-, down-, and left-arrow keys. This should tip you off. The menu allows 1-2-3 to convert the numbers 8, 6, 2, and 4 into their cursor-movement equivalents.

If you built this macro and are working along, you have probably noticed several of its limitations. For one thing, you can move only one cell at a time across the worksheet. For another, you must enter some number, even if it is just 0, in each cell you pass through. Another limitation is that you must press Enter and enter a direction between entering numbers. It would be nice if you could go directly to the next cell without having to press Enter.

You should also notice that this macro menu does not work like most macro menus. In most menus, you make your selection by using the left- and right-arrow keys to point to options in the menu. You can also type the first character of the option you want.

Our example, however, assumes that the keypad is being used for numeric entry and that the cursor keys are disabled. They, therefore, cannot be used to move the menu cursor. You can make selections in this menu only by pressing the first (and only) character of an option. As it turns out, this is exactly what you want to do, because pressing the first character simulates pressing the arrow key to move the worksheet cursor.

The Accumulator Macro

Many spreadsheet users are familiar with the difficulty of creating year-to-date totals in their worksheets. For example, suppose that you created the sheet shown in figure 12.27.

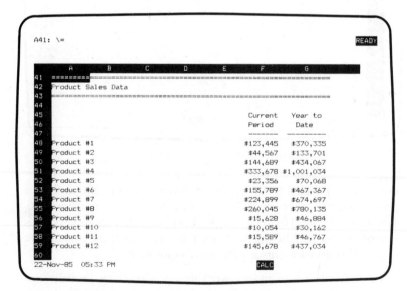

Fig. 12.27. Worksheet with month and Y-T-D.

Now suppose that you want to accumulate the current period amounts into the year-to-date total. This can be done by defining each cell in column G with a formula like

G48 = G48+F48

This circular reference adds the amount in cell F48 (the current period number) to the amount in cell G48 (the year-to-date amount) each time the model is recalculated. For example, if we recalculate this model, the result would look like figure 12.28, which is exactly what we want. But what would happen if we accidentally pressed Calc again? The sheet would look like figure 12.29, which is definitely not what we want—we've erroneously double-counted the numbers in the current column. You run this risk anytime you create this type of circular reference. We can, however, create a macro that accomplishes the job of accumulating year-to-date totals.

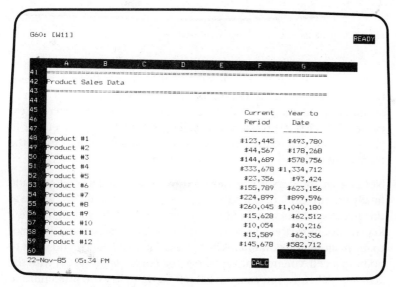

Fig. 12.28. Worksheet after recalculation.

In our original example, what would happen if there were no formulas in the cells in column G, just numbers? This would eliminate the risk of accidental double-counting. But we also want to add the data in the two columns, which requires some sort of formula.

Thanks to Steve Miller of Lotus Development Corporation, the simple macro illustrated in figure 12.30 solves this problem perfectly.

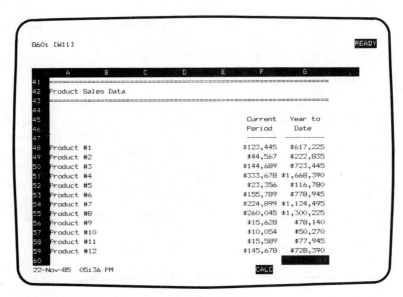

Fig. 12.29. Worksheet after a second recalculation.

Let's go through the macro one step at a time. To use this macro, place the cursor on the cell at the top of the column in which you want to accumulate the total—in this case, column G. Then the macro is executed. The first expression *edits* cell G48, then moves the cursor to cell F48 (one cell to the left) and adds the number in that cell to the number in cell G48.

Notice that the cursor was moved down one cell, left one cell, and finally up one cell ({DOWN}{LEFT}{UP}) to reach cell F48. Why was this necessary? Once you enter EDIT mode, the left- and right-arrow keys do not move the cursor from cell to cell, but cause the edit cursor to move along the edit line. When you are in EDIT mode and want to point to a cell, you must always move the cursor *up* or *down* with the arrow keys before you can move it left or right. Try the procedure to see what we mean.

The next step is a simple formula-to-number conversion. This line of the macro converts the results from a simple addition of two numbers to an even simpler single number.

The third line moves the cursor down one row; then the magic begins. The fourth line can be translated as: Create a range name called TEST. Assign that name to the range that includes the current cell and the cell immediately to the left of the current cell; then determine the

Fig. 12.30. Accumulator macro.

value for the @COUNT function for that two-cell range. The statement beginning with {IF... contains a logical test. The function can be translated as: If the value of the @COUNT function is greater than or equal to one, then delete the name TEST, BRANCH to the cell named \a, and continue processing. (This is a simple loop.) If the value of @COUNT for the range TEST does not meet the condition, then delete the name TEST and stop processing.

You may be thinking "Whoa!" Having gone through this macro once, let's go back through it, in a little more detail, to explain why we did some of the things we did. For example, notice that the TEST range was defined as *two* cells wide. We did this to include any rows for which there is a month but not a year-to-date.

This macro checks the pair of cells in columns F and G to see whether both are empty. If they are empty, the macro assumes that the end of the column of numbers has been reached. If either cell is not empty, the macro continues until it reaches the bottom of the column.

This macro can be written another way, using the FOR command. The FOR command, a looping command, calls a macro subroutine a specific number of times. This macro is quicker than the macro in figure 12.30 but fails if the Y-T-D column is blank.

In the version of the macro shown in figure 12.31, the macro begins by defining a range name over the year-to-date column. Then the FOR

NEW WITH
R2

NEW WITH
R2

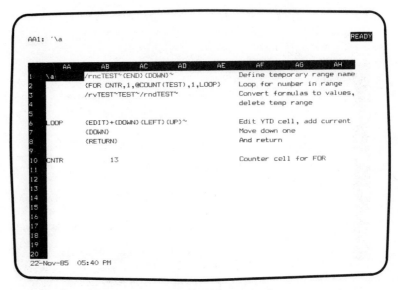

```
AA1: '\a                                                          READY

              AA        AB       AC       AD       AE       AF       AG       AH
 1     \a          /rncTEST~{END}{DOWN}~              Define temporary range name
 2                 {FOR CNTR,1,@COUNT(TEST),1,LOOP}   Loop for number in range
 3                 /rvTEST~TEST~/rndTEST~             Convert formulas to values,
 4                                                    delete temp range
 5
 6     LOOP        {EDIT}+{DOWN}{LEFT}{UP}~           Edit YTD cell, add current
 7                 {DOWN}                             Move down one
 8                 {RETURN}                           And return
 9
10     CNTR           13                              Counter cell for FOR
11
12
13
14
15
16
17
18
19
20
22-Nov-85   05:40 PM
```

Fig. 12.31. Accumulator macro using the FOR command.

NEW WITH

R2

statement calls the subroutine loop once for every nonblank cell [determined by the @COUNT(TEST) segment] in the range. The Loop macro edits each cell in the year-to-date column. After the FOR finishes, the /Range Value command is used to convert formulas to values.

Subroutines are commonly used in programming to simplify large, complex programs. Many large programs use certain routines repeatedly in different parts of the program. In addition, many common routines are used by most programs. These routines can be broken out into subroutines, which are miniature programs in their own right. They can be accessed by subroutine calls in the larger program.

Creating Your Own Help Screens

Like 1-2-3, many of the new and exciting commercial programs come with on-line help. Thanks to 1-2-3's macro capabilities, you can add help screens to your 1-2-3 worksheets.

The macro that allows you to create on-line help screens is fairly simple. It relies on 1-2-3's /Range Name and GOTO commands. Before the macro is built, you must create a *help screen* in your worksheet. You can do this by entering in a series of cells anywhere in the sheet the message, or messages, you want to convey to your users. The help screen in this example is confined to one window of data.

After the help screen is created, you must give the upper left corner of the range a name. We suggest "Help" because it is simple and to the point. Figure 12.32 shows a sample help screen. Notice that we've placed the screen at cell A100 in the worksheet. Although this place is convenient for the help screen, you can put it anywhere you want on the worksheet. Remember, cell A100 in our example is named HELP. The macro in figure 12.33 takes us to the help screen.

The first statement creates a range name, HERE, and assigns it to the current cell. The second line of the macro moves the cursor to the range named HELP—in this case, to cell A100. The {?} in the third line causes the macro to pause and wait for input from the keyboard.

At this point, the help screen would be visible on the computer display. You can take your time reading the messages on the screen, then press Enter when you are finished. When any key is pressed, the {?} command will be satisfied, and the macro will resume processing.

This macro not only brings us help, but also returns us automatically to where we were. The statement in the fourth line of the macro, {GOTO}HERE, returns the cursor to the cell that was named HERE a moment before. In other words, the macro automatically returns us to the point where we started.

The final step in this macro erases the name HERE from 1-2-3's memory. This housekeeping step is taken so that there will be no conflict between the old HERE area and the new HERE area when the macro is used again.

Deleting the range name HERE is very important. Whenever you create a range name in the 1-2-3 worksheet, 1-2-3 will automatically insert the range name in place of the cell reference that defines the same cell in any formulas that refer to the cell. In other words, if you named cell A15 HERE, the formula

+A15+A16

would change to

+HERE+A16

Now, suppose that you go ahead with your work and do not delete the range name and that, at some later time, you decide to use the help macro again. In the course of accessing the help screens, that macro names the current cell HERE. This new cell—which could be anywhere in the sheet—will now be used instead of A15 in our formula. This could mess up a carefully planned worksheet.

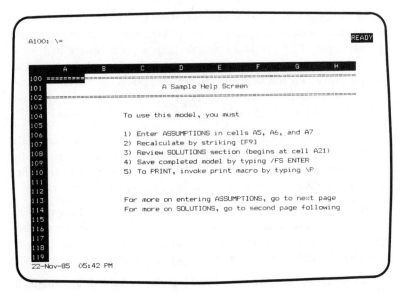

Fig. 12.32. A user-defined help screen.

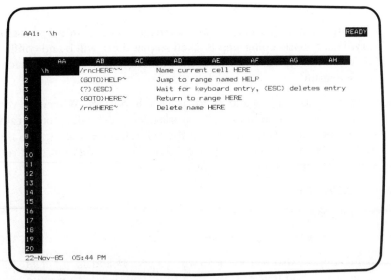

Fig. 12.33. The help screen macro.

Although this macro is very useful, you could use menus to create even more sophisticated help. For example, suppose that you had more help messages than could be squeezed on one screen. You would need a macro that allows you to view more than one screen before returning to the origin.

By slightly modifying our original macro, you could accomplish this change. The new macro is shown in figure 12.34.

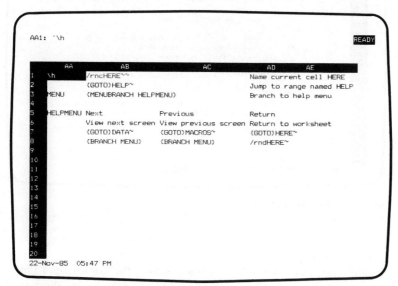

```
AA1:  '\h                                                              READY

         AA         AB                AC              AD        AE
1       \h     /rncHERE~~                          Name current cell HERE
2              {GOTO}HELP~                          Jump to range named HELP
3     MENU     {MENUBRANCH HELPMENU}                Branch to help menu
4
5     HELPMENU Next              Previous           Return
6              View next screen View previous screen Return to worksheet
7              {GOTO}DATA~       {GOTO}MACROS~       {GOTO}HERE~
8              {BRANCH MENU}     {BRANCH MENU}       /rndHERE~
9
10
11
12
13
14
15
16
17
18
19
20
22-Nov-85  05:47 PM
```

Fig. 12.34. A more sophisticated help macro.

Notice that this macro includes a fairly complex menu that can be used to select one of three options: View next page, View previous page, or Return to worksheet. The first two steps of the macro work precisely as before. Once the help is in view, however, the macro changes significantly. If the HELP area is located at cell A100, the control panel of the worksheet will look like figure 12.35 when the first help screen is displayed.

By pointing with the cursor, or by pressing the first letter of the desired alternative, you can either move ahead or back one page, or return to the main worksheet. If you return to the worksheet, the macro will be completed in the same way it was in the simpler example—by returning to the range named HERE, then deleting that range name.

If, however, you choose to go forward or back one screen, the cursor will move in the desired direction, and the menu above will repeat, thanks to the BRANCH command. The menu will appear as long as you choose the Next or Previous options.

```
A100: \=                                                        MENU
Next  Previous  Return
View next screen
           A       B       C       D       E       F       G       H
100 ==============================================================
101                        A Sample Help Screen
102 ==============================================================
103
104              To use this model, you must
105
106              1) Enter ASSUMPTIONS in cells A5, A6, and A7
107              2) Recalculate by striking [F9]
108              3) Review SOLUTIONS section (begins at cell A21)
109              4) Save completed model by typing /FS ENTER
110              5) To PRINT, invoke print macro by typing \P
111
112
113              For more on entering ASSUMPTIONS, go to next page
114              For more on SOLUTIONS, go to second page following
115
116
117
118
119
22-Nov-85  05:49 PM                      CMD
```

Fig. 12.35. Help screen with menu.

This macro could be revised even more to accommodate a more complex set of help screens. For example, suppose that in your current model you have four help screens covering the topics **Data** Entry, **Macros**, **Printing**, and **Saving**. You could create the macro illustrated in figure 12.36 that would allow the user to select directly any of the four options.

This macro is essentially the same as the macro in the previous example, except that this one gives the user the choice of one of four specific areas of help, instead of just offering the "Page back" and "Page forward" options. This kind of indexed help comes close to that offered by the 1-2-3 program itself.

Wouldn't it be nice if we could name these help macros \? Using the ? would closely parallel many other programs that use this symbol to call for help; but, as we have seen, 1-2-3 allows only letter names for macros.

Printing with a Macro

Macros can be used to automate complex tasks that are repeated frequently. Printing a large worksheet is such a task. There are several steps involved in readying the worksheet for printing: specifying the print range; aligning the paper in the printer; and specifying such op-

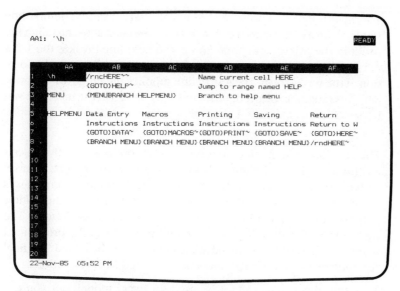

Fig. 12.36. Help macro with four menu options.

tions as borders, headers, footers, and margins. Although the design of
a printing macro will vary from application to application, the sample
model in figure 12.37 demonstrates many of the ways a macro can help
with this task.

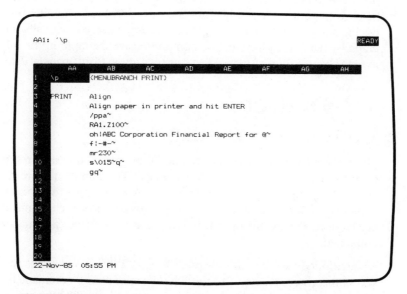

Fig. 12.37. Print macro.

This macro looks complex, but it is really very simple. The first line sends control of the macro to a menu that directs that user to align the paper in the printer and press Enter. The next line invokes the 1-2-3 **/Print Printer Align** command, which informs 1-2-3 about the location of the top of form. The fourth line supplies the range for the print job. This range can be predetermined and entered in the macro or can be specified at execution time with a {?} command (for example, r{?}~).

The next lines assign values to the 1-2-3 print options. Line five inserts a centered title (including the current date) in the report. Line six adds a footer that supplies the page number. The next command sets the right margin to 230, and the following line instructs the printer (in this case an Epson FX-100) to print in a compressed mode. The /q~ command makes the macro step up one level in the print menu so that the /g~ (GO) command in the next line can be issued. The final /q~ returns 1-2-3 to READY mode after the report is printed.

Note that this macro cannot be used for every model, but you can create a macro like it to print your frequently used reports.

Creating Graphs

In much the same way, you can use macros to issue quickly the commands required to produce common graphs. For example, 1-2-3 can be used to perform monthly financial analysis. This job includes producing a few graphs. We have created a simple macro that calls the graph by name for plotting. The comprehensive example in the following chapter shows a macro that creates a graph from financial data.

NEW WITH
R2

1-2-3's Macro Command Language

The remainder of this chapter provides a complete command reference for 1-2-3's macro command language. The commands are divided into groups based on their functions. Within these groups, each command is discussed, and an example is given of how the command can be used. Finally, any tips or tricks are noted for using each macro command.

As mentioned earlier in this chapter, Release 2 of 1-2-3 contains two sets of macro commands: (1) the limited set of macro commands—/x commands—originally included in Release 1A and (2) the macro

Command Language developed and proved in Symphony. Commands from Release 1A have corresponding commands in the command language. To help you recognize pairs of corresponding commands, table 12.4 and the following discussion of commands indicate whenever two commands—one from 1A and one from the command language—perform similar functions.

NEW WITH
R2

Macro Command Grammar

NEW WITH
R2

The format of /x macro commands is based on the way that 1-2-3 commands are invoked from command menus. The command begins with a / (slash), followed by the letter *x* and another letter that selects the appropriate subcommand. Arguments, when needed, follow the command. Each argument is terminated by a ~ (Enter).

An example of the /xi (eXtended IF) macro command,

/xisales>1000~/xq~

reads: If the value of sales is greater than 1,000, then quit macro execution. The macro command descriptions discuss the /x macro commands in detail.

The new macro commands from the Symphony Command Language have a special grammar that is similar to @function grammar. The general format of macro commands is

{KEYWORD}

or

{KEYWORD argument1,argument2,...,argumentN}

with arguments 1 through N separated by commas. Examples of macro commands are

{BLANK SALES}
    Has the same effect as **/R**ange **E**rase on the range named
    SALES

{BEEP} or {BEEP N}
    Causes the speaker to emit a short beep; a good function to
    indicate that the user has made an error. The second form
    allows you to select one of four different tones.

{GETLABEL "Enter label: ",first field}
    Causes macro to stop processing temporarily to allow user
    to enter a label; places the entry in a cell called *first field*.

NEW WITH
R2

{indicate "Bye"}
   Substitutes BYE for the standard 1-2-3 indicator in the upper
   right corner of the screen.

In the statements above, the command keywords are BLANK, BEEP, GETLABEL, and INDICATE. Notice that, in the last example, the keyword is not entered in capital letters. 1-2-3 doesn't care whether you use capital or small letters for entering keywords. However, for the sake of clarity, keywords in this chapter are in capital letters.

Macro statements can have one or more arguments following the macro keyword. Just as in @ functions, the arguments for macro keyword commands can be of three types: a number, a string value, or a range.

The rules for macro keyword command arguments differ slightly from those for functions. First, you can't use string-value formulas for arguments in macro command keyword statements that expect the string format. Macros are entered as text into the worksheet, and the string formulas are not processed in the macros' values. (Some exceptions to this rule are described later in this chapter, in the macro command descriptions.) Second, you can use a single-cell address for a range. In other words, the address A1 and the range A1..A1 are used in the same way.

Macro Command Groupings

1-2-3 macro commands can be placed into six different groups: commands for logical operations, commands for branching and subroutines, commands for testing keyboard input, commands for storing and deleting, commands to process sequential files, and a general category of maintenance-oriented commands. Table 12.4 lists the 1-2-3 macro commands; Release 1A macro commands are listed next to the corresponding new commands.

Commands for Logical Operations

Commands for logical operations include all the macro commands used for conditional testing. For example, suppose that you want to test the value in a cell before performing a calculation. 1-2-3 provides three different commands for testing the value: the IF or /xi command, the ONERROR command, and the FOR command.

Table 12.4[1]
Macro Commands in Release 2 of 1-2-3

Commands for Logical Operations

{FOR counter,start, stop,step,macro}	For loop command. Loop count is placed in \<counter\>
{FORBREAK}	Breaks out of FOR loop
{IF condition} or /XIcondition~	Conditionally executes statements after IF
{ONERROR branch, [message]}	Traps errors, passing control to \<branch\>

Commands for Branching and Subroutines

{BRANCH location} or /XGlocation~	Macro continues at \<location\>.
{DEFINE loc1:Type1, loc2:Type2,...}	Specifies cells for subroutine args
{DISPATCH location}	Branches indirectly via \<location\>
{MENUBRANCH location} or /XMlocation~	Prompts user with menu found at \<location\>
{MENUCALL location}	Like MENUBRANCH except that control returns to the statement after the MENUCALL
{name} or /XCname~	Macro subroutine call to routine \<name\>
{QUIT} or /XQ	Ends macro execution
{RESTART}	Cancels a macro subroutine
{RETURN} or /XR	Returns from a macro subroutine

Commands for Testing Keyboard Input

{GET location}	Accepts a single character into \<location\>
{GETLABEL prompt, location} or /XLprompt~location~	Accepts a label into \<location\>

[1] In this table, the following conventions apply: all 1-2-3 macro command keywords and /x commands are presented in uppercase, and terms for arguments that follow macro commands are shown in lowercase.

{GETNUMBER} prompt, location} or /XNprompt~location~	Accepts a number into <location>
{LOOK location}	Places first character from type-ahead buffer into <location>

Commands for Storing and Deleting

{CONTENTS dest.,source, [width],[format]}	Stores contents of <source> to <destination>
{LET location, expression}	Places value of expression in <location>
{PUT range,col, row,value}	Puts value into col,row within range
{BLANK location}	Erases the cell or range

File Manipulation Commands

{CLOSE}	Closes a file opened with {OPEN}
{FILESIZE location}	Records size of open file in location
{GETPOS location}	Records file pointer position in location
{OPEN filename,mode}	Opens file for reading, writing, or both
{READ bytecount, location}	Copies specified number of characters from file to location
{READLN location}	Copies next line from file to location
{SETPOS file-position}	Sets a new position for the file pointer
{WRITE string}	Copies a string to the open file
{WRITELN string}	Copies a string plus a carriage-return line-feed sequence to the open file

Maintenance-Oriented Commands

{BEEP [number]}	Sounds one of the computer's four beeps
{BREAKOFF}	Disables {BREAK} key
{BREAKON}	Enables {BREAK} key
{INDICATE string}	Resets control panel indicator to <string>
{PANELOFF}	Suppresses display of control panel
{PANELON}	Displays control panel
{RECALC location, [condition], [iteration]}	Recalculates formulas in range, row-by-row
{RECALCCOL location, [condition], iteration]}	Recalculates formulas in range, column-by-column
{WAIT time-serial-num}	Waits until specified time
{WINDOWSOFF}	Suppresses redisplay of current window
{WINDOWSON}	Enables redisplay of current window

The IF or /xi Command

The IF command (Release 2) is used to make a macro execute conditionally one or more instructions as the result of a logical test. By using this command, you can implement the kind of IF-THEN-ELSE logic common to many high-level programming languages. The general form of the command is

> {IF logical-expression}(command(s) to execute if true)

or

> /xilogical-expression~(command(s) to execute if true)

The IF and /xi (Release 1A) commands are similar to the IF command in BASIC and are functionally identical. If the logical expression is true, then the remaining macro commands on the same line are executed. If the expression is false, execution skips the commands after the IF or /xi command on the current line and continues on the next line. (The rest of the discussion refers to both forms as the IF command.)

The IF command is commonly used to branch conditionally to another macro routine or to call a subroutine. You can do this easily. Place a BRANCH command or a subroutine call after, and on the same macro line as, the IF command.

Suppose, for example, that you want to test the value in a single-cell range called NEW RECORD. If the value in NEW RECORD is Y (for Yes), you want to add a new record to a database. Otherwise, you want to modify an existing record in the database. Your macro will include the following statements:

```
{IF new record="Y"}{BRANCH new_routine}
{BRANCH mod_routine}
```

The first line is contained in a single cell. The part of the cell following the IF portion is called the THEN clause. The THEN clause is executed only if the result ot the logical test is true. In this case, the THEN clause contains the keyword BRANCH, followed by the range name NEW_ROUTINE. (BRANCH is often used with IF.) The macro will branch to NEW_ROUTINE if the value of NEW RECORD is equal to Y.

The second line contains the ELSE clause, which is executed only if the result of the logical statement in the IF statement is false. In this example, the ELSE clause also contains a BRANCH statement, but the range to branch to is called MOD_ROUTINE. Note that in this case, the THEN clause transfers control to another routine. If the macro statements in the THEN clause do not transfer control, the line below the IF statement (the ELSE clause) will be executed after the statement(s) in the THEN clause.

The IF statement adds significant strength to 1-2-3's macro language. However, the one disadvantage of the IF statement is that if you want to execute more than one macro command after the logical test, the THEN clause must contain a branching statement or a subroutine call. What's more, if the code in the THEN clause does not branch or execute a QUIT command, the macro will continue its execution right through the ELSE clause.

The ONERROR Command

NEW WITH
R2

The processing of 1-2-3 macros is normally interrupted if a system error (such as Disk drive not ready) occurs during execution. The ONERROR command provides a means to let a macro continue executing even though a system error has occurred. The general format of the command is

{ONERROR branch-location,message-location}

The best place to put an ONERROR statement is directly above where you think an error may occur. For example, suppose that your macro is about to copy a portion of the current spreadsheet to a disk file, using the /File Xtract command. A system error will occur if the drive is not ready or the disk is full. Therefore, you should include a strategically placed ONERROR command (see fig. 12.38).

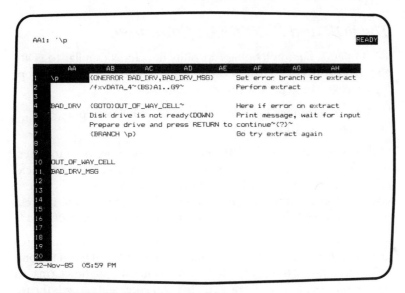

```
AA1:  '\p                                                          READY

        AA       AB       AC       AD       AE       AF       AG       AH
1  \p       {ONERROR BAD_DRV,BAD_DRV_MSG}        Set error branch for extract
2          /fxvDATA_4~{BS}A1..G9~               Perform extract
3
4  BAD_DRV  {GOTO}OUT_OF_WAY_CELL~               Here if error on extract
5          Disk drive is not ready{DOWN}        Print message, wait for input
6          Prepare drive and press RETURN to continue~{?}~
7          {BRANCH \p}                          Go try extract again
8
9
10 OUT_OF_WAY_CELL
11 BAD_DRV_MSG
12
13
14
15
16
17
18
19
20
22-Nov-85  05:59 PM
```

Fig. 12.38. ONERROR statement to retry disk access.

In this example, the ONERROR statement will cause the macro to branch to a cell called BAD_DRV if an error occurs. A copy of the error message that 1-2-3 issues is entered in a cell called BAD_DRV_MSG. (This argument is optional.) Then, the first statement in the BAD_DRV routine positions the cursor to an out-of-the-way cell (cleverly called OUT_OF_WAY_CELL). Next, the message *Disk drive is not ready* is entered in the spreadsheet, followed by *Prepare drive and press Return to continue*. The macro pauses for the user to press Return. Finally, the macro branches back to PROC to try again.

As a general rule, you should always make sure that your ONERROR statement is executed by the macro before an error takes place. Therefore, you may want to include an ONERROR statement near the start of your macros. Because you can have only one ONERROR statement in effect at a time, you should take special precautions to write your macros so that the right message appears for each error condition.

Ctrl-Break presents a special problem for the ONERROR statement. Because Ctrl-Break actually causes an error condition, the ONERROR statement is automatically invoked. Therefore, a good technique when you plan to use the ONERROR statement is to disable Ctrl-Break after you have debugged your macro. (See the discussion of the BREAKOFF command.) By disabling Ctrl-Break, you can prevent the confusion that might arise with an untimely error message.

The FOR and FORBREAK Commands

1-2-3 offers a built-in looping capability in macros (similar to FOR–NEXT loops in BASIC). The FOR command is used to control the looping process. The general form of the command is

{FOR counter-location,start-number,stop-number,step-
    number,starting-location}

The start-number, stop-number, and step-number are used to determine how many times a group of macro commands (the loop) is executed. The starting-location indicates where the first macro command in the loop resides. The counter-location is the address where you want to store the counter that 1-2-3 keeps track of.

Suppose, for example, that you want to build a macro that computes factorials. There are several ways to accomplish this, but the FOR command offers one of the easiest alternatives. Figure 12.39 shows a macro that computes the factorial of a number you enter and records the result in the current cell.

There are several points to notice about this macro. The first line of the \f routine uses the LET command. The LET command stores a number (or a string) at a specified cell location; in this case, the number to be stored is 1, and the specified cell location is a cell named PREVIOUS NUMBER. The LET command is particularly useful for initializing variables.

Next, the GETNUMBER command waits for the user to enter a number, which is then stored in a cell called FACTORIAL. Notice that the GETNUMBER command lets you include a string for prompting the user. The string appears in the control panel when the GETNUMBER command is executed.

1-2-3 begins the FOR command by evaluating the start-, stop-, and step-number values. In this case, they are, respectively: 1, FACTORIAL, and 1. 1-2-3 also initializes the counter-location cell, COUNTER, with the start-number value. Next, the program tests the value in the

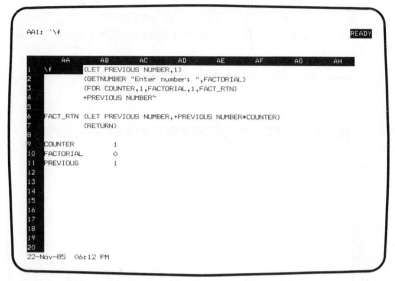

```
AA1:  '\f                                                    READY

         AA      AB        AC        AD       AE       AF       AG       AH
1    \f          {LET PREVIOUS NUMBER,1}
2                {GETNUMBER "Enter number: ",FACTORIAL}
3                {FOR COUNTER,1,FACTORIAL,1,FACT_RTN}
4                +PREVIOUS NUMBER~
5
6    FACT_RTN {LET PREVIOUS NUMBER,+PREVIOUS NUMBER*COUNTER}
7                {RETURN}
8
9    COUNTER        1
10   FACTORIAL      0
11   PREVIOUS       1
12
13
14
15
16
17
18
19
20
22-Nov-85  06:12 PM
```

Fig. 12.39. Factorial macro using the FOR command.

counter-location cell to see whether it is less than the stop-number. If the result of the test is true, 1-2-3 executes the routine at the starting-location, FACT_RTN. If the result of the test is false, 1-2-3 proceeds to the next macro command after the FOR command.

The subroutine FACT_RTN uses the LET command to reassign the value in PREVIOUS NUMBER. In this case, the value used for reassignment is derived by multiplying PREVIOUS NUMBER by the value in COUNTER.

When 1-2-3 finishes executing FACT_RTN (that is, when it encounters the RETURN statement, a command specifically designed for ending subroutines), the program returns to the FOR command and increases the value in counter by 1 (the step-number). The entire process of testing the COUNTER cell against the stop-value, executing the FACT_RTN, and incrementing the value in the COUNTER cell is repeated until the value in the COUNTER cell exceeds the stop-value. When the FOR command is completed, the macro assigns the formula +PREVIOUS NUMBER to the current cell.

If you wish to end the processing of a FOR command prematurely, you can use the FORBREAK command. When you use this command, 1-2-3 interrupts the processing of the FOR command and continues execution with the command following the FOR.

For example, suppose you are using the Factorial model again, and you want to end processing when you reach 15 decimal places of precision, the maximum precision that 1-2-3 is capable of handling. To stop processing, you can use the FORBREAK command as it appears in figure 12.40.

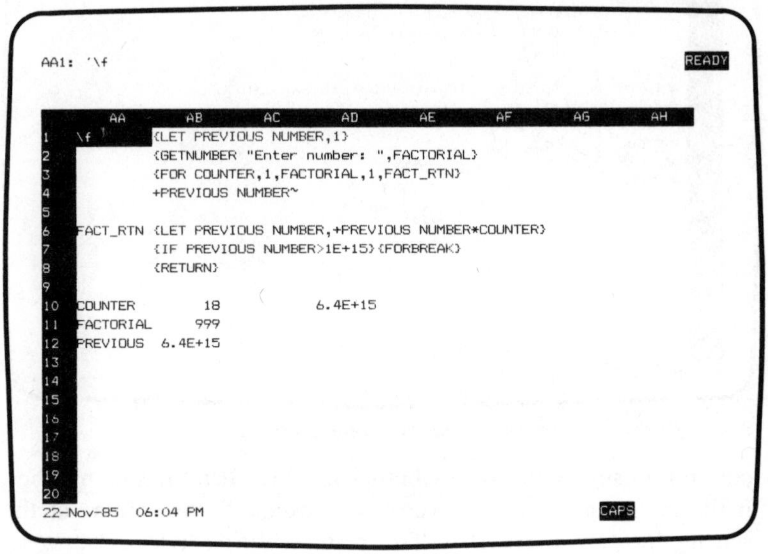

```
AA1: '\f                                                              READY

        AA        AB        AC        AD        AE        AF        AG        AH
1  \f        {LET PREVIOUS NUMBER,1}
2            {GETNUMBER "Enter number: ",FACTORIAL}
3            {FOR COUNTER,1,FACTORIAL,1,FACT_RTN}
4            +PREVIOUS NUMBER~
5
6  FACT_RTN  {LET PREVIOUS NUMBER,+PREVIOUS NUMBER*COUNTER}
7            {IF PREVIOUS NUMBER>1E+15}{FORBREAK}
8            {RETURN}
9
10 COUNTER        18            6.4E+15
11 FACTORIAL      999
12 PREVIOUS   6.4E+15
13
14
15
16
17
18
19
20
22-Nov-85  06:04 PM                                                    CAPS
```

Fig. 12.40. Factorial routine with the FORBREAK command.

Commands for Branching and Subroutines

The original release of 1-2-3 offered two different techniques for instructing a macro to continue executing at a specific cell location. One technique is a simple branch, and the other is a menu-branch. These commands are similar to the GOTO statement in BASIC. There was also a means of calling a macro as a subroutine, similar to the GOSUB statement in BASIC. Release 2 expands the Release 1A commands by offering such additional capabilities as the ability to pass arguments to subroutines and to call menus as subroutines.

The BRANCH Command (/xg and BRANCH)

BRANCH (Release 2) is the simplest macro command for getting 1-2-3 to read keystrokes starting at a new location. The general format of the command is

    {BRANCH location}   (keyword command)

or

    /xglocation~   (Release 1A command)

The keyword command and the Release 1A command perform identically.

Suppose, for example, that three separate companies are under your corporate umbrella, and you have written a macro for adding and modifying records in a corporate personnel database. Depending on how the user of the macro responds to the Enter Company (R, A, or C): prompt, you want the program to branch to a different place in the macro and prompt the user further for data specific to that company. Figure 12.41 shows a portion of the macro.

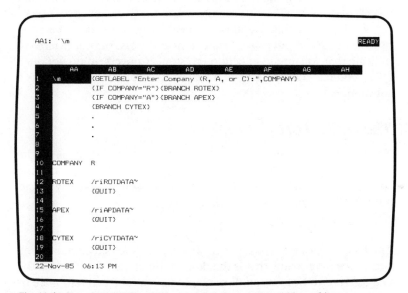

Fig. 12.41. Use of BRANCH and IF commands for conditional branching.

The BRANCH statements in the \m macro cause the flow of macro execution to shift to the different company routines. In this example, the BRANCH statements are coupled with IF statements to shift execution conditionally, depending on the user's response. After the macro executes a company routine, the QUIT statement at the end of the routine causes macro execution to stop.

You may prefer that execution return to the \m macro or to another macro after completing the company routine. This can be done in one of two ways: (1) you can replace the {QUIT} statements at the end of subroutines with {BRANCH \m} statements to return to \m; or (2) you can replace the BRANCH statements in \m with subroutine calls (discussed in the next section), followed by a BRANCH to the point where execution should continue.

There are two important points about BRANCH statements. First, they cause a permanent shift in the flow of statement execution (unless you use another BRANCH statement). Second, BRANCH statements are most often used in combination with IF statements.

The QUIT Command (QUIT or /xq)

The QUIT (Release 2) command causes macro execution to stop as soon as the QUIT is executed. It is particularly useful, in conjunction with an IF statement, to stop macro execution when a condition is satisfied. 1-2-3 will stop automatically at the end of a macro, even without a QUIT statement. (Execution stops when the program encounters a blank cell or a cell that contains a numeric value.) However, it is good practice to always put a QUIT statement at the end of your macros to indicate that you intend execution to stop. (Conversely, do not put a QUIT command at the end of a macro that you intend to call as a subroutine.)

The DISPATCH Command

NEW WITH
R2

The DISPATCH command is similar to the BRANCH command. The DISPATCH command, however, branches indirectly to a location specified by the value contained in the location pointed to by the argument. The form of the command is

{DISPATCH location}

The location given as the DISPATCH argument should contain a cell address or range name that is the destination of the DISPATCH. If the cell referred to by location does not contain a valid cell reference or range name, an error occurs and macro execution either stops with an error message or transfers to the location in the current ONERROR command.

The location must be a cell reference or range name that points to a single cell reference. If the location is either a multicell range or a range that contains a single cell, the DISPATCH acts like a BRANCH statement and transfers execution directly to location.

The BRANCH example shown in figure 12.41 is modified, in figure 12.42, to use DISPATCH.

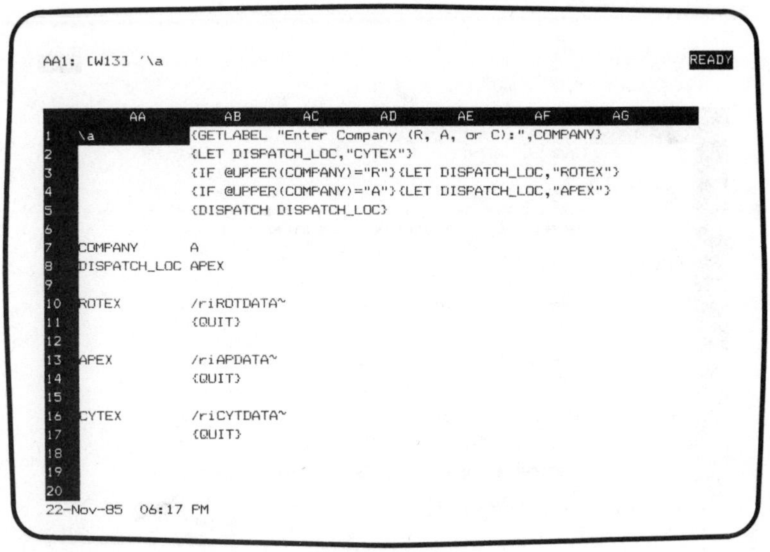

```
AA1: [W13] '\a                                                    READY

           AA          AB      AC       AD        AE       AF        AG
 1    \a              {GETLABEL "Enter Company (R, A, or C):",COMPANY}
 2                    {LET DISPATCH_LOC,"CYTEX"}
 3                    {IF @UPPER(COMPANY)="R"}{LET DISPATCH_LOC,"ROTEX"}
 4                    {IF @UPPER(COMPANY)="A"}{LET DISPATCH_LOC,"APEX"}
 5                    {DISPATCH DISPATCH_LOC}
 6
 7    COMPANY         A
 8    DISPATCH_LOC APEX
 9
10    ROTEX           /riROTDATA~
11                    {QUIT}
12
13    APEX            /riAPDATA~
14                    {QUIT}
15
16    CYTEX           /riCYTDATA~
17                    {QUIT}
18
19
20
22-Nov-85   06:17 PM
```

Fig. 12.42. Example of the DISPATCH command in a macro.

The MENUBRANCH Command (MENUBRANCH or /xm)

MENUBRANCH (Release 2) is a variant of the simple BRANCH command. Instead of immediately branching to a new location, MENU-BRANCH temporarily halts execution of the macro so that you can respond to menu choices. After a choice has been made, the MENU-BRANCH command causes the macro to branch accordingly. The form of the command is

{MENUBRANCH location}

or

/xmlocation~

For example, suppose that you have the corporate personnel database again, and you have entered the macro in figure 12.43.

When the MENUBRANCH statement is executed, 1-2-3 displays in the control panel the menu beginning at the cell ROTEX_MENU. Note: The /**R**ange **N**ame **L**abel **R**ight command was used to assign the name ROTEX_MENU to the cell in which the label Production resides. Production is the first menu item.

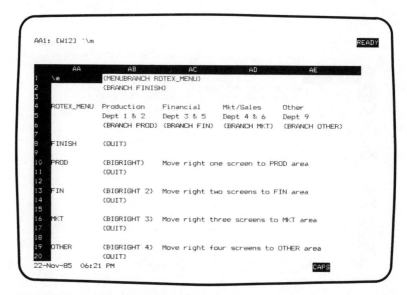

Fig. 12.43. Macro using the MENUBRANCH command.

The menu is displayed in the control panel, just like 1-2-3's command menus. You can select the desired menu item either by moving the cursor with the arrow keys or by pressing the first letter of the menu item. The bottom line of the control panel contains a description of the menu item currently highlighted by the user. For instance, when you move the cursor to Financial, the capsule description Dept 3 & 5 appears.

Now suppose that you want to select the second menu item (Financial). You select it the same way you do any 1-2-3 menu item, by pressing Return after you've located the cursor on your choice, or by entering the first letter of the menu item. The menus that you create with the MENUBRANCH command are just like the 1-2-3 command menus.

After you've selected Financial from the menu, the next statement to be executed is {BRANCH FIN}. If, instead of selecting a menu item, you press the Esc (Escape) key, 1-2-3 stops displaying the menu items and executes the next macro command after the MENUBRANCH command, {BRANCH FINISH}.

Modeling Tip: If you have a multilevel menu structure, you can make the Esc key function as it does in the 1-2-3 command menus (backing up to the previous menu). After the current MENUBRANCH command, place a BRANCH to the previous level's MENUBRANCH. When you press the Esc key, this BRANCH will back you up to the previous menu.

There are a few simple rules for using the MENUBRANCH (or /xm) command. The menu invoked by the MENUBRANCH consists of one to eight consecutive columns in the worksheet. Each column corresponds to one item in the menu. The upper left corner of the range named in a MENUBRANCH statement must refer to the first menu item; otherwise, you will get the error message Invalid use of X menu macro command.

Each menu item consists of three or more rows in the same column. The first row is the menu option name. You should try to keep the option name items short enough so that they will all fit on the top line of the control panel. If the length of the option name exceeds 80 characters, 1-2-3 will display the menu items split across two rows of the control panel.

Be careful to choose option names that begin with different letters. If you have two or more options in a menu with the same first letter and try to use the first-letter technique, 1-2-3 will select the first option it finds with the letter you specified.

The second row in the menu range is the item description, which is displayed on the bottom row of the control panel when the cursor is on the corresponding menu item. The description may be up to 80 characters of text describing the menu item. The description row must be present, even if it is blank.

The third and subsequent rows of the menu range contain the macro commands to be executed if this menu item is selected. Macro commands are read down the column beneath the menu item until a BRANCH, a blank cell, or a QUIT statement is encountered.

The MENUCALL Command

NEW WITH
R2

The MENUCALL command is like MENUBRANCH except that 1-2-3 executes the menu macro as a subroutine. Suppose that you replace the MENUBRANCH command in figure 12.44 with a MENUCALL (see fig. 12.44.)

When you use a MENUCALL, 1-2-3 returns to the statement immediately following the MENUCALL whenever it reads a blank cell or a {RETURN}. For example, suppose that you select the Financial menu option, which causes 1-2-3 to branch to FIN. The first statement in FIN moves the cursor down four rows. When 1-2-3 encounters the RE-

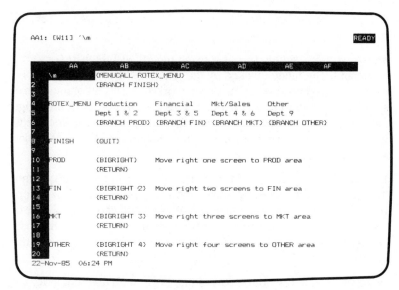

```
AA1: [W11] '\m                                                      READY

         AA          AB          AC          AD          AE     AF
1    \m          {MENUCALL ROTEX_MENU}
2                {BRANCH FINISH}
3
4    ROTEX_MENU  Production    Financial    Mkt/Sales    Other
5                Dept 1 & 2    Dept 3 & 5   Dept 4 & 6   Dept 9
6                {BRANCH PROD} {BRANCH FIN} {BRANCH MKT} {BRANCH OTHER}
7
8    FINISH      {QUIT}
9
10   PROD        {BIGRIGHT}     Move right one screen to PROD area
11               {RETURN}
12
13   FIN         {BIGRIGHT 2}   Move right two screens to FIN area
14               {RETURN}
15
16   MKT         {BIGRIGHT 3}   Move right three screens to MKT area
17               {RETURN}
18
19   OTHER       {BIGRIGHT 4}   Move right four screens to OTHER area
20               {RETURN}
22-Nov-85   06:24 PM
```

Fig. 12.44. Use of the MENUCALL command in the menu example.

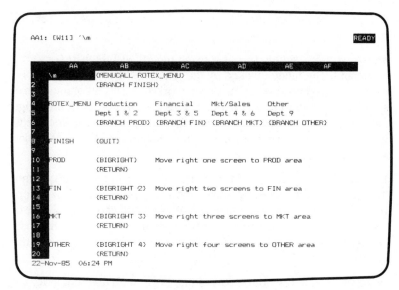
NEW WITH
R2

TURN statement, though, the flow of execution shifts back to the statement following the MENUCALL, the {BRANCH FINISH} statement.

Keep in mind that pressing Esc has the same effect with MENUCALL as it does with MENUBRANCH. Execution shifts to the statement following the MENUCALL statement. You can use only the technique described in the MENUBRANCH command modeling tip (using the Esc key) if this is also what you want to do when the MENUCALL command finishes executing.

The advantage of MENUCALL is that you can call the same menu from several different places in a macro and continue execution from the calling point after the MENUCALL is finished. This is the advantage you get from using subroutines in general.

Subroutines ({name} or /xc)

The MENUCALL statement should give you some feel for calling subroutines. However, quite a bit more can be involved in calling standard (nonmenu) subroutines.

Calling a subroutine is as easy as enclosing the name of a routine in braces or issuing a /xc command (for example, {totals} or /xctotals~). When 1-2-3 encounters a name in braces or a /xcname~, the program shifts execution to the named routine. Then, when the routine is finished (when 1-2-3 encounters a blank cell or a {RE-TURN}), execution shifts back to the command.

NEW WITH
R2

Why use subroutines? You can duplicate a simple subroutine by using two BRANCH commands. Figure 12.45 compares using a subroutine to the use of BRANCH commands.

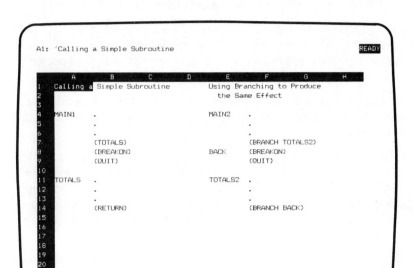

Fig. 12.45. Comparison of subroutine call to BRANCH commands.

By naming the {BREAKON} statement BACK, you can have 1-2-3 branch to BACK when TOTALS2 is completed. But suppose you want to call TOTALS2 again from somewhere else in the macro. Unless you want 1-2-3 to branch to BACK again, you must change the BRANCH statement at the end of the routine. This requirement severely restricts the usefulness of the double-branch method. If you use the subroutine method, you can call the subroutine from different places in the macro without having to change the routine's statements each time.

The DEFINE Command

NEW WITH
R2

An important new subroutine feature in Release 2 is the ability to pass arguments, using the keyword version of the subroutine call only. The form of the subroutine call with arguments is

{routine-name optional-argument1,optional-argument2,...}

where the routine name is followed by a space and by one or more arguments, separated by commas, before the closing brace.

A subroutine called with arguments must begin with a DEFINE statement that associates each argument with a specific cell location. The form of the DEFINE statement is

{DEFINE argument1:type,argument2:type,...}

where argument1, argument2, etc., are names or cell references for the cells in which to place the arguments passed from the main program. Type is either STRING or VALUE. Type is optional; if not present, the default is STRING.

If an argument is of type STRING, the text of the corresponding argument in the subroutine call is placed in the indicated cell as a string value (label).

If an argument is of type VALUE, the corresponding argument in the subroutine call is treated as a formula, and its numeric or string value is placed in the argument cell. An error will occur if the corresponding argument in the subroutine call is not a valid number, string, or formula. You do not, however, have to put a string in quotation marks or have a leading + sign in a formula, using cell references.

Suppose that you have an application where you must repeatedly convert strings to numbers and display the numbers in Currency format. Rather than enter the same code at several different places in the macro, you decide to write a subroutine. Figure 12.46 shows how the subroutine might appear.

Note that all range names in this example are defined using the /**R**ange **N**ame **L**abel **R**ight command.

The first statement in the MAIN macro is a GETLABEL statement that reads a string value into the cell named INPUT_STRING. The second statement in the MAIN routine calls a subroutine named STR_2_NO and passes the arguments INPUT_STRING (the name of the cell containing the input string) and RETURN_NUMBER (the name of the cell where the formatted number is to be stored).

The STR_2_NO subroutine begins with a DEFINE statement, which defines where and how the arguments passed to the subroutine from the MAIN macro are to be stored. Any subroutine that receives arguments passed from its calling macro must begin with a DEFINE statement.

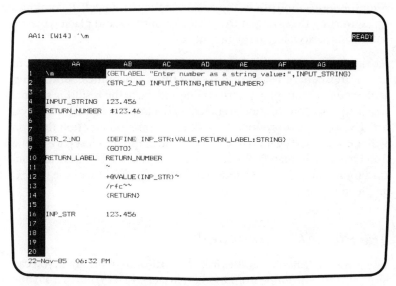

Fig. 12.46. Example of a subroutine call with parameters.

The DEFINE statement in STR_2_NO specifies two cells, INP_STR and RETURN_LABEL, that will hold the two arguments passed from the caller. Note that if the number of arguments in the subroutine call does not agree with the number of arguments in the DEFINE statement, an error will occur.

NEW WITH

R2

The DEFINE statement specifies that the first argument in the subroutine call is to be evaluated and its value placed in INP_STR. Since the first argument is the cell reference INPUT_STRING, the value in cell INPUT_STRING—the string "123.456"—is placed in INP_STR.

The DEFINE statement specifies that the text of the second argument in the subroutine call is to be placed into cell RETURN_LABEL as a string. Because the text of the second argument is RETURN_NUMBER, the string RETURN_NUMBER is placed in cell RETURN_LABEL.

The cell containing the second argument is located in the body of the subroutine. This technique is used to allow the subroutine to return a value to a location designated by the caller. In our example, the location RETURN_NUMBER is passed to the subroutine as a string value. The subroutine uses the passed value as the argument of a {GOTO} statement that places the cursor on the output cell. This technique is one of two primary ways to return information to the calling routine. The other way to return information is to place it in a specified cell that is used every time the subroutine is called.

NEW WITH
R2

After the subroutine places the cursor on the output cell, it continues by converting the string in INP_STR to a number and placing the resulting numeric value in the output cell.

Passing arguments to and from subroutines is important if you want to get the most out of 1-2-3's macro subroutine capabilities. Subroutines with arguments simplify macro coding and make the resulting macros easier to trace. Subroutine arguments are almost essential when you are developing a subroutine to perform a common function that you will use again and again. They are also one of the trickiest parts of the 1-2-3 macro commands. You will be able to master the use of subroutine arguments without serious difficulty, however, if you use the example in figure 12.46 as a guide.

NEW WITH
R2

The RESTART Command

Just as you can call subroutines from the main macro program, you can also call one subroutine from another. In fact, as 1-2-3 moves from one subroutine to the next, the program saves the addresses of where it has been. This technique is called *stacking,* or saving addresses on a stack. By saving the addresses on a stack, 1-2-3 can trace its way back through the subroutine calls to the main macro program.

If you decide that you don't want 1-2-3 to return by the path it came, you can use the RESTART command to eliminate the stack. You will not need to use this command until you are an expert at writing macros. Once you reach this point, though, this command is very helpful. The form of this command is

{RESTART}

The RETURN and /xr Commands

There are two ways to end a subroutine. The normal way is with a RETURN (Release 2) or /xr command. When 1-2-3 reads the RETURN, it returns to the main program (or other subroutine) at the location after the subroutine call. Do not confuse RETURN with QUIT, which ends the macro completely. RETURN can be used with the IF statement to return conditionally from a subroutine.

1-2-3 also ends a subroutine and returns to the calling routine when the program encounters, while executing the subroutine, a cell that is either blank or contains a numeric value. Although this method of returning from a subroutine works, the RETURN or /xr command is preferred because it documents the fact that a particular macro is intended to be a subroutine. The form of this command is

    {RETURN}

or

    /xr

Commands for Testing Keyboard Input

1-2-3 offers several special commands for testing keyboard input. These commands make it easy to perform simple edit checks on the input before storing it in the spreadsheet.

The GET Command

Suppose that you are writing an inventory macro and want to prompt the user to make a one-keystroke choice to enter data on premium- or regular-quality widgets. Figure 12.47 shows how you might prompt the user.

NEW WITH
R2

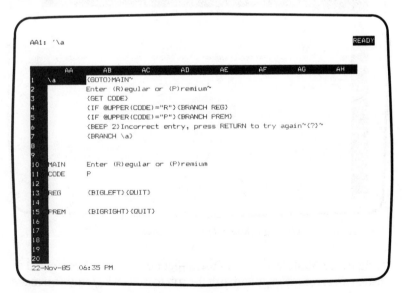

```
AA1:  '\a                                                    READY

        AA      AB      AC      AD      AE      AF      AG      AH
1   \a          {GOTO}MAIN~
2               Enter (R)egular or (P)remium~
3               {GET CODE}
4               {IF @UPPER(CODE)="R"}{BRANCH REG}
5               {IF @UPPER(CODE)="P"}{BRANCH PREM}
6               {BEEP 2}Incorrect entry, press RETURN to try again~{?}~
7               {BRANCH \a}
8
9
10  MAIN        Enter (R)egular or (P)remium
11  CODE        P
12
13  REG         {BIGLEFT}{QUIT}
14
15  PREM        {BIGRIGHT}{QUIT}
16
17
18
19
20
22-Nov-85  06:35 PM
```

Fig. 12.47. The GET command for one-character input.

The GET command is used here to pause while the user enters a single letter from the keyboard and to store that entry in a cell named CODE. Notice that the macro enters the user-prompt in the cell named MAIN. If you want a prompt to appear in the control panel rather than in the spreadsheet, you must use the GETLABEL or GET-NUMBER commands.

The GETLABEL and /xl Commands

Suppose that in another inventory model you want to prompt the user for a part description. You can use the GETLABEL command (Release 2) to accomplish this. The general form of the command is

{GETLABEL prompt,location}

or

/xlprompt~location~

Figure 12.48 shows how you can use the GETLABEL command.

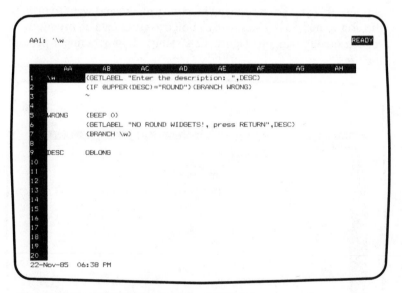

Fig. 12.48. The GETLABEL command for string input.

As figure 12.50 shows, you can use a second GETLABEL command to display an error message and wait for you to press a key after you make an incorrect entry. Remember, though, that whatever you enter in response to the prompt is stored in DESC.

Both forms of the command are identical except for one /xl command feature. If you write the /xl command as

/xlprompt~~

the label entered in response to the prompt will be placed at the current location of the cursor. You cannot do this with the GETLABEL command because 1-2-3 will give you an error message if there is no location argument. Why would you want to use this feature? With the GETLABEL command, you must specify the location where the label will be placed in the text of the macro. This makes it difficult to use the GETLABEL command in a subroutine where the location of the destination cell changes with each subroutine call. The /xl command is much more convenient in such situations.

The GETNUMBER and /xn Commands

Other variations of the simple GET command are the GETNUMBER (Release 2) or /xn commands. GETNUMBER is exactly like GETLABEL but is used for numbers. GETNUMBER accepts the entry as a formula and enters its numeric value in the indicated cell. The form of the command is

{GETNUMBER prompt,location}

or

/xnprompt~location~

The GETNUMBER and /xn commands work differently. With GETNUMBER, a blank entry or a character entry has a numeric value of 0. With /xn, however, if the entry is a blank or a character entry that is not a valid formula, an error message occurs, and the user is re-prompted for a number. This difference can be very useful in some applications. If, for example, you accidentally press the "q" key (a letter) instead of the "1" key, the /xn command will return an error message. Also, the /xn command can be used in the form

/xnprompt~~

to read a numeric value into the current cell instead of into a specified location. (See the discussion at the end of the GETLABEL section.)

Figure 12.49 shows how GETNUMBER can be used in an inventory macro.

The LOOK Command

NEW WITH
R2

Typically, after a macro has begun its execution, you can interrupt it only with Ctrl-Break. Otherwise, the characters you enter are stored until the macro completes its execution. However, 1-2-3 offers a spe-

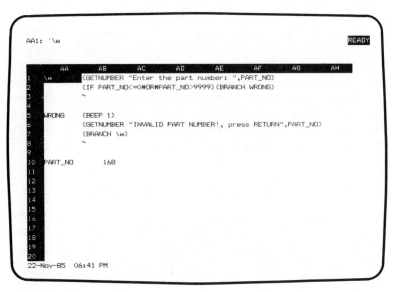

```
AA1:  '\w                                                              READY

           AA        AB        AC        AD        AE        AF        AG        AH
1    \w         {GETNUMBER "Enter the part number: ",PART_NO}
2               {IF PART_NO<=0#OR#PART_NO>9999}{BRANCH WRONG}
3               ~
4
5    WRONG      {BEEP 1}
6               {GETNUMBER "INVALID PART NUMBER!, press RETURN",PART_NO}
7               {BRANCH \w}
8               ~
9
10   PART_NO         168
11
12
13
14
15
16
17
18
19
20
22-Nov-85  06:41 PM
```

Fig. 12.49. The GETNUMBER command for numeric data entry.

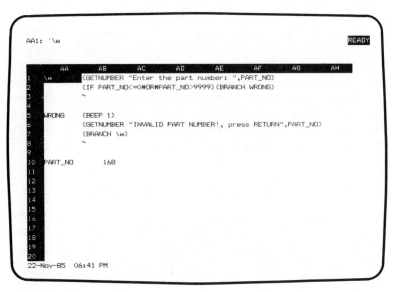
NEW WITH
R2

cial command, the LOOK command, that temporarily interrupts processing. The general form of the command is

{LOOK location}

When the look command is executed, the keyboard type-ahead buffer is checked, and the first character is copied into the indicated location. What this means is that you can type a character at any time and the macro will find it when the LOOK command is executed. The contents of location can then be tested with an IF statement. Because the character is not removed from the type-ahead buffer, you must make provisions to use it or dispose of it before the macro needs keyboard input or ends.

As a simple test of the LOOK command, try the example in figure 12.50. This macro causes the speaker to beep until you press any key. Each time the LOOK command is encountered, 1-2-3 checks the keyboard buffer and copies the first character found into location INTERRUPT. Then an IF statement checks the contents of INTERRUPT and branches accordingly. The GETLABEL command at the end serves to dispose of the keystroke that interrupted the loop.

A more helpful use of the LOOK command occurs when you have built a lengthy macro to process, for example, a stock portfolio database, and you want to be able to stop processing at certain points in the macro. You can enter a LOOK command, followed by an IF statement

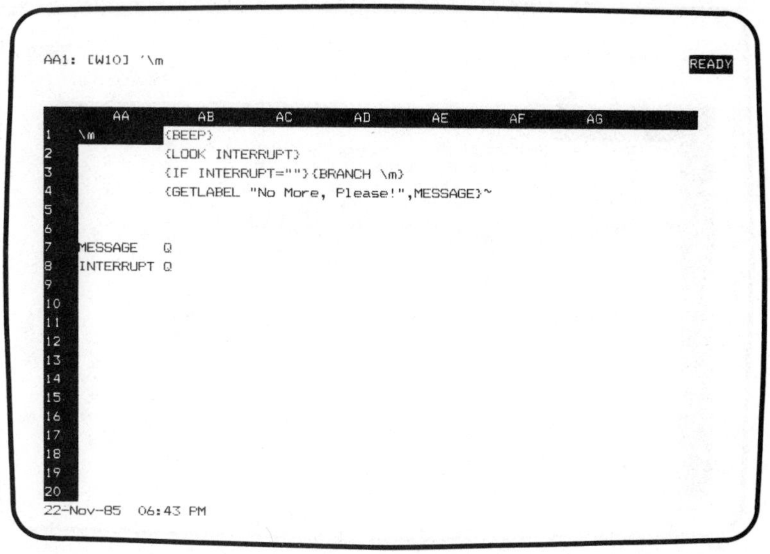

```
AA1: [W10] '\m                                              READY

         AA        AB       AC      AD      AE      AF      AG
1    \m            {BEEP}
2                  {LOOK INTERRUPT}
3                  {IF INTERRUPT=""}{BRANCH \m}
4                  {GETLABEL "No More, Please!",MESSAGE}~
5
6
7    MESSAGE       0
8    INTERRUPT     0
9
10
11
12
13
14
15
16
17
18
19
20
22-Nov-85  06:43 PM
```

Fig. 12.50. The LOOK command to stop a beeping macro.

similar to those that appear in figure 12.14, at several places in the
macro. Then, if you press a key, the macro stops the next time a LOOK
is executed. If you do not touch the keyboard, the macro continues
processing. In this example, the LOOK command is preferable to the
GET command, which always stops the macro to wait for an entry.

Commands for Storing and Deleting

1-2-3 has several different commands for storing and deleting the contents of cells. These commands do not work with input directly from
the keyboard but with values already in the spreadsheet.

The LET Command

NEW WITH
R2

The simplest of the storing commands, the LET command, stores a
number or a string value in a cell. The general form of the LET command is

    {LET location,number} or {LET location,string}

As mentioned previously, this command is particularly useful for initializing cells used as variables in a macro. The Factorial example is
repeated in figure 12.51 to show two good examples of the LET
command.

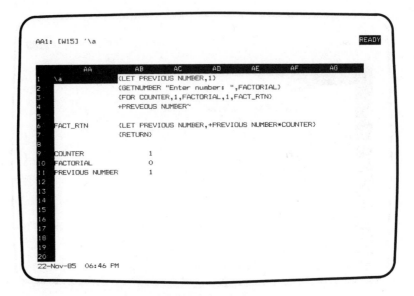

Fig. 12.51. The LET command in the factorial routine.

NEW WITH

R2

In this example, the first LET command uses a simple number to initialize the cell called PREVIOUS NUMBER. In the second LET command a formula is used.

You can use also strings with the LET command. In fact, you can use even a string formula. For example, if the cell named FIRST contains the string "Robert" and LAST holds the string "Hamer", the statement

{LET name,first&" "&last}

will store "Robert Hamer" in NAME.

Like the DEFINE command, the LET command allows you to specify :STRING and :VALUE suffixes after the argument. The STRING suffix stores the text of the argument in the location, whereas the VALUE suffix evaluates the argument as a string or numeric formula and places the result in the location. When a suffix is not specified, LET stores the argument's numeric or string value if it is a valid formula; otherwise, the text of the argument is stored. For example

{LET name,first&" "&last:VALUE}

will store "Robert Hamer" in NAME, whereas

{LET name,first&" "&last:STRING}

will store the string *first&" "&last* in NAME.

The LET command can be duplicated by moving the cursor to the desired location with {GOTO} and entering the desired value into the cell. However, the LET command has the major advantage that it does not disturb the current location of the cursor. The /Data Fill command can also be used to enter numbers, but not to enter string values. Overall, the LET command is a convenient and useful means for setting the value of a cell from within a macro.

The PUT Command

NEW WITH

R2

The LET command works fine for storing a number or label entry in a specific target cell. However, LET does not work when the target location is addressed by a row and column offset within a range of cells. For this situation, the PUT command is used. The general form of the PUT command is

{PUT range,column-number,row-number,expression}

where *range* is a range of cells, *column-number* and *row-number* are 0 or a positive integer, and *expression* is a number or label. Figure 12.52 shows the results of different variations of this command. Keep in mind that the row and column numbers follow the same conventions that functions follow. (The first column is number 0, the second is number 1, etc.)

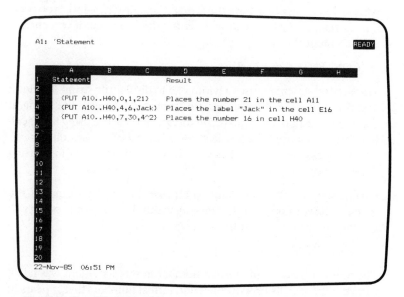

Fig. 12.52. Use of the PUT statement.

The CONTENTS Command

Suppose that you want to copy a number from one cell to another, change the copied number to a string, and format the string to look like a formatted number. Based on the macro commands you have seen so far, this would be a lengthy process, especially the process of formatting the string.

The CONTENTS command is designed to do all of the above in one step. The general form of the command is

{CONTENTS destination-loc,source-loc,width,format-number}

The width and format-number are optional. If not specified, the CON-TENTS command uses the column width and format of the source lo-cation to format the string.

Suppose, for example, that you want to copy the number 123.456, which resides in cell A21, to cell B25, and change the number to a string while you copy. The statement for this step is

{CONTENTS B25,A21}

The contents of cell B25 will be displayed as the string "123.456" with a left-aligned label-prefix character.

Next, suppose that you want to change the width of the string when you copy it. Rather than have the string display as "123.456," you want it to display as "123.4." You will get the desired result if you change the statement to

{CONTENTS B25,A21,5}

This second statement uses a width of 5 to display the string. The least significant digits of the number are truncated to create the string. If the number cannot be displayed in the specified width using the speci-fied format, a string of asterisks "*****" is placed in the cell instead. (This works just like 1-2-3's normal spreadsheet formatting commands.)

Finally, suppose that you want to change the display format of the string while you copy it and change its width. The following string will change the display format to **Currency 0**.

{CONTENTS B25,A21,5,32}

The number used for the format number in this statement was taken from the list of CONTENTS command format numbers that appears in table 12.5. The result of the statement is the number $123.

Table 12.5
Numeric Format Codes for CONTENTS Command

Code	Destination String's Numeric Display Command
0	Fixed, 0 decimal places
1-15	Fixed, 1 to 15 decimal places
15-31	Scientific, 0 to 15 decimal places
32-47	Currency, 0 to 15 decimal places
48-63	Percent, 0 to 15 decimal places
64-79	Comma, 0 to 15 decimal places
112	+/- Bar Graph
113	General
114	D1 (DD-MMM-YY)
115	D2 (DD-MM)
116	D3 (MMM-YY)
121	D4 (Full International)
122	D5 (Partial International)
119	D6 (HH:MM:SS AM/PM time format)
120	D7 (HH:MM AM/PM time format)
123	D8 (Full International time format)
124	D9 (Partial International time format)
117	Text format
118	Hidden format
127	Current window's default display format

In the following examples of the CONTENTS command with 123.456 as the number in cell A21, the width of column A is 9, and the display format for cell A21 is Fixed 2.

{CONTENTS B25,A21}	Displays the number 123.45 in cell B25, using the Fixed 2 format.
{CONTENTS B25,A21,4}	Displays the number, using a width of 4 and the Fixed 2 format. The result is "****".
{CONTENTS B25,A21,5,0}	Displays the number 123 in cell B25, using the Fixed 0 format.

The CONTENTS command is rather specialized but very useful in situations that require converting numeric values to formatted strings. CONTENTS can convert long numeric formulas to strings, using the Text format. This application is particularly useful for debugging purposes.

The BLANK Command

NEW WITH
R2

Blanking out a range of cells, A1..A10, for example, can be accomplished by the following macro statement:

    /reA1..A10~

The BLANK command duplicates this function. Its general form is

    {BLANK location}

The BLANK command was introduced in the Symphony Command Language because the Symphony equivalent of /**R**ange **E**rase is less convenient to use within a macro. The BLANK command has no particular advantage over /**R**ange **E**rase in 1-2-3.

File Manipulation Commands

NEW WITH
R2

These six macro commands give 1-2-3 the capability of opening, reading, writing, and closing a sequential data file containing ASCII text data. This capability allows 1-2-3 applications to read and write files used by other business applications. The /**F**ile Import and /**P**rint File commands provide a limited capability to manipulate foreign files, but the group of macro file-manipulation commands provides a capability equal to the sequential file commands in BASIC or other programming languages.

Warning: The file manipulation commands are programming commands. To read from and write to foreign files successfully, you must understand exactly how these commands work and how the sequential files you are manipulating are organized. If you write to a file used by another business program, be sure to back up the file before trying to write to it from within 1-2-3.

If you keep this warning in mind, this group of commands can open up the world of outside files to your 1-2-3 applications. Should you need to process external data files, these commands make it possible to do the job, using 1-2-3.

NEW WITH
R2

The OPEN Command

NEW WITH
R2

To work with an external file, you need to open it. The open command tells 1-2-3 which file you want to work with and whether you want to read only, write only, or do both.

1-2-3 allows one external file to be open for processing. If you want to work with more than one file in your application, you will have to open each file before using it, then close it again before opening and using the next file.

The form of the open command is

{OPEN filename,access-mode}

The filename argument is a string, an expression with a string value, or a single-cell reference to a cell that contains a string or a string expression. The string must be a valid DOS filename or pathname. A file in the current directory can be specified by its name and extension. A file in another directory may require a drive identification, a subdirectory path, or a complete DOS path in addition to the filename and extension.

The access-mode argument is a single character string that specifies whether you want to read only ("R"), write only ("W"), or both read from and write to the file ("M").

"R" (Read)   Read access opens an existing file and allows access with the READ and READLN commands. You cannot write to a file opened with Read access.

"W" (Write)   Write access opens a new file with the specified name and allows access with the WRITE and WRITELN commands. Any existing file with the specified name will be erased and replaced by the new file.

"M" (Modify)   Modify access opens an existing file with the specified name and allows both read (READ AND READLN) and write (WRITE and WRITELN) commands.

The OPEN command succeeds if it is able to open the file with the access you requested. If the OPEN command succeeds, macro execution continues with the cell below the OPEN. Any commands after the OPEN in the current cell are ignored.

The OPEN command will fail with an ERROR if the disk drive is not ready. You should use an ONERROR command to handle this contingency.

If the access mode is READ or MODIFY but the file does not exist on the indicated directory, the OPEN command fails, and macro execution continues with the macro commands after the OPEN command in the current cell. You can place one or more macro commands after the OPEN command in the same cell in order to deal with the failure. The most common practice is to place a BRANCH or a subroutine call after the OPEN to transfer to a macro that deals with the failure. Here are some examples (with explanations) of the OPEN command

{OPEN "pastdue","R"}{BRANCH fixit}
Open the existing file named PASTDUE in the current directory for reading. If the file cannot be opened, branch to the routine **fixit**.

{OPEN "c:\data\clients.dat",w}
Open the new file named CLIENTS.DAT on drive c, subdirectory data, for writing.

{OPEN file,m}/XGretry~
Open the file whose name is in cell FILE for Modify access. If the file cannot be opened, branch to the routine **retry**.

Figure 12.53 shows examples of macros that use all of the file commands except the READ and WRITE commands (which are similar to the READLN and WRITELN commands). The macro named \O uses the OPEN command to open a user-specified file. This macro illustrates how to deal with disk drive not ready and file not found errors. After prompting you for the filename, an ONERROR command sets the error jump to the routine that handles such problems as the drive not being ready. Next, the OPEN command is used with the BRANCH that follows it. This BRANCH handles such problems as "a file not found" error.

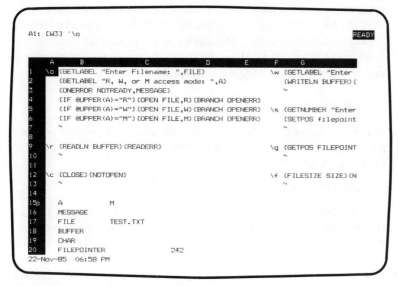

Fig. 12.53. Macros to illustrate use of file macro commands.

The CLOSE Command

The {CLOSE} command closes a currently open file. If no file is open, the CLOSE command has no effect. CLOSE does not take an argument. The CLOSE command is particularly important for files that you are writing or modifying. You can lose the last data written to a file that you don't close.

Although, under most circumstances, 1-2-3 automatically takes care of a file that you do not close, you should make it a practice to use CLOSE when you are finished using any file opened with OPEN. Better safe than sorry. Use of the CLOSE command is illustrated in the macro labeled \c in figure 12.17.

The READ and READLN Commands

READ and READLN are your two means of reading data from an external text file. Use READ to read a specified number of characters into the worksheet, as when you read the next record from a database. Use

NEW WITH

R2

READLN to read a line of text from a file whose lines are delimited by a carriage-return, line-feed combination. You would, for example, use READLN to read the next line from an ASCII text file.

If you attempt to read past the end of the file, if no file is open, or if the file was opened with Write access, the READ or READLN command is ignored, and macro execution continues in the same cell. Otherwise, after the READ or READLN command is completed, macro execution continues on the next line. This allows you to place a BRANCH or subroutine call after the READ or READLN to handle the problem of an unexecuted READ or READLN statement.

NEW WITH

R2

The READ Command

The READ command, starting at the file pointer's present position, reads a specified number of characters from the file that is currently open. The form of the READ command is

{READ bytecount,location}

in which bytecount is the number of bytes to read, starting at the current position of the file pointer, and location is the cell to read into. READ places the specified number of characters from the file into the location cell as a label. Bytecount can be any number between 1 and 240, the maximum number of characters in a 1-2-3 label. If bytecount is greater than the number of characters remaining in the file, 1-2-3 reads the remaining characters into location. After the READ command finishes, the file pointer is positioned at the character following the last character read.

The READ command is useful primarily when you want to read a specific number of characters into the buffer. A data file that contains fixed-length records, for example, is read conveniently by the READ command with bytecount equal to the record length.

READ generally should not be used with ASCII text files from a word processor or text editor. Such files generally have variable length lines terminated with a carriage-return, line-feed sequence and are read better with the READLN command. Although figure 12.53 does not contain an example of the READ command, READ is used much like the READLN in the figure's \r macro.

NEW WITH

R2

The READLN Command

The READLN command reads characters from a file into the cell specified by location, either until the two-character Carriage-Return

Line feed sequence is encountered or until 240 characters have been read. The file pointer is positioned one character past the last character read (at the beginning of the next line). The READLN command form is

{READLN location}

A 1-2-3 PRN file generated by the /Print File command is an example of a file that should be read using READLN. READLN is best suited to reading files that are print images. The macro labeled \R in figure 12.53 illustrates the use of READLN.

The WRITE and WRITELN Commands

NEW WITH

R2

The WRITE and WRITELN macro commands write characters to an open file. The WRITE command writes the characters passed to it and positions the file pointer just beyond the last character written. The WRITELN command, which operates in a similar fashion, also places a carriage-return, line-feed sequence after the last character written and positions the file pointer just beyond the carriage-return line feed.

If the file pointer is not at the end of the file, 1-2-3 overwrites the existing characters in the file. If the file pointer is at the end of the file, 1-2-3 extends the file by the number of characters written. And if the file pointer is past the end of the file (see discussion of SETPOS command, later in this section), 1-2-3 extends the file by the amount indicated before writing the characters.

For these two commands to work, a file must be opened with Write or Modify access. If the command succeeds, macro execution continues on the next line. If the command fails, execution continues on the same line. This allows you to place additional macro commands after the WRITE or WRITELN to be executed only in case of a problem.

The WRITE Command

NEW WITH

R2

The WRITE command writes a string of text to the currently open file. The WRITE command has the form

{WRITE string}

The argument string can be a literal string, a range name or cell reference to a single cell that contains a string, or a string expression. Because WRITE does not place a carriage-return, line-feed sequence at the end of the string, multiple WRITEs can be made to concatenate text on a single line. WRITE is well suited to creating or updating a file that contains fixed-length database records. Although there is no example of the WRITE command in figure 12.53, the WRITE command is used in much the same way as is the WRITELN command in the \w macro.

The WRITELN Command

The WRITELN command is identical to the WRITE command except that it places a carriage-return, line-feed sequence after the last character written from the string. The WRITELN command form is

{WRITELN string}

WRITELN is useful when the file being written or updated uses the carriage-return line feed to mark the end of its lines or records. (The WRITE command is also useful.) In many applications, several WRITEs are used to write a line to the file; then a WRITELN is used to mark the end of the line. The WRITELN command is illustrated in the \w macro in figure 12.53.

File Utility Commands

Three file utility commands are most useful when you are developing an application with random-access file operations. The key to random-access file operations is the capability to reposition the file pointer to the start of a specific record. The SETPOS, GETPOS, and FILESIZE commands provide this capability.

The SETPOS Command

The SETPOS command sets the position of the file pointer to a specified value. The form of the command is

{SETPOS file-position}

File-position is a number, or an expression resulting in a number, that specifies the character at which you want to position the pointer. The first character in the file is at position 0, the second at position 1, and so on.

As an example, suppose that you have a database file with 100 records which are each 20 bytes long. To access the first record, you can use the commands

{SETPOS 0}
{READ 20,buffer}

To read the 15th record, you can use the commands

{SETPOS (15-1)*20}
{READ 20,buffer}

NEW WITH
R2

Nothing prevents you from setting the file pointer past the end of the file. If the file pointer is set at or past the end and a READ or READLN command is executed, the command does nothing, and macro execution continues with the next command on the same line (error branch). If the file pointer is set at or past the end and a WRITE or WRITELN command is executed, 1-2-3 will first extend the file to the length specified by the file pointer, then, starting at the file pointer, will write the characters.

Warning: If you inadvertently set the file pointer to a large number with SETPOS and write to the file, 1-2-3 will attempt to expand the file and write the text at the end. If the file will not fit on the disk, the write command does nothing, and macro execution continues with the next command on the same line (error branch). If the file will fit on the disk, 1-2-3 extends the file and writes the text at the end.

If a file is not currently open, SETPOS does nothing, and execution continues with the next macro command on the same line as the SETPOS command. Otherwise, when the SETPOS command is completed, execution continues on the next line of the macro. This allows you to place a BRANCH command or a subroutine call after the SETPOS command to handle the problem of an unexecuted statement. SETPOS is illustrated in the \s macro in figure 12.53.

The GETPOS Command

NEW WITH
R2

The GETPOS command allows you to record the file pointer's current position. The form of this command is

{GETPOS location}

The current position of the file pointer is placed in the cell indicated by location, where location is either a cell reference or a range name. If location points to a multicell range, the value of the file pointer is placed in the upper left corner of the range.

The GETPOS command is useful if you record in the file the location of something you want to find again. You can use GETPOS to mark your current place in the file before you use SETPOS to move the file pointer to another position. You can use GETPOS to record the locations of important items in a quick-reference index. GETPOS is illustrated in the \g macro in figure 12.53.

The FILESIZE Command

Another file-related command, FILESIZE, returns the length of the file in bytes. The form of the command is

{FILESIZE location}

The FILESIZE command determines the current length of the file and places this value in the cell referred to by location. Location can be a cell reference or range name. If location refers to a multicell range, the file size is placed in the cell in the upper left corner of the range. FILESIZE is illustrated in the \f macro in figure 12.53.

Maintenance-Oriented Commands

The catch-all group of maintenance-oriented commands includes commands to sound your computer's speaker, control the screen display, and selectively recalculate portions of the spreadsheet. Two commands in this group, WINDOWSOFF and PANELOFF, can increase significantly the execution speed of large macros.

The BEEP Command

By using the BEEP command in a macro, you can have 1-2-3 sound your computer's speaker in one of four tones. The BEEP command is good to use when the user has made an error, entering data. (For a good example of how and when to use the BEEP command, see figure 12.48.) The form of the command is

{BEEP number}

in which number is an optional tone number between 0 and 3.

The INDICATE Command

You can use the INDICATE command to change the indicator in the upper right corner of the screen to display a message you choose. The general form of the command is

{INDICATE string}

in which the string can be any length up to five characters. If the string is longer, 1-2-3 uses only the first five characters. Suppose, for example, that you want to display the message START in the upper right corner of the screen. You can use the following INDICATE command

{INDICATE START}

Unless you clear your indicator, using the command

    {INDICATE}

will display the START message until you exit from 1-2-3.

To blank out the indicator completely, you can use the command

    {INDICATE ""}

When you use the INDICATE command, remember that you have to enter an actual string. You cannot use a cell address or range name.

The WINDOWSON and WINDOWSOFF Commands

A big problem with 1-2-3 macros is that the screen shifts around when macros are executing; with complex macros, this problem can be extreme. The screen's shifting is a problem for two reasons: 1-2-3 takes time to redraw the screen, which slows macro execution, and the shifting screen can be unnerving to the unsophisticated user of an application that is automated with macros.

By using the WINDOWSOFF command, you can freeze the lower part of the screen and have just the control panel show the changes that occur as a result of the macro steps. This feature is particularly helpful if the purpose of your macro is to automate an application that will be used by an unsophisticated 1-2-3 user. While the macro is performing the application, the screen can be frozen with WINDOWSOFF. Then, after the macro has finished its processing and the results are ready, the WINDOWSON command can be used to restore the normal activity of the display screen.

However, if something goes wrong with your macro while the WINDOWSOFF command is in effect, you can get into trouble. Unless you have a simple one-line macro already preset for issuing the WINDOWSON command, you may have to reboot 1-2-3 and start your application all over again to recover the use of the screen. Therefore, it is wise to develop and test your macros without the WINDOWSOFF and WINDOWSON commands; add these commands to the debugged and tested macro.

The PANELOFF and PANELON Commands

You can also control the redrawing of the control panel with the PANELOFF and PANELON commands. The PANELOFF and PANELON

NEW WITH
R2

NEW WITH
R2

NEW WITH
R2

commands behave exactly like the WINDOWSOFF and WIN-
DOWSON commands.

Using the WINDOWSOFF and PANELOFF commands can have a significant effect on macro execution time. In one complex application,
use of the WINDOWSOFF and PANELOFF commands to freeze the
screen completely reduced macro execution time by 50 percent, from
5 to 2 1/2 minutes. Speed improvement will depend, of course, on the
particular application.

The macro shown in figure 12.54 demonstrates how you can use the
WINDOWSOFF and PANELOFF commands to eliminate screen shifting and to reduce execution time. The example's first FOR statement
takes 14 seconds to execute on an IBM PC. The second loop, after the
WINDOWSOFF and PANELOFF commands, takes 7 1/2 seconds.

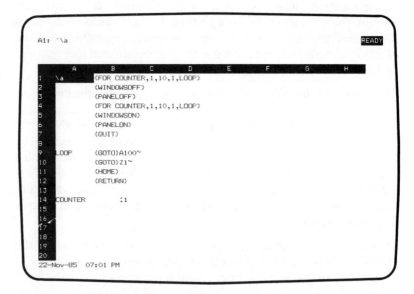

Fig. 12.54. Use of the WINDOWSOFF and PANELOFF commands.

The BREAKOFF Command

The easiest way to stop a macro is to issue a Ctrl-Break command.
However, 1-2-3 can eliminate the effect of a Ctrl-Break while a macro
is executing. By including a BREAKOFF command in your macro, you
can prevent the user from stopping the macro before its completion.
Note: Before you use a BREAKOFF statement, you must be certain that
the macro is fully debugged.

BREAKOFF is used primarily to prevent the user from interrupting a process and destroying the integrity of data in the spreadsheet. You will not need to use BREAKOFF unless you are developing extremely sophisticated macros; but, in such applications, BREAKOFF can be an important safeguard against user-caused problems.

To restore the effect of Ctrl-Break, use the BREAKON command. You will probably want a simple one-line macro that issues a BREAKON, just in case something happens during execution to your original macro. You may also want to make sure that the last statement in your macro before QUIT is BREAKON.

Because any Ctrl-Break commands in the keyboard buffer will be executed as soon as the BREAKON command is executed, be sure that the BREAKON is at a place where the macro can safely stop. Figure 12.55 demonstrates how you can use the BREAKOFF and BREAKON commands to prevent the factorial calculation from being interrupted in the Factorial example.

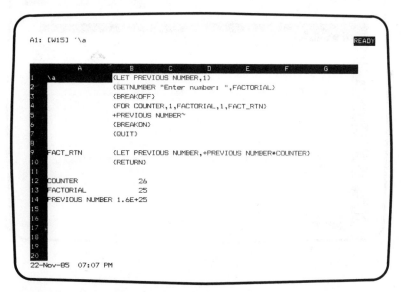

Fig. 12.55. Use of the BREAKOFF and BREAKON commands.

The WAIT Command

The WAIT command in a macro can delay execution of statements that follow the WAIT until an appointed time. The general form of the command is

{WAIT serial-time-number}

NEW WITH

R2

The serial-time-number must contain a date plus a time. If you want the macro to wait until 6:00 PM today to continue, you can use the expression {WAIT @INT(@NOW)+@TIME(18,00,00)}. If you want the macro to pause for 50 seconds, you can use the expression {WAIT @NOW+@TIME(00,00,50)}.

The WAIT command was introduced in the Symphony Command Language, in which it is used primarily with Symphony's communications features.

The WAIT command is less useful in 1-2-3, although you may find that including time delays in your macros is sometimes useful. You could use a WAIT function, for example, to display an instruction on the screen, pause a few seconds while the user reads the instructions, and continue macro execution (see fig. 12.56.)

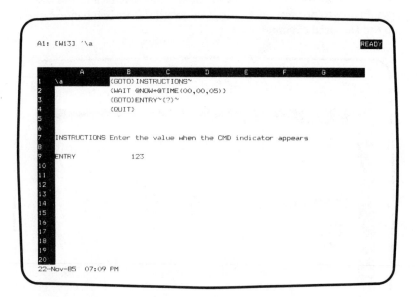

Fig. 12.56. Use of the WAIT function to display instructions.

NEW WITH

R2

Controlling Recalculation

Two macro commands, RECALC and RECALCCOL, allow you to recalculate a portion of the worksheet. This feature can be useful in large spreadsheets where recalculation time is long and where you need to recalculate certain values in the worksheet before you proceed to the next processing step in your macro. The commands for partial recalculation have the form

NEW WITH
R2

{RECALC location,condition,iteration-number}

and

{RECALCCOL location,condition,iteration-number}

in which location is a range or range name that specifies the cells whose formulas are to be recalculated. The condition and iteration number arguments are optional.

If the condition argument is included, the range is recalculated repeatedly until condition has a logical value of TRUE (1). Condition must be either a logical expression or a reference to a cell within the recalculation range that contains a logical expression. If condition is a reference to a cell outside the recalculation range, then the value of condition, either TRUE (1) or FALSE (0), will not change, and condition will not control the partial recalculation.

If the iteration-number argument is included, the condition argument must also be specified (the value 1 makes condition always TRUE). The iteration-number specifies the number of times that formulas in the location range are to be recalculated.

The RECALC and RECALCCOL commands differ in the order in which cells in the specified range are recalculated. The RECALC command performs the calculations by row—all the cells in the first row of the range, then all the cells in the second row, etc. The RECALCCOL command performs the calculations by column—all the cells in the first column of the range, followed by all the cells in the second column, etc. In both commands, only cells within the specified range are recalculated.

Use RECALC to recalculate the range when the formulas in the range refer only to other formulas in rows above or to the left of themselves in the same row in that range. Use RECALCCOL to recalculate the range when formulas in the range refer only to other formulas in columns to the left or to cells above themselves in the same column.

Just a word of caution here: You may have to use CALC if formulas in the range refer to other formulas located below and to their right, or if formulas refer both to cells in rows above and to the right and to cells in columns below and to the left.

You need to include in the range only those cells you want to recalculate. The formulas in the recalculation range can refer to values in cells outside the range; however, those values are not updated by the RECALC or RECALCCOL.

When either the RECALC or RECALCCOL command is executed, the partial recalculation occurs immediately. However, the results do not appear on screen until the screen is redrawn. Macro execution may continue for some time before a command that updates the screen is executed. In the interim, the recalculated numbers, although not visible on screen, are available for use in calculations and conditional tests.

If the macro ends and you want to be sure that the recalculated numbers are on screen, use the PgUp and PgDn keys to move the window away from and back to the recalculated range. The act of looking away and back again will update the screen and display the current values in the recalculated range.

You may need to use {CALC}, {RECALC}, or {RECALCCOL} after macro commands such as LET, GETNUMBER, and {?}, or after 1-2-3 commands such as /Range Input within a macro. You do not need to re-calculate after invoking 1-2-3 commands such as /Copy and /Move; 1-2-3 automatically recalculates the affected ranges after such commands, even during macro execution.

Caution: Recalculating a portion of the worksheet can cause some formulas (those outside a recalculated range that reference formulas within the range) to fail to reflect current data. If this should occur in your application, be sure to perform a general recalculation at some point before the end of your macro.

In Chapter 13, you will find a complete 1-2-3 application that includes the use of several of the macro commands discussed in this chapter.

13

A Comprehensive Model

The comprehensive model in this chapter integrates all the main elements of 1-2-3—spreadsheet, database, macros, and graphics—in one worksheet. This model demonstrates how all the main elements discussed previously work together to create a unified whole.

The model is designed for a corporate controller, Mr. Dudley Eyeshade, who finds that he must frequently answer questions from the president and sole proprietor, Mr. John Paul Gherkins, about financial trends in Mr. Gherkins' pickle business—Gherkins, Inc. For example, Mr. Gherkins may ask Mr. Eyeshade to prepare reports that show the fluctuation in net income from one month to the next over the course of the year. He may ask Mr. Eyeshade also about fluctuations in such items as current assets, working capital, gross sales, etc. Along with these items, Mr. Eyeshade finds that he must report from time to time on the status of several key financial ratios and how they relate to prior status from months and years past.

A General Description of the Model

Although this model is called the "Financial Ratio Model," it does much more than just compute financial ratios.

The steps for using the model are very simple. First, Mr. Eyeshade supplies the data for the model by entering Balance Sheet and Income Statement figures on the last day of each month. After entering that month's data, he invokes an *accumulator* macro that adds the monthly Income Statement figures to the year-to-date totals in the column to the right of the monthly figures.

After the Income Statement figures have been accumulated, the controller invokes a second keyboard macro. This macro saves certain key financial ratios that Mr. Eyeshade believes he may want to use later in a database.

These records are kept in a database so that Mr. Eyeshade can evaluate trends in the key ratios and financial statement items. For example, he may want to search the database for the net income value for December, 1984, and compare it to the level of net income for the current month. He may also want to search the database for twelve months of net income values and evaluate the movement in the values.

After Mr. Eyeshade has selected the information from the database, he can graph the data to enhance the report before presenting it to Mr. Gherkins. Mr. Eyeshade has his choice of several different types of graphs for the report. In our example, he uses simple line and bar graphs and a pie graph.

After each graph is created, Mr. Eyeshade saves it in a graph (.PIC) file. Once all the .PIC files have been created, he exits from 1-2-3 and enters the PrintGraph program where he prints the graphs one after the other.

After using the model routinely for several months, Mr. Eyeshade added a menu-driven macro system for routine data entry, reports, and graphs that are generated each month. With this menu system, Mr. Eyeshade's clerk, who knows almost nothing about 1-2-3, is able to enter the data each month and produce the reports and graphs.

The Spreadsheet

The *spreadsheet* refers to the portion of the model that is used to enter the Balance Sheet and Income Statement figures for a given month. Figure 13.1 shows the figures for the last month entered: July, 1985.

Notice that in column F, the rightmost column of both the Balance Sheet and the Income Statement, there are columns of percentages labeled "Common Size." In the Balance Sheet portion, the common- size column represents each item as a percent of total assets. In the Income Statement portion, the column size represents each item as a percent of gross sales. The term *Common Size* is used because it gives the financial analyst a way to evaluate trends over time in financial statements even though the amount of total assets and sales may have changed. The analyst can get an idea of the underlying movement of funds.

```
             A          B          C          D          E          F
1    ===============================================================
2    Balance Sheet
3    ===============================================================
4                                                   Balance on    Common
5                                                   07/31/85       Size
6                                                   ----------    ----------
7          Assets
8
9    Cash                                            $275,000        8%
10   Marketable Securities                             35,000        1%
11   Accounts Receivable                  1,256,000
12      Allowance for Doubtful Accounts       8,000
13      Net Accounts Receivable                     1,248,000       39%
14   Inventory                                         359,000       11%
15   Prepaid Expenses                                   70,000        2%
16   Other                                              23,000        1%
17                                                   ----------
18      Total Current Assets                         2,010,000       62%
19
20   Property, Plant, and Equipment         956,700
21      Accumulated Depreciation            123,700
22      Net P, P, and E                              833,000        26%
23   Investment - Long-term                           396,000       12%
24                                                   ----------
25      Total Noncurrent Assets                      1,229,000       38%
26                                                   ----------
27      Total Assets                                $3,239,000      100%
28                                                   =========
29
30          Liabilities
31
32   Notes Payable                                   $276,000        9%
33   Accounts Payable                                  378,000       12%
34   Accrued Expenses                                   98,000        3%
35   Other Liabilities                                  25,000        1%
36                                                   ----------
37      Total Current Liabilities                     777,000       24%
38
39   Long-Term Debt                                    333,000       10%
40
41          Stockholders' Equity
42
43   Common Stock, $1.00 par value                    440,000       14%
44   Paid-in Capital                                   361,000       11%
45   Retained Earnings                               1,328,000       41%
46                                                   ----------
47      Total Stockholders' Equity                   2,129,000       66%
48                                                   ----------
49      Total Liabilities and Net Worth             $3,239,000      100%
50                                                   =========
51
52
```

```
53    ==========================================================
54    Income Statement
55    ==========================================================
56                               Month Ended              Common
57                                07/31/85      Y-T-D       Size
58                               ----------   ----------
59    Gross Sales               $732,730   $5,656,407      100%
60       Less: Returns and Allowances  4,167     70,833       1%
61                               ----------   ----------
62    Net Sales                  728,563    5,585,574       99%
63    Cost of Goods Sold         468,947    3,855,667       68%
64                               ----------   ----------
65    Gross Margin               259,616    1,729,907       31%
66    Operating Expenses         201,042    1,306,667       23%
67    Depreciation                12,016       84,112        1%
68                               ----------   ----------
69    Earnings Before Interest and Taxe  46,558   339,128    6%
70    Interest Expense             7,043       53,578        1%
71                               ----------   ----------
72    Earnings Before Taxes       39,515      285,550        5%
73    Income Taxes                10,342       73,158        1%
74                               ----------   ----------
75    Earnings After Taxes        29,173      212,392        4%
76    Cash Dividends                   0       76,389        1%
77                               ----------   ----------
78    Net Income                 $29,173     $165,176        3%
79                               =========   =========
80
81    ==========================================================
82    Financial Ratios
83    ==========================================================
84    INDICATORS OF SOLVENCY
85       Debt/Equity Ratio                0.29 Total Debt/Total Equit
86       Times Interest Earned            6.33 Income Before Interest
87
88    INDICATORS OF LIQUIDITY
89       Net Working Capital        $1,233,000 Current Assets - Curre
90       Net Working Capital/Assets       0.38 Net Working Capital/To
91       Current Ratio                    2.59 Current Assets/Current
92       Quick Ratio                      2.01 (Cash+Marketable Secur
93       Cash Ratio                       0.40 (Cash+Marketable Secur
94
95
96    FUNDS MANAGEMENT RATIOS
97       Receivables/Annualized Sales     0.14 Net Accounts Receivabl
98       Days Sales Outstanding             51 Receivables/Sales rati
99       Payables/Cost of Goods Sold      0.07 Accounts Payable/(12*C
100      Days Purchases in Payables         24 Payables/Cost of Goods
101      Annualized Inventory Turnover   15.68 12*Net Sales this mont
102      Days Sales in Inventory            23 360/Inventory Turnover
103      Month's Sales/Fixed Assets       0.87 Net Sales/Net P, P, an
104
105   PROFITABILITY RATIOS (Annualized)
106      Return on Sales                  4.0% Earnings After Taxes/
107      Return on Total Assets          13.4% (Earnings After Taxes
108      Return on Shareholders' Equity  16.4% Earnings After Taxes/
```

Fig. 13.1. Balance Sheet and Income Statement for model application.

Common-size figures allow Mr. Eyeshade to perform a quick visual inspection of the percentages to see whether he incorrectly entered any Balance Sheet or Income Statement items. He can also review these percentages against any past percentages that he may remember from the previous session or have jotted down. None of these percentages is actually saved in the database.

As a further check on data in the spreadsheet's Balance Sheet portion, Mr. Eyeshade set up a pair of formulas just below the Total Liabilities and Equity line. These formulas (found in cells A51 and A52, respectively) determine whether the Balance Sheet is out of balance and display the out-of-balance amount. The formulas use @IF functions and 1-2-3's string conversion and concatenation capabilities and display a message that shows either the out-of-balance amount or nothing (when the Balance Sheet is in balance). The formulas are

```
@IF(@ROUND(E27-E49,Ø)>Ø, "ASSETS EXCEED LIABILITIES BY "&
   @STRING(E27-E49,Ø),"")
```

and

```
@IF(@ROUND(E49-E27,Ø)>Ø, "LIABILITIES EXCEED ASSETS BY "&
   @STRING(E49-E27,Ø),"")
```

NEW WITH
R2

If assets exceed liabilities by more than 0.5, the first formula displays the message ASSETS EXCEED LIABILITIES BY concatenated with the out-of-balance amount. If liabilities exceed assets by more than 0.5, the second formula displays LIABILITIES EXCEED ASSETS BY concatenated with the out-of-balance amount. Figure 13.2 shows the display when assets exceed liabilities and equity by $1,000.

Both formulas display the null string if assets and liabilities are in balance; nothing appears on the screen or in the Balance Sheet report. (Fig. 13.1A shows the result when the Balance Sheet is in balance.)

Placing these formulas at the bottom of the Balance Sheet provides a simple, highly visible means of verifying that the Balance Sheet is balanced. Wherever possible, Mr. Eyeshade uses such automatic error-checking devices in his models.

In the Income Statement, notice the Y-T-D column (column E) to the left of the Common Size column. This is where the year-to-date values for the various items in the Income Statement are stored. Although none of these values is stored in the database, they allow the controller to compare data from a given month against the accumulated total for the year.

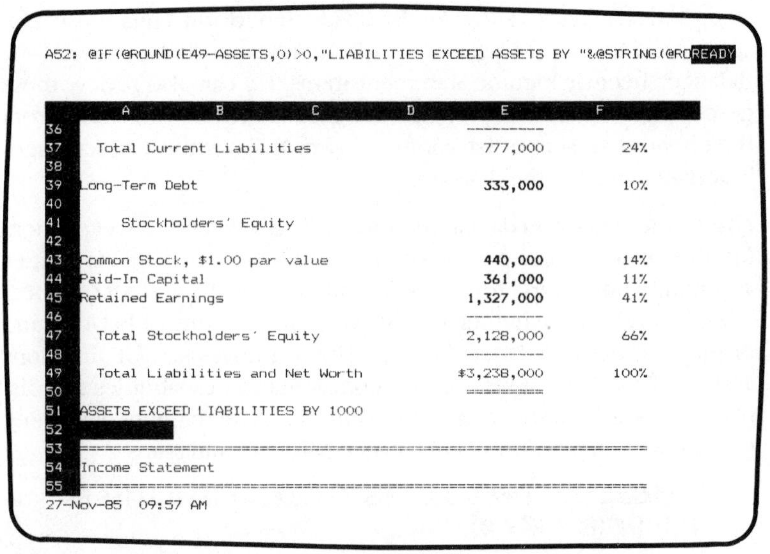

```
A52: @IF(@ROUND(E49-ASSETS,0)>0,"LIABILITIES EXCEED ASSETS BY "&@STRING(@RO  READY
```

	A	B	C	D	E	F
36					————	
37	Total Current Liabilities				777,000	24%
38						
39	Long-Term Debt				333,000	10%
40						
41	Stockholders' Equity					
42						
43	Common Stock, $1.00 par value				440,000	14%
44	Paid-In Capital				361,000	11%
45	Retained Earnings				1,327,000	41%
46					————	
47	Total Stockholders' Equity				2,128,000	66%
48					————	
49	Total Liabilities and Net Worth				$3,238,000	100%
50					=======	
51	ASSETS EXCEED LIABILITIES BY 1000					
52						
53	==					
54	Income Statement					
55	==					

27-Nov-85 09:57 AM

Fig. 13.2. Message displayed when the Balance Sheet is out of balance.

A final point to notice about this part of the model is the distinction between Currency and Comma formats. 1-2-3 allows you to conform to the accounting convention of using dollar signs in the first and last entries of financial statement entries and omitting them everywhere else.

Macros as a Keyboard Alternative

When originally developing this model, Mr. Eyeshade created two simple macros: one that accumulates totals in the year-to-date column of the Income Statement, and another that automatically enters records into the database. The name of each macro appears to the left of its first cell entry.

For example, if you glance at cell AA4 in figure 13.3, you will see the label \a. This label has two purposes. First, by using the /Range Name Labels Right command, you make \a the range name for cell L2, the first cell of the macro. Second, the appearance of the macro to the right of \a serves to document the macro's name.

The accumulator macro, \a, is the first macro that is actually used by Mr. Eyeshade. This macro takes the monthly income statement values supplied by Mr. Eyeshade in column D and adds them to the year-to-date values in column E.

```
AA11: [W6]                                                           READY

         AA       AB       AC       AD       AE       AF       AG
 1  MACROS - Macros for the Financial Ratio Model
 2
 3         Accumulator Macro to add month to YTD in Income Statement
 4  \a     {GOTO}Y-T-D~                              Goto Y-T-D Column
 5  ALOOP  {IF @CELLPOINTER("type")="l"}{DOWN}{BRANCH ALOOP}   Skip labels
 6         {IF @CELLPOINTER("type")="b"}{BRANCH AEND}  Quit if cell is empty
 7         {EDIT}+{UP}{LEFT}{DOWN}~                  Add month to YTD
 8         {EDIT}{CALC}~                             Convert to value
 9         {DOWN}{BRANCH ALOOP}                      Cursor down and contin
10  AEND   {RETURN}
11
12
13
14
15
16
17
18
19
20
22-Nov-85  11:09 AM                                           CAPS
```

Fig. 13.3. Macro to add Current Month to Y-T-D in Income Statement.

When he set up the macro, Mr. Eyeshade used the **/R**ange **N**ame **L**abel **D**own command to assign the name **Y-T-D** to cell E57 (the top of the Y-T-D column). The macro begins by moving the cursor (using the range name **Y-T-D**) to the top of the Income Statement's Y-T-D column.

Next, the macro enters a loop (a set of commands that executes repeatedly) to process the entries in the Y-T-D column. This macro loop is called ALOOP. The second row of the macro (the top of the loop) checks for a label in the Y-T-D column's current cell. If a label is present, the cursor is moved down and the loop repeated. If no label is present, the next row of the macro checks whether the current cell is empty. If it is empty, the end of the Y-T-D column has been reached, and the loop has finished; otherwise, the macro proceeds to add the month to the Y-T-D.

When the loop has finished, the last statement in the macro executes a {RETURN}. That is, as soon as the cursor reaches an empty cell, the macro branches to the subroutine named AEND. At this point the macro ends by executing a {RETURN}.

Within the loop, the macro begins processing the Y-T-D entry by having 1-2-3 enter EDIT mode. You might think that the next step is to move the cell pointer left immediately and point to the cell to be added to the year-to-date value; however, this is not the case. If you use the ← and → cursor-movement keys when you first enter EDIT mode, 1-2-3 thinks that you want to move the cursor left or right in the second line of the control panel and not in the worksheet. To get around this problem, you begin by using the ↑ cursor-movement key. This causes 1-2-3 to move the cell pointer up one cell and shift to POINT mode. Now you can point to the appropriate cell entry.

Once the appropriate cell address has been added to the year-to-date Income Statement value, the next step is to use {EDIT}{CALC}~ to convert this newly created entry from a formula to a value.

The final step in the macro loop is to move the cursor down and return to the top of the loop. The loop is repeated until the bottom of the Y-T-D column is reached.

The second macro, \d, is shown in figure 13.4. This macro takes specific values from the Income Statement and Balance Sheet and copies them to fields within the database. Begin the macro by positioning the cursor to the very top of the database. The statement in cell AB13 uses a range name called DATABASE that represents the cell A116. This cell is the first cell in the first row of the database. Figure 13.5 shows the database portion of the spreadsheet.

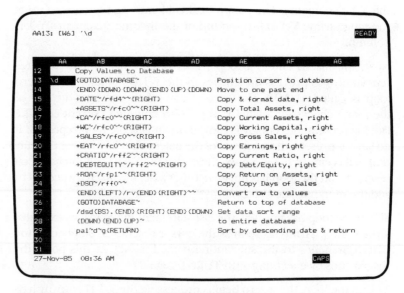

Fig. 13.4. Macro to update Financial History database.

```
A111:  'DATABASE                                                    READY

        A         B         C         D         E         F
110 =================================================================
111 DATABASE
112 =================================================================
113                                              MONTH
114    RECORD                          WORKING    GROSS     MONTH
115      DATE  TOT ASSETS CUR ASSETS   CAPITAL    SALES      EAT
116  07/31/85 $3,239,000 $2,010,000 $1,233,000  $732,730  $29,173
117  06/30/85 $3,202,976 $1,907,543 $1,160,483  $729,652  $26,612
118  05/31/85 $3,192,286 $1,893,724 $1,167,836  $726,572  $24,269
119  04/30/85 $3,181,407 $1,843,487 $1,118,712  $722,683  $24,833
120  03/31/85 $3,175,632 $1,875,261 $1,091,880  $717,947  $25,481
121  02/28/85 $3,158,517 $1,888,461 $1,154,019  $714,820  $22,582
122  01/31/85 $3,142,910 $1,821,474 $1,085,296  $713,267  $23,201
123  12/31/84 $3,118,964 $1,810,432 $1,131,818  $709,580  $22,898
124  11/30/84 $3,084,112 $1,758,559 $1,094,167  $705,182  $22,137
125  10/31/84 $3,081,261 $1,762,365 $1,072,725  $704,854  $23,101
126  09/30/84 $3,043,640 $1,867,870 $1,092,085  $704,000  $26,308
127  08/31/84 $3,028,681 $1,844,625 $1,071,413  $701,632  $26,541
128  07/31/84 $3,013,676 $1,764,898 $1,059,416  $700,554  $27,008
129  06/30/84 $2,991,601 $1,768,636 $1,061,479  $697,503  $24,048
22-Nov-85  11:21 AM                                  CALC       CAPS
```

Fig. 13.5. Financial History database.

The next step in the macro is to position the cell pointer down one row below the last entry in the database to begin entering the following record. The next statements in the macro enter formulas that reference certain items, such as the Record Date, Total Assets, Current Assets. Working Capital, etc., to the database, one item at a time. The documentation in column AE to the right of the macro indicates the values that are copied. After all the formulas are set up, the /**R**ange **V**alues command converts the formulas to values in the current database row.

As each cell in the database is set up, the formats of the cells for the items copied to the database are entered using the /**R**ange **F**ormat command.

Finally, the last four lines of the \d macro are used to sort the database automatically in descending order according to the date. In the third and second to last lines (cells AB27 and AB28), the statement reads

    /dsd{BS}. {END}{RIGHT}{END}{DOWN}{DOWN}{END}{UP}~

This statement automatically resets the **D**ata-Range to include the record just added, including the special case when this record is the only record in the database. The last line in the macro sets the primary key to the first column of the database and initiates the sort.

The Database

The *database* refers to the area of the spreadsheet that contains the monthly records of key ratios as well as the Balance Sheet and the Income Statement items. To illustrate how Mr. Eyeshade might want to manipulate the database, let's look at three different examples.

In the first example, suppose that Mr. Eyeshade is asked by Mr. Gherkins, the president, to find the gross sales and earnings after taxes for January 31, 1984. A logical way to get this information is by using the /Data Find command. Figure 13.6 shows the Criterion range (L112..L113) and part of the Input range (which corresponds to the entire database (A115..J146). The single record found as the result of the command is highlighted in reverse video.

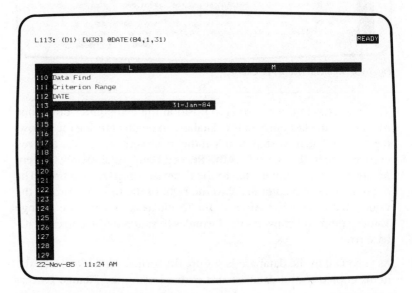

Fig. 13.6A. Criterion for /Data Query.

In the second example, Mr. Gherkins wants to know the trend in working capital throughout the first six months of 1985. The controller chooses the /Data Query Extract command for this application. Again, the Input range is the entire database (A115..J146). Figure 13.7 shows the Criterion range (L121..L122) used to select the records. Notice that the criteria are shown in Text format. The Output range for this Extract operation is the range L126..M126. Figure 13.7 also shows the values in the Output range (L127..M132) that are copied as a result of the command.

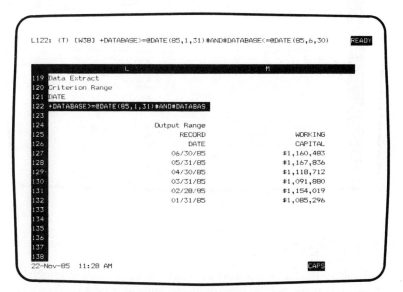

```
A134:  (D4)  30712                                                    FIND

        A          B            C           D          E         F
124  11/30/84 $3,084,112 $1,758,559 $1,094,167   $705,182   $22,137
125  10/31/84 $3,081,261 $1,762,365 $1,072,725   $704,854   $23,101
126  09/30/84 $3,043,640 $1,867,870 $1,092,085   $704,000   $26,308
127  08/31/84 $3,028,681 $1,844,625 $1,071,413   $701,632   $26,541
128  07/31/84 $3,013,676 $1,764,898 $1,059,416   $700,554   $27,008
129  06/30/84 $2,991,601 $1,768,636 $1,061,479   $697,503   $24,048
130  05/31/84 $2,962,020 $1,701,132 $1,006,475   $693,041   $25,537
131  04/30/84 $2,939,631 $1,814,346 $1,056,518   $692,004   $21,674
132  03/31/84 $2,936,500 $1,675,854 $1,015,673   $690,824   $26,006
133  02/29/84 $2,922,458 $1,684,678 $1,033,158   $690,289   $23,351
134  01/31/84 $2,903,961 $1,682,436 $1,002,948   $688,450   $21,267
135  12/31/83 $2,891,879 $1,779,420 $1,095,574   $686,639   $22,339
136  11/30/83 $2,889,668 $1,720,860 $1,026,998   $685,821   $27,259
137  10/31/83 $2,868,248 $1,654,943   $972,434   $685,073   $26,496
138  09/30/83 $2,864,642 $1,696,249 $1,042,317   $684,348   $23,122
139  08/31/83 $2,831,978 $1,695,048 $1,004,192   $681,827   $22,862
140  07/31/83 $2,830,797 $1,644,616   $986,548   $680,687   $21,246
141  06/30/83 $2,799,154 $1,607,371   $957,749   $680,000   $20,470
142  05/31/84 $2,788,738 $1,601,230   $963,565   $679,317   $22,278
143  04/30/83 $2,759,173 $1,575,963   $947,576   $677,506   $20,832
22-Nov-85  11:25 AM
```

Fig. 13.6B. Result of /Data Query Find.

```
L122:  (T)  [W38] +DATABASE>=@DATE(85,1,31)#AND#DATABASE<=@DATE(85,6,30)   READY

                        L                              M
119  Data Extract
120  Criterion Range
121  DATE
122  +DATABASE>=@DATE(85,1,31)#AND#DATABAS
123
124                Output Range
125                  RECORD                      WORKING
126                   DATE                        CAPITAL
127                  06/30/85                   $1,160,483
128                  05/31/85                   $1,167,836
129                  04/30/85                   $1,118,712
130                  03/31/85                   $1,091,880
131                  02/28/95                   $1,154,019
132                  01/31/85                   $1,085,296
133
134
135
136
137
138
22-Nov-85  11:28 AM                                          CAPS
```

Fig. 13.7. Extract of working capital for 1st half 1985.

Mr. Eyeshade might want to print the results of the **Extract** as they appear in the worksheet. To do this, he would specify the **Range** to be printed for the **/Print Printer** menu, and the results of the **Extract** are printed on the printer.

In the final example, Mr. Eyeshade wants to determine the months with the highest earnings-after-tax levels over the last two years. He could use a /Data Query Extract command again to copy the results of the search to a separate area of the worksheet. He decides, however, that he wants to re-sort the entire database and perform a simple visual review of the highest values. He uses the /Data Sort command with the Primary-Key set to the monthly earnings-after-tax column (column F). He also specifies descending order so that the months with the highest levels of earnings after taxes will appear at the top.

Before Mr. Eyeshade executes the sort, he first double-checks the Data-Range designation. He makes sure that the range is A116..J146. He then presses Go from the Sort command menu. Figure 13.8 show the result of the Sort.

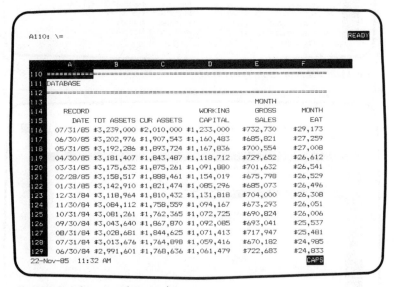

Fig. 13.8. Database sorted on earnings.

Graphics

Graphics is the final feature of the comprehensive mode. Although Mr. Eyeshade could create several different kinds of graphs, he decides to create and print three simple graphs: a line graph, a bar graph, and a pie graph. This group of graphs will give you a general idea of how graphs are created and displayed in this integrated model.

Mr. Eyeshade first creates a line graph to plot the points for the working capital levels for the first half of 1985 that were copied to the Output range in the second database example previously mentioned. He first selects **Line** as the /**Graph Type** and then sets his data range. To do this, he uses the /**Graph A** command and the range M127..M132, shown in figure 13.7. If he graphs the command at this point, he will get the results shown in figure 13.9 after he selects **View**.

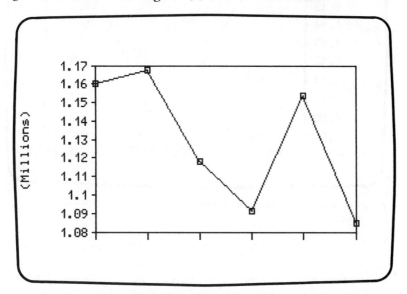

Fig. 13.9. First view of Working Capital graph.

To dress up the graph, Mr. Eyeshade can choose graph options. For example, he might decide to use graph titles and labels for the x-axis. To add the graph titles, he uses the **Graph Options Titles** command. For the main title, he sets the **First** option to "Gherkins, Inc." For the subtitle, he sets the **Second** option to "Working Capital Levels."

It isn't necessary for Mr. Eyeshade to give the y-axis a scale indicator, however. 1-2-3 automatically indicates the scale along the y-axis. In figure 13.9, for example, the scale indicator is (Millions). If he chose to do so, Mr. Eyeshade could suppress the scale indicator for the y-axis by using the /**Graph Options Scale Y-Scale Indicator No** commmand (see Chapter 9).

To set up the labels for the x-axis, Mr. Eyeshade uses the range corresponding to the dates that were extracted. To enter the range, he chooses **X** from the graph menu and enters *L127..L132* for the range. The results of Mr. Eyeshade's selections are shown in figure 13.10.

Notice that the order of the months displayed in the graph goes from June to January. To reverse the order of the months, Mr. Eyeshade can

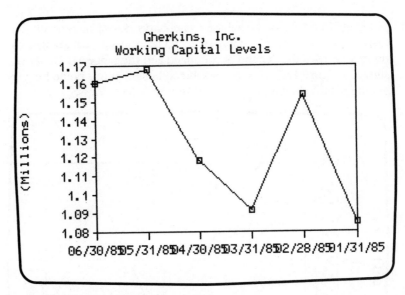

Fig. 13.10. Working Capital graph with titles.

do a **/Data S**ort on the **Data-Range** of L127..M132 with the **Primary-key** set to the date; for example, L127. If he selects **A**scending order for the **S**ort, he can get the graph to display the months from January to June, as shown in figure 13.11.

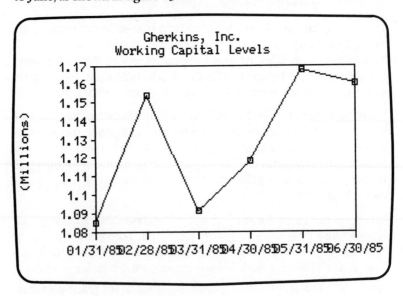

Fig. 13.11. Completed Working Capital graph.

To print this graph later, Mr. Eyeshade uses the /Graph Save command. This command saves the current graph in a .PIC file to print later after all the other graphs are created. Mr. Eyeshade also uses the /Graph Name Create command to save the current graph settings for later use.

The next type of graph that Mr. Eyeshade might select is a bar graph of the same data. To create this graph, he simply selects Bar from the /Graph Type menu. When he enters View from the /Graph menu, the results shown in figure 13.12 appear on the screen.

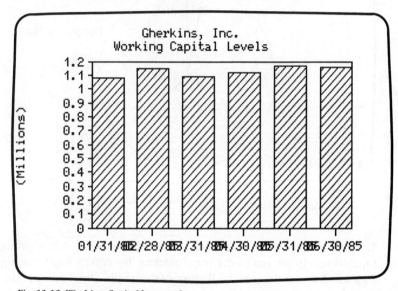

Fig. 13.12. Working Capital bar graph.

Again, Mr. Eyeshade uses the /Graph Save command to save the current graph for printing, and /Graph Name Create to save the current graph settings for later sessions.

The final graph Mr. Eyeshade creates is a pie graph called "Current Liabilities Jul–85." The slices of the pie are Notes Payable, Accounts Payable, Accrued Expenses, and Other Liabilities.

The first step that Mr. Eyeshade takes in creating the graph is to select Pie as the /Graph Type. Next, he sets the A range as E32..E35 (see fig. 13.1A), corresponding to July's values for the components of current liabilities listed above. In creating the Titles for the graph, Mr. Eyeshade again uses "Gherkins, Inc." for the First title. The Second title that he chooses is "Current Liabilities Jul–85." To name the slices, he uses the /Graph **X** command and designates A32..A35 (see fig. 13.1A) as the range for the x-axis labels. Figure 13.13 shows what happens after Mr. Eyeshade selects **View.**

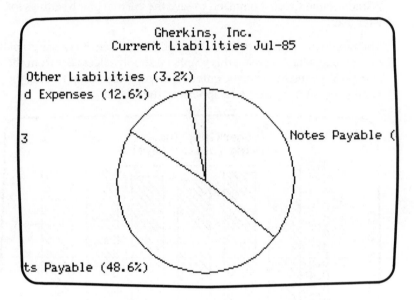

Fig. 13.13. Current Liabilities pie graph.

To make the pie wedges stand out, Mr. Eyeshade uses 1-2-3's shading capabilities. In an out-of-the-way location, he enters four shading codes and selects them as the **B** range of the graph. The shading codes are values from 0 to 7. Mr. Eyeshade enters a shadow code of 100 to make the Other Liabilities wedge "explode" from the pie. Figure 13.14 shows the result.

Once again, Mr. Eyeshade saves the current graph for printing with the /Graph **S**ave command. He also uses the /Graph **N**ame **C**reate command to save the settings for possible later use.

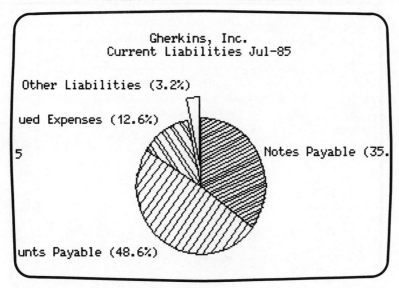

Fig. 13.14. The pie graph with an exploded wedge.

Printing the Graphs

To print the graphs he has created, Mr. Eyeshade must exit from 1-2-3 and enter the PrintGraph program either through the Lotus Access System or from DOS, depending on his preference at the time. Once he has entered the PrintGraph program, he may select several different print options. For this example, we assume that he uses defaults rather than any special options. Also, he selects all three graphs at once from the list of available .PIC files and prints them one after the other. The results of the PrintGraph program appear in figure 13.15.

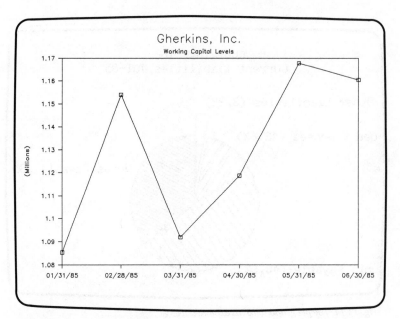

Fig. 13.15A. Finished line graph.

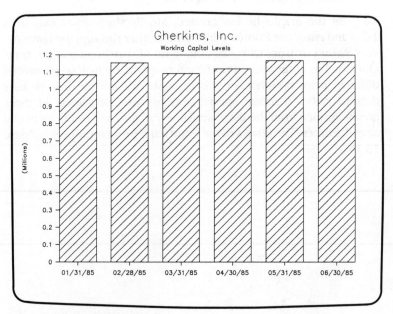

Fig. 13.15B. Finished bar graph.

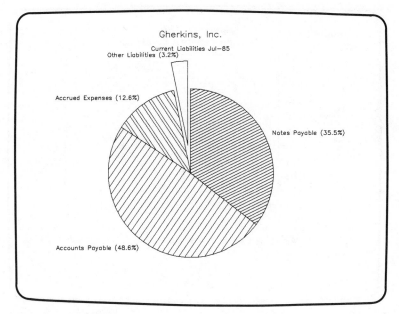

Fig. 13.15C. Finished pie graph.

Enhanced Working Capital Graph

Noting a recent rapid growth of working capital, Mr. Eyeshade wants to examine the relationship of working capital to sales over the past 12 months to see whether greater sales explain the rise of working capital. He uses 1-2-3's /Data Regression command to determine the relationship between working capital and sales and displays the results in an enhanced version of the Working Capital line graph (fig. 13.16).

The enhanced Working Capital graph is produced by running the /Data Regression command with the extracted Working Capital values for the past 12 months as the dependent variable (Y-Range), and the corresponding Sales for the past 12 months as the independent variable (X-Range). The Sales values are extracted and sorted along with the Working Capital values in the same manner as we extracted Working Capital values previously.

The /Data Regression output is a set of regression coefficients and statistics. The regression coefficients in this case are the constant and coefficient for Sales, the independent variable. The statistics measure

NEW WITH

R2

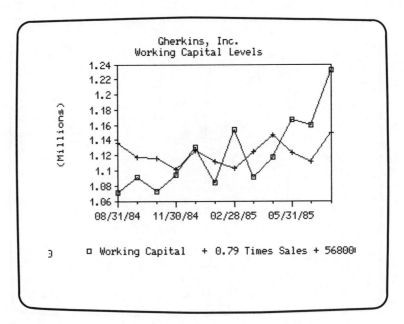

Fig. 13.16. Working Capital graph with regression line.

how closely the regression results describe the behavior of the dependent variable in terms of the independent variable.

To graph the regression results, Mr. Eyeshade uses the regression coefficients to calculate the fitted monthly values of working capital,
which he plots against the actual working capital amounts. He then
plots fitted values for working capital as the B range in the Working
Capital graph (see fig. 13.17).

Mr. Eyeshade uses legends to distinguish between the two lines on the
graph. He creates the legend for the working-capital line by typing in
the text for the A range legend, but he creates the legend for the fitted
line by entering a cell reference preceded by a backslash for the B
range legend.

The cell reference for the B legend refers to a cell containing the text
for the legend. In this case, the cell contains the string formula

```
@STRING(R132, 2)&" Times Sales +
   "&@STRING(@ROUND(S127. -3), 0)
```

(see fig. 13.18). This formula converts the regression coefficient for
Sales and the regression constant from numeric values to string values

and concatenates them with the string " Time Sales + " (see fig. 13.18).
The resulting string value is used as the legend in the graph.

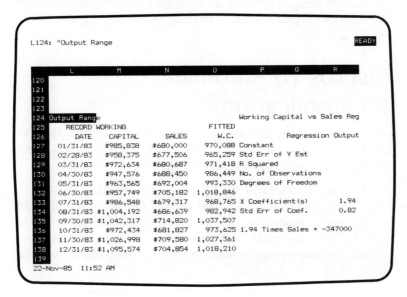

Fig. 13.17. Data for the enhanced working capital graph.

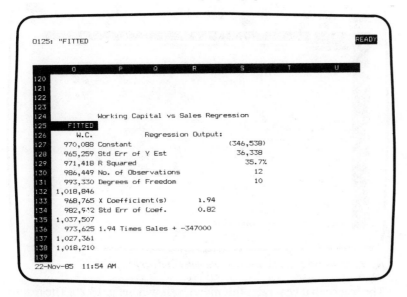

Fig. 13.18. /Data Regression output for working capital versus sales.

The resulting graph shows Mr. Eyeshade that the recent growth in working capital is greater than can be explained by sales growth. Armed with this graph, Mr. Eyeshade is ready to recommend that Mr. Gherkins take action to stabilize or reduce working capital to the previous year's levels.

Macros To Automate the Application

After using the Financial Ratios Model himself for a time, Mr. Eyeshade has decided to have his clerk enter the data and generate every month the reports and graphs shown to Mr. Gherkins.

Mr. Eyeshade decides that the clerk can enter the data and run the reports successfully if led through each of the steps with a macro. Based on his assessment of the clerk's abilities, Mr. Eyeshade decides to build a set of macros that automates routine data entry, report generation, and graph preparation steps with the macro menu shown in figure 13.19.

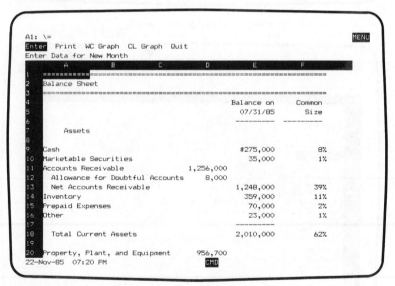

Fig. 13.19. Macro Menu for routine data entry and reports.

The macro that generates this menu is shown in fig. 13.20. The macro labeled \m invokes the menu labeled MENU. When the user invokes one of the menu options, the corresponding subroutine is invoked, followed by a return of control to the \m macro that recalls the menu.

The user can exit the menu system by selecting the **Quit** option, which executes a /xq (e**X**tended **Q**uit) macro command. Mr. Eyeshade also assigns the label \0 to the \m macro to invoke the macro automatically when the worksheet is loaded with **/File Retrieve**.

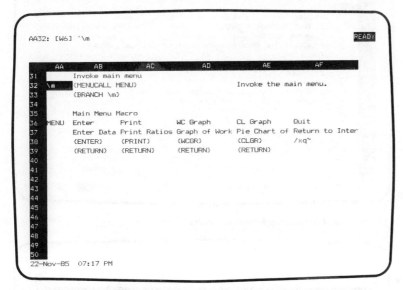

```
AA32: [W6]  '\m                                                      READY

        AA        AB          AC          AD          AE          AF
31                Invoke main menu
32      \m        {MENUCALL MENU}                     Invoke the main menu.
33                {BRANCH \m}
34
35                Main Menu Macro
36      MENU      Enter       Print       WC Graph    CL Graph    Quit
37                Enter Data  Print Ratios Graph of Work Pie Chart of Return to Inter
38                {ENTER}     {PRINT}     {WCGR}      {CLGR}      /xq~
39                {RETURN}    {RETURN}    {RETURN}    {RETURN}
40
41
42
43
44
45
46
47
48
49
50
22-Nov-85  07:17 PM
```

Fig. 13.20. Macro commands to display menu.

Figure 13.21 shows the ENTER subroutine called when the user selects the **E**nter option from the menu. The ENTER subroutine prompts the user for the date with a GETLABEL command. After accepting the date as a text string, the @DATEVALUE function in the LET command on the next line converts the string to a date value. The IF command on the third line checks that a valid date value was obtained. If a valid date value was not obtained, an error message is displayed, and execution returns to the top of the ENTER macro to obtain a valid date.

When a valid date is obtained, execution continues at ENTR1, which displays a screen of instructions for the data entry that follows. These instructions are shown in figure 13.22.

The instruction screen is invoked by a {GOTO} statement, followed by a GETLABEL that prompts the user to press Enter when ready to enter data. Then another {GOTO} statement positions the cursor to the top of the data entry area, and a {?} statement accepts all entries made until the user presses Enter again.

NEW WITH
R2

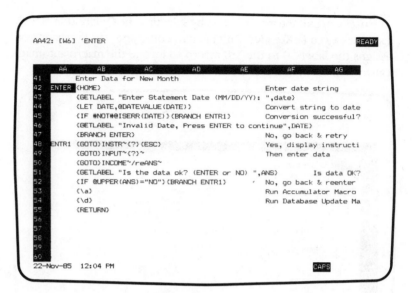

Fig. 13.21. ENTER subroutine called from the menu.

Fig. 13.22. Instructions for data entry.

After entering the data, you use another GETLABEL command to ask whether the data is OK. If the answer is no, execution branches back to the data entry step. Otherwise, the accumulator macro (\a) and the database macro (\d) run and control returns to the menu.

After data is entered for the month, the clerk can print the Financial Ratios Report along with hard copies of the Balance Sheet and Income Statement, using the **Print** option on the menu. The **Print** option calls the PRINT subroutine, which is shown in figure 13.23.

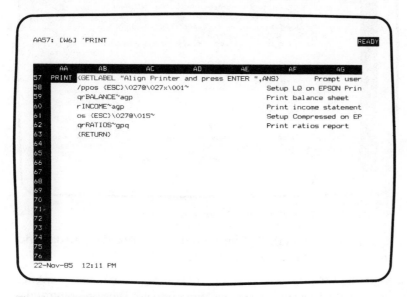

```
AA57: [W6] 'PRINT                                                    READY

        AA        AB          AC          AD          AE          AF          AG
57  PRINT {GETLABEL "Align Printer and press ENTER ",ANS}         Prompt user
58       /ppos {ESC}\027@\027x\001~                      Setup LQ on EPSON Prin
59       qrBALANCE~agp                                   Print balance sheet
60       r INCOME~agp                                    Print income statement
61       os {ESC}\027@\015~                              Setup Compressed on EP
62       qrRATIOS~gpq                                    Print ratios report
63       {RETURN}
64
65
66
67
68
69
70
71
72
73
74
75
76
22-Nov-85  12:11 PM
```

Fig. 13.23. PRINT subroutine called from menu.

The PRINT subroutine prompts the user to align the printer, then sets up the printer to print the Balance Sheet, Income Statement, and Ratios Report before returning to the menu.

Two menu options generate graphs. The first generates the enhanced Working Capital graph, and the second generates the Current Liabilities pie graph. The macro to generate the enhanced Working Captal graph is named WCGR (fig. 13.24).

The macro first prompts the user for the beginning date and ending date for the graph. As in the ENTER macro, the dates are entered as string values and converted to date values using the LET macro command and the @DATEVALUE function. This method is more convenient than having the user enter the date as, for example, @DATE(85,07,31). An *IF* command checks for invalid dates and returns the user to the date entry if an invalid date is found.

After the beginning and ending dates are entered, the WCGR macro performs a **/Data Query Extract** on the database into the data area shown in figure 13.17. The command extracts values of the date,

NEW WITH

R2

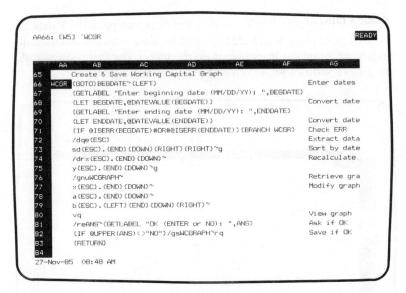

```
AA66: [W5] 'WCGR                                                    READY

         AA      AB       AC       AD       AE       AF       AG
65           Create & Save Working Capital Graph
66   WCGR  {GOTO}BEGDATE~{LEFT}                              Enter dates
67         {GETLABEL "Enter beginning date (MM/DD/YY): ",BEGDATE}
68         {LET BEGDATE,@DATEVALUE(BEGDATE)}                 Convert date
69         {GETLABEL "Enter ending date (MM/DD/YY): ",ENDDATE}
70         {LET ENDDATE,@DATEVALUE(ENDDATE)}                 Convert date
71         {IF @ISERR(BEGDATE)#OR#@ISERR(ENDDATE)}{BRANCH WCGR}  Check ERR
72         /dqe{ESC}                                         Extract data
73         sd{ESC}.{END}{DOWN}{RIGHT}{RIGHT}~g               Sort by date
74         /drx{ESC}.{END}{DOWN}~                            Recalculate
75         y{ESC}.{END}{DOWN}~g
76         /gnuWCGRAPH~                                      Retrieve gra
77         x{ESC}.{END}{DOWN}~                               Modify graph
78         a{ESC}.{END}{DOWN}~
79         b{ESC}.{LEFT}{END}{DOWN}{RIGHT}~
80         vq                                                View graph
81         /reANS~{GETLABEL "OK (ENTER or NO): ",ANS}        Ask if OK
82         {IF @UPPER(ANS)<>"NO"}/gsWCGRAPH~rq               Save if OK
83         {RETURN}
84
27-Nov-85  08:48 AM
```

Fig. 13.24. Macro to create enhanced working capital graph.

Working Capital, and Sales from records in the database with dates between the beginning date and ending date.

Next, the WCGR macro performs a /**D**ata **S**ort command to arrange the extracted data into ascending order by date. The **S**ort command is invoked right after the **E**xtract command, without having to go all the way back to the main command menu. The SORT range is defined using the End key to expand the cursor to "paint" all the data that was extracted in the previous extract step.

After the sort is completed, the /**D**ata **R**egression command is rerun over the extracted and sorted Working Capital and Sales values. Then the graph definitions for the Working Capital graph are retrieved, and the preliminary graph is viewed. The user must press any key at this point to continue the macro execution.

The WCGR macro finishes by redefining the graph data ranges over the entire extracted data and redisplaying the graph. After the user reviews the graph and presses any key, a final prompt asks whether the graph is acceptable. If the answer is no, the macro returns to the menu without saving the graph. Otherwise, the finished graph is saved for later printing with the file name WCGRAPH.PIC.

The WCGR macro assumes that the data query and data regression are both set up beforehand so that the macro merely needs to redefine the existing ranges used by these commands. This works well in Mr. Eye-

NEW WITH
R2

shade's ratio model, but some applications might require macros capable of setting everything up from scratch.

The second graph option calls the macro CLGR that generates a pie graph of current liabilities by category (fig. 13.25). This simple macro recalls the pie graph definitions and displays the graph for the current month on the screen. The user must press a key for macro execution to continue. The macro next asks whether the graph is acceptable. If the graph is unacceptable, the macro returns to the menu without saving the graph. If it is approved, it is saved for printing under the name CURRLIAB.PIC before the macro returns to the menu.

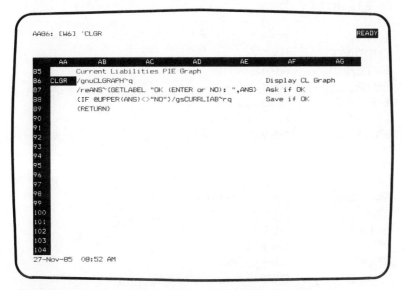

Fig. 13.25. Macro to create pie graph of current liabilities by category.

The macros in the macro menu subsystem make extensive use of range names. Figure 13.26 shows a listing of the worksheet range names generated by the /Range Name Table command to document the range names that are used.

If you have further questions about how the financial ratios worksheet is set up, refer to figure 13.27, a complete cell listing of the financial ratios worksheet.

NEW WITH
R2

```
AEND          AB10
ALOOP         AB5
ANS           AB91
ASSETS        E27
BALANCE       A1..F51
BEGDATE       M106
CA            E18
CLGR          AB86
CRATIO        D91
DATABASE      A116
DATE          E5
DEBTEQUITY    D85
DSO           D98
EAT           D75
ENDDATE       M107
ENTER         AB42
ENTR1         AB48
INCOME        A53..F79
INPUT         A7..E79
INSTR         AB93
MACROS        AB1
MENU          AB36
PRINT         AB57
RATIOS        A81..J108
ROA           D107
SALES         D59
WC            D89
WCGR          AB66
Y-T-D         E58
\A            AB4
\D            AB13
\M            AB32
\O            AB32
```

Fig. 13.26. Table of range names used in the worksheet.

```
A1: \=
B1: \=
C1: \=
D1: \=
E1: \=
F1: \=
AA1: [W6] 'MACROS
AB1: ' - Macros for the Financial Ratio Model
A2: 'Balance Sheet
A3: \=
B3: \=
C3: \=
D3: \=
E3: \=
F3: \=
AB3: 'Accumulator Macro to add month to YTD in Income Statement
E4: 'Balance on
F4: "Common
AA4: [W6] '\a
AB4: '{GOTO}Y-T-D~
AF4: 'Goto Y-T-D Column
E5: (D4) 31259
F5: "Size
AA5: [W6] 'ALOOP
AB5: '{IF @CELLPOINTER("type")="l"}{DOWN}{BRANCH ALOOP}
AG5: 'Skip labels
E6: "----------
F6: "----------
AB6: '{IF @CELLPOINTER("type")="b"}{BRANCH AEND}
AF6: 'Quit if cell is empty
A7: '      Assets
AB7: '{EDIT}+{UP}{LEFT}{DOWN}~
AF7: 'Add month to YTD
AB8: '{EDIT}{CALC}~
AF8: 'Convert to value
A9: 'Cash
E9: (C0) U 275000
F9: (P0) +E9/$ASSETS
AB9: '{DOWN}{BRANCH ALOOP}
AF9: 'Cursor down and continue
A10: 'Marketable Securities
E10: U 35000
F10: (P0) +E10/$ASSETS
```

```
AA10: [W6] 'AEND
AB10: '{RETURN}
A11: 'Accounts Receivable
D11: U 1256000
A12: '  Allowance for Doubtful Accounts
D12: U 8000
AB12: 'Copy Values to Database
A13: '  Net Accounts Receivable
E13: +D11-D12
F13: (P0) +E13/$ASSETS
AA13: [W6] '\d
AB13: '{GOTO}DATABASE~
AE13: 'Position cursor to database
A14: 'Inventory
E14: U 359000
F14: (P0) +E14/$ASSETS
AB14: '{END}{DOWN}{DOWN}{END}{UP}{DOWN}
AE14: 'Move to one past end
A15: 'Prepaid Expenses
E15: U 70000
F15: (P0) +E15/$ASSETS
AB15: '+DATE~/rfd4~~{RIGHT}
AE15: 'Copy & format date, right
A16: 'Other
E16: U 23000
F16: (P0) +E16/$ASSETS
AB16: '+ASSETS~/rfc0~~{RIGHT}
AE16: 'Copy Total Assets, right
E17: "---------
AB17: '+CA~/rfc0~~{RIGHT}
AE17: 'Copy Current Assets, right
A18: '  Total Current Assets
E18: @SUM(E9..E17)
F18: (P0) +CA/$ASSETS
AB18: '+WC~/rfc0~~{RIGHT}
AE18: 'Copy Working Capital, right
AB19: '+SALES~/rfc0~~{RIGHT}
AE19: 'Copy Gross Sales, right
A20: 'Property, Plant, and Equipment
D20: U 956700
AB20: '+EAT~/rfc0~~{RIGHT}
AE20: 'Copy Earnings, right
A21: '  Accumulated Depreciation
```

```
D21: U 123700
AB21: '+CRATIO^/rff2^^{RIGHT}
AE21: 'Copy Current Ratio, right
A22: '  Net P, P, and E
E22: +D20-D21
F22: (P0) +E22/$ASSETS
AB22: '+DEBTEQUITY^/rff2^^{RIGHT}
AE22: 'Copy Debt/Equity, right
A23: 'Investment - Long-term
E23: U 396000
F23: (P0) +E23/$ASSETS
AB23: '+ROA^/rfp1^^{RIGHT}
AE23: 'Copy Return on Assets, right
E24: "----------
AB24: '+DSO^/rff0^^
AE24: 'Copy Copy Days of Sales
A25: '  Total Noncurrent Assets
E25: @SUM(E22..E24)
F25: (P0) +E25/$ASSETS
AB25: '{END}{LEFT}/rv{END}{RIGHT}^^
AE25: 'Convert row to values
E26: "----------
AB26: '{GOTO}DATABASE^
AE26: 'Return to top of database
A27: '  Total Assets
E27: (C0) +CA+E25
F27: (P0) +ASSETS/$ASSETS
AB27: '/dsd{BS}.{END}{RIGHT}{END}{DOWN}{DOWN}
AF27: 'Set data sort range
E28: "=========
AB28: '{END}{UP}^
AE28: 'to entire database
AB29: 'pa1^d^g{RETURN}
AE29: 'Sort by descending date & return
A30: '    Liabilities
AB31: 'Invoke main menu
A32: 'Notes Payable
E32: (C0) U 276000
F32: (P0) +E32/$E$49
G32: 1
AA32: [W6] '\M
AB32: '{MENUCALL MENU}
AE32: 'Invoke the main menu.
```

A33: 'Accounts Payable
E33: U 378000
F33: (P0) +E33/$E$49
G33: 2
AB33: '{BRANCH \m}
A34: 'Accrued Expenses
E34: U 98000
F34: (P0) +E34/$E$49
G34: 3
A35: 'Other Liabilities
E35: U 25000
F35: (P0) +E35/$E$49
G35: 100
AB35: 'Main Menu Macro
E36: "---------
AA36: [W6] 'MENU
AB36: 'ENTER
AC36: 'PRINT
AD36: 'WC GRAPH
AE36: 'CL GRAPH
AF36: 'QUIT
A37: '   Total Current Liabilities
E37: @SUM(E32..E36)
F37: (P0) +E37/$E$49
AB37: 'Enter Data for New Month
AC37: 'Print Ratios Report
AD37: 'Graph of Working Capital
AE37: 'Pie Graph of Current Liabilities
AF37: 'Return to Interactive 1-2-3
AB38: '{ENTER}
AC38: '{PRINT}
AD38: '{WCGR}
AE38: '{CLGR}
AF38: '/XQ~
A39: 'Long-Term Debt
E39: U 333000
F39: (P0) +E39/$E$49
AB39: '{RETURN}
AC39: '{RETURN}
AD39: '{RETURN}
AE39: '{RETURN}
A41: '   Stockholders ' Equity
AB41: 'Enter Data for New Month

```
AA42: [W6] 'ENTER
AB42: '{HOME}
AF42: 'Enter date string
A43: 'Common Stock, $1.00 par value
E43: U 440000
F43: (P0) +E43/$E$49
AB43: '{GETLABEL "Enter Statement Date (MM/DD/YY): ",DATE}
A44: 'Paid-in Capital
E44: U 361000
F44: (P0) +E44/$E$49
AB44: '{LET DATE,@DATEVALUE(DATE)}
AF44: 'Convert string to date
A45: 'Retained Earnings
E45: U 1328000
F45: (P0) +E45/$E$49
AB45: '{IF #NOT#@ISERR(DATE)}{BRANCH ENTR1}
AF45: 'Conversion successful?
E46: "---------
AB46: '{GETLABEL "Invalid Date, Press ENTER to continue",DATE}
A47: '  Total Stockholders' Equity
E47: @SUM(E43..E46)
F47: (P0) +E47/$E$49
AB47: '{BRANCH ENTER}
AF47: 'No, go back & retry
E48: "---------
AA48: [W6] 'ENTR1
AB48: '{GOTO}INSTR~{?}{ESC}
AF48: 'Yes, display instructions
A49: '  Total Liabilities and Net Worth
E49: {C0} +E37+E39+E47
F49: (P0) +E49/$E$49
AB49: '{GOTO}INPUT~{?}~
AF49: 'Then enter data
E50: "=========
AB50: '{GOTO}INCOME~/reANS~
A51: @IF(@ROUND(ASSETS-E49,0)>0,"ASSETS EXCEED LIABILITIES BY "&@STRING(@ROUND(ASSETS-E49,0),0),"")
AB51: '{GETLABEL "Is the data ok? (ENTER or NO) ",ANS}
A651: 'Is data OK?
A52: @IF(@ROUND(E49-ASSETS,0)>0,"LIABILITIES EXCEED ASSETS BY "&@STRING(@ROUND(E49-ASSETS,0),0),"")
AB52: '{IF @UPPER(ANS)="NO"}{BRANCH ENTR1}
AF52: 'No, go back & reenter
A53: \=
B53: \=
```

```
C53: \=
D53: \=
E53: \=
F53: \=
AB53: '{\a}
AF53: 'Run Accumulator Macro
A54: 'Income Statement
AB54: '{\d}
AF54: 'Run Database Update Macro
A55: \=
B55: \=
C55: \=
D55: \=
E55: \=
F55: \=
AB55: '{RETURN}
D56: "Month Ended
E56: (D4) +DATE
F56: "Common
D57: (D4) +DATE
E57: "Y-T-D
F57: "Size
AA57: [W6] 'PRINT
AB57: '{GETLABEL "Align Printer and press ENTER ",ANS}
AG57: 'Prompt user
D58: "---------
E58: "---------
AB58: '/ppos {ESC}\027@\027x\001~
AF58: 'Setup LQ on EPSON Printer
A59: 'Gross Sales
D59: (C0) U 732730
E59: (C0) 5656407
F59: (P0) +E59/$E$59
AB59: 'qrBALANCE~agp
AF59: 'Print balance sheet
A60: '  Less: Returns and Allowances
D60: U 4167
E60: 70833
F60: (P0) +E60/$E$59
AB60: 'rINCOME~agp
AF60: 'Print income statement
D61: "---------
E61: "---------
```

```
AB61: 'os {ESC}\027@\015*
AF61: 'Setup Compressed on EPSON
A62: 'Net Sales
D62: +SALES-D60
E62: 5585574
F62: (P0) +E62/$E$59
AB62: 'qrRATIOS*gpq
AF62: 'Print ratios report
A63: 'Cost of Goods Sold
D63: U 468947
E63: 3855667
F63: (P0) +E63/$E$59
AB63: '{RETURN}
D64: "---------
E64: "---------
A65: 'Gross Margin
D65: +D62-D63
E65: 1729907
F65: (P0) +E65/$E$59
AB65: 'Create & Save Working Capital Graph
A66: 'Operating Expenses
D66: U 201042
E66: 1306667
F66: (P0) +E66/$E$59
AA66: [W6] 'WCGR
AB66: '{GOTO}BEGDATE*{LEFT}
AF66: 'Enter dates for graph
A67: 'Depreciation
D67: U 12016
E67: 84112
F67: (P0) +E67/$E$59
AB67: '{GETLABEL "Enter beginning date (MM/DD/YY): ",BEGDATE}
D68: "---------
E68: "---------
AB68: '{LET BEGDATE,@DATEVALUE(BEGDATE)}
AF68: 'Convert beginning date
A69: 'Earnings Before Interest and Taxes
D69: +D65-D66-D67
E69: 339128
F69: (P0) +E69/$E$59
AB69: '{GETLABEL "Enter ending date (MM/DD/YY): ",ENDDATE}
A70: 'Interest Expense
D70: U 7043
```

```
E70: 53578
F70: (P0) +E70/$E$59
AB70: '{LET ENDDATE,@DATEVALUE(ENDDATE)}
AF70: 'Convert ending date
D71: "---------
E71: "---------
AB71: '{IF @ISERR(BEGDATE)#OR#@ISERR(ENDDATE)}{BRANCH WCGR}
AG71: 'Check ERR
A72: 'Earnings Before Taxes
D72: +D69-D70
E72: 285550
F72: (P0) +E72/$E$59
AB72: '/dqe{ESC}
AF72: 'Extract data for graph
A73: 'Income Taxes
D73: U 10342
E73: 73158
F73: (P0) +E73/$E$59
AB73: 'sd{ESC}.{END}{DOWN}{RIGHT}{RIGHT}~g
AF73: 'Sort ascending by date
D74: "---------
E74: "---------
AB74: '/drx{ESC}.{END}{DOWN}~
AF74: 'Recalculate Regression
A75: 'Earnings After Taxes
D75: +D72-D73
E75: 212392
F75: (P0) +E75/$E$59
AB75: 'y{ESC}.{END}{DOWN}~g
A76: 'Cash Dividends
D76: U 0
E76: 76389
F76: (P0) +E76/$E$59
AB76: '/gnuWCGRAPH~
AF76: 'Retrieve graph
D77: "---------
E77: "---------
AB77: 'x{ESC}.{END}{DOWN}~
AF77: 'Modify graph ranges
A78: 'Net Income
D78: (C0) +EAT-D76
E78: (C0) 165176
F78: (P0) +E78/$E$59
```

```
AB78: 'a{ESC}.{END}{DOWN}~
D79: "=========
E79: "=========
AB79: 'a{ESC}.{LEFT}{END}{DOWN}{RIGHT}~
AB80: 'vq
AF80: 'view graph
A81: \=
B81: \=
C81: \=
D81: \=
E81: \=
F81: \=
G81: \=
H81: \=
I81: \=
J81: \=
AB81: '/reANS~{GETLABEL "OK (ENTER or NO): ",ANS}
AF81: 'Ask if OK
A82: 'Financial Ratios
AB82: '{IF @UPPER(ANS)<>"NO"}/gsWCGRAPH~rq
AF82: 'Save if OK
A83: \=
B83: \=
C83: \=
D83: \=
E83: \=
F83: \=
G83: \=
H83: \=
I83: \=
J83: \=
AB83: '{RETURN}
A84: 'INDICATORS OF SOLVENCY
A85: '  Debt/Equity Ratio
D85: (F2) (E32+E39)/E47
E85: 'Total Debt/Total Equity
AB85: 'Current Liabilities PIE Chart
A86: '  Times Interest Earned
D86: (F2) +E69/E70
E86: 'Income Before Interest and Taxes/Interest Expense
AA86: [W6] 'CLGR
AB86: '/gnuCLGRAPH~q
AF86: 'Display CL Graph
```

```
AB87: '/reANS~{GETLABEL "OK (ENTER or NO): ",ANS}
AF87: 'Ask if OK
A88: 'INDICATORS OF LIQUIDITY
AB88: '{IF @UPPER(ANS)<>"NO"}/gsCURRLIAB~rq
AF88: 'Save if OK
A89: '  Net Working Capital
D89: (C0) +CA-E37
E89: 'Current Assets - Current Liabilities
AB89: '{RETURN}
A90: '  Net Working Capital/Assets
D90: (F2) +WC/ASSETS
E90: 'Net Working Capital/Total Assets
A91: '  Current Ratio
D91: (F2) +CA/E37
E91: 'Current Assets/Current Liabilities
AA91: [W6] 'ANS
AB91: '
A92: '  Quick Ratio
D92: (F2) @SUM(E9..E13)/E37
E92: '(Cash+Marketable Securities+Receivables)/Current Liabilities
A93: '  Cash Ratio
D93: (F2) @SUM(E9..E10)/E37
E93: '(Cash+Marketable Securities)/Current Liabilities
AA93: [W6] 'INSTR
AD93: 'DATA ENTRY FOR NEW MONTH
A96: 'FUNDS MANAGEMENT RATIOS
AC96: '   Enter data only in
AE96: U 'Highlighted
AF96: ' cells.
A97: '  Receivables/Annualized Sales
D97: (F2) +E13/(D62*12)
E97: 'Net Accounts Receivable/(12*Net Sales for month)
A98: '  Days Sales Outstanding
D98: +D97*360
E98: 'Receivables/Sales ratio * 360
AC98: 'Use the cursor keys to move to the next cell
A99: '  Payables/Cost of Goods Sold
D99: (F2) +E33/(D63*12)
E99: 'Accounts Payable/(12*Cost of Goods Sold)
AC99: 'At the end of each entry. Pressing the ENTER
A100: '  Days Purchases in Payables
D100: +D99*360
E100: 'Payables/Cost of Goods Sold ratio * 360
```

```
AC100: 'key ends the data entry.
A101:  '  Annualized Inventory Turnover
D101:  (F2) +D63*12/E14
E101:  '12*Net Sales this month/Inventory
A102:  '  Days Sales in Inventory
D102:  360/D101
E102:  '360/Inventory Turnover
AC102: 'Be sure that the balance sheet balances at
A103:  '  Month's Sales/Fixed Assets
D103:  (F2) +D62/E22
E103:  'Net Sales/Net P, P, and E
AC103: 'the end of data entry. If it is out of balance,
AC104: 'a message appears below the total liabilities
A105:  'PROFITABILITY RATIOS (Annualized)
AC105: 'and equity line.
A106:  '  Return on Sales
D106:  (P1) +EAT/D62
E106:  ' Earnings After Taxes/Net Sales
L106:  'BEGDATE
M106:  (D4) 30317
A107:  '  Return on Total Assets
D107:  (P1) (EAT+D70)*12/ASSETS
E107:  ' (Earnings After Taxes + Interest Expense)/Total Assets
L107:  'ENDDATE
M107:  (D4) 30682
AC107: 'The system asks you if the data is ok after
A108:  '  Return on Shareholders' Equity
D108:  (P1) +EAT*12/E47
E108:  ' Earnings After Taxes/Total Stockholders' Equity
AC108: 'the end of data entry. If you say no, the
AC109: 'system will reenter data entry mode.
A110:  \=
B110:  \=
C110:  \=
D110:  \=
E110:  \=
F110:  \=
G110:  \=
H110:  \=
I110:  \=
J110:  \=
A111:  'DATABASE
A112:  \=
```

```
B112: \=
C112: \=
D112: \=
E112: \=
F112: \=
G112: \=
H112: \=
I112: \=
J112: \=
E113: "MONTH
A114: "RECORD
D114: "WORKING
E114: "GROSS
F114: "MONTH
H114: "DEBT TO
I114: "RETURN
A115: "DATE
B115: "TOT ASSETS
C115: "CUR ASSETS
D115: "CAPITAL
E115: "SALES
F115: "EAT
G115: "CUR RATIO
H115: "EQUITY
I115: "ON ASSETS
J115: "DSO
L115: 'Data Extract
A116: (D4) 31259
B116: (C0) 3239000
C116: (C0) 2010000
D116: (C0) 1233000
E116: (C0) 732730
F116: (C0) 29173
G116: (F2) 2.5868725869
H116: (F2) 0.2860497886
I116: (P1) 0.1341747453
J116: (F0) 51.388829792
L116: 'Criterion Range
A117: (D4) 31228
B117: (C0) 3202976
C117: (C0) 1907543
D117: (C0) 1160483
E117: (C0) 685821
```

```
F117: (C0) 27259
G117: (F2) 2.48
H117: (F2) 0.3465
I117: (P1) 0.13
J117: 71
L117: 'DATE
A118: (D4) 31198
B118: (C0) 3192286
C118: (C0) 1893724
D118: (C0) 1167836
E118: (C0) 700554
F118: (C0) 27008
G118: (F2) 2.5
H118: (F2) 0.3245
I118: (P1) 0.13
J118: 63
L118: (T) +DATABASE>=$BEGDATE#AND#DATABASE<=$ENDDATE
A119: (D4) 31167
B119: (C0) 3181407
C119: (C0) 1843487
D119: (C0) 1118712
E119: (C0) 729652
F119: (C0) 26612
G119: (F2) 2.55
H119: (F2) 0.286
I119: (P1) 0.12
J119: 53
A120: (D4) 31137
B120: (C0) 3175632
C120: (C0) 1875261
D120: (C0) 1091880
E120: (C0) 701632
F120: (C0) 26541
G120: (F2) 2.39
H120: (F2) 0.319
I120: (P1) 0.13
J120: 63
A121: (D4) 31106
B121: (C0) 3158517
C121: (C0) 1888461
D121: (C0) 1154019
E121: (C0) 675798
F121: (C0) 26529
```

```
G121: (F2) 2.62
H121: (F2) 0.3575
I121: (P1) 0.14
J121: 80
A122: (D4) 31078
B122: (C0) 3142910
C122: (C0) 1821474
D122: (C0) 1085296
E122: (C0) 685073
F122: (C0) 26496
G122: (F2) 2.42
H122: (F2) 0.3465
I122: (P1) 0.13
J122: 73
A123: (D4) 31047
B123: (C0) 3118964
C123: (C0) 1810432
D123: (C0) 1131818
E123: (C0) 704000
F123: (C0) 26308
G123: (F2) 2.41
H123: (F2) 0.319
I123: (P1) 0.12
J123: 61
A124: (D4) 31016
B124: (C0) 3084112
C124: (C0) 1758559
D124: (C0) 1094167
E124: (C0) 673293
F124: (C0) 26051
G124: (F2) 2.47
H124: (F2) 0.363
I124: (P1) 0.14
J124: 82
L124: "Output Range
P124: 'Working Capital vs Sales Regression
A125: (D4) 30986
B125: (C0) 3081261
C125: (C0) 1762365
D125: (C0) 1072725
E125: (C0) 690824
F125: (C0) 26006
G125: (F2) 2.54
```

```
H125: (F2) 0.33
I125: (P1) 0.13
J125: 66
L125: "RECORD
M125: "WORKING
O125: "FITTED
A126: (D4) 30955
B126: (C0) 3043640
C126: (C0) 1867870
D126: (C0) 1092085
E126: (C0) 693041
F126: (C0) 25537
G126: (F2) 2.45
H126: (F2) 0.3245
I126: (P1) 0.12
J126: 65
L126: "DATE
M126: "CAPITAL
N126: "SALES
O126: "W.C.
Q126: 'Regression Output:
A127: (D4) 30925
B127: (C0) 3028681
C127: (C0) 1844625
D127: (C0) 1071413
E127: (C0) 717947
F127: (C0) 25481
G127: (F2) 2.39
H127: (F2) 0.297
I127: (P1) 0.12
J127: 54
L127: (D4) 30347
M127: (C0) 985838
N127: (C0) 680000
O127: @IF(N127<>0,+$S$127+N127#$R$133,"")
P127: 'Constant
S127: -346538.14702
A128: (D4) 30894
B128: (C0) 3013676
C128: (C0) 1764898
D128: (C0) 1059416
E128: (C0) 670182
F128: (C0) 24985
```

```
G128: (F2) 2.64
H128: (F2) 0.363
I128: (P1) 0.11
J128: 83
L128: (D4) 30375
M128: (C0) 958375
N128: (C0) 677506
O128: @IF(N128<>0,+$S$127+N128*$R$133,"")
P128: 'Std Err of Y Est
S128: 36337.799438
A129: (D4) 30863
B129: (C0) 2991601
C129: (C0) 1768636
D129: (C0) 1061479
E129: (C0) 722683
F129: (C0) 24833
G129: (F2) 2.54
H129: (F2) 0.2915
I129: (P1) 0.11
J129: 53
L129: (D4) 30406
M129: (C0) 972634
N129: (C0) 680687
O129: @IF(N129<>0,+$S$127+N129*$R$133,"")
P129: 'R Squared
S129: (P1) 0.3570221068
A130: (D4) 30833
B130: (C0) 2962020
C130: (C0) 1701132
D130: (C0) 1006475
E130: (C0) 726572
F130: (C0) 24269
G130: (F2) 2.61
H130: (F2) 0.2915
I130: (P1) 0.11
J130: 53
L130: (D4) 30436
M130: (C0) 947576
N130: (C0) 688450
O130: @IF(N130<>0,+$S$127+N130*$R$133,"")
P130: 'No. of Observations
S130: 12
A131: (D4) 30802
```

```
B131: (C0) 2939631
C131: (C0) 1814346
D131: (C0) 1056518
E131: (C0) 697503
F131: (C0) 24048
G131: (F2) 2.5
H131: (F2) 0.3245
I131: (P1) 0.12
J131: 63
L131: (D4) 30467
M131: (C0) 963565
N131: (C0) 692004
O131: @IF(N131<>0,+$S$127+N131*$R$133,"")
P131: 'Degrees of Freedom
S131: 10
A132: (D4) 30772
B132: (C0) 2936500
C132: (C0) 1675854
D132: (C0) 1015673
E132: (C0) 690289
F132: (C0) 23351
G132: (F2) 2.59
H132: (F2) 0.3355
I132: (P1) 0.12
J132: 68
L132: (D4) 30497
M132: (C0) 957749
N132: (C0) 705182
O132: @IF(N132<>0,+$S$127+N132*$R$133,"")
A133: (D4) 30741
B133: (C0) 2922458
C133: (C0) 1684678
D133: (C0) 1033158
E133: (C0) 713267
F133: (C0) 23201
G133: (F2) 2.47
H133: (F2) 0.3025
I133: (P1) 0.11
J133: 57
L133: (D4) 30528
M133: (C0) 986548
N133: (C0) 679317
O133: @IF(N133<>0,+$S$127+N133*$R$133,"")
```

```
P133: 'X Coefficient(s)
R133: (F2) 1.9362145786
A134: (D4) 30712
B134: (C0) 2903961
C134: (C0) 1682436
D134: (C0) 1002948
E134: (C0) 684348
F134: (C0) 23122
G134: (F2) 2.59
H134: (F2) 0.352
I134: (P1) 0.12
J134: 74
L134: (D4) 30559
M134: (C0) 1004192
N134: (C0) 686639
O134: @IF(N134<>0,+$S$127+N134*$R$133,"")
P134: 'Std Err of Coef.
R134: (F2) 0.8216823386
A135: (D4) 30681
B135: (C0) 2891879
C135: (C0) 1779420
D135: (C0) 1095574
E135: (C0) 704854
F135: (C0) 23101
G135: (F2) 2.56
H135: (F2) 0.3135
I135: (P1) 0.11
J135: 60
L135: (D4) 30589
M135: (C0) 1042317
N135: (C0) 714820
O135: @IF(N135<>0,+$S$127+N135*$R$133,"")
A136: (D4) 30650
B136: (C0) 2889668
C136: (C0) 1720860
D136: (C0) 1026998
E136: (C0) 709580
F136: (C0) 22898
G136: (F2) 2.67
H136: (F2) 0.308
I136: (P1) 0.11
J136: 58
L136: (D4) 30620
```

```
M136: (C0) 972434
N136: (C0) 681827
O136: @IF(N136<>0,+$S$127+N136*$R$133,"")
P136: @STRING(R133,2)&" Times Sales + "&@STRING(@ROUND(S127,-3),0)
A137: (D4) 30620
B137: (C0) 2868248
C137: (C0) 1654943
D137: (C0) 972434
E137: (C0) 681827
F137: (C0) 22862
G137: (F2) 2.45
H137: (F2) 0.352
I137: (P1) 0.12
J137: 75
L137: (D4) 30650
M137: (C0) 1026998
N137: (C0) 709580
O137: @IF(N137<>0,+$S$127+N137*$R$133,"")
AC137: '           Press ENTER to begin.
A138: (D4) 30589
B138: (C0) 2864642
C138: (C0) 1696249
D138: (C0) 1042317
E138: (C0) 714820
F138: (C0) 22582
G138: (F2) 2.57
H138: (F2) 0.3025
I138: (P1) 0.11
J138: 55
L138: (D4) 30681
M138: (C0) 1095574
N138: (C0) 704854
O138: @IF(N138<>0,+$S$127+N138*$R$133,"")
A139: (D4) 30559
B139: (C0) 2831978
C139: (C0) 1695048
D139: (C0) 1004192
E139: (C0) 686639
F139: (C0) 22339
G139: (F2) 2.6
H139: (F2) 0.341
I139: (P1) 0.11
J139: 69
```

```
D139: @IF(N139<>0,+$S$127+N139*$R$133,"")
A140: (D4) 30528
B140: (C0) 2830797
C140: (C0) 1644616
D140: (C0) 986548
E140: (C0) 679317
F140: (C0) 22278
G140: (F2) 2.51
H140: (F2) 0.352
I140: (P1) 0.1
J140: 78
D140: @IF(N140<>0,+$S$127+N140*$R$133,"")
A141: (D4) 30497
B141: (C0) 2799154
C141: (C0) 1607371
D141: (C0) 957749
E141: (C0) 705182
F141: (C0) 22137
G141: (F2) 2.65
H141: (F2) 0.308
I141: (P1) 0.11
J141: 59
D141: @IF(N141<>0,+$S$127+N141*$R$133,"")
A142: (D4) 30467
B142: (C0) 2788738
C142: (C0) 1601230
D142: (C0) 963565
E142: (C0) 692004
F142: (C0) 21674
G142: (F2) 2.39
H142: (F2) 0.33
I142: (P1) 0.11
J142: 65
D142: @IF(N142<>0,+$S$127+N142*$R$133,"")
A143: (D4) 30436
B143: (C0) 2759173
C143: (C0) 1575963
D143: (C0) 947576
E143: (C0) 688450
F143: (C0) 21269
G143: (F2) 2.48
H143: (F2) 0.341
I143: (P1) 0.11
```

```
J143: 68
O143: @IF(N143<>0,+$S$127+N143*$R$133,"")
A144: (D4) 30406
B144: (C0) 2737433
C144: (C0) 1572624
D144: (C0) 972634
E144: (C0) 680687
F144: (C0) 21246
G144: (F2) 2.5
H144: (F2) 0.352
I144: (P1) 0.11
J144: 77
O144: @IF(N144<>0,+$S$127+N144*$R$133,"")
A145: (D4) 30375
B145: (C0) 2715848
C145: (C0) 1612148
D145: (C0) 958375
E145: (C0) 677506
F145: (C0) 20832
G145: (F2) 2.51
H145: (F2) 0.3575
I145: (P1) 0.11
J145: 79
O145: @IF(N145<>0,+$S$127+N145*$R$133,"")
A146: (D4) 30347
B146: (C0) 2710753
C146: (C0) 1587850
D146: (C0) 985838
E146: (C0) 680000
F146: (C0) 20470
G146: (F2) 2.47
H146: (F2) 0.352
I146: (P1) 0.11
J146: 77
O146: @IF(N146<>0,+$S$127+N146*$R$133,"")
O147: @IF(N147<>0,+$S$127+N147*$R$133,"")
O148: @IF(N148<>0,+$S$127+N148*$R$133,"")
O149: @IF(N149<>0,+$S$127+N149*$R$133,"")
D150: @IF(N150<>0,+$S$127+N150*$R$133,"")
A151: '{?}{DOWN}{BRANCH \z}
O151: @IF(N151<>0,+$S$127+N151*$R$133,"")
O152: @IF(N152<>0,+$S$127+N152*$R$133,"")
```

```
0153:  @IF(N153<>0,+$S$127+N153*$R$133,"")
0154:  @IF(N154<>0,+$S$127+N154*$R$133,"")
0155:  @IF(N155<>0,+$S$127+N155*$R$133,"")
0156:  @IF(N156<>0,+$S$127+N156*$R$133,"")
```

Fig. 13.27. Cell listing of Financial Ratios worksheet.

Conclusion

The comprehensive model is an ideal conclusion for *Using 1-2-3* because it gathers all of the elements of 1-2-3 into one powerful model. The application includes a spreadsheet that uses some of the techniques from Chapters 3, 4, 5, 6, 7, and 8. The graphs included in this example build on the commands from Chapters 9 and 10. The financial database was created using the tools developed in Chapter 11. The macros in the model draw heavily on concepts developed in Chapter 12.

This book has examined every facet of 1-2-3. We hope that you have found the examples of each command and function helpful and our observations informative. It's now up to you to begin using 1-2-3 to help you solve your own problems. Remember, the model above is just one illustration of the fact that the four elements of 1-2-3—spreadsheet, graphics, data management, and macros—can be merged together to form a powerful model. The possible applications for 1-2-3 are limitless. Now that you are familiar with all of 1-2-3's capabilities, you should have no trouble thinking of ways to use 1-2-3 in your business. Just use your imagination!

If you want to learn still more about 1-2-3, you should subscribe to Que's periodical, *Absolute Reference: The Journal for 1-2-3 and Symphony Users. Absolute Reference* is an excellent source of ongoing information about 1-2-3. To learn more about this exciting opportunity, see the announcement inside the back cover of this book.

Index

More Computer Knowledge from Que

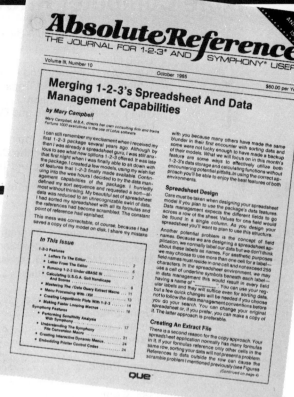

LEARN MORE ABOUT LOTUS SOFTWARE
WITH THESE OUTSTANDING BOOKS FROM QUE

1-2-3 Macro Library

by David P. Ewing

This best-selling reference contains more than 100 examples of 1-2-3 macros. Explanations help you apply many of these macros to your 1-2-3 worksheets. Included are examples of macros for 1-2-3's spreadsheet, data management, and graphics applications, as well as macros for file and print operations. For beginners and experts alike.

1-2-3 for Business

by Leith Anderson and Douglas Cobb

Now that you've mastered 1-2-3, learn how to manage your business with this powerful program. Step-by-step instructions show you how to build fourteen practical business applications, using all the features of 1-2-3. The book includes models for Fixed Asset Management, Ratio Analysis, and Project Management.

1-2-3 Tips, Tricks, and Traps

by Dick Andersen and Douglas Cobb

A must for 1-2-3 users. This book explains 1-2-3's little-known features and offers advice for problem areas, or traps. Tips include shortcuts for creating macros, producing graphs, and using Data Tables. Tricks help with special problems that may arise when using 1-2-3.

1-2-3 Financial Macros

by Thomas W. Carlton

This book will show you how to develop complex spreadsheets and database models controlled by macros. Expanding applications introduced in *1-2-3 Macro Library*, this book contains macro applications for accounting, budgeting, forecasting, and analysis, plus macros for a stock portfolio model and project management.

Mail to: Que Corporation • P.O. Box 50507 • Indianapolis, IN 46250

Item	Title	Price	Quantity	Extension
174	1-2-3 Macro Library	$19.95		
34	1-2-3 for Business	$16.95		
127	1-2-3 Tips, Tricks, and Traps	$16.95		
187	1-2-3 Financial Macros	$19.95		
		Book Subtotal		
		Shipping & Handling ($1.75 per item)		
		Indiana Residents Add 5% Sales Tax		
		GRAND TOTAL		

Method of Payment:

☐ Check   ☐ VISA   ☐ MasterCard   ☐ American Express

Card Number _____ Exp. Date _____

Cardholder Name _____

Ship to _____

Address _____

City _____ State _____ ZIP _____

If you can't wait, call **1-800-428-5331** and order TODAY.

All prices subject to change without notice.

Que Command-Menu Map
for
Lotus® 1-2-3®, Release 2

This color indicates the features new with Release 2 of Lotus® 1-2-3®.

WHEN IT COMES TO 1-2-3, QUE BOOKS HAVE THE PERFECT SOLUTIONS

WHEN IT COMES TO 1-2-3,
QUE BOOKS HAVE THE
PERFECT SOLUTIONS

Function Key Operation

Key	Function
Alt-F1 (Compose)	Used with other keys to make International Characters
Alt-F2 (Step)	Shifts 1-2-3 into single-step mode for debugging macros
F1 (Help)	Accesses 1-2-3's on-line help facility
F2 (Edit)	Shifts 1-2-3 into EDIT mode. Allows contents of cells to be altered without retyping entire cell
F3 (Name)	In POINT mode, displays list of range names. Pressed a second time, it switches to full-screen display of range names
F4 (Abs)	Changes relative cell address into absolute or mixed address
F5 (Goto)	Moves cursor to cell coordinates (or range name) provided
F6 (Window)	Moves cursor to other side of split screen
F7 (Query)	Repeats most recent Data Query operation
F8 (Table)	Repeats most recent Data Table operation
F9 (Calc)	Recalculates worksheet
F10 (Graph)	Redraws graph defined by current graph settings

Cursor-Movement Keys

Key	Function
← →	Used to move cursor one column left or right
↑ ↓	Used to position cursor one row up or down
Home	Returns cursor to cell A1. When used with End key (End+Home), positions cursor at active end of worksheet. Also used in EDIT mode to jump to beginning of edit line.
End	When entered before any of the arrow keys, positions cursor in the direction of the arrow key to the cell on the boundary of an empty and filled space. Also used in EDIT mode to jump to end of edit line.
PgUp	Used to move up an entire screen
PgDn	Used to move down an entire screen
Ctrl ←	Moves cursor left one screen
Ctrl →	Moves cursor right one screen

Frequently Used 1-2-3 Functions

Mathematical Functions

@ABS(number or cell reference)
@EXP(number or cell reference)
@INT(number or cell reference)
@LN(number or cell reference)
@LOG(number or cell reference)
@SQRT(number or cell reference)
@RAND
@ROUND(number,places rounded to)
@MOD(number,divisor)

Financial Functions

@NPV(discount,rate,range)
@IRR(estimate,range)
@PV(payment,interest,term)
@FV(payment,interest,term)
@PMT(principal,interest,n)
@RATE(future value,present value,n)
@TERM(payment,interest,future value)
@CTERM(interest,future value,present value)
@SLN(cost,salvage value,life)
@DDB(cost,salvage value,life,period)
@SYD(cost,salvage value,life,period)

Logical Functions

@IF(a,vtrue,vfalse)
@N(range)
@S(range)

String Functions

@FIND(search string,overall string,start number)
@MID(string,start position,length)
@LEFT(string,length)
@RIGHT(string,length)
@REPLACE(original string,start number,length,replacement string)
@LENGTH(string)
@EXACT(string1,string2)
@LOWER(string)
@UPPER(string)
@PROPER(string)
@REPEAT(string,number)
@TRIM(string)
@STRING(number to convert,decimal places)
@VALUE(string)
@CHAR(number)
@CODE(string)
@CLEAN(string)

Date and Time Functions

@DATE(year number,month number,day)
@DATEVALUE(date string)
@NOW
@TIME(hour,minute,second)
@TIMEVALUE(time string)
@SECOND(time number)
@MINUTE(time number)
@HOUR(time number)

Announcing a major new learning breakthrough for Lotus® 1-2-3® trainers!

Introducing the *Que Learning System*—the clearest, most comprehensive program to help you train students or colleagues in Lotus 1-2-3.

The *Que Learning System* contains all the materials you need to explain clearly the use of 1-2-3: workbooks, instructor's guides, textbooks, disks, transparencies, and slides. But you purchase only the components you need—in the quantities you want.

To introduce you to the *Que Learning System*, we'll send you a FREE information kit, which includes:

- A 40-page booklet of guide and workbook sample pages
- Information on how you can customize the *Que Learning System* to your specific training needs

- Outlines of eight different *Que Learning System* programs, including Lotus 1-2-3 Introduction and Macros; Symphony®; WordStar®; MultiMate®; dBASE III®; and IBM PC XT™, and DOS.

To get your free information kit as soon as possible, order yours today.

FREE INFORMATION KIT

Call toll free 1-800-428-5331 (Ext. 13) or tear out and mail this postage-paid card immediately.

☐ YES! I'd like my FREE, no-obligation *Que Learning System* information kit. Rush mine *right now*!

Name _____

School/Company _____

Address _____

City _____ State _____ ZIP _____

Phone (_____) _____

Get one issue of

Absolute Reference
THE JOURNAL FOR 1-2-3™ AND SYMPHONY™ USERS
absolutely FREE!

If you use 1-2-3® or Symphony®, reading *Absolute Reference* is a must! And to prove how valuable a reference tool *Absolute Reference* is, we'll send you a sample issue FREE!

This informative monthly newsletter is filled with concise, helpful articles and features designed to offer you the most help in the shortest time—tailored to fit your busy schedule.

In each issue, you'll find:

- Tips on using Lotus® products more effectively
- Models showing how 1-2-3 and Symphony can be used to solve a variety of specific problems and perform various analyses

- Questions and answers
- Guest columns by Lotus experts
- Reviews of new Lotus-related products
- Examples of macros, graphs, database, communications, word-processing applications, and much more!

Thousands of Lotus users are convinced that *Absolute Reference* is a tremendously helpful tool. Ask for your FREE copy—we think you'll be convinced, too. There's no risk or obligation on your part, so request yours *now*.

Call toll free 1-800-227-7999 (Ext. 501) or tear out and mail this postage-paid card and drop it in the mail today.

☐ YES! Send my FREE issue of *Absolute Reference* immediately, with no obligation to subscribe. I understand I'll receive an invoice after getting my free issue, and may either write "cancel" on the invoice or subscribe to receive more issues.

Rates for subscribers: Within the U.S., 12 issues, $60; 24 issues, $105 (Save $15!). Outside the U.S., 12 issues, $80; 24 issues, $135 (Save $25!). Payable on International Money Orders drawn on U.S. banks only.

If subscribing now, I'm paying by

☐ Check ☐ VISA ☐ MasterCard ☐ American Express

Card Number _____ Exp. date _____

Signature _____

Name _____

School/Company _____

Address _____

City _____ State _____ ZIP _____

Phone (_____) _____

Prices subject to change without notice.

BUSINESS REPLY CARD

FIRST CLASS   PERMIT NO. 9918   INDIANAPOLIS, IN

POSTAGE WILL BE PAID BY ADDRESSEE

Que Corporation
P.O. Box 50507
Indianapolis, IN 46250

NO POSTAGE
NECESSARY
IF MAILED
IN THE
UNITED STATES

BUSINESS REPLY CARD

FIRST CLASS   PERMIT NO. 9918   INDIANAPOLIS, IN

POSTAGE WILL BE PAID BY ADDRESSEE

Que Corporation
P.O. Box 50507
Indianapolis, IN 46250